The Dead Saints Chronicles

A Zen Journey through the Christian Afterlife

David Solomon

with John Anthony West

Quotations from the website www.nderf.org and www.adcrf.org are printed with permission from Jeffery Long, M.D. and Jody Long.

Names have been occasionally changed to protect privacy.

Copyright © 2016, by David Solomon and Delynn Solomon. (DS Media Pub, LLC) All rights reserved. DS Media Pub, LLC. Third printing 2021

No part of this publication may be reproduced, stored in a retrieval system, or transmitted, in any form or by any means, electronic, mechanical, photocopying, recording, scanning, or otherwise, except as permitted under Section 107 or 108 of the 1976 United States Copyright Act, without the prior written permission of the publisher, or authorization through payment of the appropriate per-copy fee to the Copyright Clearance Center, Inc., 222 Rosewood Drive, Danvers, MA 01923, 978-750-8400, fax 978-646.8600, or on the Web at www.copyright.com. Requests to the publisher for permission should be addressed to the Permissions department, (TBA).

Bible Citations

Unless otherwise noted, all Scripture quotations are from the King James Version of the Holy Bible (Authorized Version). First published in 1611.

Readers should be aware Internet Web sites offered as citations and/or sources for further information may have changed or disappeared between the time this was written and when it was read. Limit of Liability/Disclaimer Warranty: While the publisher and author have used their best efforts in preparing this book, they make no representations or warranties with respect to the accuracy or completeness of the contents of this book and specifically disclaim any implied warranties of merchantability or fitness for a particular purpose. No warranty may be created or extended by sales representatives or written sales materials. The advice and strategies contained herein may not be suitable for your situation. You should consult with a professional where appropriate. Neither the publisher not author shall be liable for any loss of profit or any other commercial damages, including but not limited to special, incidental, consequential or other damages.

Publisher Information:
Library of Congress Cataloging-in-Publication Data
    Solomon, David
    The Dead Saints Chronicles: A Zen Journey through a Christian Afterlife / David Solomon with John Anthony West
    p. cm.
    Includes bibliographical references and reference notes
    ISBN: 978099724549-3
    1.   Death and Dying 2. Spirituality.

Printed in the United States of America
3rd Edition

POSTSCRIPT:

After a journey through thirty-four months with brain cancer, David transitioned from this life to the next on April 18th, 2016 at 3:10 a.m. in his home in Virginia Beach, Virginia.

Shortly after sending his manuscript to print, his health rapidly declined. His mind was sharp and his fingers continued to type up until 34 hours before passing. He continued to complete his part of the second and third books, now in the editing phase. David had the pleasure of receiving the first printing of his book, the joy of having a book signing, two live stream interviews, and a radio interview just 10 days before his passing.

His hope was that all would be curious enough to question, bold enough to search for an answer, and in all things grow in Love.

Delynn Solomon
In Love and Light

Legal Notice:

The Dead Saints Chronicles discuss suicide NDEs as part of NDE research. The authors DO NOT ENDORSE, ENCOURAGE OR ADVOCATE FOR SUICIDE IN ANY WAY, SHAPE OR FORM! If you are feeling suicidal, please know help is available. Though you may feel alone, YOU ARE NOT ALONE! If you are in crisis, call 911 IMMEDIATELY, or contact the Suicide Crisis Hotline in your state or country. Call 1-800-273 TALK (8255).

For Ben and Angela

Contents

Foreword: *Dannion Brinkley*

Part I: Nebari
Chapter 1: Premonitions — 1
Chapter 2: The Race, the Research, & the Dead Saints Epiphany — 7
Chapter 3: Death Is a Lie Humans Tell Themselves — 23
Chapter 4: Earth University — 37
Chapter 5: Rice Paper Teachers — 53
Chapter 6: Dreams: Night School — 69
Chapter 7: The Apprentice Gardener — 85
Chapter 8: The Spiritual Journal — 101
Chapter 9: Life Review — 111
Chapter 10: The Judgment — 119
Chapter 11: We Die in Character — 131

Part II: Afterlife Bonsai
Chapter 12: Is Our Mission Finished? — 141
Chapter 13: Death Step by Step — 153
Chapter 14: Transformations — 181
Chapter 15: You Do Not Die Alone — 201
Chapter 16: The Body of Light — 217
Chapter 17: Heaven—The Kingdom of Light — 223
Chapter 18: Ghosts, Apparitions, & Earthbound Spirits — 239
Chapter 19: Tragedy, Evil & Hell — 249

Part III: Bonsai Secrets
Chapter 20: The Governing Laws of Religion Are Not Absolute — 263
Chapter 21: Pre-Existence — 289
Chapter 22: An Uncomfortable Possibility — 301
Chapter 23: Jesus, Planetary Headmaster — 315
Chapter 24: The 13th Path — 339

Afterword: by John Anthony West

The Way of the Dove
By Paul Solomon

...the way of the dove is simple:

Every being can live in the way of the dove,
and all religions can follow in the way of the dove
because the way of the dove is not a religion
for one may say 'I am religious and a dove'

The way of the dove is never instead of
always in addition to
it is a journey without a beginning
and without a known destination

For when all beings live in the way of the dove
all beings will live in peace
and the journey will continue in peace
then there will be a beginning with no end

The way of the dove is undertaking
a seeking to be from which no one can fail
for as long as today is today
there still is a way to walk in the way of the dove

One can never fail for it is the next step
not the last, that one walks in the way of the dove
neither shall any dove condemn a mis-step along the way
for it is not in the nature of a dove to so speak in any discouraging way

A dove seeks always to honor life and all that live
and seeks to speak encouragement and praise
a dove entices and seeks to be joined
in striving to walk in the way of wellness and wholeness

Healing is always offered
but never the dis-eased be condemned
for displaying a symptom, a stumbling step,
that seems not to walk in the way of the dove

No dove is demanding of another
for every dove knows the value of the way
and every dove knows that any being who can
will walk without push or shove

A dove will not take when it is not offered
but instead will rejoice that he has it
and the dove will know what one has
is not what brings joy or contentment

Nor will doves hesitate to accept what is offered
for doves know the joy of giving
and would not deprive another the joy of sharing
for a gift is the mark of the dove.

FOREWORD
by
Dannion Brinkley

New York Times and international bestselling author of
Saved by the Light and The Secrets of the Light

There are very few things I do not know about death and dying, because I have had one death and two near-death experiences. After being struck by lightning in 1975, I was pronounced dead, and yet I was more alive than ever before, as I journeyed through the Hereafter with 13 Beings of Light. Three years later, I was struck by lightning again. This time I was only knocked out for 40 minutes, after being thrown through the bedroom window. In 1989, I had my first real near-death experience during open heart surgery to replace my aortic valve. Then, as the result of brain surgery to drain five subdural hematomas, I had my second near-death experience. So, after all of these experiences, and the time I've spent on the Other Side, I understood why David Solomon asked me to write this forward. As you might have figured out, I have quite a famous reputation as an experienced dead man! But, I must admit, quite unlike David, I didn't know anything about death before I died myself.

David, on the other hand, has conducted a remarkably in-depth study of the Near-Death Experience since he was first diagnosed with a terminal brain tumor. After receiving this shocking diagnosis in June 2013, David, with the help of his wife, Delynn, embarked on a fantastic journey to verify the reality of the Afterlife, beginning with the comfort of their Christian viewpoint. As a Christian minister, and a leading expert on Biblical interpretation, David did not narrow his search to strictly Christian theology. I feel this book is an incomparable guide for people who are trying to find a way to reconcile their belief in the Afterlife. Most people are afraid of "what's next," but this book is about one man's journey to find out exactly what IS next!

In fact, *The Dead Saints Chronicles,* is an intimate account of David courageously coming to terms with his own life and death and with the sincere hope of helping others facing similar situations. So in an open-minded approach, David's research led him to scour all religious, spiritual and mystical evidence available on the subject. From the work of Dr. Jeffrey Long, David gained a vast understanding of the presence of Jesus in many near-death experiences he'd studied. From Dr. Raymond Moody's lifelong investigation of the Near-Death Experience, David garnered a great insight into the basic stages of the Near-Death Experience. However, through his own research, David was actually able to add to Dr. Moody's original list of consistent NDE fundamentals.

What caught my eye more than anything in *The Dead Saint's Chronicles* was David's statement at the beginning of the book. It absolutely astounded me. 'When Doctor Ma entered the emergency room, closed the blue curtain for privacy, and she bluntly told me, "Mr. Solomon, we found a mass in your brain,' no matter how unafraid you think you are of death, no matter what your religion, when a doctor tells you that you have what might be a terminal illness, the news is catastrophic. Suddenly death became real. It was no longer a "philosophy" or just something, that had to happen when I got old. In that moment, two years of Dead Saints research looking for answers to abstract Christian theological debates about death and the Afterlife suddenly became the central focus of my life."

Largely written during David's battle with terminal Glioblastoma brain cancer, the book is also a deeply personal account of how he relates his life's work to his own tenuous mortality. Through journal entries, recordings of dreams and after-death communications from deceased loved ones, and autobiographical reflections, David is able to give theology, spirituality, and overwhelming concepts like death and the Afterlife a relatable immediacy. Part educational volume, part guide, and part memoir, *The Dead Saints Chronicles* is unlike anything written to date. Intended for all types, backgrounds, and creeds, the book challenges readers to expand their thinking while providing all the lessons they need to recognize, understand, and eventually experience the state of Heaven.

David's journey to the Hereafter includes "live reports" from a "dazzling white light shining through his bedroom window panes." His heroic approach to his life and his inevitable transition is truly phenomenal! I enjoyed this book immensely. It is extremely well written and definitely belongs in everyone's personal library.

Blessings,   *Dannion*   *"Dead   Saint"*   *Brinkley*

Part I

Nebari

Takanohashi sensei, my deceased Bonsai teacher, appeared in a dream and gruffly said "Nebari!"—pointing at an old azalea trunk and its thick, exposed roots. Nebari is a Japanese word, which means "root," specifically the visible spread of roots above the growing medium at the base of a Bonsai. Thus the book was divided and Part I became Nebari—the "roots" of the Dead Saints Chronicles

1
Premonitions

June 1994

I dreamed I was in Heaven.

I found myself standing side by side with a group of twenty new spirit arrivals in a small, vaulted, travertine stone room. To my right, the entire wall of the building was missing, opening up to a spectacular view of a great gulf which separated us from a grand shining metropolis I can only call the Holy City of God. It was made of dozens of overlapping golden domes that glowed like golden halos against a crystalline glacier-blue sky sprinkled with stars, galaxies, and nebulae.

Everything within me wanted to fly through the space opened up by the missing wall, bridge the chasm[1], that seemed only a few miles away, enter the Holy City, and have all wisdom and all knowledge bestowed upon me. The pull on my soul was overpowering.

The stone building, I stood in was simple and unadorned, like a humble mountaintop shrine or sanctuary, but it seemed a way station or portal to the Holy City. Those of us standing together were being prepared for our next step in spiritual growth. New "Light Bodies" had been created for our new life in spirit. They floated, lined up side by side, just a few feet in front of us. These new Light Bodies appeared solid to me, I stood facing their backs, so I could not see their faces. I don't remember if I knew any of these souls, but I did know all of us had died back on Earth.

"How did I die?" I had no memory of the event.

An unfamiliar Voice suddenly commanded all of us to step forward into our respective new Light Bodies, as if we were an incorporeal, spiritual "mist" that could easily blend into them. As I stepped forward, laughter erupted.

"No, not that one, silly! The next one!"

I moved into the correct body and when I did so, I saw my former spiritual mentor, Paul Solomon, in the corner of the room. He looked as I remembered him when he died, just three months ago. White beard, white hair, big belly. Yes, it was Paul. Instead of being shocked, it seemed completely natural my dead friend should be here.

He motioned "Follow me" with his finger.

Suddenly, we were no longer in the quaint little mountaintop shrine, but were walking next to each other on an oak-leaf covered mountain trail somewhere in the wooded highlands of the Shenandoah Valley. We walked quietly for a short distance, before he spoke to me:

"You know David; it would be a shame you pass over before completing your book. You have a unique ability to put together very abstract ideas. Connect the dots. You don't have much time." He gave me the distinct impression my life was in danger.

The Afterlife encounter with Paul ended abruptly. I awoke with tears streaming down my face, just as the morning sun was rising. Images of the Holy City filled my mind. What had just happened? It seemed as though I had been in *Heaven for years*, but somehow I was still breathing. I could feel the warmth of the tears, now cooling on my face. Sunlight bounced off the rafters of the vaulted ceiling of my condominium. I was back on Earth in good ol' 1994.

I dreamed I went to Heaven, but I didn't die. How could that be? For the moment, it was just another vivid dream put into the back pocket of my mind.

God waited. I lived out my life.

January 18, 2013

Fast forward 19 years.

Once again, I dreamed of death. I was driving across a bridge spanning high above a deep river canyon, when suddenly, the bridge and all the cars on it collapsed into the river below. I didn't see or feel the collapse. I only observed from above.

The next thing I knew I was standing inside a small ferry with a couple dozen other passengers who sat quietly watching the scenery pass by the ferry windows. The ferry itself was nothing like an actual commercial Seattle ferry, but was more like a city bus, with seats on both sides and vertical floor-to-ceiling aluminum poles to hold onto.

This "death ferry" was clipping along over deep green and blue tropical waters between islands similar to the San Juan's where I lived in Washington's Puget Sound. Snow covered the small mountains down to the water's edge, which would have been impossible on this warm, sunny dream day.

Out the windows, I could see angels or spirits flying next to our ferry bus like spiritual tugboats pulling us towards (presumably) heavenly shores I could not yet see.

I was standing near the rear and noticed the seats were all taken and I was the only passenger standing along with a tall, older woman standing at the front. She had sharp features and pure white hair tied tightly tied into a braided ponytail. She stood angelic. Her face glowed with white Light. She was looking directly at me with incredible bright blue eyes and a warm smile. She seemed familiar. I thought she might have been my great grandmother, but in mid-dream, I wasn't sure.[2]

She seemed to be our spiritual guide across the great waters we were now traversing, heading for our unknown destination.

"I just died, didn't I?" I asked, as if it were a fact, not a question.

She responded in my mind but without moving her lips with a simple, "Yes." No shock. Just a confirmation. Most of the others on the ferry had died as well, but seemed unaware they were dead. To me it was quite clear. *I had died.*

I then woke up. The Afterlife visitation by Great Grandma Miller was the first since Paul Solomon's visit two decades ago. It was interesting, but nothing felt out of the ordinary. Life moved merrily along. I had no worries at all.

May 15, 2013

Five months later, on May 15, I walked through the backdoor of our home into the Egyptian Spa healing room. Suddenly, without warning, I had a gut wrenching realization I was going to die soon. This was a real premonition. Out of the blue with no apparent connection to anything else.

The moment was palpable. Unmistakable. I could reach out and touch it. I knelt on the cold marble floor and spoke aloud, "*Lord, at least if you are going to take me, give me three years to see my daughter graduate high school.*"

Over the weekend, I began to feel dizzy. I thought I had a simple ear infection.

June 10, 2013

Three weeks later, I leaned over to pinch off tiny, green Shimpaku needles from my favorite bonsai, planted in a four-foot high brown glazed, clay pot. I stood back to check my work. Looking underneath the tree to see if I needed to cut more, I nearly lost my balance. I felt nauseous, ran inside the house into the bathroom, and vomited. My legs felt strangely disconnected from my body, like Pinocchio wooden legs. I mentioned the weird symptoms to my wife, Delynn, and she said, "Oh, that's exactly what I feel when I get vertigo."

After dinner, Delynn and I took a stroll through the gardens surrounding our home. Sunbeams poked through the spruce trees. Birds chirped in the cool of the evening. The sound of gravel crunching underfoot required no words. It was a perfect, peaceful evening, but walking through the dizziness was challenging. I had practiced and taught T'ai Chi for years where balance is everything— and mine was dreadfully off.

I blew it off thinking I had a simple inner ear infection.

June 12, 2013

Three weeks later, on Wednesday evening, June 12, I received a call from John, a longtime friend, I hadn't heard from in over a year. He asked me if I was alright.

I told him, "I'm okay. Why?"

"I had a dream last night you were in trouble. I was told to call you."

"John, I am fine," I said.

We talked for a few minutes, but quickly the call was over. It didn't even occur to me to put the pieces of it all together: *The after-death warning from Paul Solomon and Great Grandma Miller. The spa premonition. John's call. My dizziness.*

The clock was ticking...

---

1 Deep gorges, canyons, and great gulfs represent symbolic barriers of the boundary separating Heaven and Earth often encountered during near-death experiences. (See chapter 13, *Death Step by Step*).

2 On July 26th, 2013, I told my mother about the "death ferry" dream. She showed me a photograph of Great Grandma Miller who had died when I was 16-years-old. I instantly

recognized the woman from my dream as my Great Grandmother. Mom's photo showed her hair in a different style than I saw in my dream—her hair tied up in a braided ponytail—the same braided ponytail Great Grandma had when she was laid to rest, a fact I could not have known, since I did not attend her funeral.

2

The Race, the Research, & the Dead Saints Epiphany

"I said to the man who stood at the gate of the Year, "Give me a light that I may tread safely into the unknown." And he replied, "Go out into the darkness and put your hand into the hand of God. That shall be to you better than light and safer than a known way."
~Minnie Haskins (England, 1875-1957)

On Thursday, June 13, 2013, as I neared completing two years of NDE (Near Death Experience) research, I was diagnosed with GBM IV (glioblastoma multiforme stage IV) a very rare, aggressive form of terminal brain cancer with a median survival rate of 15-18 months, and no recorded instances of permanent remission. The catastrophic news halted midstream, the completion of Akio Botanical, a five-acre Japanese landscaping project that surrounded our home in Washington State.

Ted Kennedy died of GBM just 15 months after his initial diagnosis and he famously used to say until he passed, "I am still here." As of December 13, 2015 as I prepare to bring this book to print, I pass my own thirtieth month of survival. So I, like the venerable senator, can also say, "I am still here!"

The waters ahead may be turbulent and treacherous, but the sky is clear, and I accept my fate, however it plays out. The scientist in me even sees this as an opportunity to explore, in a unique fashion, the unknown territory called The Afterlife. It faithfully and objectively records the challenges of finishing a writing project, wholly devoted to all aspects of dying and after death survival (physical, psychological, philosophical, religious and scientific) before the lethal tumor in my own head takes me away.

My NDE studies were initially both intensive and wide-ranging but without a focus. My ultimate aim was to someday write a book on the subject, but frankly, knowing myself, it probably would have never happened. This is where the story acquires its plot. By the time the cancer diagnosis bomb dropped, my NDE "hobby" had already assembled a vast trove of near-death research.

If my life had an expiration date, it appeared I had better get to work writing. After months of iterating the outline, the *Chronicles* burgeoned into a Trilogy... three separate but complementary explorations of a single grand theme.

Book I: *A Zen Journey through the Christian Afterlife*
Book II: *Training Wires of the Soul*
Book III: *The Armageddon Stones*

Between the apparently inescapable prognosis and my own instinct, I knew the writing project would be a race to the finish, one that would continue right down to the very last moments of my life. It was as though it was orchestrated by God, angels, and deceased friends and teachers on the "other side." It was a work that had to get done.

The Race

Despite debilitating *brain fog* and fatigue from radiation and chemo treatments, I wrote with a *Blues-Brother-Mission-from-God* vigor. The *Chronicles* materialized steadily, often daily. Mystics would call it revelation, or artist's inspiration. Atheists, skeptics and materialists call it hypothesis formation in order to make it reasonably acceptable to their academic colleagues.

I would wake up with insights and direction. My mind was always pondering, always asking, "Lord, how should I write this?" Sometimes insights came in the form of a dream or just a "knowing." Answers and new realizations would come late at night and I often had to text myself so as not to forget the words by morning. While I never stopped thinking about the book, often brain fog from GBM would limit my ability to write. Hours of rest would become days of rest, then weeks. It's hard enough to write, even with a normally functioning brain!

At times, I wanted to abandon the *Chronicles* and focus only on my family and my bucket list. Sometimes I despaired. I was dying! But then, the Hand of God would reach down, slap me upside the head with some new inspiration, and pull me out of bed. I'd get a phone call from some friend I hadn't heard from in thirty years. He'd send me a dream or a thought of how to proceed with a chapter, the title of a book I should read, or perhaps just a sunrise I should experience. So the *Chronicles* became my Afterlife training ground, teaching me ever more about the Earth School we attend, our divine "boot camp."

My book would be the culmination of forty years of personal experiences, Eastern and Western spiritual practice, scientific/scholarly research into a variety of related fields, ongoing journal work and dream analysis. *The Dead Saints Chronicles* would set out to validate the vivid descriptions of the mysterious Afterlife realm recorded by the Dead Saints throughout human history. My prognosis assured my own entry into that realm in the not-so-distant future, lending it an immediacy and a unique perspective; a book about the Afterlife unlike anything written to date.

Dead Saints Epiphany

Why the *Dead Saints*?

In early November 2012, during my usual 20-minute morning drive to the local 76 gas station for my favorite coffee, I was casually musing about my near-death research when suddenly the words *Dead Saints* and *Apostle Paul* appeared in a vision.

In that instant, *I knew* all my NDE research would become a book, and Dead Saints would be part of the title. In that instant, I also *knew* how the book would be structured. It was inspired by Paul, the Apostle, who, 2000 years ago, wrote his Epistles directed to the saints. It was the specific word he applied to those Christians who had had an encounter with God, Christ and unconditional love. That experience transformed their lives and freed them from the fear of death. It was just such a mystical and transformative experience of brilliant Light that turned Saul of Tarsus, a notorious persecutor of Christians, into Paul the Apostle.

While that ecstatic moment on the Road to Damascus is common knowledge, less well known is another experience of Paul's that may have been what we today would recognize as a classic NDE:(2 Corinthians:1-4)

> *It is not expedient for me doubtless to glory. I will come to visions and revelations of the Lord. I knew a man in Christ above fourteen years ago, (whether in the body, I cannot tell; or whether out of the body, I cannot tell: God knoweth;) such a one caught up to the third Heaven. (A place beyond the stars) And I knew such a man, (whether in the body, or out of the body, I cannot tell: God knoweth;) How that he was caught up into paradise, and heard unspeakable words, which it is not lawful for a man to utter.*

The accounts of Paul's conversion describe it as miraculous, supernatural, or otherwise revelatory in nature. The NDE testimonies shared in modern times are similar to St. Paul's experience. Thus, Dead Saints refer to those who have gone through and been transformed by their NDE.

The term *Dead Saints* differs from the Catholic, Buddhist, Muslim, or Hindu "saints" who are known and revered for their piety, devotion and miracles. These *Dead Saints* represent a unique *Class* of saint, usually ordinary people who after actually, if only briefly, dying, return alive to this side of life with absolute KNOWLEDGE of the immortality of the soul and a concomitant loss of the fear of death.

But with that experiential knowledge comes a sense of urgency. The Mission must be completed; they have so much to do and so little time to do it in. These contemporary Dead Saints may acquire spiritual gifts and some become interested in the paranormal. Like Paul, they share a newfound love for the Being of Light (in the Christian case, Jesus Christ) they encountered while "out-of-the-body."

Flashback: Near-Death Research Project Launched in July 2011

By late July 2011, I was engaged in disciplined research, cataloging about fifty near-death testimonies a day from blogs posted on NDERF.org, but as yet I had only a vague intention of using that research "someday" as the foundation of a book. NDE researchers had done a thorough job establishing the reality of near-death experiences, but few had systematically indexed, analyzed, commented upon and connected the dots of the myriad, profoundly paradigm-changing details brought back from the Afterlife.

Gradually, I realized connecting those dots was to be my Mission. I believed (and still believe) that worldwide acceptance of the near-death phenomenon could have momentous worldwide consequences. Thus, the seed for *The Dead Saints Chronicles* was sown, took root and grew.

Near-Death Lightning: October 5, 2011

I was reading the near-death experience of Christopher, a 60-year-old Vietnam vet from North Carolina, who died during surgery to remove his left lung. Without warning, I began laughing hysterically. I felt continuously zapped by a thousand volts of *humor*. The room and I appeared to be sealed in a bubble of holiness and absolute gentleness. The laughter turned into uncontrollable sobbing. Time lost meaning. Only the moment mattered. I could barely speak. I dropped to my knees and repeated over and over, "Oh, my God! *Oh, my God!*"

I spent the next several days floating in that holy softness so often described by those who have died and returned to life. I could tolerate no cussing or yelling. When I walked outside in our Japanese garden, everything looked more alive, perhaps an unseen connection between the plants, birds, rabbits and myself. I felt such peace for a few days. I thought I *was* in Heaven.

I wondered, what triggered such a dramatic event?

There were clues. During Christopher's surgery, before dying on the operation table, he began speaking aloud in what appeared to be a two-way conversation. After Christopher was resuscitated, one of the surgeons later approached him to discuss the surgery and talk about the remarkable conversation that happened:

[Surgeon standing at Christopher's bedside begins speaking]
You're probably wondering why I'm standing here.
Christopher replied, 'You want to tell me some more about my dying?'
No, that's not the reason why.
'Well, what's up, doc?'
I've been performing these same surgical procedures for the past 25 years and something happened here today I've never experienced before. It's had such a profound effect on me that I have to tell you about it.
'Okay, go ahead.'
We had you wide-open and were removing a special kind of fat tissue from your heart to use to tie-up your fistula when all of a sudden you started talking out loud. Surprised, we all jumped back from the table as we initially thought you had come out from underneath the anesthesia, but when we checked our instruments, we found, no, you were still under...still unconscious...so we just stood there and listened while you talked.

'What did I say?' [He had no recall of anything that had happened while this was going on.]

It's not so much what you said as it was to whom you were talking to.

'Who was that?'

'You were talking to Jesus Christ.'

When he said this, I thought he was some kind of a nut. I didn't really know what to say, but I noticed he seemed to be a little astonished.

'Well, was He talking back or was I just hollering out into the void?'

He quickly said, 'We couldn't hear any other voices, but it sounded like you were engaged in a two-way conversation.'[1]

My encounter could be described by the Christian term, "slain in the spirit," but I have experienced this first hand among large groups of believers during laying-on-of-hands healing services, and *felt* the movement of the Holy Spirit (associated with laughing and crying), but my living room encounter was much more intense.

It then occurred to me I must have invoked Jesus' Holy Presence while visualizing the NDE. I wasn't praying at the time. I wasn't asking for an experience. It just happened. My encounter raised an important question: "How could the simple act of reading a dying man's near-death meeting with Jesus Christ evoke such a profound experience for me? Could this happen to others who read about near-death experiences?

I began to believe others could tune in to an NDE testimonial like Christopher's and vicariously share it. I gave the direct encounter with Jesus a name. *Near-Death Lightning.* A term that became an important thesis in the *Chronicles*.

The Method, Early Insights, Sudden Unanticipated Urgency

For the most part, I have selected significant, but not-always-obviously related snippets from innumerable NDE accounts which, when woven together, address timeless and universal questions about the purpose of life and death, the physics of the Cosmos, the reality of God, and the proof of immortality. Often it was seemingly minor details brought back by the Dead Saints, viewed in the context of theology, mythology and philosophy that brought these normally abstract subjects to life and provided meaningful insights into the nature of the Universe itself.

With the advent of the internet, NDE reports have increased exponentially. For the first time in human history, technology has given ordinary people the ability to post extraordinary individual experiences on popular dedicated websites and reach massive audiences without going through the expense and time of publishing a book.

The Dead Saints Chronicles include near-death experiences of both children and adults, drawn from accounts of some 5000 people, who describe what it is like to be dead. We learn from people who have faced death and who came back to life KNOWING death is not something to fear; death is literally an illuminating transition to a greater reality ruled by Love.

These are the stories of those changed lives, or Dead Saints as it were, who have died (physically or mystically) and journeyed beyond this life and this Earth to a divine dimension of celestial Light and color, who received life changing counsel from Jesus, from God-like Beings, angels, even deceased family members, and who were able to retain and bring back this apostolic message. Their stories of personal transformation (sometimes bestowing upon them supernatural powers, such as healing and prophecy) and their unalterable sense of a universal love are qualities in keeping with the generally accepted definition of *saint*.

Are Dead Saint Experiences Holy?

If the Apostle Paul can be transformed by his encounter with a dazzling Light from Heaven, can people who today experience the same Light receive divine revelations as holy and life changing as St. Paul? Can these Dead Saints, who have glimpsed paradise, return to life with holy conversations? Why would their experiences be any less holy than Paul's?

While addressing these questions, I draw mainly from Judeo/Christian accounts. This is not meant to disparage or exclude other spiritual traditions. It is simply that the bulk of the available NDE evidence comes from the West and in all likelihood is what most of our audience will be familiar with.

More often than not, the truths brought back by the Dead Saints through direct personal experience are infused with a humble authority. One writes:

> *I found myself embracing solitude rather than wasting time retelling a story; NDE is not a mandate, not a commissioning to holiness. I can, as any other human being, make a claim to holiness, without ever being touched by the Sacred. And the mindless repeating of story, a story that cannot ever be fully told, is loath to me. I am a simple, uninteresting, semi-rational, ordinary, human being (my wife sometimes doubts that). And I*

am constantly making mistakes, laughing about them or apologizing. And still in search of an answer.[2]

Some NDEs are more equal than others. Though always intense and unforgettable, not all NDEs are equally transformational. Some experience a Christ-like change. However, the NDE is not a guaranteed free pass to endlessly serene sainthood. Not everyone, upon returning to life on Earth, is turned from a caterpillar into a butterfly. Some become sad and angry, having lost "Heaven" and feel they were given little choice about returning to life in order to carry out their Mission. Some accepted their Mission and returned, but by no means did all accept their return to Earth willingly. Others came back still feeling all too human, burdened by all the struggles beset them prior to their NDE. To be clear, NDEs are not equal licenses to sainthood. These sacred experiences do not equally transform the heart and mind.

Seven Near-Death Triggers

One central theme in *the Dead Saints Chronicles* is you don't have to be physically dead to have a near-death experience. While death and near-death accounts commonly gain the most attention and are considered more "authentic," there are four additional triggers, which can lead to an NDE, but do not involve injury or death of the physical body.

Table 1 describes the injury and non-injury events that may trigger an NDE, containing one or more of the 23 Death Elements (See chapter 13).

Invariably, the near-death experience is a "born-again" experience—consistent with, but not restricted to, Christian values. The Dead Saints aspire to charity, service, and a love for all humanity, as do all other spiritual traditions. Eyes are opened, hearts are touched, life will never again be the same, but the newly canonized saints typically have the same obstacles to overcome, the same lessons to learn after their resurrection as they did before they died. The Dead Saints come back with a new perspective. They discover Earth is a University. Their classes, designed by God, are still in session, with exams remaining to be studied for and passed. Now these students have the gift of a new heart, new perspective, and a new hope in which to tackle those daily challenges.

Seven Near-Death Triggers	Description
#1: Physical-Death	**Clinical Death of the physical body**
#2: Near-Death	**Severe/moderate injury** to the physical body, including coma
#3: Multiple-Death	**Severe/moderate injury** to the physical body during a multiple casualty event. NDE survivor witnesses and communicates with non-survivors as they die.
#4: Fear-Death	**Non-injury**, core-dying event caused by belief death is imminent. *(Term coined by Dr. Jeffery Long, M.D.)*
#5: Shared-Death	**Non-injury** core dying event experienced by the living in the presence of a dying person. Living are acutely conscious and awake during the experience. (Term used by Dr. Jeffery Long, M.D., and Dr. Moody, M.D., Ph.D.)
#6: Mystical-Death	**Non-injury** core dying event triggered by deep meditation, prayer, hypnosis, astral travel, Near-Death Lightning, Holy Spirit, (i.e., Christian born-again), or appear spontaneously without cause. Sometimes referred to as an STE. (Spiritual Transformative Experience) or SOBE (Spiritual Out-of-Body Experience)
#7: ADC (after-death communication) / NELE (near-end of life event)	**Non-injury** core dying event experienced through a dream involving an after-death communication (ADC) from deceased loved ones, (which may occur years, months or days before death) or a near-end of life event (NELE) (seeing and talking while conscious or semi-conscious to deceased friends and family, weeks, days or hours before death.

Table 1

Linda describes her prayer one year after her near-death experience:

> *I don't know what I am supposed to do, who I am to see, or what I should say. I don't even know what to think. I am always requesting what I think would be best for me. God, I don't know what is best for me. My life is yours. Whatever you want for me is fine. If I am to lie here in this bed, sick and disabled for the rest of my life, whether it is twenty minutes or twenty years, that's fine. Whatever happens is fine. I know you love me. Then I added, 'I make one request, however. Please, if I am to live, let me be useful in some way —for YOU.'* [3]

Dr. Jeffrey Long asked in the original version of the web based NDRF.org study Questionnaire "Has your life changed specifically as a result of your experience?" Of those responding, 73.1 percent answered, "Yes." He concluded from his ongoing study that the majority, but not all, NDERs experienced changes in their lives as a result of the near-death experience.[4]

Authenticity of Dead Saint Experiences (Term to be interchangeable with NDEs)

I have written the *Chronicles* with a distinct Christian and Eastern bent that reflects my training and I include many of my own Christian-oriented dreams and personal experiences of the Afterlife. My material has been culled from the thousands of Dead Saint experiences that make up the world's NDE English inventory. I have chosen Afterlife testimonies I believe to be authentic, real, and "off the cuff"—that ring true and do not attempt to impress or proselytize.

NDEs are not rare. It is estimated by near-death researchers one out of 25 people (4.2%) in the US have experienced several core elements of the dying experience.[5] Calculating this statistic equates to more than 12 million Afterlife tales in the US alone, a statistic that may be off by as much as 50%. It has also been estimated more than 25 million individuals worldwide have had an NDE in the past 50 years.

NDEs that occur on the operating table in hospitals are thought to be widely underreported because doctors and healthcare practitioners are not open to them.[6] Research has shown "patients remain silent because nobody believes them when they first try to talk about it and fear being labeled as crazy."[7] Christians may keep their experiences to themselves, fearing ridicule because the dead are not supposed to awake until Judgment Day. Sometimes children do not recognize the unusual nature of their experience, as was the case for 4-year-old, Colton in (the movie and book), *Heaven is for Real*.

The Dead Saint's near-death visions are typically described as very vivid-*more than just a dream-more real than real*, and often the most beautiful, dramatic experience of their lives. Looking back on the NDE, the saint perceives physical existence as the dream. Moreover, the saints describe communication akin to what we regard as telepathy. Every word is communicated without actual verbal words. They never feel like they are hearing anything auditory at all:

> *People would just look at each other, and often even with some mouth movements, but messages would come through so quickly, without any effort, and from the inside, rather than outside of self.*[8]

Are the Dead Saints divinely inspired voice recorders playing back *exactly* what is being dictated to them, or does the brain *significantly* filter their experience? From my research, each Dead Saint encounter is unique. Afterlife experiences that occur in a non-corporeal state, must be interpreted by the human brain when the Dead Saint returns to the physical body. The vision or dream images of the saint are converted to words and symbols that are interpreted through the filter of the human brain-mind's experiences including: vocabulary, culture, religion, beliefs, fears and age. Interestingly, some researchers have found that a surprising number of children "felt like an adult in a child's body" during their NDE.[9]

Some researchers theorize the NDE is a result of an intense belief in God and the Hereafter, but as we will see, NDEs happen as frequently with unbelievers as believers. It appears, at times, deep religious beliefs significantly affect the interpretation of Afterlife encounters when re-told to the faithful, but the basic framework of the experience remains intact. There may be overlapping themes of *brilliant Light* and *unconditional love* in all non-materialistic phenomena, but they always intersect with and are informed by the *unique matrix of the individual's personality and social circumstances.*

Regardless whether the quasi-scientific anecdotal approach I employ in the *Chronicles* is accepted, I believe the cumulative evidence gathered is enough to convince—except for die-hard materialists—that even one valid Dead Saint "white crow"[10] will disprove "all crows are black."

Can Christianity's Beliefs Accommodate the Dead Saint Experience?

You may wonder if your religion (or, for that matter, lack of religion) can accommodate the Dead Saint experience. Christians may ask whether these encounters will confirm their belief in Jesus Christ as Savior and the Son of God. Christian writers have written many books on NDEs that most often reflect their Biblical beliefs about Heaven and the Afterlife, sometimes rejecting NDEs that do not support their views.

Some preachers feel the widespread practice of accepting personal spiritual experience, or the near-death experience as "authoritative" is misleading Christians. They feel many people are "augmenting the Bible with extra-biblical data, proclaimed as "new" revelations from the Holy Spirit, and misplacing their faith in an alleged mystical experience."[11] The fear among some churches is they will make the spiritual experience as valid as the written Word of God. I believe this is the crux of the matter. Perhaps, their spiritual experience *IS as valid* and *holy* as the Word of God.

The basis behind the fear of the personal, spiritual experience can be found in the Evangelical Reformation led by Martin Luther, who taught, "enthusiasm" for the mystical experience, "Clings to Adam and his children from the beginning to the end of the world—fed and spread among them as poison by the old dragon. It is the source, power, and might of all the heresies, even that of the papacy and of Mohammed. Therefore, we should and must insist that God does not want to deal with us human beings, except by means of his external word and sacrament. Everything that boasts of being from the Spirit apart from such a word and sacrament is of the Devil."[12]

Martin Luther's teachings are why some Christians regard the NDE as a type of "demonic possession," a view derived from a single St. Paul line in 2 Corinthians 11:14, where he writes Satan may disguise himself as an "angel of light." I have only read of one such "counterfeit angel" NDE out of 5000 in my database where a being poses as a "smiling angel" clothed in bright white garments.[13]

A lone "counterfeit angel" should not be accepted as a reason to dismiss wholesale the thousands of real, life altering, Dead Saint encounters with a holy, loving Being of Light and with Jesus; transformative encounters which validate and clarify our faith. These are not cruel charades devised by the Devil.

St. Paul says in his letter to Galatians 5:22-23 that we will know them by their fruits:

The fruit of the spirit is love, joy, peace, patience, kindness, goodness, faithfulness, gentleness, and self-control. Against such, there is no law.

The Dead Saints show ability to distinguish good from evil even in the midst of a near-death state. Their encounters with Jesus and the Being of Light describe angels and Beings exhibiting unconditional love and forgiveness. The saints discern the being of darkness (Satan), as the antithesis of Light, and while created by God, is deceitful, and does not generate love, forgiveness, holiness or goodness.

Please be assured, NDE studies and spiritual experiences will neither become a "religion of the resuscitated" nor will they replace the Word of God as reported in the Holy Bible and the sacred texts of other religions. It will become clear from NDE testimonies there may be some misunderstanding of what has been passed down to us centuries ago, but God's Word remains holy and complete. It is my belief, the Dead Saint experience is a contemporary "continuation" of God's Word. We should consider their sacred experiences carefully and weigh them against the Spirit of Truth.

Strict, doctrinaire, literal Christian beliefs appear to be changing. In the last two years, movies based upon NDEs and sojourns in Heaven continue to attract blockbuster audiences. Why is the Word of God not being sought as the *only guide* for many Christians? Ponder this question as we take up a walking stick and begin our Zen journey through the *Chronicles*.

Reporting the Afterlife

The doctors have given my life an early expiration date. Over 150,000 people die every day somewhere on the planet. So, my death, whether it comes tomorrow or in the next few months, will be just one of hundreds of thousands who will be led through the "Grand Central Station" of death to a final destination somewhere in the Realms of Heaven.

Think of me as a "dying journalist" in the fox hole with pen and pad in hand, reporting "live" from the Earth side of Heaven's gates. My reports offer an unusual opportunity to look beyond the veil, to see what I see, to hear what I hear, to visualize what I dream, and to present salient, unambiguous evidence from the foxhole that Heaven is real, and that consciousness survives death.

Whether or not some scientist or university eventually manages to prove the existence of the Afterlife to the satisfaction of debunkers matters little. I believe the evidence presented will convince everyone else consciousness is eternal, and that our true native and original spiritual state exists in the Realms of Heaven, our true home. This reiterated truth, carrying the imprimatur of direct personal experiences, is as powerfully expressed by today's Dead Saints as the venerable, time-honored words of our ancient prophets, sages, and saints.

While this manuscript is technically no more than bits of data on my computer as I write this, it really feels more like a thick, ancient, worn leather manuscript, illuminated throughout with sacred symbols and prayers. It is not a Bible, but a Canon of sacred Afterlife experiences that become a lens, magnifying truths about God and Heaven, a new *Magna Carta Liberatum* for all faiths.

Definitions and Terms

I feel it's necessary to clarify terms used in the *Chronicles,* how my journal notes are woven into the book, and the format that makes this work unique.

I refer to the *Being of Light* encountered by the Dead Saints using many synonyms: The Creator. The Christ. Jesus Christ. The Living One. The Source of Life. Living Love. Living Water. The Son of God. The Messiah. God. These terms are meant to be interchangeable and not to reference a particular religion.

Ongoing After-death communications (ADCs), approaching-death dreams (ADDs), and premonitions about death I received during the dying process, are chronicled and integrated into the story when appropriate. Chronicle journal notes begin June 13, 2013, when my brain cancer was discovered. They are inserted throughout the book by Chronicle number. Day 1 is Chronicle 1, and so on. They are included for content and may be out of sequence. My experiences before June 13, 2013, are referenced by date instead of Chronicle number.

I use Japanese gardens and Bonsai metaphors throughout the book to tell *the Dead Saints Chronicles* story. In the process, I refer to the term '*Zen*',[14] not the religion, but to the core essence of Zen, which states wisdom can only come from direct experience, not through doctrine or dogma. Each religion has its mystical branch, and as my path took me from Christianity, to Eastern thought and back again, I employ the Zen philosophy to shed light on aspects of the Afterlife modern Christians may be curious about. Through Zen mysticism, or the belief in gaining knowledge from direct experience, I utilize those who have had direct experience of death—the Dead Saints—to glean a better understanding about what truly lies beyond the veil.

Zen attempts to describe *what is* rather than *what is not*. In other words, "Things are what they are." The Zen philosophy (via the Koan- e.g., "What is the sound of one hand clapping?") attempts to resolve paradoxes, which cannot be resolved by the rational mind. Answers are invoked by prayer / contemplation / meditation—with the solution coming as a flash, a realization of the truth, and from whence does this answer come?

The answer, in the Christian vernacular, is it comes from the Holy Spirit, the spirit of Truth revealing what is real as opposed to what is illusion or fantasy. It is an answer born not from the rational mind, organized religion, formal education or inculcated beliefs, but from the mind of God, the Living One, the Christ, the Source of Life and Light *within and without you.*

Let me explain why I emphasize and italicize the above sentence.

There is great debate among non-Christians, non-believers, and metaphysical students whether Jesus Christ was a historical man or a created archetype of a mythical Christ. Their ongoing belief is that Jesus was a myth created to represent the Christ Consciousness within us.

Early second century followers of Christ called Gnostics recognized the paradox of Jesus Christ without and the Spirit of Christ within. They describe *'The Kingdom of the Father'* as the Light within us that also exists in and around all things, a Light personified in the historical figure of Jesus Christ. This theology appears on the surface to be in conflict with traditional Christian beliefs of a sovereign Jesus, but I assure you, it is not. The resolution to the paradox will be found through reading and pondering hundreds of Dead Saint experiences. "The pondering" is the Zen part of your journey.

Of Jesus' real, historical existence, there is no doubt. When He touched me in 1981 and 2011, my faith became a KNOWING. Like the Dead Saints who encounter Jesus in the Afterlife, the experience of touching the hem of His garment changes us forever. It is not mythical, nor is it philosophical. To those who have not had the experience, there is no way to explain it, other than to document my own approaching-death experiences of Jesus Christ and those Dead Saint testimonies of the Being of Light chronicled throughout the book.

The Christian Afterlife

The term *Christian Afterlife* became a part of the title of the *Chronicles* for several reasons:

1) To prove that the Being of Light and Jesus of Nazareth are real.
2) To interpret the deeper message of the Christ hidden in the Bible.
3) To resolve Christian theological dilemmas about Heaven and the Afterlife.

Beneath the Zen and the Christian Afterlife themes, brain cancer presented me with a formidable obstacle to writing. On June 13 2013, when Doctor Ma entered the emergency room, closed the blue curtain for privacy, and she bluntly told me, "Mr. Solomon, we found a *mass in your brain,*" no matter how unafraid you think you are of death, no matter what your religion, when a doctor tells you that you have what might be a terminal illness, the news is catastrophic. Suddenly death became real. It was no longer a "philosophy" or just something that had to happen when I got old. In that moment, two years of Dead Saints research looking for answers to abstract Christian theological debates about death and the Afterlife suddenly became the central focus of my life.

Cancer forced me to find real answers to these eternal questions. It allowed me to open my heart to dreams, to revelations about the Bible, God, Christ, and the Afterlife I would never have grasped without the cancer experience.

Let me be clear. Whatever your belief system, whether Christian, Buddhist, Hindu, Muslim or Atheist (which is the belief, often passionate, in disbelief) this book is intended for people of all types and creeds. My ultimate hope is EVERYONE from any background will be able to find inspiration within its pages.

~Afterlife Journalism has become for me all about penning one by one the ten thousand details of unconditional love. ~Chronicle 940

---

1 *Christopher R Possible NDE,* #932, 09.07.06, NDERF.org. Christopher R NDE phone interview July 7, 2014. Printed with permission.
2 *Herbert M's NDE,* #322,10.29.03, NDERF.org
3 *Linda S probable NDE,* #1011, 02.03.07, NDERF.org
4 Jeffrey Long, M.D. with Paul Perry 2010. *Evidence of the Afterlife: The Science of the Near-Death Experience.* New York: HarperCollins. p. 177.
5 G. Gallup and W. Proctor 1982. *Adventures in Immortality: A Look Beyond the Threshold of Death.* New York: McGraw-Hill.
6 Pim van Lommel, M.D. 2007. *Consciousness Beyond Life, The Science of the Near-Death Experience.* New York: HarperCollins. p. 9.
7 R. F. Hoffman 1995. Disclosure Habits After Near-Death Experience: Influences, Obstacles, and Listener Selection. *Journal of Near-Death Studies 14*: 29-48.
8 *Amy C NDE,* #2386, 10.09.10, NDERF.org
9 P.M.H. Atwater, LH.D. 1999 & 2003. *The New Children and Near-Death Experiences.* Bear & Co: Rochester, VT. p. 52. Originally published in 1999 by Three Rivers Press under the title: *Children of the New Millennium: Children's Near-Death Experiences and the Evolution of Humankind.*
10 The White Crow theory proposed by William James in 1848 was a popular metaphor to illustrate one of the problems with inductive reasoning. A billion observations can lead to an induction, but it only takes ONE contrary observation to invalidate the whole chain of reasoning.
11 Rev. Robert S. Liichow October 2007. THE SUFFICIENCY OF SCRIPTURE. Truth Matter Newsletters. Vol 12, Issue 10.
12 Bayer Oswald 2007. *Theology the Lutheran Way.* Grand Rapids, MI. Eerdmonds. p. 53.
13 Unverified source. Experience is suspect because of reported 115-degree high

temperature and delirium. A young person sees a being clothed in bright white garments with a bright happy angelic face with arms outstretched saying, 'Come with me and all of your worries and problems will be over. When he asked the being, 'What would happen to my younger brother and sister whom I protect from my mean sadistic older brother?' The being turned dark and grimaced at him and said harshly, 'Forget about them, think about yourself!' It threw up its arms, covered its face, and said 'Nooooooo' as it retreated back into a dark tunnel.

14 Note: Zen originated with Taoism, a philosophy called the "The Way" or "Tao" founded in the writings of Lao Tzu, who authored the *Tao Te Ching* in the middle 6th century BC in Hunan, China. His writings appeared nearly simultaneously with the writings of Buddha, and the two modes of thought later blended together in Japan, in Zen Buddhism and integrated into the discipline of Bonsai. Zen is a continuation of Taoism with Buddhist concepts and language.

3

Death is a Lie Humans Tell Themselves

If life, or consciousness failed to survive death, there would be neither any meaning to life nor any ultimate justice. Nevertheless, many people believe that life does not continue after death. Yet, as we often discover in life, what we believe may have little or nothing to do with reality.
~ *Sogyal Rinpoche*

It was October 29, 2014. I was only a week away from sending the rough draft of the *Chronicles* to John Anthony West for editing, when Takanohashi sensei, my deceased Bonsai teacher, appeared in a dream and gruffly said *"Nebari!"*—pointing at an old azalea trunk and its thick, exposed roots. Nebari is a Japanese word which means *root, specifically the visible spread of roots above the growing medium at the base of a Bonsai.*

When I studied with Takanohashi sensei in Japan in the late 1980's, he always uttered the word *Nebari* with great passion. This was the second time he had visited me during an after-death communication (ADC) dream, the last time only a few months ago on August 8. He had died in 1997, but I had not seen him since 1989. I said to him in the dream, "You're alive!" He just grinned at me, and then the dream was over.

So on October 29, after he said *Nebari* in his gruff Japanese, there appeared in my dream a round sour dough loaf of bread on a cutting board. I saw my dream-self cut two slices of bread, the two slices were placed one on top of the other and cut in half, then I woke up.

I immediately interpreted the meaning of the bread, (as in *"feed us this day our daily brea*d") as a reference to the spiritual word explored in the *Chronicles* and how I was to write it. I was supposed to cut the book literally in two. So I did. I rearranged chapters, made edits, and the book flowed better. I cut in half an impossibly long 600-page tome—so thank you, Takanohashi sensei, Bonsai master, and now master editor. My first 11 chapters have become Part I, Nebari-the "roots" of the *Dead Saints Chronicles*.

~There is no prescribed path to death. Mine is being recorded and laid out here for all to see. ~Chronicle 819

A Life Threatening Game

It was summer 1975. I was 16 and experimenting with a hashish enhanced version of the "pass out" game with my sister and an older friend. Little did I know at the time how dangerous this foolish trick had become. One in 16 adolescents have played the choking game, a deadly playground fad that cuts off the oxygen supply to the brain, causing a 'high' sensation. Along with the risk of asphyxiation, the choking game comes with a chance of seizures that can cause brain damage.

I do not want to share specific details about this dumb trick, because I do not want to give anyone ideas. Anyway, according to my 14-year-old sister who was present, sometime after the "big squeeze," I suddenly collapsed and fell on the floor, my eyes rolled into my head so only the whites showed, my body went into convulsions and I stopped breathing for about a minute. During this brief time, I saw an image of a red tricycle I rode as a young child, (which I verified later), but nothing else I could remember. When I awoke, John D.—my best friend who "setup" the dangerous experiment—was laughing hysterically, but my sister was freaking out because I had stopped breathing.

I immediately KNEW I had died and my heart had stopped.

For a very long minute, I... was... dead.

Technically, I experienced two core aspects of a near-death experience. First, the knowledge I had died. Second, the vision of a partial Life Review. I was certainly unconscious and apparently dead as my sister recounts, but I would call it a sort of a *near-death twilight zone*.

Before my NDE, I was afraid of death. Very afraid. I would lay in bed at night imagining what it would be like to die. It was a horrible, morbid fear that would follow me for days. I thought, "Someday I am going to die" and the knowledge would hit me like a knife in the gut, that "I will literally, really die someday."

I could not imagine... not being.

I could not imagine... non-existence.

For me, it was about surviving death—that my personality and consciousness could cross the dark threshold and somehow be preserved. Many of us, I believe, have gone through this mental exercise sometime in our life. The provocative question lingers almost daily.

Does our consciousness survive when we die?

Immediately after my NDE, I still feared death. I came to consciousness knowing I had died and it frightened me. A few weeks later, however, I had a dream that seemed to be memories I had forgotten from my NDE. It is important to describe this, not only because dreams became a central part of my life during those early teenage years, but also because that "dream" was my own, personal "born-again" experience that permanently established my relationship with Jesus Christ.

Furthermore, and more importantly, I believe for most of us, dreams are our most accessible vehicle for "piercing the veil" between the celestial Realms of Light and Earth University. Dreams make communication possible with the spirit beings, long lost friends, angels, and with God. Dreams are non-physical, sometimes traumatic, events that sometimes trigger certain "core" Death Elements commonly associated with death and near-death experiences recorded in the *Chronicles:*

> *This dream began in a setting of a high-rise hotel building that was set against a bright blue sky. I had some unknown purpose for going into the building, but I suspected it had to do with robots and electronics, because a robot was in the elevator with me and small flat TV sets were hanging on its elevator walls. (Flat TV's didn't exist in 1975). I had this strange sensation as the elevator went higher up into the sky within the building that we were moving higher into the future. The elevator brought me to one of the upper floors, and I was surprised when I stepped out of the open elevator door, my white 1967 Chevy station wagon was there waiting for me to drive me even higher up the hotel. So I*

began driving the wagon up these green-carpeted ramps that went higher up several floors until I saw a man wearing a red, hotel bellman outfit.

I stepped out of the station wagon, and he motioned to me with his finger, "follow me." I followed him until I realized I was no longer in the hotel, but walking in a "fog." I looked behind me and hundreds of people were following me. It was morning, and the sun was just beginning to rise. The fog finally thinned out with the sunrise and I realized when the fog cleared, I was walking near my house on Coconut Lane in Virginia Beach, where I then lived.

I was staring at the large disk of the morning sun, when suddenly the sun itself began floating towards me and gently landed in front of me near my house. As the sun touched the ground, it transformed into Jesus Christ. I faced Him and fell immediately at His feet on my knees, clutching repeatedly the green grass beneath me, weeping and crying. I noticed to my left there was a young woman, about the same age as me, with short, slightly curled black hair, also kneeling; also weeping and crying. I could not see her face. We both were making a "promise" to do something. The "something" we promised the Lord, I do not know. Jesus spoke to us for some time, but again, I did not remember His words.

I awoke, sobbing. Forty-years later, I still remember every detail of the dream. It was real, more real than memories I've had at any time in my life. The dream experience helped ease my fear of death, but left many questions in my mind. One that stood out was the importance of completing my "Mission"—a task which I have no memory. The second, "Who was the girl kneeling next to me?" Apparently, the Mission Christ gave us was a partnership, a connection I would not make for nearly forty-years.

The dream appeared to be additional memories surfacing from my near-death experience, because it highlights several Death Elements (See chapter 13): An elevator (tunnel); scenes from the future; a bellman (angel) directing me; people walking through a fog (veil); the Sun (bright Light) turning into Jesus Christ (Light Being); a Mission for living; and prostration (perceived holiness).

Remarkably, decades later, this dream would have a near-death corollary. A woman who died during childbirth, but who was brought back to life, also saw the sun transform into Jesus Christ:

The next thing I was aware of was lying on my back on some type of bed, within a dimly lit room. I noticed the window looked like the one in the delivery room, but I recalled it had been shaded and now was not shaded. It looked like the sun was rising and that too seemed strange since it was close to noon when I went into the delivery room. Then as I gazed at the sun, it kept coming closer to the window, getting larger, speeding up, and getting brighter. My thought was that the Earth and the Sun were about to collide and I was witnessing the end of the world. The ball of Light came through the window with the sound of a swift wind, and I saw it was an awesome image of illuminating white Light that was Jesus.[1]

Afterlife Questions

I never told Mom, Dad, or even my Pastor, Tracy Floyd, about the NDE or my dream of Jesus—which would have revealed my foolish attempt to get high. I had been active in the United Church of Christ Youth Group every Sunday since we moved to Virginia Beach in 1972, but dreams and near-death experiences...were not their specialty. After my Dead Saint experience, my thirst to know the world of the unseen (not just be titillated by it) soared. I wanted to know everything about death and the Afterlife.

I would not have long to wait.

Six months later, on the evening of January 8, 1976, I awoke late one night to a loud "snapping sound." For some reason, I looked out my second story window to see if I could find the source of the noise. To my astonishment, and I wasn't sure, but I thought I saw a woman standing in the middle of the street below. Then, as suddenly, she disappeared. The next morning, Mom told me Great Grandma Miller had died. I wondered, "Was she the woman I saw last night?"

Mom flew out to California for her funeral, but she never told me how Grandma wore her hair in the open casket funeral. After my cancer struck in June 2013, I told Mom about the "death ferry" dream of Great Grandma Miller's prediction of my future death. I described her distinct appearance and her silver, braided ponytail. Mom pulled out a 1957 photo of her family, and there she was...just as I had seen her in my premonition! I can only guess Grandma Miller's visit that night in 1976 (and I believe it was her), and her warning/preparation visit in my dream three years ago surely means...she is my guardian angel!

Mom was my source of spiritual wisdom at the time, an "unconventional" Christian who, in addition to church, was a member of a *Search for God* study group at the Association for Research and Enlightenment (ARE) in Virginia Beach. I asked her about dreams and how to interpret them. Hearing my interest, she suggested I join her study group and research the works of Edgar Cayce, the renowned "Sleeping Prophet." In addition to my Youth Group Bible Studies, the ARE opened other possibilities I had never considered; that we could learn to pray and meditate and receive answers from God through dreams. They became the Saturn V rocket, which lifted my sight ever higher towards Heaven.

I began keeping a Dream Log, and recorded continuously nearly two years of dreams until I was eighteen—dream logs I still have stored in boxes. In my Junior High school year, I completed a college elective in Parapsychology at the ARE. It was there I was introduced to the near-death work of Raymond Moody M.D., through his book *Life after Life*, which subsequently sold 20 million copies. His work became a bookmarker in the back of my own mind—a seed planted that wouldn't begin growing until I began researching NDEs as a pastime in July 2011.

Why we Fear Death

As I began my NDE research in July 2011, I searched the *Chronicles* for answers to questions about why people attend church, temple or a spiritual retreat. Were they afraid of death? Was faith or belief in the Afterlife (or eternal life) enough to ease their fear of dying? These questions morphed into a spiritual treasure hunt when I discovered Christians and non-Christians, despite a strong faith in God, were still afraid of the same things, which made me shiver at night. Where did these deep-seated fears come from?

The Christian mystic, Dion Fortune, talks about the root of our fears in her little book, *Through the Gates of Death:*

"So, what makes death so terrible? Is it the pain of dying? No. Morphine can deaden that. Most death-beds are peaceful when the times comes, and few souls go out struggling." Why, then, do we fear death so? Firstly, it is the fear of the Unknown." [2]

There are other reasons we fear death including a fear of God's Judgment in the Afterlife. For others, it may be the dread of separation from those we love, but *the fear of the unknown* is the one thing which makes death terrible for people of ALL faiths.

How differently would we set out to cross the threshold of Death were our minds at rest?

Death Is a Lie Humans Tell Themselves

The title to this chapter, *Death is a Lie Humans Tell Themselves*, is a quote taken from a Dead Saint. What does it really mean?

There may be just one thing in the universe a human being cannot do and that is we cannot imagine not being. If we try to imagine ourselves as dead, we may conjure up a body in a casket, a funeral, and lots of flowers, solemn words and mourners dressed in black. We are still here in the present; simply observing from another vantage point.

However, everything, involving fear, to any extent, is rooted in a belief in death. Most of the top ten best sellers are about murder, death and dying. We are entertained vicariously by war and movies that imitate or re-enact death: *The Walking Dead*, is still the #1 television series and is entering its 6th season.

We thrill at being scared to death, entertaining ourselves through dangerous death-defying feats, creating faster and faster ways to propel ourselves from one place to another and allowing access to more and more methods for killing ourselves and each other. We attempt to corral death with costly coffins of impenetrable metals and as a final insult to death, we toy with cryogenics and cloning as a last ditch effort to achieve physical immortality.

Exploring Death: Not Living in the Present

The most popular and widely used method for exploring death remains the choice not to be alive in the present. The mind can easily put itself somewhere else, choosing to live outside present-time. We live in the past and blame it for being inadequate in the present or we live in the future and dread what might or might not be. Thus, our fantasies allow us to escape living in the now. We are as good as dead to the present.

Of course, we are not really dead, only pretend-dead, but there is little difference. Both allow us to escape what is around us in the present moment. How often does the mind wander from this experience and go to tomorrow, next week, or last week? And this moment is lost. We will not remember what was said. We will have to check someone's notes. Then we lose that moment as we try to recapture this one. All because we were so busy living in another time instead of the present. We killed the moment which brings life.

When we live in the present moment, we experience what is real. We do not experience fear, disappointment and death. We are stimulated by our surroundings and enthusiastic about what we are doing.

The less conscious we are of life, the *deader* we are. When Jesus says, "Let the dead bury the dead," he is referring to the living as "dead"—unconscious to life. The total lack of consciousness is a step deeper into the fantasy of annihilation and non-existence, but it is not real either. Total lack of consciousness can deprive us of the physical body, but it is not real, and it is not the same as death.

Death Is Birth into Life

The Dead Saints often describe death as a birth into life—the Afterlife. That death is not real and an untruth accepted and taught by humankind. David, an 18-year-old atheist until his near-death experience, encountered Jesus:

I was 18 years old when I felt immense pain in my chest. I had been diagnosed with an irregular heartbeat which I had my whole life. I felt my heart stop beating and then I experienced blackness. The next thing I know I'm looking at my body. Then I see myself, but have no real feeling of "oh, that's me." I didn't care. It was an empty vessel. Big whoop. I didn't need my glasses and I no longer had Tourette's Syndrome. I felt a warm Light behind me and when I turned around, I was in this beautiful warm sunny garden. Everything was alive. Then I heard His voice...

He [Jesus] said, 'Death is a lie men tell themselves. We never truly die. *You leave this Earth once you've learned all you can and then return to the spirit world.'*

He showed me they [the dead] can see us whenever they desire, but we here in the physical world have complete free will. There was a part in this beautiful world where I wanted to go. But he said, no, that if I went there I couldn't come back. Suddenly, a beautiful Light shown towards us. It was a Light I knew was Jesus.

He said, 'You must go back now.'

And I said, 'No. I wanna stay.'

He replied, 'You promised you would do this. You have much left to do.'

With that, I was slammed into my body and I awoke gasping for breath.[3]

Janet, who died from an injected drug of unknown type, came back astounded that the beliefs and untruths about death could not continue:

Three of us were in an empty house, making lots of preparations to do complete house decorating. Walls stripped, etc. We were in the kitchen. The two men with me were not drug addicts, but recreational drug users. They had been given a drug. They had small needles to inject with it. I was given an injection.

...They lived. I collapsed and died.

I know the next details, as I observed, was in a different dimension. Between them, they picked up my body and moved me into the main hallway. Lying on the floor, they checked for a pulse, to hear any breathing, and then gave me mouth-to-mouth resuscitation, using movements to press on my chest for lungs. Nothing happened. I lay there lifeless.

They gave up and were in shock, so they leaned back on the radiator and didn't know what to do, rolled themselves cigarettes, and smoked them looking at my body lying upon the floor, discussing wrapping my body in bin liners and how to get rid of me, and dispose of the body.

...Meanwhile, I had risen up. I could see through the floorboards...into the floor above...I saw the wooden framework within the building as I was rising up. I was just going higher up and higher up through the building...I was in the banisters...moving through the floors... walls...a totally different dimension...I was a living entity that could move through things...that did not appear to be solid as they had been to me before. I saw them, but moved through them....no emotion....no joy, no sadness, no pain, nothing like that at all...but then, something, I don't quite know what, made me turn around. Then I saw myself on the floor. They had finished their cigarettes, and then one said I was 'dead.'

My instant reaction was 'they think I am dead.' That is a lie. It cannot be allowed. **The lie of death is not acceptable. My complete whole being found the untruth just unacceptable. I could not allow it. It could not be allowed in the entity I had become, or was.** *It was principled, all consuming, in a way I find hard to describe other than it could not sustain that which was not truth. It was truth...and very, very alive...*

The men were spooked a bit by me and started to tell other people I had come back from the dead. I thought I would not be believed, so, kept a lot to myself. But I had, and have, a complete certainty we do not die. We continue to live, but in a different dimension as a different type of entity. There should be no fear of death. None whatsoever.[4]

Fears about Death

The only thing that allows fear to exist is our belief in it. Fear appears to be real, but it is an illusion. So what is fear? A definition coined by Zig Zigglar: ***False Evidence Appearing Real*** perhaps best describes it. Fear is a fantasy we create to prove to ourselves something is real. It stems from a belief in lack or limitation. It is a belief that something...like God's love for you... can be withheld from you. It is not the truth.

Fear has many soldiers. Worry. We believe it's alright to worry. For example, if your daughter is two hours late coming home, you worry. Was she in a car accident? Was she raped? Or, God forbid, even killed? You may go through every possible scenario, imagining all the bad things that could happen. Your daughter walks through the door two hours late. You scold her and ground her for a month. In the end, your fears were unwarranted.

Fear is a fantasy imagining bad things happening. Fear causes you to lie to God, yourself, and others. Instead of fear, we should invoke prudence to make our decisions.

The Fear of Pain

Besides modern medicine and morphine drips to ease suffering, patients who are dying find themselves floating outside the physical body, erasing all pain. Kathleen had a medical emergency on the operating table when she experienced her NDE:

> *I was so afraid to die. I was afraid of the pain I thought I would feel. Then I heard the doctors say, oh Lord, we're losing her! I then felt a pulling whoosh up and then was at the ceiling watching it all! I felt no pain at all. I did, however, feel the fainting sick feeling you get before passing out and I felt light and heard a buzzing noise. I then watched the doctors working on me. He (the doctor) was swearing terrible. I remember thinking, good Lord, He (God) can hear him! I was embarrassed for them all in the ER. I then went up but don't remember moving. I just was in a really beautiful meadow of sorts, trees, stream, fish, grass, etc.*
>
> *Then, I was in a place of the most beautiful silver white color - that's the best way I can describe the color of this place! The feeling was one of utter joy and love!! I mean real complete love. Not of this Earth. And peace, such peace!* [5]

The Fear of Loss

Beverly was raised in a conservative Jewish family in Philadelphia. The culture was materialistic and judgmental. Bookish, shy and serious, she went through her teens as an atheist. Since learning of the Holocaust at age eight, she had turned angrily against any early belief in God. How could God exist and permit such a thing to occur? At age 17, just after graduating high school, she was devastated when a sudden, fatal heart attack took the life of her father. When he died, she felt abandoned. To add insult to injury, she learned during the mourning period that the prayers of her mother, sister and herself did not count because they were women. Furious, she turned to Eastern mysticism for comfort. During the summer of 1970, she moved to California, looking for adventure, a new life, and inner peace. Then, while staying in Venice Beach outside of Los Angeles in July 1970, she had a motorcycle accident which led to her near-death experience after being transported by ambulance to the hospital ER:

> *I lay down on the bed, becoming an agnostic as many atheists do in times of trial, and prayed from the bottom of my heart for God to take me. Somehow, an unexpected peace descended upon me. I found myself floating on the ceiling over the bed looking down at my unconscious body. I barely had time to realize the glorious strangeness of the situation—that I was me but not in my body —when I was joined by a radiant being bathed in a shimmering white glow. Like myself, this being flew but had no wings. I felt a reverent awe when I turned to Him; this was no ordinary angel or spirit, but he had been sent to deliver me. Such love and gentleness emanated from his being, I felt I was in the presence of the Messiah.*
>
> *...I then remember traveling a long distance upward toward the Light. I believe I was moving very fast and through an immeasurable vastness, but this entire realm seemed to be outside of time and space. Finally, I reached my destination. It was only when I emerged from the other end that I realized I was no longer accompanied by the being who had brought me there. But I wasn't alone. There, before me, was the living presence of the Light. Within it, I sensed an all-pervading intelligence, wisdom, compassion, love, and truth. There was neither form nor sex to this perfect Being. It, which I shall in the future call He, in keeping without our commonly accepted syntax, contained everything, as white Light contains all the colors of a rainbow when penetrating a prism. And deep within me came an instant and wondrous recognition: I was actually facing God.* [6]

Beverly's actions after the accident revealed her transformation. In the past, she was painfully shy and felt herself unworthy of being loved. No longer an atheist, she went out with her head swathed in bandages and landed a job in one week, made many friends, and got involved in her first real romance. Since then, she has married and become a mother. Although it's been 36 years since her heavenly voyage, Beverly's memory of her Dead Saint experience never diminished. Even in the face of ridicule and disbelief, she never doubted its reality. Nothing that intense and life changing could possibly have been a dream or hallucination.

She concludes her testimonial on NDERF offering inspiring counsel to anyone who fears the oblivion of death, or who grieves the loss of family or friend:

> *For anyone who grieves or fears annihilation in death, I assure you of this: there is no death, nor does love ever end. Modern physics assures us matter does not die, but is instead transformed into energy. I see the body as a coat housing the immortal consciousness within. When our Mission is complete we remove the coat and take on our glorious form, complete with the full spiritual understanding we vainly seek during our Earth days.* **Then, having graduated this temporary school, we get our report card in the life review, with extra credit for love, forgiveness, and service to others.** *Now we can continue on our journey unencumbered, free, and truly alive. Someday you who are reading this and I will be together in this realm of Love, Light, and unending bliss.*[7]

Fear Blinds Us

Everything in this life is dying from the minute it's born. It's one thing to say it, to repeat it and know it intellectually. It's quite another to actually sit there and see it, really see it, and it's a very strange experience. All the things we all think so important—wealth, having a partner, a big house, possessions in a hundred years' time, will be gone or belong to somebody else! We don't matter, not in the greater scheme of things. We take years accumulating wealth to ensure security, and then we die. Clichéd though it may be...we can't take it with us. We all know this. So why do we do it?

The lie or illusion of death blinds us to the truth about eternal life. It does not matter what religion we believe in. If we act as if life will end when we die, then fear rules our life. You do not know the Christ, the Living One. As the Zen saying goes, "You do not know what you do not do."

The Zen of Death

Enlightened men and women over the millennia have tried to communicate transformational mystical experiences through language but language is, by its very nature, inadequate for the task. Words cannot describe experiences that are, by their very nature, indescribable and ineffable. This limitation is captured by an ancient Chinese teaching tale about a stonecutter who was training his son to sharpen swords. Teaching was difficult. Too much pressure cut the sword edge too deeply. Too light pressure would not properly sharpen the blade. Teaching the correct pressure was only communicated through "doing and experiencing," not by words written or spoken. The same applies to playing a violin or hitting a baseball or riding a bicycle. Words, however wise, written in books are but skeletons—frameworks for the truth, but not the truth itself.

Such puzzles/paradoxes can drive the mind mad, but this Zen tale essentially attempts to describe the importance of gaining knowledge by direct experience. Is death a lie? I can only share the sacred periphery of an answer through the dry bones of words. To invoke a realization of the Truth, to KNOW it for ourselves we must experience what death is NOT.

*~A few hours after reading the end of Chapter 1 of "An Autobiography of a Yogi,[8] Yogananda describes his miraculous capture of two kites as a child. Two hours later, Delynn and I attended a Cirque du Soleil's Kooza, in Virginia Beach. In the show, the hero flew two kites. One kite was flown by a young boy at the beginning of the show to represent his childhood, and one kite at the end of the show, symbolizing the freedom of innocence he found at the end of his life. As we shall see later in the Chronicles, it was another breadcrumb revealing the Law of 2's. ~***Chronicle 794**

---

1 *Elizabeth S NDE*, #2113, 02.02.10, NDERF.org
2 Dion Fortune 1968. *Through the Gates of Death*. Great Britain: Society of Inner Light. p. 7.
3 *David NDE*, #3240, 01.14.13, NDERF.org
4 *Janet M NDE*, #2639, 03.14.11, NDERF.org
5 *Kathleen's NDE*, #213, 03.02.03, NDERF.org
6 *Beverly B NDE-like*, #1031, 02.25.07, NDERF.org
7 Ibid. *#1031*.
8 Paramahansa Yogananda 1981, 1987, 2007. *Autobiography of a Yogi*. Authorized by the International Publications Council of Self-Realization Fellowship.

4
Earth University

*~ADC DREAM: It was my 56th birthday, 2015. In the dream, I was having a birthday party, when **Felton Jones** sat next to me on the sofa. Even though he had passed away in 2007 at the age of 86, he was apparently very much alive in my dream. The birthday party was potluck and he had picked out a plate of what looked to be some sort of tempura vegetables to eat. Felton seemed rather coy and did not speak much—at least I don't remember anything he said. It was definitely him.*
~Chronicle 589

April 1982
Hearthfire Lodge, New Market, Virginia

    I was staring out a second floor window of Hearthfire Lodge when an old, brown 60's Oldsmobile drove up in a thick cloud of dust that settled on the massive 100-year-old spruces lining the drive. The car circled the roundabout in front of the house and parked nearby. A thin, tall, graying man stepped out of the car and stood looking up at the house. I couldn't see from the second floor, but my mentor, Paul Solomon, had already come out the front door and was welcoming someone he seemed to know well.

We soon learned our unexpected mystery guest was Felton Jones. We had all heard that name. Paul had often talked about the Zen master he had studied with back in '70's. No one could have guessed, looking at him, and meeting him, that this lanky, matter-of-fact, chain-smoking American, was in any way a spiritual master, especially in so exacting and so traditional a Japanese art as Bonsai! But so he was. And what was he doing here? I had been learning Christian and Eastern mysticism from Paul Solomon in our little country school, but Zen was so.... Zen. It was something I didn't rationally understand.

When Felton Jones showed up, he never identified himself as a teacher, Zen master, or even a *sensei* of Bonsai.[1] Actually, as I subsequently learned, if you ask three different teachers of Zen if they are Zen masters, they will all deny it anyway!

It was mid-morning and a warm spring day. There were 12 of us living at Hearthfire at the time, including Paul Solomon. He and Felton talked briefly, then without explanation, they left in Paul's yellow Pacer in another cloud of gravel dust. Really? We all thought there would be some kind of Bonsai demonstration or class. We were mystified. And with the ubiquitous cell phone a couple of decades into the future, there was no way to satisfy our curiosity. We just hung around, waited...and waited.

Hours later, they returned with a dozen small nursery specimens, azaleas, junipers, and pines, one for each of us at the Lodge. Each plant was to be become a trained Bonsai, a term that means literally "tree in a pot." Paul and our small class, spent most of the afternoon gently guided by the Bonsai master, pruning, shaping, and wiring our trees. Hours went by.

When Felton got to me, he asked me to choose one of the plant specimens on the table. I had no idea how to choose a good Bonsai, but I settled on a pretty, two-foot high, small leafed red azalea. It hadn't bloomed yet. It seemed to have a nice trunk, but it looked like an Azalea bush, not a Bonsai. He and I stared at the tree for a few minutes, when suddenly he took his concave Japanese cutters and pruned off one of the major trunks on the plant. I was shocked. How could he cut off that much?

"There, you go, David. Just trim the dead branches. Other than that, we are done. You can't wire this tree during spring, because there is too much water in the bark. Enjoy the flowers when they bloom. It will

---

Hearthfire Lodge Blog: 1982

P.M.H. Atwater visited Hearthfire Lodge and shared her NDE with our student group.

Elisabeth Kübler-Ross visited Hearthfire Lodge to give a talk about Death and Dying.

become a beautiful Bonsai, but it will take years to fill in the branch I cut off. Next year you can do more." I knew Felton was communicating something more than horticultural advice to me, but I couldn't get his meaning.

Paul pulled me aside, "David, the personality you put out front to people is your importance. He just pruned it off. He is suggesting you develop new branches to fill it in again, a process that will take many years."

I'd always wanted to be the good student," but that came as a shock and it stuck with me. It's something I've pondered for years, even to this day.

Some of the trees were ready for root pruning, and so we spent time learning that. A few of the pines were put in clay Bonsai pots, transforming them into classic Bonsai. It was an amazing and profound afternoon. Except for Paul, it was our first encounter with this rarified and quintessentially Japanese Art. Somehow, through the fledgling trees we were experiencing conception, gestation and birth. We were no longer Bonsai virgins! They were our new babies. It was awesome.

We were asked to put our Bonsai away and gathered inside the Library for a "talk." Felton settled in as well for the class. It had been several years since Paul had seen him and he had told us the story of how they met a number of times. However, this was different. The Zen Master was present, in our midst.

Paul looked to Felton, who replied, "This is your story. Don't look at me!" He lit a cigarette and got comfortable. Paul pulled out his Meerschaum pipe, and began:

[Paul speaking]

In 1974, a woman approached me and asked if I wanted to meet a Zen master who taught Bonsai in Atlanta.

She said, 'I have a feeling what he is really teaching has little to do with these trees he is bending into shape, but I don't know really what it is and he won't say, so why don't you go and see him.'

I had always heard about ancient eastern spiritual schools dramatized by Kwai Chang Caine in the popular 1970's series, Kung-Fu. It absolutely fascinated me. So I went to see him.

As I recall, when I arrived at the school of Bonsai in Atlanta, I saw this six-foot-American meandering out to me. I had expected a short, white haired Japanese master. He was not at all what I expected. We walked quietly together through traditional Japanese landscaping and ponds, to shaded benches that held hundreds of these miniature trees, all of them Bonsai. Some of them looked like a little tree you would see on a mountain beside the ocean where they were bent in a windswept direction, one side bare from the salt spray and the branches moving out to the other side. The Bonsai were done so perfectly they didn't look as if the hand of man shaped them. They were actually modeled in that way and yet they were living things. It was exceptionally fascinating. There were little forests with dozens of trees growing on a slab of rock. Dozens of trees and a perfect forest. In fact, the forest might include a mountain, a lake or a cliff, and ferns, in this little miniature world.

Paul explained. As I walked through the garden with Felton, I noticed some peculiar things about him. First, he was never in a hurry. I was so excited with everything that was going on around me I would ask three questions before he would answer the first one. I couldn't get him to move any faster. And the slower he got, the more impatient I got. But the man didn't even seem to notice. In fact, he was so much in communication with the nature around him that I was there as an observer, and got the distinct impression he was apologizing to the garden for my presence.

[*Paul turned and looked directly at Felton sitting next to him*]

'I began to realize you were teaching me something, but not by pointing it out to me, and by not telling me what the lesson was. I had the option of not even noticing it was a lesson.'

[*Felton said nothing and stared into his cloud of cigarette smoke*]

Paul continued. We went to sit down and chat about what you were doing. I had heard you working with some students in forming a tree and I heard you say, 'In wiring branches in a particular direction, you must realize this is a living being. Don't think of it as a plant. Think of it as a soul, and this soul needs to be molded in a particular direction. These training wires are like life's experiences that bend your nature in a particular direction so you are made more beautiful by the pressure of these wires that mold your being.'

I was listening to you give these people fantastic spiritual truths, when all of a sudden it occurred to me; you were not really teaching horticulture or botany or even Bonsai. You were teaching them spiritual growth and the laws of the universe. What a brilliant mind! So slow. So understated, acting as if he was not brilliant.

[*Paul stopped speaking. He sometimes used the "pregnant silence" between sentences to make his point. Long seconds passed.*]

You acted disinterested in me, but as a perpetual student, I needed to ask, 'I know the ancient masters had a rule, if the student couldn't notice a lesson, the teacher couldn't give it to him. You had to be ready for the lesson in order to receive it. You had to be able to ask the question in order to get the answer. I realize you are not going to sit here and tell me you are a teacher of spiritual growth, but I can see you are and I want to learn from you.'

[Felton glared at Paul with a look that could melt steel.]

You looked hurt I could make such an accusation. And in your very slow, soft way that still twisted the knife, you said, 'I am not a spiritual teacher. I do not teach spiritual lessons.'

[Paul grinned at Felton, 'How peculiar. I wonder what he does believe in?]

But I didn't quite know how to ask. The best I could say was, 'What do you mean?' I know you are teaching more than how to torture these plants. It is a bigger lesson. I can hear that in what you are saying to these students. What do you mean you are not a spiritual teacher?'

You looked a little confounded, but answered:

'What you are accusing me of suggests I would separate life from its essence. What I teach is life. The relationship to the universe. Not this on a spiritual level and this on a practical level, and this on a physical level. I don't rip these things apart. It is all one law. Spiritual growth is growth—that's all. I don't believe there is any such thing as a spiritual teacher. If a person separated that part of their life and tried to teach that, they would be teaching an error in the first place.'

[Paul turns to Felton]

Well, I was duly impressed and that's when I asked you to teach me. A few uncomfortable moments went by, but you just shrugged your shoulders and said, 'All right, let's work with a tree for a few moments and then I will come back and we will talk about it.'

You gave me a pine tree that was sort of rag-tag. It didn't look like a Bonsai at all. It looked like something he had picked out of somebody's garbage can and put in front of me. It had literally thousands of dead, miniaturized little brown pine needles in it. You explained the pine needles had been reduced in size by clamping its roots and cutting them back. You gave me a little pair of tweezers and told me to pick out every one of those little brown pine needles.

[Paul stared at our class]

I was not so dense I couldn't recognize a lesson in patience. Everybody laughed, but Felton sat absolutely deadpan.

So, I took those tweezers and said, 'If it kills me I am going to do it and sat there at that table picking out those little pine needles one by one. I wondered if I really had to do this or if you thought it was just for me. But I kept plucking and plucking. Hours went by and I had just plucked one side of the tree. My mind began to think about work at my office and all sorts of other things I could be doing. I kept thinking Felton should be talking to me. He could be teaching me fantastic lessons while I am plucking these damn little pine needles!'

You let it go on for hours and I didn't think you would ever get back to me. Later on, you wandered off stopping here and there to comment on work done by one of your students. By the time you got back to my plant, and me, I had developed quite a relationship with my rag-tag little pine tree. I was beginning to see the tree in a completely different way.

[Paul looked at Felton]

You began to talk with me about the tree. You asked me, 'If you were going to shape that into a more beautiful shape, what would you do?'

I looked around at some of the other trees you had shaped and looked at my tree and thought, I don't see any way this tree can get into a shape like one of those other trees. If I bend all of these branches that way, it still wouldn't do it. Even if I cut this branch or another, it still isn't right. I couldn't imagine anything beautiful in that tree. It was like a rag-tag, dirty little girl without her hair combed.

You just stared at the tree while I struggled to decide about its shape and direction. Suddenly, it occurred to me, 'Well, maybe windswept, because most of the branches go in one direction anyway.'

[Felton suggested Paul begin working on his Bonsai]

'Why don't we just work on it and see if anything comes out of it for you?'

I watched you take the pruning shears, cut, wire them, and push them around. It really didn't look all that gentle, in the way you did it. I didn't see how the trees survived it. So, I picked up the shears, held my breath, and started to cut one of the pine branches.

At first, I thought you would go through the ceiling, 'Don't do that! You didn't ask for permission first!'

I said, 'What do you mean?'

'You have to talk to the life in the tree so it understands what you are going to do to it, so it will cooperate with you. That's how you are going to find out what direction it wants to go in.'

I wondered, 'Oh, you are going to tell me how to talk to the spirit in the tree. I see. Alright, how do I do it?'

[*Felton explained*]

'Talk to it.'

I sat there looking at this ridiculous little scruffy pine tree and had no idea how that pine tree was going to talk back to me. There is nothing harder than trying to talk out loud to a tree feeling it is just a tree. But I tried. I asked it what direction it wanted to go and it was so ridiculous I almost giggled. You watched you and me didn't smile. I could see little fleeting glimpses of a sense of humor at my discomfort in trying to communicate with the tree.

Sighing, you said, 'If you could see the tree as a human being, what would being look like?'

I began to describe this dirty, skinny little girl with combat boots and uncombed hair.

You urged me, 'Close your eyes and see that little girl standing before you.'

I thought that was easy enough. 'I closed my eyes and I could see the little girl.'

[*Felted prompted Paul on*]

'Now talk to her. Don't talk to the tree. Talk to her, the spirit of the tree and ask what she would like.'

With my eyes closed, the image began to come. 'First of all,' she said, 'you've already washed my face.' And I saw her face differently after that.

'My hair is ready for combing and shaping.'

As the images came, I opened my eyes and looked at the tree again, and saw it with brand new eyes. It was a different tree, and the tree was excited, as I was to cut it. It no longer felt that I was going to cut a branch and it was going to bleed. It was more like a girl who was going to get a haircut and when she was finished, she knows she is going to look beautiful. There was a spirit coming from the tree, and both you and I began to communicate with it.

Before we finished late that afternoon, we had pruned and wired the tree into an exquisitely beautiful, little Bonsai that was windswept and had the bark missing on one side. You showed me how to paint the bare part of the pine with sulfur, which turned it white so it looked as if it had been bleached by the sun and salt spray. You could almost smell the ocean by looking at it.

I was thrilled! I really felt as if I had seen the transformation of a soul from something uncontrolled to something beautified by nature itself. It didn't look like the hand of man shaped it.

[Paul began speaking to Felton]

After this experience, I said, 'I would like to study with you. I have an idea you can cause me to learn more than I can learn by accident. You can take me in a short time and teach me more in one year than I can learn in five years on my own. Will you take me on as a project and shape my mind like yours?'

You looked at me and said, 'This is not a part time job. Could you leave your Fellowship church, close its doors, wash my teacups in my kitchen, make my bed, sweep my floors and pick the pine needles off the dirty, scruffy pines and do all of these things if I never say anything wise to you?'

It hit me like a ton of bricks. I had started the Fellowship in 1972. It was like my child, a living being, something that was a part of me, and to close it would be like closing a part of my life. However, at the same time, there was this great opportunity to study with a great Zen master. These two highly valuable things were being weighed in the balance for me, and it seemed to me the life of the Fellowship would continue even if its doors were closed. I made the decision. 'Yes. I will come here and be your student.'

You turned to me and said, 'That being true, I cannot teach you.'

I was not expecting that sort of reply. I thought I had sorted it out and had done exactly the right thing. And I said with tears running down my face, 'Why?'

[Felton looked unmoved]

You gave me two reasons. 'For one thing you are too emotional about it, and secondly, if you could close your Fellowship and come here, then I have need of learning from you because I couldn't close this Bonsai school and come stay in your Fellowship.'

Well, I felt I had learned more in that short exchange in those few seconds than I could have learned in a lifetime out there looking for it. The experience affected me profoundly. I asked Felton if I could meet his teacher someday. He said, 'the teacher only makes that decision.... if he wants to meet you.'

I asked, 'How will I know?'

[Felton looked at Paul as if it were the most absurd question he had ever asked]

I realized it was, so he dropped the subject. We parted with a handshake and a smile and he left for the day to go about his business.

It wasn't long after that I moved the Fellowship headquarters from Atlanta to Virginia Beach. I got a call one day from a man at the Norfolk Botanical Gardens who said he knew Felton, the Bonsai teacher from Atlanta. He said, 'I've studied with him for quite some time and I have a tree here I would like to bring to you. Perhaps, you could work with it and see if you would like to continue learning Bonsai like you did with Felton some time ago.'

I asked him to come out and he brought a stunning black pine Bonsai that was still in training wires. I noticed the man was oriental. He sat down with me and we looked at the tree together. After a few moments of conversation, he left the tree with me, giving me the impression it was a gift from Felton. Later in the day, I thought I'd call Atlanta, assuming Felton had sent me the tree. When I spoke to Felton, he said, 'I didn't give that tree to you.'

I questioned, 'Who did?'

'He did.'

I wondered, 'Why should one of your students want to give me a tree?'

That's when you told me, 'That wasn't one of my students. That was my Teacher.'

I was incredulous, 'My God! I spent ten minutes with that man and hadn't asked him a single question! All these years I waited to meet him, and I don't even have sense enough to recognize the presence of this teacher! How could I have missed it?'"

[Paul got on the phone to Norfolk Botanical Gardens and asked if the oriental man was still around]

I finally got the Teacher on the phone and told him I was not quite sure how to take care of the Bonsai he left and asked if I could see him again. He very graciously consented to come back out and talk to me about the care and feeding of the little Bonsai tree he had left. I found myself sitting with this gentle man, peering at the little Bonsai tree.

This time, I was captivated by every word and gesture from him. How could I have missed the signs? The sharpness and clarity of his presence, his slow and purposeful movements?

Then the most spectacular thing happened; as we sat there, he began to refer to the tree sitting before us. 'As I was training this branch, instead of bending in a new and beautiful direction, it was stiff and ready to break.'

He explained softly, 'That was the period when you decided to teach instead of publish your work.'

I stammered, 'What do you mean? How did do you know?'

He quietly said, 'This tree was put in training wires at the time my student told me of you. Since then, I have watched you in the branches of this tree. Everything you have done has been reflected in this image of you. If I met resistance in a branch, I knew you were experiencing resistance in what you were doing, in your work or in your personal life.'

I was astonished. This Teacher, who I had never even met, had been participating in every experience of my life for the past three years. Looking at the Bonsai, I realized every branch had been a point of communication between the Teacher and me. He had been teaching me through the tree. He never forced me to learn anything. He never manipulated me by bending the branches in ways they did not want to go. He only made gentle suggestions to me through the tree, to grow in a more beautiful, harmonious direction.

I knew he had come very, very close, and had somehow been allowed to touch the periphery of a genuine school of ancient mysteries, much like Kwai Chang Cain in Kung-Fu...but without the Shao-Lin Temple. I asked the Teacher the question that persisted in my mind. 'Are there places, perhaps in China or Japan, where priests and priestesses provide instruction to students who become spectacular individuals who know how to respond to every situation in life?'

'There may be such a place,' he answered, 'but you are already enrolled in the highest possible graduate school on this planet. You have never been without a teacher. You study at the feet of the Light who created this little Bonsai, who created your body and your mind, who puts before you every day the necessary lessons you need to grow and become more beautiful. Why would you go in search of something less than what you already have?'

Then he told me the story of another young man who had gone in search of one of these hidden, ancient schools in Japan. This young monk had traveled from China, searching for a fabled mountain top Buddhist Monastery where enlightened masters lived. He eventually found the school, was enrolled, and began a lifelong career of study and discipline. His first learning experience was attending dinner. As he left his room and walked down the long, tatami mat hallway to the dining room, he noticed a broom leaning against the wall and some dust nearby on the floor.

He noticed the dust and the broom were still there the next day. He went back to his room and meditated, still waiting for the classes to start. After his afternoon meditation, he went again to the dining room for dinner. The broom and the dust remained, and now a mop and a bucket sat a little further down the hallway.

'How careless,' he thought. 'This school was supposed to be the best available.'

Irritated, he went to eat. When he returned, the mess in the hallway remained. 'I'm going to tell someone about this,' he muttered. 'In fact, I'm not sure I want to stay here. If the masters of this school can't manage things better than this, they can't teach me very much.' Within a week, the young man left the school, unaware the lessons had already been placed before him. Even as he walked out the temple doors, he was waiting for the lessons to begin—still ignoring the mop and the bucket.

Following my encounter with the Teacher, I dropped my search for an ancient school of the mysteries. I accepted his advice and decided to concentrate on the lessons God's Earth University presented to all of us every day. We entered this school the day we were born. Since our birth, God has been carefully designing and presenting the perfect lessons we need in order to strengthen our ability to master life on Earth—our ability to respond appropriately, with compassion, kindness and wisdom, to every situation that arises. Through this school of life, we are being shaped daily in more beautiful and harmonious directions.

Not all schoolteachers on this planet are slight, gentle, Bonsai masters bearing tiny trees. Teachers come in many disguises. The training wires in this school can come in all shapes, sizes and personalities.

No waiter or waitress was ever rude to us in a restaurant for no reason. No cashier was ever impatient for no purpose. No family member ever created trauma for us when you did not have something to learn from it.

In this school of life, it is impossible to need a particular lesson without that lesson appearing. It is impossible for a lesson to appear without your needing it. The next lesson is always ready and waiting. The mop and the bucket are always out in the hallway. God, our source of Life and Light, has placed them there so we will stumble over them if necessary. Each time we walk by without seeing them, the teacher's purpose is to move them a little closer to the middle of our path.

Whatever the lesson we face, we have two choices: pick up the mop and start scrubbing, or push it out of the way and say, 'Isn't it ridiculous somebody left this here?'

Paul continued, 'Enrollment in Earth University is mandatory. The only elective is whether we do it consciously or not. Some people are sleeping through their classes. Others are awake, paying attention, taking notes, studying old tests, learning the correct answers for when the teacher calls on them. Guess who gets better scores and passes to the next grade? When we make the decision to pay attention and to participate in our lessons on purpose, life takes on new meaning. We feel less victimized when the plumber overcharges, the car breaks down or the promotion falls through. We feel less defeated if our marriage struggles. We feel less alone if we become ill. We are students in the school of life, whose headmaster is the Source of Life, the Source of our Consciousness itself, the Divine we call God. Our Inner Teacher. Take notes.

Paul stopped talking and grinned at everybody. He turned to Felton and cleared his throat, 'I think dinner is ready. It's time to eat.' And with that our evening class was done.[2]

As I remember that special evening in 1982, I recall feeling I was given a teaching that was very wise-something I should really pay attention to. However, I wondered what I was really striving to learn in that little country school we called Hearthfire Lodge? Was it the Eastern secret to enlightenment? Or the Christian secret of Jesus Christ?

The concept of our planet as one BIG SCHOOL is a common theme throughout the *Chronicles*. Jean sees Earth as a testing ground to apply spiritual lessons:

> *I was told the Earth is like a **big school**, a place where you can apply spiritual lessons learned and test yourself, under pressure, to see if you can actually "live" what you already know you should do.*[3]

Another near-death testimony pre-supposes God has laid out our life's purpose and lessons before we are born. Pat writes:

> *I was at a water fountain with a man in a long white linen robe tied around the waist with a cord. He told me, 'Basically, the Earth is a place to walk the walk and literally live the way it should be done. It was made clear to me some people come to the Earth to work on only one aspect of themselves, while others come to work on several aspects. Then there are others who come to not*

only work on their own nature, but also to help the world as a whole.

The other side does not have the physical pressures having a body has. Here on Earth, you must feed and clothe that body and provide shelter for it from the elements. You are under continual pressure of some sort, to make decisions that have a spiritual base. You are taught on the "other side" what you are "supposed to do," but can you LIVE it under these pressures on Earth? From what I saw and heard there...on the other side...it is all about relationships and taking care of each other. Perfection is not expected of people...but learning is expected and considered good progress.

All of our experiences in a lifetime tend to follow some sort of pattern...and often will recreate the same lessons...only in a different way, and under various circumstances. This is how you know what you are here to learn and test. If you examine the patterns...certain themes will become clear.

I was shown a library filled with gold covered books. These are the lives of people on Earth where their life plan is laid out and what they hope to achieve through certain key experiences. From what I was shown, people have free choice as to how to get to these preset key experiences. They can take a meandering path of experiences or a more direct route, but there are certain events that are preset and will happen...no matter what. Each of those key events are benchmarks and one's reactions to them will show how much they have learned and what more needs to be done, or learned. [4]

Sue reiterates the importance of learning our lessons:

From these two near-death experiences, I have learned a couple of things. From the first, in good child form, I got the impression there were lessons I needed to learn and if I learned them quickly, I could play the rest of my life. It seemed there was a certain amount of time allotted to this lesson learning and if I was astute, I could get through it and then play. (I do not believe I have been very good at the lessons. However, quite a few folks have said it looks a lot like I'm playing all the time these days. Who knows, maybe I am?) [5]

One Dead Saint commentary communicates the concern many may have about mistakes we have made in life. Can we flunk out of Earth University? Sure we can. Some of us may feel we have already, but it is not a sentence to a dark place in eternity. During Bridget's NDE, Jesus explained to her to be 'flesh' is to 'sin':

> *'You were flesh. And with flesh is biology and psychology and instinct and desire and mechanism and ego and the serving thereof. To be flesh is to sin and that is the nature of being. There is no fault in being human.*[6]

It perhaps also gives an answer to the question, "If we are automatically forgiven for our sins and mistakes, why should we care about paying attention to our lessons in life?" From a spiritual perspective, the idea of Earth University makes a lot of sense. However, from a Christian perspective, why should we concern ourselves with mastering the lessons of Earth University? We are going to Heaven anyway, right? What difference does it make?

Parable of the Scuba Dive[7]

Entering Earth University with all its quizzes, exams, and finals, is analogous to Scuba Diving. When you plan a dive, you usually choose a beautiful setting, like the Virgin Islands, Hawaii, or the Great Barrier Reef in Australia. Ideally, you wait for a peaceful, clear day, with bright blue sky, with the island and palm trees in the distance, warm sunshine, and beautiful aqua, green, and blue waters of the reefs.

Then you put on heavy, restrictive, cumbersome equipment. You strap tanks on your back, and put a mask over your face, which limits your vision. You put a regulator in your mouth that allows you to breathe but not talk, and fins on your feet that make it awkward to walk.

Then you fall off the boat, usually backwards, and tumble into a different world. From that moment on, the world you were living in no longer exists. Your experience of this exciting "underwater" world is limited to the equipment you are occupying, but as you adjust to your equipment, it feels less and less restrictive. You are neutrally buoyant and can easily float through "inner space" and...quickly...almost too quickly...it becomes difficult to remember what it was like "up there" in the sunlight. You don't have much time to think about it because you are focusing on breathing, how much air you have left in your tanks, kicking your fins, and taking in the beautiful, sometimes dangerous underwater life.

It is very much like this when you are born into a physical body in Earth University. Taking on a body is restrictive and cumbersome; a prison compared to the pre-conception freedom "on the boat" before our descent into the terrestrial waters.

And as long as we struggle with our need to breathe, and move around in this world; our need to make a living guaranteeing personal security; getting distracted by entertainment and excitement, depending on our lizard "human" brain to survive, we forget the spiritual world we came from.

However, the Dive Master, who planned our dive, our excursion into Earth University, knows why we came down here. He knows the life purpose we once understood, what we had to explore, and what Mission we were supposed to accomplish. He is still there providing us with air to keep us alive and pertinent lessons to help us learn and grow.

It is interesting to hear what people talk about when they come back up to the boat after a dive. Coming back up is remarkably like a near-death experience. After you resurface, you take off your scuba gear (physical body), recover your natural ability to breathe air—the breath of your Source of Life, —and jabber about what happened "down there." Do you know what divers talk about? You would think the conversation would be dominated about the exhilarating reefs and the fabulous Technicolor fish—and it is, if that is all the divers experienced. However, when a diver encountered threatening things, the electric eels, the poisonous scorpion fish, the barracudas, the sharks-the dangers down there become the exciting things that animate us.

That seems to be what fascinates, even obsesses us in life-the dangers and the problems. We are so wrapped up dealing with dangers and problems, and just struggling to survive in Earth University reality, we forget why we were put here.

Waking Up in Heaven

The dive led by the Dive Master is still, always, underway. We are all still breathing. If we recollect hard enough, we may remember that heavenly boat waiting on the surface. However, if we have plenty of air left in the tanks, what's the hurry? The underwater garden we have been swimming through has captivated our thinking since the day we were born. But that was so long ago we have almost forgotten the sunshine and the friends we left behind on the surface. We have become so mesmerized by our Earth University reality that we think it is not only real, but is *the only reality*.

Heaven and the sparkling Light is waiting for us on the surface. However, as I said, most of us believe we have plenty of air, so there's no rush to swim back to the surface. And, frankly, because we are still here, our life purpose and Mission are not yet finished.

That's just the big picture. At any moment, despite our Earth University syllabus, we can "change our major," and graduate with honors.

It is the ultimate conundrum.

We don't have to run out of air, have a near-death experience, or have a terminal illness to discover Heaven. Christ taught, and I paraphrase Luke 17:21, "Heaven is also right here, right now, not only swimming in front of you in the beautiful underwater garden of life, but swimming within you."

We've read it. We've heard it. And perhaps, we think we intellectually understand what Jesus said, but do we really believe it? The Dead Saints insist Heaven is not separated by religion, and is more about the state of love we achieve, than a place we go. The states of love we can attain are many ("In my Father's House are many mansions"); they are separated by love, not according to belief system.

Readers of every faith and belief should consider paying attention. Earth University is real. The school is real. Someday, when you die, you will stand before God and review every action and non-action, every thought and dream, their consequences for both good and evil, and you will realize God spoke to us every day in the mop and bucket lessons he presented to us in Earth University, lessons designed to make you more realized; lessons carefully crafted to help you overcome fear; lessons personally designed to teach you the laws of love and about the Planetary Headmaster in charge of those laws.

---

1 Felton was born on a farm in eastern North Carolina in 1921. Educated at Duke University, he majored in botany and minored in zoology and geology. Although interested in Bonsai in his early teens, he wouldn't actually start studying it until the mid-1950s when Frank Nagata of Los Angeles took him in as a student. Felton would subsequently study with John Naka, before he opened his own Sho-Ko-En School of Bonsai in Atlanta in 1967.
2 Story excerpted from Paul Solomon lecture 1982. *The Planetary Mystery School.* See also, De Rond, Grace 2000. The Fellowship Primer, Paul Solomon. Ireland, UK. The Paul Solomon Foundation. pp. 19-33.
3 *Jean R NDE,* #2932, 01.18.12, NDERF.org
4 *Sue C NDE,* #2927, 01.18.12, NDERF.org
5 *Pat P NDE,* #1228, 10.11.07, NDERF.org
6 *Bridget F NDE,* #1654, 07.21.08, NDERF.org
7 Based on the scuba diving analogy, Paul Solomon, Gary and Mary Anna Keller 1985. *Love and Fear, Only Two Powers Exist.* Timberville, VA: The Master's Press. pp. 7-8.

5
Rice Paper Teachers

Prolific writer, near-death researcher, P.M.H. Atwater, uncovered previous near-death research showing a link between NDE states and transformation of first-century Buddhism in China and Japan:

Mahayana Buddhism suddenly merged at that time, a reflection of near death "visions" that depicted caring and enlightened individuals reaching back to help others less fortunate. Before then, only Hinayana

Buddhism existed—a singular path that encouraged severance of all earthly ties.[1]

Kwai Chang Caine, fictional hero of the 1970's TV series, *Kung Fu*, was a young monk studying martial arts in an ancient Chinese Shaolin Temple. One of his first instructors was blind, old master Po.

Caine was the grandfatherly Po's favorite pupil and it was he who bestowed upon Caine his curious nickname "Grasshopper."

That was derived from an exchange where the naive young Caine asked the old blind master how he could function without seeing. Po asked Caine to close his eyes and describe what he could hear. Caine reported he could hear the water flowing in a nearby fountain and birds in a nearby cage. Po then asked if Caine could hear his own heartbeat or the grasshopper at his feet (Caine hadn't noticed the grasshopper until that moment). Incredulous, Caine asked Po, "Old man—how is it you hear these things?" Po's response was, "Young man. How is it you do not?" From that point on, Po affectionately called Caine "Grasshopper."

It was the first of many tests, trials and initiations. However, in order to graduate from the Shaolin Temple, Kwai Chang had to pass the "rice paper test."

"Only when you can walk across the rice paper without tearing it, will your footsteps not be heard," old Po explained. Initially failing, years later the young monk tried again; this time he walked the rice paper without leaving a trace, and was allowed to graduate from the Temple.

That story is an excellent example of the student on the arduous path to "becoming conscious" who, in mastering the lessons of life, becomes a Teacher in turn.

Thus, teachers who have mastered an art or craft on Earth University, I call "Rice Paper Teachers." I use the term to separate them from the myriad other teachers we may meet over the course of our lives and who teach us. Not only the formal teachers in our schools and universities who guide our academic progress, and our parents, family and friends, who do so much to shape our characters, but also the uncredentialed, and often-unwitting "professors" of Earth University we stumble across on our path. Some may be homeless people; some ex-wives, some business associates...a janitor; a gardener.

Looking back, it seems to me, and it may be universally true, that the teachers who were hardest on us, we learned the most. In ancient traditions, these teachers are called "Initiators," a term Paul Solomon often used to separate teachers who were consciously aware of their role, versus unconscious teachers who still taught us major lessons, but were unaware they were doing so. The Initiator's job is to kick us in the butt, push us off the cliff, force us to face and learn lessons we otherwise might not have faced or learned.

Over the course of our Earth University experience, we all have Rice Paper Teachers. Some we recognize, some we don't. Some may "look" like spiritual teachers, others do not. Most we can "see" walking among us on the great University campus, but some watch over us from above, guiding us during dreams from the Realms of Light, and from time to time, poke through the veil to walk with us and instruct us. One central theme binds these Rice Paper Teachers. They have a major impact on the direction of our lives. They are typically masters of an art, a science, or even business. There is a quality in the manner in which they live their lives, a softness in the voice, and a clarity in their thought. They are not typically famous and the majority of them are hardly perfect.

All Rice Paper Teachers have staff members and faculty who support them. It's important to get to know them too.

Earth University: Staff, Teaching Assistants & Syllabus

Enrollment in Earth University presupposes the idea a Syllabus was designed for each of us before we were born. A syllabus is often either set out by an "exam board," or prepared by a "professor" who supervises or controls the course quality. Both syllabus and curriculum are often fused and usually given to each student during the first class session so the objectives and the means of obtaining them are clear. A syllabus usually contains specific information about the course, teaching assistants, and an outline of what will be covered in the course. A schedule of test dates and the due dates for assignments, along with the grading policy for the course and specific classroom rules are also given.

Twelve Earth University Lessons

All major religions describe 12 paths or lessons that are presented to us in Earth University. While it is beyond the scope of the *Chronicles* to address these lessons individually, it is important to point out their prevalence in Scripture. In the Hebrew tradition the 12 paths were represented by the 12 sons of Jacob; Reuben, Simeon, Levi, Judah, Dan, Naphtali, Gad, Asher, Issachar, Zebulun, Joseph, and Benjamin.

The 12 sons of Jacob also reflected the 12 constellations in the zodiac.

A 6th century mosaic of the zodiac reflects this belief on a tiled floor of the Beth Alpha Synagogue in Israel, and in six other early era synagogues. The rabbis who built their synagogues with depictions of the zodiac may have been illustrating Ezekiel's vision of a divine chariot driven by God (represented by the sun) that ordered the movement of the 12 constellations, the moon and the stars. Regardless of their intent, what in Heaven's name were they doing? How could they create tiled mosaic pictures in a synagogue? Did they not read the second commandment in Exodus 20:4-5 about worshipping graven images? An explanation to the mystery may be forthcoming from Hebrew scholars who say the second commandment could be interpreted conditionally, "make no graven images...which you worship."

Early Christian founding fathers prohibited the making of zodiacs in the early church until after the Middle Ages. According to archeologists, "There is not one zodiac mosaic in a church that dates before the Middle Ages."[2] Though the U.S. is an overwhelmingly Christian country, a survey by the Pew Forum in 2009 found 23% of American Christians still expressed a belief in astrology.[3] An ancient and honorable enemy to be sure, in principle, the zodiac is the antithesis and enemy to monotheistic religions. So why did the Hebrew priests have the floors of their synagogues tiled with them? And why do a significant percentage of Christians believe in it?

Dead Saint's Vision of a Zodiac Wheel

William describes 12 spokes of a large wheel representing the constellations of the zodiac, revealed to him during his NDE:

> *I would have to say this occurred about halfway through my last NDE. My last NDE was not one single trip but actually seven trips. I would leave my body, not only to escape the tremendous pain I was in, but also to continue those things I was being instructed in on the other side. It was during the third or fourth trip when I was taken in a room that had a large wheel on the*

floor, at the end of each spoke of the wheel stood a pillar. **The wheel had 12 spokes and subsequently there were 12 pillars at the end of each spoke. Each pillar also contained 12 crystals and 12 symbols. Some of these symbols were representative of the astrological star constellations of the zodiac.**[4]

As William describes above, at the end of each spoke was *a pillar*. When I refer to the lessons we experience in Earth University, I am referring to these 12 pillars. Each of the 12 pillars represents and revolves around the following 12 major life lessons:

Alrightness	Intuition	Sexuality
Purity of Heart	Loyalty	Balance
Creativity	Discipline	Money
Judgement / Discernment	Communication	Power

While our lessons involve electives from all 12 pillars, most of us focus on one pillar at a time. It is our strength, but it can also be our weakness. Each pillar has its strengths, weaknesses, and purpose. The permutations of pillar lessons combined are many, but ultimately originate from these 12. Later, the 12 lessons were personified by in Jesus's choice of 12 apostles, and symbolically memorialized in the Book of Revelation by the Virgin with a crown of 12 stars and the description of the Holy City with 12 gates, 12 stones, and 12 fruits of the Tree of Life in the celestial New Jerusalem.

Joseph Weiss, in his excellent book, *The Gospel in the Stars,*[5] helps set a Biblical foundation behind this *6000-year-old astronomical/astrological mystery*. I highly suggest you get a copy and carefully study it, as it answers from a Judeo/Christian point of view, many questions about the purpose of God's handiwork written in constellations and stars in the heavens.

Masonic Pewter Ceremonial Water Pot

The symbol of 12 kept showing up in my life. John, a long-time friend, was visiting my home at Akio in December 2012 to install his latest version of the HydroSonic InfraSound Relaxation System[6] in my Egyptian Spa room. During his stay, he saw a heavy, antique 8-inch-high serpent snouted hammered pewter water pot sitting on my library shelf. When he saw it, he nearly jumped out of his skin.

"Where did you get that?"

Surprised at his reaction, I said, "When Delynn cleaned out the garage a few months ago, she found it buried at the bottom of a cardboard box."

He turned it over and on the bottom of the pot was the traditional Mason compass and ruler, but instead of a "G" in the center, there was a 12-spoked zodiac wheel with the pewter metal smith stamp "Etain Fin." We could see with a magnifying glass at the center of the wheel, an Ouroboros—a serpent swallowing its tail.

I asked John, "What is it?"

He looked exasperated. "I'm only a 3rd degree Mason, but the last time I saw one that remotely looked like your pot was on a ceremonial Masonic altar. You *are not supposed to have this*."

"So now what?"

"Well, hold onto it. Keep it safe. Maybe God will someday reveal to you why." I put pot aside hoping we could solve the riddle together someday. We never got the chance. John lost his fight with cancer ten months later on October 20, 2013. I've searched the internet. The symbol has never been seen on any known Masonic artwork. Nobody knows or they won't tell. Today, it reverently rests on my altar waiting for an answer.

Teachers and Tutors

Sometimes in the midst of our learning schedule, we may seek further guidance. As an ancient Eastern proverb declares, "when the student is ready, the Teacher appears" or in some cases, a *Guru* appears." Of course, the same thing happened with John the Baptist and with Jesus. These great teachers found their students. Perhaps, this is what happened to me.

When I look back over my life, I realize I may have had great, unseen, ethereal "Rice Paper Teachers" guiding me. When I go back to my journals and re-read my dreams, I could probably name a few who would visit me from time to time, and you may guess some of them as you read further in the *Chronicles*, but for now I will keep them to myself.

Paul Solomon was my first "physical" Rice Paper Teacher. I remember very clearly the first of my many journeys with him, forty days after my first visit to Hearthfire Lodge. It was October 8, 1979. Destination: Australia. My job: travel assistant. I had absolutely no idea what to expect, or what was expected of me, nor any idea of what I would be learning. I was 20 years old, a kid.

But like Master Po, who called Kwai Chang, *"Grasshopper,"* so Paul had already anointed me *the Dweeper*. I guess he came up with the nickname by combining my first name "Dwayne" with my half-closed, squinting Japanese eyes.

Not only did I get a new nickname, I got a new name. Early on, while traveling with Paul Solomon in 1979, he suggested I consider changing my name to represent the spiritual change in my life during baptism[7] to reflect the new man I wanted to become. My own choices of names came down to Michael or David. Michael seemed too gentle. I had always adored the leadership, strength and spiritual commitment of King David. I needed that. I was always a bit too shy, too laid back, too reclusive, too much like a monk. After baptism, like Paul Solomon, who changed his name a decade earlier from William Bilo Dove, I changed my name from Dwayne to David, and was known for a few years as David Earley.

By 1984, Paul had become more like a father to me than a teacher, and often would refer to me as his 'adopted son.' So, to reflect the man who was like my second father, I adopted his surname to complete my name change and was baptized in the Jordan River in Israel, David Ben Solomon, which I later made official at the Rockingham County Courthouse in Virginia.

My job description was simple. I was to arrange the air travel with a local travel agent. I packed and carried his suitcases, washed and ironed clothes, retrieved the morning paper, filled his metal thermos with hot Folgers instant coffee several times a day, packed in his black, leather shoulder bag, seven of his meerschaum pipes with his favorite blend of cherry and mango tobacco-and kept them packed since he smoked throughout the day, and when necessary, I cooked. It was my responsibility to make sure he got to lectures on time, had transportation, and made all his personal appointments.

Paul left everything in my hands to screw up, and so I did. After a few months of touring Australia, (Sydney, Melbourne, and the southeastern Gold Coast), we were off to Christchurch, New Zealand.)

As our plane left the ground, I suddenly realized I had left the case with all his expensive suits on a hanger on the back of the hotel door. It took me an hour to work up the courage to tell Paul. He barely reacted. Of course, as soon as we landed, I called the hotel to have them check the room for the clothes. They found the suit bag and arranged to send it back on the next flight out. And, I made more-or-less the same mistake with the ill-fated suit bag on the return home through Hawaii. Luckily, again we got it back.

As with Master Po and Kwai Chang, the objective was to cultivate *mindfulness*-an awareness of my actions, my thoughts, and my own state of consciousness. It was not about the suit bag ...which in fact I never left behind again. Over the years, I put Paul Solomon through any number of awkward situations, but for me, the lesson each time involved becoming aware of my role and responding to the needs of others. They were mop-and-bucket lessons—for it is only by becoming conscious of the lesson, we give ourselves the chance to master it.

We can read thousands of Dead Saints testimonials and see them, especially in aggregate, as a unique introduction to the higher wisdom. They should convince all but the terminally unteachable that we are immortal. However, they will not, in and of themselves, teach patience, service, or the art of listening. They will not teach us, or teach anyone else, how to love or how to be present in the moment.

Paul Solomon also widened my focus. He taught me the Earth University syllabus involved more than an awareness of personal surroundings. It was necessary for me and for all of us to be conscious of our local and our global environment. This was why he read The *Washington Post* religiously every day. The inner spiritual world of communication, intuition and dreams should not be divorced from the secular outer world that is its framework.

My first year on the job was devoted to service. It was a simple enough teaching that would have a profound and complicated impact. At times, it was frustrating, because it seemed I was missing all the good stuff being taught in Paul's classes and lectures. Though I was able to keep journal notes and reflect upon the spiritual truths Paul so generously sowed, it was tempting to try to tell everyone I met in the outside world about these great truths. But seeing to Paul's personal needs, i.e., filling pipes, keeping coffee brewed, filling the taxing daily double role of secretary/assistant, left me little or no socializing time at all.

He kept me focused on the importance of paying attention to detail—the little things that are recorded in our *Book of Life* and that we will be held responsible for during our Life Review and Judgment at the end of our lives. Paul commonly pointed out to me about little things and innocent errors I did unconsciously—errors that *miss the mark* that will appear ultimately important in the life we will all review when we die. He referenced Scripture in the Song of Solomon 2:15:

> *Catch all the foxes. Those little foxes before they ruin the vineyard of love for the grapevines are blossoming. They could go in and out among those vines and nip at them.*

That is why the constant admonition to keep a journal. I needed to notice the little foxes spoiling the vines in my life. They are not obvious. While they do not seem important, they spoil the young vines of spiritual growth I planted every day in the garden of my heart.

Many Earth University lessons that Rice Paper Teachers teach may be found in the Bible. With his Southern Baptist background, Paul Solomon was particularly good at illuminating Bible passages that were not normally recognized for the wisdom enshrined within them. These passages also commonly find unwitting expression in the accounts of the Dead Saints.

The Foundation to All Learning: Alrightness

In the Gospel of Matthew (22:37) a lawyer of the Pharisee tests Jesus about His understanding of the Law, "Master, which is the greatest commandment in the law?" Jesus responded by saying, 'Thou shalt love the Lord thy God with all thy heart, with all thy soul, and with all thy mind.' This is the first and greatest commandment, and the second is like unto it: "Thou shalt love thy neighbor as thyself." On these two commandments hang all the Law and the Prophets.'"

We might elaborate, adding, *"On these two commandments hang all of the lessons we will ever learn."* Arguably, the most ignored injunction in Christ's gospel is love thy neighbor as thyself. Learning to love thyself...*unconditionally*...is a lesson Paul Solomon coined *alrightness*.[8]

The seeking of alrightness may be the single most powerful motivating force known to humanity. Almost everything we do is directed toward establishing or proving our alrightness *in the eyes of our neighbor*. A lack of inner alrightness instills fear and it is fear that makes us take foolish and ill-considered actions that are not in our own best interest. We decorate our homes to demonstrate our alrightness. The clothes we often choose project our alrightness. If we truly examine what we say and think, we find much of it is driven by the need to be acceptable to others. It is easy enough to test the hypothesis on the material plane. How many things would you have bought if you knew nobody else would ever see them?

I do not condemn surrounding ourselves with beautiful things— harmoniously designed material creations carry the imprimatur of the Creator—they communicate our feelings about alrightness. We should, therefore, be honest with the motives that drive us to surround ourselves with material things. It's not about right and wrong or how much we spent. It's about motive and intent.

Where does this all-consuming quest for alrightness come from, anyhow? What might be viewed as the signature aspect of contemporary society has been in place throughout recorded history, but it has generally been regarded very differently. What, over the millennia, the sages, saints, mystics, prophets, philosophers, rishis, gurus, masters and dervishes have railed and inveighed against as evil incarnate, our current worship of materialism has effectively sanctified.

What the prophet of Ecclesiastes excoriated as the "vanity of vanities" (aka 'Alrightness') is now extolled in its various guises as the ultimate aim in human life. "Success" "ambition" "renown" "fame" "respect" "admiration" "popularity" and "wealth" is the best we can expect out of life ...since that is all there is.

The English novelist Samuel Butler famously wrote, "Analogies may often be misleading, but they are the least misleading thing we have." Therefore, to return to our scuba diving analogy, even though our novice diver knows he could run out of air in a given amount of time, he is tempted to "push" the dive longer than he should. Why? "Success" "ambition" "respect" "admiration" "popularity" "wealth"— material underwater entertainments that keep our novice diver distracted enough, long enough, that he fails to notice his air tank has almost no air pressure left. None. The air pressure needle is in the "red zone." At this point, it becomes more difficult to breathe.

When this happens, divers have two alternatives. They make an emergency accent to the surface—follow the analogy—because you have brain cancer or some life threatening disease, or you buddy breathe to the surface—have a Dead Saint experience; find God or Jesus and become born-again. Until an "underwater dark night of the soul" forces our novice diver out of his materialistic reverie, he gives little thought to ascend to the Light realm above, where (Heaven) is all "air."

Can Somebody Else Bestow Alrightness on us?

Central to the engulfing Alrightness fantasy is the belief someone else can bestow alrightness upon us. Many people spend whole lives building careers, accumulating more money than they can possibly spend, all to impress other people with their alrightness. It is what motivates the political arena—that ongoing three-ring exercise in futility, in which the least fit to lead, fight to lead. True, with sufficient drive, hunger and luck some will reach the top of their chosen field. Only then, at the zenith of their careers, will they realize it didn't work, not really. The masses may regard them as successes, even role models, paragons of alrightness. However, if they have not established their own inner alrightness, victory will be both ephemeral and hollow...and at some profound level, they know it. If they did not know it, they would not behave the way they do.

However, most of us have been brain and heart washed into a set of beliefs in the name of science and reason that are, upon examination, neither scientific, nor reasonable; we embrace values that have no value. It is not really our fault. Much that we take for granted we have learned in our schools. Crystallizing over time, both the credulous belief system along with its valueless values, are handed down unquestioned as though ordained.

It is at this point, then, that the accumulated testimonials of the Dead Saints, brought back from the Realms of Light, take on significance. *Materialist* debunkers try to debunk the NDE phenomena, attributing these profound and compelling experiences to brain-manufactured hallucinations, but the power of these accumulated anecdotal accounts resists the debunker-a vast public is not buying it.

A common thread runs through virtually every retelling. The resuscitated Dead Saints have shed their wet suits, fins, and air tanks. For them, worldly delusions and concerns, the obsession with alrightness, have all been left behind or at least put in their rightful place. The core of their message, their bottom line, always comes down to learning love at all its levels. Upon their return, that conviction serves as their introduction into the Greater Mysteries.

The Greater and Lesser Mysteries

Paul Solomon divided Earth University lessons into the Lesser and Greater Mysteries; the esoteric (hidden/inner) and the exoteric (public/written) traditions. The Lesser Mysteries included the arts, sciences, mathematics, religious texts, stone masonry, to name but a few. Typically, the lesser mysteries could be acquired from books, or orally transmitted from teacher to student.

The Greater Mysteries were not discussed. They were experiential. If you can't recognize the lesson, you're not ready for it. So what was the purpose of being exposed to these Greater Mysteries? The Greater Mystery lessons trickled down in a sort of hierarchy under the foundation of honesty, personal integrity, and love. These *foundation stones* were the basis of everything Paul taught, and the basis of every lesson I learned. Early on, I could see Paul was trying to hone my character. In the midst of learning these lessons, I learned essential skills and experiences I needed later in life, including those used to build my company and the writing of this book.

At first, I felt like the *Karate Kid*. I often thought, "Why am I washing his clothes, cooking his food, filling his pipes, planning his trips, recording his lectures, radio and television engagements?" I was the shadow who never received attention. When will I get to learn the real secrets of life? When would I ever get to teach?

Some of the mop and bucket mysteries thrown in front of me were obvious. The first day I went to Hearthfire Lodge, Paul Solomon asked me to clean off the spiders from the ceiling corners of the back porch. I hated spiders. I had a fear of them since childhood. How did he know? From that moment on, it seemed he knew exactly what was missing in my character needing attention. Just like Felton Jones who had cut off the front of my Bonsai tree, revealing my need to show off and present myself more "knowledgeable" than others, Paul kept pruning my tree even more.

Many of the lessons seemed reasonably obvious. The lesson of Service-awareness of the needs of others. Persistence. Consistency. Organization. Journaling. Cleanliness. Discipline. Focus in meditation and prayer. Awareness and attunement to God's presence. Alrightness. Caring and kindness. I believe I have learned much from these classroom exercises, and I know I have much more to learn and much I am still trying to grasp. The lessons *I am still learning today* are embarrassingly long: holding children and people accountable for their actions; paying attention and being fully present during a conversation; communicating clearly; procrastinating what could be done now; mastering anger; praying more often; telling no white lies; patience— not going off half-cocked; better control of appetites and desires; being less of a lone wolf, and more sociable; being in charge of my own thoughts and being more conscious of my actions, words, and keeping verbal promises.

Teachers in Disguise

In 1980, Paul suggested I move to NYC to study business and several spiritual disciplines. While I detail more of my NYC adventures in Book II of the *Chronicles*, *Training Wires of the Soul*, an important observation I want to make here was that during the 18 months I lived in New York City from 1980-81, and during my NDE research (2011-13) and the writing of the *Chronicles* beginning July 2013, I became convinced —focused spiritual discipline attracts supernatural phenomena. At least, so it was for me. The New York chapter of my life was rich in such events.

There is an especially vivid one I'll tell, but will preface it by an excerpt from the 2007 NDE of Linda who, one year after her full recovery, had a vision of beautiful angelic spirits who seemed to have charge over every individual going about their daily lives on the city streets. One day she was driving down a busy street and stopped at a red light to watch an odd scene unfold before her. A delivery truck had parked on the right about a half-block ahead.

Linda watched as the driver walked around to the traffic side of his truck and began unloading his cargo with oncoming traffic approaching. Inside her car, she said aloud in her little southern voice, "Oh honey, you shouldn't do that, it's dangerous." Then she saw an angel hovering near the truck driver:

> *Perhaps it was because I had sent a loving and concerned thought about the delivery mans' well-being that the spirit turned her loving gaze on me. For a brief moment, our eyes met. She smiled at me, then, hovering over the unsuspecting man, returned her attention to her charge who was oblivious to the heavenly presence and was busily going about his business. I was thunderstruck.*
>
> *Barely breathing for fear the vision would leave, and mesmerized by the vision, I was reluctant to take my eyes off the beauty of the scene; however, from my peripheral vision, I became aware of even more compelling lights. When I was able to tear myself away from the spirit, I glanced slowly at the vista around me and everywhere I looked, every single person in my view had beautiful, loving spirits attending them. People walking nonchalantly down the sidewalk were accompanied by spirits. From within cars, unfettered by physical barriers, I could see the glow and form of beings around the occupants. I saw joggers with flutters of light streaking behind them as their spirit kept pace. As people entered and left buildings, light beings followed.* [9]

As the Saints repeatedly insist, you and I are never alone. However, back in 1980, walking the dirty, dangerous streets of New York at 21, I was, as of yet, oblivious to the unseen presences of hovering angels.

New York City Homeless Bag Lady

I was itching to get outside on this bright sunny day and I decided, for no particular reason, to take a walk down Broadway. Soon, also for no particular reason, I was suddenly feeling happy, walking along the busy street—all smiles which was for me unusual. People, who know me, generally think of me as the "serious" one. So, in this happy, smiley mood I did something I'd never done before in my life. I just started smiling at people as I strolled along, trying to make those unsmiling New Yorkers smile back at me.

Do you know how difficult it is to get a smile back in New York City? This was a metropolis of eight million who appeared

to me to be self-important, self-conscious, impatient people, who have a business meeting or something else urgent to get to, and who instinctively distrust anyone who might be smiling ... especially for no particular detectable reason.

Paul Solomon had sometimes commented about that studiously cultivated, severe, grown-up city look. If such people see someone strolling down the sidewalk with a silly smile on their face, the assumption was they must be on drugs or had something else mentally wrong with them.

So I was busy smiling away... (Which was curiously unsettling, actually, since I'd never done such a thing before). Walking south, at the corner of 92nd Street, there was a fruit and vegetable stand across the street and I thought I'd pick up a few things to bring back to the apartment. Before crossing Broadway, I noticed a bag lady, her shopping cart stuffed with everything she possessed in the world. She was leaning against a brick wall next to the fruit stand; one of the countless bag ladies of New York—solitary, impoverished women, usually old, pushing all of their worldly possessions along before them in a shopping cart, picking over trash cans near food markets for their food, and dozing in doorways. She was just one of thousands we walk past without a further thought. There was nothing to distinguish this one from any other.

As I crossed the street, I saw she was sniffling and wiping her nose with a Kleenex. Without thinking, as I approached her, I gave her a big smile. To my surprise, she nodded and smiled back at me—really the only person, so far, who had done so. I thought: How interesting! I stopped just in front of the fruit stand and looked back to where she had been. She had walked away from the wall, out to the middle of the sidewalk and was just staring at me nodding and smiling.

Suddenly, and without warning, a holy presence hit me like a lightning bolt. I dropped to my knees, right there in the middle of the sidewalk, and began bawling. I didn't know what was happening. I felt like I'd been plugged into a million-volt electric outlet. She didn't move and I didn't move. I didn't know what to do. I was so shocked I was afraid to get any closer to her. After about five minutes, she turned and went back to her place against the brick wall. I got up and walked back to my apartment. Had this been an angel?

Reflecting, I kind of felt the way the nine other lepers described by Luke the Physician must have felt—the nine didn't go back to Christ and thank him for the healing. As the story is told, only one of the ten healed lepers who came back to Christ to thank him. (Luke: 17:12-14)

A few weeks later, Paul Solomon flew up to New York to visit me. I told him about the bag lady. I asked Paul, "Was that an angel I met?

He said, "No. That was Jesus Christ."

(Author's note: While, needless to say, I cannot "prove" Paul's assertion, it is worth noting in NDE accounts; encounters with Jesus Christ in disguise are not uncommon. Significantly, they show up in accounts of people of other religions, no religion, and even hitherto self-described atheists.)

Ken R. Vincent, Ed.D. researched modern people who have also experienced visions of Jesus in disguise (Migliore, 2009, pp. 137-139).[10] In meditation, a woman saw a vision of Jesus:

> *I went forward, alone, toward an old man who stood at the very end of the rose-covered arches. I stopped before him. He asked me if ministry was what I really wanted. I replied affirmatively. He then used his thumb to make the sign of the cross on my forehead, my hands, my feet, my lips, and over my heart-in that order. Then he said, 'Go in peace.' I wondered who he was. He looked at me with sad eyes and said, 'Don't you know me?' With His words, the illusion of the old man fell away, and I realized that He was* Christ. (Sparrow, 1995, pp. 150-51).[11]

Encountering the Christ in the disguise of a Bag Lady on the streets of New York City taught me a great lesson. I took a risk to smile in a hostile environment and found Christ. God allowed me to take into my heart and soul that very real presence of Jesus—an experience magnified thirty years later during His visit in my living room in 2011 while reading an NDE, (chapter 2), being touched by His Presence in moment of Near-Death Lightning.

*~ Zen Tradition teaches that after satori (or first awakening to one's true nature), a student can begin to put into practice **what they have learned** from their realization. ~Chronicle 174*

---

1 P.M.H. Atwater 2007. *The Big Book of Near-Death Experiences*. Charlottesville, VA: Hampton Roads Publishing Co. p. 400.
2 Walter Zanger, August 24, 2014. *Jewish Worship, Pagan Symbols*. Bible History Daily.
3 Pew Forum on Religion and Public Life, U.S. Religious Landscape Survey, Summary of Key Findings, http://www.pewforum.org/2009/12/09/many-americans-mix-multiple-faiths/
4 *William C's NDE*, #119, 04.29.02, NDERF.org
5 Joseph A. Weiss 1972. *The Gospel in the Stars*. Originally published in 1882, *The Gospel in the Stars: or, Primeval Astronomy*. Kriegal Publications: Grand Rapids, MI.
6 CymaSonics, LLC. Virginia Beach, VA. (757) 574-4384. Email: info@cymasonics.com.
7 While not often practiced today, changing the name at Baptism was common in early Christian times. Jesus changed the name of the disciple Simon to Peter meaning "Rock" to reflect his future role in the church. Saul's name was changed to Paul. Meaning of the name change can be found in Eph. 4:24 "And that ye put on the new man, which after God is created in righteousness and true holiness." This means that Christians are called to become new men by God. The old man is dead and new man is

born through baptism.
8 Term "alrightness" and spelling coined by Paul Solomon. See also, Paul Solomon, Gary and Mary Anna Keller 1985. *Love and Fear, Only Two Powers Exist.* The Master's Press: Timberville, VA.
9 *Ibid. #1011.* NDERF.org
10 Vince Migliore, 2009. *A Measure of Heaven.* Folsom, CA; Blossom Hill Books. pp. 137-139.
11 Ken R. Vincent 1995. Ed.D. *Journal of Near-death Studies*, pp. 142-143. See also, G. Scott Sparrow 1996. *I Am With You Always. True Stories of Encounters with Jesus.* Bantam Books. pp.150-151.

6
Dreams: Night School

"If there be a prophet among you, I the Lord will make myself known to him in a vision, and will speak to him in a dream." (Yahweh speaks to Aaron and Miriam in Numbers 12.6)

Since I was 16, I began recording my dreams in a journal. Dreams became so much a part of my life, that during the day, I would still be pondering about the dreams occurring from the previous night. Sometimes I would dream I was flying; at other times I would become aware I was dreaming within the dream and be able to control the dream, an ability known as lucid dreaming.

And the more I recorded my dreams, the more they became alive. If I forgot a dream, I would often begin remembering last night's dream as I fell asleep the following night. It was like tapping into an indelible recording.

I dreamed almost every night and I dreamed in color. They were most often symbolic, but very detailed – epic novels that would take thirty minutes to write down. I learned to interpret my dreams and after a few years, I was able to listen to other people's dreams and discovered I could interpret their dreams as well. I don't know how I knew the meaning of the dream, but somehow I would just know. My dream world often drifted into my own private Twilight Zone where I "zoned out." Much like the *Secret life of Walter Mitty*, my dream life was a world none of my friends and family knew about. It was more real than my waking life.

While the *Chronicles* primarily walk us through the testimonials of the Dead Saints and their near-death experiences, from time to time I insert significant approaching-death dreams (ADDs), dreams containing death symbology, especially applicable to terminally ill or dying patients, and after-death communications (ADCs), dreams containing dialogue from deceased loved ones, when appropriate. As I approach "my appointed time," these types of dreams have become more intense, more numerous and more "near-death-like." I've integrated dreams as part of our Zen Journey through the Christian Afterlife, a tale that helps explain the opening of the veil, allowing the Lord to communicate with us from Heaven.

Dreams: A Night Time Classroom

When we sleep, we continue learning in our dreams at night. Every night we sleep, our soul goes through a process of analyzing and judging its own activities and thoughts. Every incident of the day, the management of lessons presented and responded to, *sets up future events*. All lessons poorly handled will be repeated.

We only need to know the past and present to know what the future likely is going to be. This is the real opportunity of dreams, so that we can avoid repeating the same lesson over and over. It's an initiation in consciousness. If one solves it there, we don't have to experience it in our outer, daily physical life.

In essence, we set up our own future, based on what happens today. So, while specific outer meetings, accidents, conversations, and realizations occur while we are awake, a great deal of communication happens in dreams. It is said, teachers and angels watch our daily lives in the Realms of Heaven and set up our future based on what we need to learn and communicate this information in our dreams—whether we remember them or not.

According to Edgar Cayce, "Dreams are the safest path to spiritual growth." Paul Solomon once said, "Dreams are the activity of the soul making a journal entry into the Book of Life." Eastern mystics call this Book, the Akashic Record—the record of our thoughts and actions during our walk through Earth University. Every minute and every second of our lives are recorded on this Akashic "fabric of space and time."

The theory goes something like this. Our brain in its thought process generates electrical impulses and transmits electrical impulses. Your physical body and mind live in an electrically charged atmosphere that is tenacious of equilibrium. Within that force field of thought, atoms and molecules are exchanging electrons and being created and reformed constantly, which means everything around you is in "flux." Things that look solid to your touch, such as your body, the walls of your house, your clothes, or the floor, anything physical, are also in constant movement and in flux.

When you think, speak, move through your environment, because of this electro-magnetic flux, a record is made in the Book of Life of your thoughts and their impact on the physical environment around you.

Dream Tutorial: How to Remember Dreams

Most people go to sleep automatically, without forethought, rather than mindfully and with a purpose. Since we spend a full third of our lifetimes sleeping this means that a whole chunk of life goes by unconsciously, and we literally throw away a third of our lives.

However, the dream state is not oblivion, a period devoted solely to recharging our physical batteries. Rather, it holds important life lessons for every one of us, *if we know how to use it*. If we practice remembering dreams, we begin to open a doorway to our Inner Teacher, who will help us understand ourselves in a way we cannot access in our normal waking state.

If we prepare nightly for sleep, (this is not as easy as it sounds!) then we are prepared to learn the lessons invariably enshrined in dreams. It is important to go to sleep relaxed, and if you want answers from your Inner Teacher, it is important to formulate your questions clearly before drifting off to asleep. (Practical advice: Take a lined journal and penlight to bed with you. If you wake up in the middle of the night with a dream, keep your eyes closed, and write down key words *without* opening your eyes. (It can be done. Those key words will help you remember the rest of the dream in the morning.)

Also, you can set your alarm to wake at a specific period (or periods) during the night to capture any dream images you might otherwise forget. Until you learn to remain in that altered state of consciousness, it is important you do not open your eyes. Doing so will speed up your brain wave rhythms to Beta, 21-30 cps (cycles per second), the normal, waking state, and you will wipe out the dream images. (Note: falling back to sleep tends to be easy when young, more difficult with age, and everyone is different. Experiment!)

Conscientious dream explorers may soon learn to realize in mid-dream, "I am dreaming." This is called lucid dreaming. It is a direct way to talk with your subconscious mind through dream images.

On January 30, 2015, I had a lucid dream where I am fighting off an attacker Kung Fu style with bamboo fighting sticks. I eventually wrestle him down to the ground, straddle him, and then begin strangling him about the neck with a string. I looked into the pupils of his eyes as the life ebbed from him. His pupils dilated as he approached death. I realized in the dream I was fighting and trying to kill myself, blaming it on the cancer. I gave up on strangling him and his pupils returned to normal. It was very, very real. ~**Chronicle 596**

With practice, you will soon be remembering several dreams a night. Your waking-state consciousness will evolve and change ...and you will know it.

Remembering dreams is a way to learn how to listen; to access levels of your consciousness you normally ignore or cannot access. Dreamland is for most of us largely unexplored, unknown territory, our personal *terra incognito,* challenging because most of us go through our lives smugly self-assured that we already know our own minds. Dream recording teaches us otherwise, but patience is a prerequisite. It is not possible for us to run around all day disoriented, pre-occupied by worldly cares and barely semi-conscious and then expect to suddenly become spiritual in dreams.

Once we learn to remember dreams, we find ourselves most often dreaming in symbols, which include mother, father, family and friends, all of whom play symbolic as well as merely physical roles in our lives. The first rule of thumb about dream interpretation is that symbols in dreams are generally (but not always) about ourselves and symbolically reflect events which occurred the previous day or recently. This is why it is important to create a dream library of people we dream about and events. Assigning a unique attribute to each person helps us interpret what our *subconscious mind is saying about us, and what God is trying to say to us about lessons we need to learn.*

Even so, a time will come when you will recognize the difference between symbolic dreams about yourself versus dreams that are truly about someone else. Moreover, there are hundreds of common dream symbols and symbolic dream actions. This chapter is just a primer--a trailer to introduce the subject and its importance. Remember, dreams recapitulate and assess the actions of the last day(s) and lay out tomorrow's lessons. The more familiar we become with the process, the more aware we become of the repetitious nature of the lessons.

From my personal experience, the more truthful we become, the *less* symbolic and the more real and lifelike our dreams become. I believe it is because we are learning to *see things as they are*. Even in the Afterlife, as we shall see, there is a temptation to lie, to fudge the truth, and even to avoid it altogether.

Remembering dreams is one thing. Interpreting dreams accurately is quite another. Our interpretation depends on the type of dream we have. Each dream is a different view of reality. The following are some of the most important and/or striking:

After-Death Communication (ADC) in Dreams

ADC DREAM: I am in the "Presidents Mansion" with Paul Solomon having a drink with him. We spoke about creating a Unified Mind, which creates the Shekinah light resting over the crown, like paintings that depict crowns of light over the apostles and Jesus. I told Paul you can't teach a student how to do this, you can only prepare them as he had done. ~**Chronicle 505**

ADC DREAM: Walking upstairs, through an opening into a humble apartment. I was surprised to see a deceased friend, Thomas Keller lying casually on a big brown round beanbag. I said, 'You're alive! How can that be?' He responded, 'What's the story about that?'—Like, why do people think I'm dead? Of course, I am alive! ~**Chronicle 593**

ADC DREAM: I saw my deceased Aunt June in the distance. She was standing among a few people I didn't recognize. No words between us. Not close up like the rest of my deceased friends who have visited. I just knew it was she. ~**Chronicle 782**

A Pew Study in 2009 found 29% of Christians (and nearly three-in-ten Americans overall) said they have felt in touch with someone who has already died.[1] Most of these ADCs happen in dreams. Communications from deceased loved ones (or with a powerful historical or spiritual entity) can be startling and sometimes life changing. Visitations from deceased family members, angels, Jesus Christ, or a Divine Being are not common, but *they are common enough that Jody Long and Jeffery Long, M.D., have devoted their* After Death Communication Research Foundation, ADCRF.org, to the subject. On the website, they provide extensive information and resources regarding after-death communication (ADC), bereavement, grief, life after death, and make available hundreds of testimonials of Afterlife communications that occur in dreams and sometimes the waking state.

In July 2013, when I first began writing *The Dead Saints Chronicles*, I had Kathy, a friend and former employee, begin setting up my own website www.deadsaintschronicles.com. (www.deadsaints.org in early 2016) Within days of setting up the website, she confided in me about a special experience where in a dream, she witnessed her ex-husband, Toby's death—exactly at the moment it occurred. Even though they were divorced, she would visit him weekly to give him his insulin medication. She felt his death was her fault, since she had failed to visit him the day before to give it to him.

The passing of her ex-husband had been very traumatic. It triggered her fears about the Afterlife, and her belief in God. I told her a similar thing happened to me when Paul Solomon died in March 1994. He was in a lot of pain from pancreatitis and had been for months. He called me the evening before his death and asked me to visit him. Normally, I would have, but I knew his nephew and a nurse assistant were there to help him, and I was tired and really didn't feel like going. I told him I would visit him the next day. Well, he died the next morning.

I never got the chance to say goodbye. "If I would've gone to see him, could I have been able to do anything at all to change what happened? I question myself about this over and over. I will never know."

I told her, "Kathy, each of us has an appointed time to die. I believe it was Paul's time to pass. I also believe it was Toby's time to pass. The miracle is Toby reached out to you in your dream during his dying experience. You were able to be there for him in spirit. I know this was very traumatic for you, but in a way, I believe, it was a gift to help you understand death is not the end. God has a way of planning these things. He sent you a message. Toby is going to be okay."

I could see through her tears she understood and my advice helped.

More ADC Dreams

Since my cancer diagnosis, my after-death communications have become more frequent. It seems my deceased friends and teachers are lining up to visit me. Most of my dream visitations are short, thirty-second clips, partly symbolic, mostly to say "we are thinking of you." Deceased relatives I haven't thought about in forty years are showing up.

I believe as we approach our appointed time, if we remember our dreams, these types of dreams occur more often.

On June 19, 2015, my stepfather, Ray, visited me the day after his death. Knowing his time was near, I'd been praying that while alive, he would help me put together his Memorial Service. At 3:00 am, Ray visited me in a vivid dream. A bright light illuminated the background behind his face. He was absolutely beaming and appeared thirty years younger. He had this message for me to deliver at his Memorial Service. "We all need to love one another more."

Nine days later, on June 26, my Great Grandpa Sarge appeared in a dream. I hadn't seen or thought of him since his death forty-years ago. He said the word *Terrapin* to me. I remembered him as broad chested and wearing a brown/white tweed sports jacket. (Mom verified this the following day). I saw him last in 1970. He died in 1983 seven years after his wife, Great Grandma Miller died. (She also appeared to me in January 2013, (an ADC Dream described in chapter 1, *Premonitions*). I do not ever remember dreaming of Great Grandpa Sarge before. When I woke up, I looked up the word *Terrapin*. It's a small turtle living in the brackish water in Virginia back bays. I didn't know if he meant I was going too slowly, as in turtle slow, or if he was telling me to pace myself. Evidently, the turtle wins the race, not the hare!

Strangely, three days after this dream, I opened my backdoor to my house, and not ten feet away on our lawn was a box turtle (not exactly a terrapin, but close enough!) staring at me! A very, very rare sight, as they are elusive creatures that usually stay hidden in the forest.

Related dreams kept coming. In mid-July 2015, I dreamed of an old Galapagos-sized tortoise, flailing on its back, unable to right itself. This was followed by a dream a few days later of a three-foot sized, bright yellow and green turtle, attempting to leave the shoreline and cross a river. I saw myself trying to hold back the heavy turtle from swimming to the other side of the river. This took a lot of effort.

The three dreams are part of the same theme. I am the turtle. The ADC dream of Great Grampa Sarge was telling me not to panic about finishing my book. Steady progress will win the race. The second dream of the flailing tortoise is true. My brain tumor is affecting my body. I am slowing down. The third dream indicates it's taking a lot of effort to hold back my turtle from crossing the river, an approaching-death (ADD) symbol, discussed later in this chapter.

ADC Markers

There are several classic markers that can help determine if your ADC is real. They include:

➢ Knowledge you died, or believe you died
➢ Time Dilation. You believe you were in the Afterlife for a long period of time

- Visitation and communication from or with deceased relatives
- Perception of a barrier symbolized by a wall, river, gorge, gate, fence, etc.
- A brilliant, dazzling Light
- View of Heaven, Holy City, angels, deceased relatives, or a Being of Light

The reader should note many Dead Saints feel they have been gone for years or at a minimum a long time, but discover when they return to the body on Earth, only a few seconds or minutes have gone by. Robert recognizes this time dilation during his NDE:

Before I was sent back I asked how long was I here and is this how it would be like for everyone else. I was told I was there for 7-years. I was dead for 1 minute 47 seconds [107 seconds].[2]

Prophetic Dreams: Biblical Examples

History has numerous examples of prophetic dreams in the Bible. Joseph, one of the most famous dreamers in the Bible, recorded his dreams in Genesis 37:1-11. They showed through easily deciphered symbols that Joseph's family would one day bow to him in respect. His brothers didn't appreciate the dream and in their hatred sold Joseph into slavery. Eventually, Joseph ended up in prison in Egypt where he interpreted some dreams of Pharaoh's cupbearer and baker. Two years later, Pharaoh himself had a dream, which Joseph interpreted. This helped prepare Pharaoh to save the Egyptians and the Israelites from a horrible famine.

In Matthew 1:20 and 2:13, Joseph would have divorced Mary when he found out she was pregnant, but God sent an angel to him in a dream, convincing him the pregnancy was of God. Joseph went ahead with the marriage. After Jesus was born, God sent two more dreams, one to tell Joseph to take his family to Egypt so Herod could not kill Jesus and another to tell him Herod was dead and he could return home.

In Matthew 2:12, the Magi who visited Jesus in Bethlehem, were warned in a dream they should not return to Herod and to depart home to their own country another way.

During Jesus' trial, Pilate's wife sent an urgent message to the governor encouraging him to free Jesus. Her message was prompted by a nightmare that convinced her Jesus was innocent and Pilate should have nothing to do with His case. (Matthew 27:19)

Modern Precognitive Dreams

In 1865, two weeks before he was shot dead, Abraham Lincoln had a dream about a funeral at the White House. In the dream, he asked someone who was in the casket and they replied, "The president of the United States." He told his wife about the dream, but neither of them took it to heart. For on the night of his assassination, he gave his bodyguard the night off.

John Brooks, a back-up defender on the U.S team, was a long shot to enter the World Cup, but an injury to a teammate, Matt, changed all that a few weeks before the 2014 Soccer World Cup. In the 86th minute of play against Ghana, Brooks took a header from a corner kick and knocked it in. It was the game-winning goal against a team that had eliminated the United States in the last two World Cup tournaments. However, what is even more remarkable, Brooks had dreamed the completely unlikely scenario two nights before; "It's unbelievable I had a dream about it," Brooks said. "I told some teammates I would score after the 80th minute and win the game and I did it—in the 86th minute... and it [the dream] was also a header from a corner."

"This was the first dream like that I've had. Hopefully it won't be the last," said Brooks. Skeptics will ascribe it to "extraordinary coincidence." Others are at liberty to regard a premonition that came true *exactly* as dreamed, (and verified by teammates) as quite something else.

Precognitive Dreams or Visions of the Near Future Are Highly Accurate

I have discovered in my research about both my own precognitions and those recorded by Dead Saints, we are sometimes afforded a view into our personal future as a *warning*. They almost always concern ourselves, our children, or family...and, unfortunately, ominous premonitions usually are accurate—especially within a 3-year period.

Carl's future son was foretold:

I was standing before Christ. The Light behind Him was so bright you could not look at Him with human eyes. He told me, 'No you must return for this reason. You will have a son born unto you, (3 years later— to the very day—my son Julian was born).[3]

In *Light and Death, One Doctor's Fascinating Account of Near-Death Experiences*, Michael Sabom, M.D., writes of Lori's premonition of her brain tumor, surgery, and NDE a year before it happened.[4] At the time of her vision, she was perfectly healthy. Similar to my premonitions in chapter 1, Lori was *"listening to her heart"* and felt she was told, *"Get your house in order or you shall surely die."* She and her husband prayed about it, and then promptly put it out of their mind. A year later, to their astonishment, everything occurred exactly as envisioned.

I had a waking (pre-brain cancer) premonition on May 16, 2012 with Soozi Holbeche, a good friend with decades of ILC[5] teaching experience. Her lovely South African accent and humor won the hearts of many thousands around the world as she often co-taught ILC with Paul Solomon during his travels during the 1970's and 1980's. Soozi and I were having a casual conversation in the foyer of the A.R.E (Edgar Cayce Foundation) in Virginia Beach, when suddenly, without warning, I began sobbing. It was as if I had been punched. Tears running down my face, I blurted out, "I will never see you again." Soozi was taken back. She just smiled at me, "David, of course, we will see each other again!" But I knew she was going to die. When she left the conference and traveled back to her home in South Africa, we stayed in close contact after my brain cancer surfaced in June 2013.

On March 16, 2014, I received the following email from Soozi:

Dear David,

Sorry not to respond to your e-mails and invitations, but I have had 2 cancerous growths removed from my head and my left leg, the latter of which went septic, so have been in hospital on drips and having other treatment for my knees. I will be in touch when I am out of these woods. Sorry you have not heard from me. Lots of love to you all.
Soozi

She died six days later on March 22.

Probable Futures

I believe when we are given a premonition in a vision or in a dream, several trajectories are presented that lead to a number of possible personal futures. However, one future may be more likely than others.

I knew time was not A-Z. I felt a suspension in time. I knew life events were in "probables."[6]

If time for all events, past and present, happen simultaneously and if seeing into the future is possible, it appears that only rarely it can be changed. Like John Brooks, we can have a view into the short-term future and see probabilities that can sneak their way into our dreams and sometimes into our waking reality that occur exactly as foreseen.

So, why do we have dreams about the future? Are they meant to warn us so we can prepare for the inevitable? Or can our actions in the present change probabilities we set in motion in the past? Do we have an option to change our "appointed time?" Is the prophetic dream "set in stone?" Will the future occur just as John Brooks saw in his dream before the 2014 World Cup?

Some Examples: A symbolic dream I had on May 18, 2014 seemed to have prophetic consequences. I dreamed of a very deep gorge, threaded by a fast raging river. A huge, but gentle King Kong straddled the gorge. He wasn't scary at all. I say "gentle" because he was helping Sharon Solomon (Paul Solomon's widow) and me across the fast moving river. Sharon jumped into his huge ape hand, and he carefully lifted her over to *the other side*. It was my turn to jump into his hand, when I woke up from the dream.

The gorge and bridges crossing rivers were recurring elements in dreams I had throughout 2014 and 2015. The symbol of a *gentle black* King Kong could represent *Death*, sometimes represented by the Grim Reaper or the Angel of Death. (See also chapter15, *You Do Not Die Alone*) I don't know why I got a gentle King Kong, but I think he is a better symbol of death than the Grim Reaper! I was concerned after I woke up from the dream thinking Sharon's life was in danger. Over the summer, I asked her about her health. She told me she felt fine.

It seemed highly unlikely she would die before me. However, six months later on November 14, 2014, Sharon had a massive heart attack that, according to her doctors, brought her within an hour of death. I called Sharon a month later, and we had a two-hour chat. I talked to her about her heart attack and reminded her of my King Kong dream eight months prior. To me, the dream clearly predicted the real possibility of her death before mine. I asked her to email me a description of her heart attack. I discovered a week prior to her dramatic event; she had a dream about deceased friends and family

I was at Hearthfire Lodge with Paul Solomon, Thomas Keller, Paul Ricioppo, and Reverend and Mrs. Dove (all deceased). We were moving, packing up everything there, moving then to Texarkana, Texas (where I moved for a time after Paul died) and from there, to Burke's Garden, Virginia, to my current home. It left me with a good feeling, but I was not able to interpret its meaning until I remembered it again soon after I had a heart attack.

Sharon disclosed more details about her medical emergency:

Thinking back on the experience and the four days I spent in the hospital, I realize something transformational occurred and I don't know exactly how to explain it. It wasn't a near-death experience in the classic sense. I didn't leave my body and view it from above. I didn't go to or through a tunnel.

What did happen I knew ...with a certainty...this dream was real-those people who I loved and had gone before me had come to reassure me. They are waiting for me and would have been there had I died then and will be there whenever I die. I have no fear of death and have been able to discuss my plans for my passing very easily." ~Sharon Solomon

Sharon feels she did not take the opportunity to die at her appointed time, which I believe it was. Of course, I am praying for her good health, but it seems our future deaths will be connected regardless of when our deaths occur and whoever crosses over first!

Interpreting Dreams

One example of dream interpretation I would like to share happened in a 1988 dream class in Japan. I asked for one of the Japanese class participants to share a dream so I could attempt to interpret it. Emiko, my wife at the time, was translating Japanese to English for me, making the task all the more difficult.

A man in his forties stood up and described a dream where he had been imprisoned for 11 years, his wrists bound with duct tape. It was a recurring dream where he could not escape. At first, the meaning of the dream escaped me, but then it occurred to me to ask him, "What happened 11 years ago?"

He thought for a moment, and then he said, "That's when my daughter left our home after a family argument."

You could feel the goosebumps run through the entire class. The man had put himself in a prison of guilt for 11 years since she left.

I asked him, "Can you forgive her for leaving?"

He broke down in tears. "I've been in so much pain. Yes. Yes. I can." The whole class was in tears.

Such Zen moments are few and far between. Wisdom comes when it comes. But in between, we need lots of practice!

Asking God for Answers in Dreams

I have endured thirty radiation sessions and sixty Temodar chemo treatments since September 2013. My tumor shrank from 20mm to

3mm, so the current therapy appeared effective. By September 29, 2014, it was time for a PET scan to see if any tendrils of my cancer had spread to other areas in my brain. PET is a high resolution MRI, where you are injected with a radioactive fluid that reveals even pinpoint cancer spots. I was in my 16th month of survival following my GBM diagnosis, so this scan was pivotal in predicting any chance for long-term survival. Our neuro-oncologist appointment with Dr. Randazzo was set for the next morning at 10:30am to go over the MRI and PET scan results.

My disorientation symptoms had increased, so we didn't know what to expect, and I wasn't that hopeful. So before we went to bed, Delynn and I prayed together and asked God to give us a dream with some guidance.

At 3:00 am later that night, I woke up with a very short, but powerful dream. In the dream, Delynn told me *"David, you are expecting unfaithful waters."* I woke up Delynn and conveyed the simple words to her. It sounded Biblical, but neither of us had heard the term "unfaithful waters" before. We did a google search and found this amazing quote from Jeremiah: 15-18. (ASV) "Why is my pain perpetual, and my wound incurable, which refused to be healed? Wilt thou indeed be unto me as a deceitful [brook], as waters that fail?"

In the Good News Translation we read, "Why do I keep on suffering? Why are my wounds incurable? Why won't they heal? Do you intend to disappoint me like a stream that goes dry in the summer?"

Delynn and I were both surprised by the short dream and Biblical reference. The Scripture specifically refers to the prophet Jeremiah who also had *a wound that would not heal.* (Jeremiah 15:18) and he complained to God, "When are you going to heal me? God basically says, "Don't you trust me? I am a spring well that never dries up." The dream was a powerful "note" from God, "I am here with you. Your continued survival is dependent on ME. *Have faith David."*

Approaching-Death Dreams (ADDs)

There is a distinct subset of dreams I have termed approaching-death dreams (ADDs). They differ from near-end-of-life events (NELEs)— (see Table 1, *Seven Near-Death Triggers,* #7, ch.2) which are conscious or semi-conscious visions of deceased loved ones seen by the person who is dying a few weeks, days, or hours before death.

ADDs represent dreams of a person approaching death and contain symbols such as luggage, airplanes, ice and oranges, snow, crossing a river, black shoes, tropical shirts, passports and tickets. In general, they describe someone who is getting ready to leave for a destination in the Afterlife.

The Angel of Death may appear or in my case, death is symbolized by a gentle, King Kong described earlier in the chapter. Sometimes approaching-death dreams may be prophetic about the time a loved one plans to leave. I have included several instances of my own approaching death dreams that have occurred over the last two years. These are just a few examples:

~I saw myself climb down from a very high oak tree to be engaged in a conversation with a group of people. They were discussing whether we should feed a beautiful white stallion who had lost its will to live, or instead, continue payments on a 3-year car lease. The question was, "Do we spend money feeding the stallion who had lost its will to live, or pay the car lease?" The advisors in the dream wanted to pay the car lease. I disagreed.

The stallion was so weak from losing its will to live, and it was quietly lying down on the ground on its side waiting to die. I stood over him and was surprised to see, instead of a black eye pupil staring at me, a brilliant, glowing white Light was shining out of its eye. It was as if his whole body was lit up from within, releasing the Light through the one eye I could see. It reminded me of Luke 11:34: 'The Lamp of the Body is the eye.'

I knelt down next to the stallion, and began gently petting his head saying, "You can do it, buddy. You can do it. Come on...hang in there, consoling him, like I was encouraging my very best friend to live."

Then I woke up. Even when I think about the moment I petted the horse with such compassion and encouragement, how absolutely gentle I expressed myself in the dream as I stared into the beautiful white Light, every time it brings tears to my eyes.

The dream became a distinct turning point in my life. I wanted to live again. I thought I had wanted to live. I was not afraid of death, but perhaps I was resigned to dying. I wasn't "acting" as if I wanted to live. I knew the meaning of the dream. The horse was my body and life. The white Light shining from the stallion's eyes was Christ, the Living One. God was trying to resurrect "David" back to life. My encounter with the brilliant, white Light in the dream had the hallmarks of a near-death experience.
~Chronicle 358

~Crossing a river holding on to a pole attached to a rope spanning the river. I observed a trout swimming below the thin ice and an orange (tropical). The ice and tropical mix is a near-death symbol for me.
~Chronicle 481

~Walking on pebbles just under the water leading towards a bridge crossing over a river. Six Sans Souci relaxed summer chairs freshly painted blue and grey set on a dock at the beginning of the pebble walkway on the shore I was standing on. Walking on the pebbles made it look like I was walking on water. ~Chronicle 504

~I remember getting a gold-covered piece of luggage for travel. ~Chronicle 524

~Looking to take an "excursion" to a tropical place. I was alone. No one was traveling with me. I waited at an airport/travel agency four hours for a flight. I was quite the impatient one. I really wanted to leave. Still, I was polite. Some of the other passengers who were going to the "tropical place" had bright blue or purple tropical shirts for their trips, everyone else wore black and white—kind of like the little girl with the red coat in Schindler's List. (Travel dream going to a tropical place, color, all indicative of crossing over at some point in the not-too-far-off future. A four-hour wait could be four months or four years.) In my desperation to leave, I found a small plane I could fly, but I didn't know how to operate it; descend, ascend, or even contact the airport tower for control instructions. I had to get to Los Angeles International Airport, which was excessively intimidating for a pilot with no experience. ~Chronicle 815

    I believe dreams are a language sent from God. Learn to remember them and interpret them. Do not let unconscious sleep rob you of the dreams the Lord has sent to teach you. The world of your subconscious is a pathway to interpret the activity and meaning of your daily life, and can be an instrument to seeing beyond the veil, a mini-death experience without the requirement of illness or death to receive messages from God. Perhaps, you will be gifted with dreams with deceased loved ones or dreams about the future. Or you may hear a dream of a loved one who is preparing to cross over and know how to interpret it. But none of these will be available to you unless you begin recording dreams, interpreting dreams, and enriching your mind with a new skill. It is rare, very rare, for someone NOT to be able to learn to remember his or her dreams. Practice will not only open a doorway to Heaven for blessings and communication from the Lord, you will prepare yourself for your own death because you will have become familiar with the Light that shines through from the Afterlife.

---

1 Pew Forum on Religion and Public Life, U.S. Religious Landscape Survey, Summary of Key Findings, http://www.pewforum.org/2009/12/09/many-americans-mix-multiple-faiths/
2 *Robert B NDE*, #2158, 02.25.10, NDERF.org

3 *Carl G NDE*, #1797, 12.15.08, NDERF.org
4 Michael Sabom, M.D. 1998. *Light and Death, One Doctor's Fascinating Account of Near-Death Experiences*. Grand Rapids Michigan: Zondervan Publishing House, paraphrased from Lori's Premonition, p. 158.
5 ILC (Inner Light Consciousness) A Course in Spiritual Evolution taught by Paul Solomon. Available at www.paulsolomon.com.
6 *Lori E STE/SOBE*, #3098, 07.28.12, NDERF.org

— 7 —
The Apprentice Gardener

An apprentice gardener does not try to shape nature, but lets nature reveal its shape, and in so doing, the garden becomes the teacher of life... It is not the gardener who makes the garden, but the garden who makes the Gardner. ~Alan Chadwick, Founder of the French Intensive, Bio-Dynamic Gardening method.

Imagine. You are dreaming you have just crossed over to the "other side."

You are in Heaven.

It is a separate reality from Earth University. All your earthly senses; sight, keener, sharper, subtler, spiritual counterparts here have replaced touch, smell, taste, and hearing in this special place. A robe of light covers your body, tied with a golden sash. Your new body floats as easily as a dandelion seed in the wind. You are happy. You are smiling.

You find yourself walking through a beautiful meadow with tall green grass and wild flowers. As you walk, you can feel the tips of the high grass on your fingertips. You can hear birds chirping in the absolute quiet and the laughter of children playing nearby.

Off in the distance, across the valley, a magnificent garden-terraced mountain rises up into a deep azure sky. Waterfalls, forests, and vivid flowered gardens cover its slopes, and a breathtaking, almost blinding white Lig

ht shines from its summit. You instinctively know it is the Light of God and it is His Light that lights up the heavens.

You want to get to know that Light and are drawn towards it like a moth to a flame. You realize you have been to this sacred mountain before. This is not the first time. You realize your life on Earth has created the Afterlife garden you now observe around you. It was created by lessons learned and experiences encountered while enrolled in Earth University—a garden you grew in your own heart. It is not the end of your journey, but an immortal latest addition to a garden project begun long ago. A worn granite and alabaster stone path gently winds its way through the meadow to the base of the mountain.

Looking up, you can see there are seven lush garden terraces clinging to its slopes—the gardens we must pass through in our Afterlife journey up the sacred mountain. Red flowers and Japanese maples predominantly mark the first garden. A large granite entry stepping-stone and a magnificent 700-year-old gnarly Black Pine Bonsai frame define the entrance.

Beneath the Bonsai, a gardener sleeps. Lying beside him is a rake, a hoe, and a shovel. An angel hovers above, whispering, *"Apprentice, it's time to wake up. It's time to finish your garden."*

Afterlife Evidence of Heavenly Gardens

The metaphorical garden is an ongoing exercise intended to heighten our level of consciousness. What we achieve (or fail to achieve) is recorded in the Great Ledger (Book of Life) of God's Kingdom. Our words and our deeds during our stay in Earth University do not simply vanish when we take leave of our physical vehicle; we shall be called to account for our lives. As Galatians 6:7 puts it, "Whatsoever a man soweth, that shall he also reap." Repeatedly, the Dead Saints bear witness to the reality of that promise (or warning, as the case may be.)

That understanding is a staple of most esoteric traditions and it may be the reason why, in so many Dead Saint accounts, Heaven is filled with plants, flowers, meadows, and beautiful panoramas.

God endows transformational power in the garden, a concept often overlooked by the Christian faith. Both literally and metaphorically, the ancients understood this power as a science. That is why, in ancient Egypt, the walls of the nobles' tomb were carved with scenes of sowing, reaping and all the other crafts that transformed raw material into refined finished products. The garden is an eternal metaphor that reveals the power of Christ hidden within plants, rocks, and animals, and all living things, the Source of Life itself— nature's *athanor*.

Heaven Is So Beautiful It Makes Earth Look Soiled

The most brilliant late Autumn Japanese maples are some of the most beautiful I have ever seen. Yet, as the *Tao Te Ching* (The ancient Chinese book of wisdom) puts it: "The whole world recognizes the beautiful as the beautiful, yet this is only the ugly."[1] This same idea is reflected by Rhea's NDE. Heaven still makes even the most beautiful places on Earth look soiled:

This place that we walked was the most beautiful place I have ever seen. It was like a grassy, hilly place filled with flowers. The colors were so bright and vivid. It makes the greenest grass here on Earth look dirty. Like Hawaii but the colors were so bright they looked like wet paint. After our short walk, he stopped and asked me if I wanted to go back with my mother and brother, or did, I want to stay. At that second, I thought of my mom and brother for the first time. I told Him (without speaking) I needed to go back with them. He smiled at me, and in the next second, I was back on the table in the doctor's office.[2]

Marilyn saw heavenly gardens during her NDE when she was 12-years-old. She was playing a horse and rider game, which consisted of tying a skipping rope around the neck of one of the other players, and while on their hands and knees, another person sat on their back and they rode the first like a horse. In the melee, the rope around Marilyn's neck became knotted and tightened to the point she could not breathe. In a panic, she tried to get her younger sister to get it off, which she tried, but could not get out the knots. She started to climb the basement stairs to have her mom help her, but felt herself fall down and slipped into total darkness, that's where she spoke with Jesus, and her NDE began:

Suddenly, I saw a white Light in the distance and thought I should try to get there, but I was too scared to move in the dark. It sounded like someone was walking towards me, but I could not see them. Suddenly I felt someone pick me up in their arms, I was

> *surrounded by Light, and I looked into the smiling face of a man who said His name was Jesus. He told me not to be frightened. He was here to take me back. He had shoulder length brown hair and dark brown eyes. He was wearing leather sandals on His feet with straps that went between His toes and tied around His ankles. He had on a long white gown with long, big sleeves with a long light blue tunic over it. There was a gold color rope tied around His waist. His voice was very soft and kind almost musical and I felt a feeling of pure love and complete safety and trust.*

Marilyn could hear birds singing, see butterflies flying and little children laughing chasing lambs, as she walked through the tall grass:

> *As we were walking up the stairs, I noticed the left side of the wall was still basement wall but...the right side of the wall disappeared and in its place was a beautiful garden full of long grass and wild flowers. I could hear birds singing and there were butterflies flying. I could see little children playing and chasing little lambs and I could hear their laughter. It looked like so much fun. I asked if I could go play with the kids and was told, no. There was no time today for that I have had you too long as it is. He made me promise to tell the world about what I saw and if I did, then when my time comes, I will be able to walk in the garden with Him.*[3]

There are dozens and dozens of Dead Saint stories describing such breathtaking Afterlife vistas: the mountains, gardens, butterflies, colors and wildlife of Heaven. In the following NDE, which occurs during an asthma attack, Anthony describes the process of building a Garden Temple on a sacred mountain over the course of 2500 years of *Heaven-time:*

> *The voice [a high spiritual being] told me I was to build a garden on the mountain and every year a brick would appear on the top of the boulder and with the bricks, I was meant to build a path up the mountain from the base to the boulder. I was told to plant trees which appeared as acorns etc. at the top of the mountain...As the years passed I watched the trees grow, the flowers and grass I planted also grew, the color of the flowers weren't of any color I have ever seen, like there was 20 different colors in the rainbow there, I couldn't describe them as there's just no frame of reference to what they looked like...The last brick that appeared on the boulder appeared some 2,500 years after I had*

first arrived. I was aware of every year. It was not dreamlike. It was "real time," if that makes any sense.

The path now stretched from the base to the boulder, but over the years, the boulder had gradually changed shape and now looked square like some sort of altar. The trees I had initially planted had grown, the bows and branches had arched, and the trunks thickened to form what I can only describe as a temple at the top of the mountain. The voice told me the first part of my job was finished and I now had to set foot upon the path. I went to the bottom of the mountain and put a foot onto the path.

...The voice was kind and patient and said it was with me and I would finish [the garden path], but I needed to learn the lessons it was teaching...I continued to the end of the path with the encouragement and presence of what I now understood to be some higher spiritual being. I reached the entrance to the tree temple, went inside, and saw the only other being I saw the entire time I was there. It had its back to me and was kneeling as though in prayer.

...I was also told the garden I had created would exist there forever, and I would return there one day. As I walked with the being back out of the tree temple, I saw for the first time other people coming to the garden and sitting on the grass, looking at the flowers, talking and laughing. The being smiled and said, 'See what you've accomplished here?'

The entire experience had taken about eight minutes from my initial [asthma] attack to being "back." I've never reported this before as I guess most people would say it was a hallucination. I can only say it was more "real" than anything I have experienced in this world.[4]

Anthony's description of laying bricks as a pathway up a bare mountain, planting trees, flowers, and various greenery, and a pathway up to a "tree temple," over many centuries, is a perfect analogy of our own journey up the sacred mountain we must traverse during our journey through Earth University. The garden in Heaven reflected the lessons, both the joy and the pain he caused others throughout time.

Carmel, who had a previous NDE at age four and encountered "Grandfather Jesus," had a second NDE forty years later, when she died of a bladder infection. During her second NDE, she again encountered Jesus and this time saw a mountain with a very large living Light at its summit:

> At first, I noticed, (Jesus the same man was waiting for me, but this time He was not alone.) There were hundreds of people there, moving about with what seemed to be purpose to me. It was dark, like this place was in space and I could see the tree again. There were no gates this time, but there was now a mountain that looked to be about 20kms away. On the top, there was a very large living Light presence. I knew this was GOD or SOURCE and this is why it is called the LIGHT.[5]

We will explore deeply the metaphor of the sacred Mountain, the garden and the Gardener as we examine and take an accounting of our own lives before we exit Earth University. On that note, let's take a closer look at the garden metaphor in Christianity.

Jesus the Gardener

Perhaps the Apostle John wanted to make a point about the garden and the gardener when he tells the story about Jesus rising from the garden tomb three days after His crucifixion. When Mary Magdalene finds the stone rolled away, and is shocked to see Jesus has disappeared, she sees a man in the garden and not recognizing Him, assumes he is the gardener:

> Jesus says to her, 'Woman, why weepest thou? Whom seekest thou?' She, supposing him to be the gardener, saith unto Him, 'Sir, if thou have borne Him hence, tell me where thou hast laid Him, and I will take Him away.' Jesus saith unto her, 'Mary.' She turned herself, and saith unto Him, 'Rabboni; which is to say, Master.' (John 20:15-16)

Scholars believe Mary did not recognize Jesus because it was early morning and too dark to see Jesus' face clearly, but the passage begs the question—why didn't she recognize His voice, since she had been His disciple for three years. I believe John was using specific language to highlight the importance of the garden itself and to acknowledge Jesus as our heavenly Gardener.

Dead Saints often describe conversations with Christ in a garden. During Linda's NDE, she had a revealing conversation with Jesus in a desert garden:

> Jesus put His arm around me in the area of what would have been my shoulder, looked me straight in the eyes and said, 'I have

*come for you, that you may know I am real.' I was totally awestruck by His presence, yet I felt a love and respect for Him that I have never felt in physical life. I followed Him to an area I can best describe as a "desert garden." We sat on large "sitting rocks," and He began to speak... He was explaining the different things of life on Earth, why it was that life on Earth was not perfect, why it was that way, and **what people on Earth had misconstrued about life and living**.*[6]

The Garden, Nature and St. Francis of Assisi

St. Francis (1182-1226) serves as a unique bridge between Eastern and Western theology. This simple Christ-like man clothed in a brown tunic tied with a rope, believed all levels of creation were endowed with consciousness including, Sun, Moon, Earth, wind, creatures, as well as human beings.

The transformation of St. Francis, along with the Apostle Paul has, is one of the most dramatic in Christian history. While St. Francis is universally known for his unconditional love, theologians often avoid commenting on his love for the natural world, no doubt, because it bordered on nature worship. This is a true anomaly in Christian literature, since his spiritual connection with birds, animals...with all nature is legendary. Francis writes, "Our Sister, Mother Earth, who nourishes and governs us, and produces various fruits with many colored flowers and herbs. Or for our Sister Water. She is very useful, and humble, and precious and pure."[7] These suggest profound links between all manifestations of Great Nature, humanity, and God; a view largely absent from Christian dogma...though in the Old Testament, thousands of years before Francis, the patriarch Job provides a precedent when he describes the Divine lessons enshrined within God's creation (Job 12: 7-9):

Ask the plants of the Earth, and they will teach you... But now ask the beasts, and let them teach you; and the birds of the heavens, and let them tell you. Or speak to the Earth, and let it teach you; and let the fish of the sea declare to you. "Who among all these does not know that the hand of the LORD has done this?

Bonnie, during her NDE, sees the Light of God in all things—mountains, people, everything:

I was shown the white Light was really made up of all the colors. I was shown the zillions of colors in the Light, more than I have seen on Earth. They were all beautiful. I don't remember the exact words, but I do remember discussing that all things were made of the Light. I asked if even mountains, and people, and the voice (which I now think was God) told me even mountains, and a long list of things, everything.[8]

Anecdotes abound of St. Francis and his reverence for and intimate relationship with all nature. In one, he and his companions were resting near the town of Bevagna, when Francis spotted a great flock of birds of all varieties nesting and chirping in the nearby trees. Awestruck, Francis left his friends and ran toward the birds, who patiently waited for him. He greeted them, as was his custom, expecting them to fly off at the sound of his voice, but they did not move. Francis asked them if they would stay awhile and listen to the Word of God.

He said to them, "My brother and sister birds, you should praise your Creator and always love Him. He gave you feathers for clothes, wings to fly and all other things you need. It is God who made you noble among all creatures, making your home in thin, pure air. Without sowing or reaping, you receive God's guidance and protection."

St. Francis treated all God's Creation with a radical reverence. Once, it is said, when he was sitting too close to a fire, his undergarments caught aflame. He refused to put out the fire, saying to a fellow Assisi brother who tried to smother it, "Dearest brother, do not hurt Brother Fire! At other times, his love for water made him wash his hands where the water would not be trodden underfoot, and his love for rocks made him walk on them reverently because Christ was the foundation, the "rock" of all Creation.

In a world where the resources of nature are routinely abused, St. Francis is a glaring anomaly. However extreme his behavior, his love for all creation and its Creator illuminates whatever he did. Catholic authors, embarrassed by Francis' unorthodoxy, try to minimize his reverence for the natural world by claiming he "exorcised" and "cleansed" the pagan spirit of nature by asceticism:

The mistake of the pagan world had been "the mistake of nature-worship..." How could they learn anything from the love of birds and flowers after the sort of love stories that were told of them? Not till the pagan spirit had been exorcised by renunciation of the enjoyment of the beauties of nature, by asceticism, that is, could a cleansed and purified love of nature, a love of nature as the mirror of its Creator, take its place. St. Francis was the exponent, the poet, the saint of that new love. In his own person he experienced the cleansing process, became the living exemplification and pattern of this purified love in a supreme degree and so was the fit instrument for the propagation of a spiritual life which, though not new in its source, divine charity, was new in its attitude to the world. [9]

However, in the light of St. Francis' thoroughly documented life story, such comments are patently absurd. Nature (God's creation) has existed for billions of years. It was pristine and sacred before humanity ever arrived on the scene. Before Christ, most world religions based their pagan beliefs on the veneration of natural phenomena they observed in Nature, developing a pantheon of matriarchal goddesses, representing the Spirit God in Mother Earth, Gaia. The Light they venerated and worshipped became part of the evolutionary process of our understanding of God.

While Christian tradition seeks to exorcise the adoration of all natural phenomena as unnecessary or evil, the transformation of St. Francis among the lilies of the field and the testimonies from the Dead Saints, reveal a sacred doorway to knowing the Being of Light, and an understanding that Mother Earth, Father God, and the Christ—Jesus Christ, are ONE.

Gospel of Thomas Describes Christ in Nature

We find an early Christian understanding of Christ in nature on a papyrus document known as the *Gospel of Thomas*. One of the earliest and oldest known Gospels dating to 130 A.D., the *Gospel of Thomas*, was unearthed in the Egyptian desert in 1945,[10] and contains a list of 114 sayings of Jesus. While many of its verses written are similar to ones spoken by Christ in the four Gospels, a few sayings of St. Thomas describe Christ as the Light in all things, including Nature.

In verse 77, Jesus said, "It is I who am the Light which is above them all. It is I who am the all. From me did the all come forth, and unto me did the all extend. Split a piece of wood, and I am there. Lift up the stone, and you will find me there."[11]

In verse 3, St. Thomas reiterates Jesus' teaching of the Father's Kingdom: "The Kingdom is *within you*, and it is *outside of you*."[12]

Christ taught the same philosophy when he served the Last Supper:

And he took bread, and gave thanks and broke it, and gave unto them saying, 'This is my body which is given for you: this do in remembrance of me. 'Likewise He took the cup after they had eaten, saying, 'This cup which is poured out for you is the new covenant in My blood.' (Luke 22:19-20)

Jesus was saying; every time you eat and drink remember the new covenant I have made with you. The bread represents His flesh, the wine His blood. Jesus is saying He is one with God in ALL THINGS in Heaven and on Earth. "How can we explain away that He meant anything differently?"

There is a consensus among scholars that the Gospel of Thomas dates to the very beginnings of the Christian era, and appears to have been written on papyrus *before* the four traditional canonical Gospels. Initially, for a few decades, scholars argued the Gospel of Thomas was a late second or third century Gnostic forgery. When it was proven to be authentic, and could be older by half a century than the four Canonical Gospels, orthodox apologists still rejected it because it presented what was believed to be a pantheistic belief Nature is identical with divinity excluding a personal relationship with Jesus Christ.

It seems modern theologians want one theme in the Gospels with little deviation. Early Christian doctrine and emperors established the worship of God, the Creator, through Jesus Christ alone. The adoration or worship of God in Nature became pagan and "of the Devil." Unable to conceive any possibility Jesus Christ ever taught such a theology, Christian theologians have consigned the Gospel of Thomas to hidden recesses of museums as another "heretical" pagan document, unworthy of general public mention or consideration to be added to the Canon of our Holy Bible.

Sacrifice of the Sparrow: A Mystical Experience

My own understanding of God expressing Himself through Nature began during my sophomore year in High School. My friends and I were hunting birds for sport with BB guns on the 25 acres of woodland adjacent to our homes. This local virgin tract in Virginia Beach was our own private refuge for fun and sport. We idled away much of our summer vacation time there.

On this day, it was late afternoon, and I hadn't yet bagged a bird. Most of the time we shot at blackbirds, but with the BB gun's low pressure air pump action and our own deplorable aim, we rarely hit our targets. Nonetheless, the process of hunting itself satisfied some savage, primal part of us somehow. I'm not sure why. I approached a row of bushes lining a ditch, and spotted a sparrow perched on a branch just ten feet away from me. Without thinking, I took aim, held my breath and pulled the trigger. It was a perfect shot. The sparrow fell dead to the ground and rolled down to the bottom of the ditch end over end.

As if in slow motion, the stricken little bird finally came to rest in the center of a large maple leaf with its lifeless eyes staring up at me, as if asking, "Why did you kill me?"

Blood spilled out of the sparrow's wound in a horrible pool next to its head. Slowly the sparrow's slight weight made the fingered edges of the limp leaf gently curl up around it like the hand of God.

The gleaming pool of blood shocked me.

For most of my teenage years, I had always believed in Jesus Christ, but He was the Man in Heaven, not the Light of God animating the sparrow, the trees, and all of Creation. The wrongness of this wanton, mindless act shocked me to the core. I never forgot it.

I never shot another living creature again.

The Zen Garden & the Art of Bonsai

Before I began writing this chapter, I took time to remove the copper training wires from my 150-year-old Western Juniper Bonsai. As Felton Jones had taught me, I began talking to the tree, and in talking realized how much I loved that tree and cared about its well-being.

The art of Bonsai is truly a love relationship. I connect myself with the tree and by extension, I am connected beyond the tree to the Divinity who created the tree. It's not exactly a conscious act, but after pruning, wiring, fertilizing, or removing wire from my tree, I feel attuned to its sensitivity, the smell of it, how healthy it is, whether it's been watered enough, or if it needs fertilizing and food. I want the tree to be happy.

It is on display inside my home on a wooden stand for a week at a time, before going back out to my balcony, where it can see the ocean, smell the air, and listen to the ocean crash on the beach.

Zen and Bonsai go hand in hand. Most Bonsai artists will tell you there is a much deeper meaning to Bonsai than just tastefully styling and dwarfing trees. As we learned from Felton Jones, the art of Bonsai is a form of spiritual significance. In Bonsai (unlike all other art forms), we mimic Mother Nature with one of Mother Nature's own creations. I have ultimate control of my tree and am writing a poem, honoring its inherent Divine nature. Bonsai is a tranquil art- invoking peace and quiet, even in the middle of stressful settings and busy cities.

The simple styled tree in its pot allows us to conjure up granite, mountains standing still, flowing water, birds flying, flowers blooming, clouds drifting, and wind blowing. It is as inevitable as any oil painting or sculpture: The shape of the trunk, every twist of a branch, the spacing of the leaves or needles provide the observer with insight into the artist's soul.

Just as Felton Jones (ch.4) literally cut away the front half of my Azalea Bonsai to teach me I must grow new branches in my own life, so to all who begin to cultivate the garden of their own lives, experience the same.

With these insights in mind, I do not expect you to become an apprentice under a Bonsai teacher just because I was formally trained in the art. It is to use the art of Bonsai and the philosophy of Zen as training wires for your own soul. Along with your own Christian (or non-Christian) background and beliefs, begin planting new seeds of thought that will soon flourish and grow in the fertile garden of your heart.

What Can We Really Learn from the Garden?

Being There, the 1979 American film comedy, addresses this question indirectly through the life story of Chauncey Gardiner (Peter Sellers), a simple-minded gardener. (Note: Peter Sellers had a near-death experience after a heart attack in 1964, a fact Shirley Maclaine reveals in her book, *Out on a Limb).*[13]

From birth, he has never left the estate of his wealthy guardian employer. The guardian dies and Chauncey, now in his sixties, is forced to leave. Everything in the outside world is new, strange and unfathomable to him. Entranced and wandering aimlessly around, he steps backward off the sidewalk and is struck by a chauffeured car owned by Ben Rand (Melvyn Douglas), an elderly business tycoon. In the back seat of the car sits Rand's wife, Eve (Shirley MacLaine). Satisfied that Chauncey has not been injured they take him back to their luxurious mansion.

No one knows where he comes from, and he can provide no useful information about himself. In the search to find out more, his benefactors come to assume he must be a wealthy and wise genius. Because of his simple, Zen-like utterances about life and gardening—his responses are taken for profundity:

> *As long as the roots are not severed, all is well. And all will be well in the garden. In the garden, growth has it seasons. First, comes spring and summer, but then we have fall and winter. And then we get spring and summer again.*

Even though these simple sayings are adapted from the 1970 novella by Jerzy Kosinski and the uncredited Robert C. Jones, they illustrate the simplicity of Zen. We are led to believe all along Chauncey is just a simple-minded, child-like gardener, whose limited intelligence makes it appear he was incompetent.

Then, in the final scene of the film, Chauncey sticks his walking stick deep into the lake, and begins casually strolling over the water like Peter the Apostle. Unlike Peter, who sinks into the water after taking but a few steps towards Christ, Chauncey continues walking towards the other side, as if walking on water is no special accomplishment. *Being There* leaves the viewer to wonder debate and question…or if we so choose, dismiss it all cynically, as a mere Hollywood fabrication.

Is there a message? Can a simple gardener, blessed with child-like innocence, who spends his life "cultivating his garden," walk on water? Can we use his example to walk on water as well?

Entry Requirements for Heaven?

It is this "simplicity of mind" that is central to the philosophy of Zen and it is a concept mirrored by Jesus in Matthew 18:3: "Verily, I say unto you, except ye be converted and become as little children, ye shall not enter into the Kingdom of Heaven."

Jesus says becoming child-like is very important: In fact, it is critical to reaching Heaven and a quality we often overlook, as we stumble through our daily lives. I accidentally discovered this "secret" on the streets of New York City in 1981, when I "childishly" smiled at the Bag Lady, and subsequently got put summarily in my place by a holy presence, I later identified as Jesus. If there is Heaven on Earth, that experience was it.

While completing this chapter, I recognized this child-like quality, was exemplified by Tyler, a young man with Cerebral Palsy whose life story was shared with me by his parents, Charlie and Maria, during a casual pool-side chat at our Virginia Beach apartment complex. (It's remarkable how many conversations at such chance hot tub/pool-side encounters take on a life of their own, when I bring up the subject of NDEs.)

Once people realize you are willing to talk about the Afterlife…often they open up.

Maria and Charlie's son had been born a normal, healthy baby, but a major defect, undetected at birth, was discovered in his heart muscle two months later. Hospitalized, at ten months old, he had open-heart surgery. Forty-eight hours after the life-saving surgery, Tyler suffered multiple strokes leaving him irremediably brain damaged and with a paralyzed left side.

The boy's early years were a challenge for his family, as he grew through his severe handicap, but grow through it, he did. Tyler became the smiling champion of the disabled, helping kids, disabled as he was, to learn to smile despite their afflictions, and he never gave up helping.

He was famous locally for his child-like simplicity and unflagging good humor. But Cerebral Palsy cut his life short. He died aged 21. His funeral was packed with the children and their parents whom he had touched with his love, his playfulness, and his smiles.

Shortly after his death, Tyler would appear to Maria in dreams, letting her know he was happy, but also that he was still caring for children-in this case children who had recently died. It was like, "Mom, I'm okay, but I am really busy right now. Can we talk later?"

Tyler's influence persisted on the earthly realm. Charlie, his father, took on the challenging job as school bus driver for handicapped children. (While writing this passage, a wonderful presence filled our room—goosebumps and all—Delynn and I both broke down in tears. We had the sense Tyler was looking down from Above, so proud of his father!)

As adults, how do we practically emulate the qualities of a child, so we might fulfill Jesus' exhortation in (Matt 18:3) to become as little children? Perhaps, we should ask ourselves, "What are the defining qualities of a little child?" One who loves unconditionally has no filters; is happy, joyful, laughs a lot, acts spontaneously and without forethought and lives in the present. Does it mean this child of God is one who never gets dirty, never is selfish, never is cruel, never is stubborn, or never throws a tantrum? Well, no. Not in this worldly dimension. Such a child is an imaginary child.

During conversations with Tyler's parents, I learned Tyler was often a handful growing up as a child and then as a teen. Even so, his overriding quality was his child-like loving approach to his peers, disabled kids like himself. That is what everyone remembers. His innocence and his love. [14]

Like Tyler, we are a blend of the good, the mischievous and sometimes even the bad. I believe most of us in this hectic world can hardly imagine re-acquiring our child-like qualities, and perhaps even more unrealistically, transform our thought processes to approximate that of an innocent child. For many Christians, the process towards innocence begins with the born-again experience. However, it is only the beginning of the path that leads up the sacred mountain to the Light of God at its summit.

One Dead Saint remembers these words of wisdom upon awakening from their NDE:

> *Pray without ceasing. Play. Love. Laugh. Live for the joy of it. Have fun. Happiness is holy. The purpose of life is joy. Savor fully the loveliness of each experience. Self-awareness is the prayer of the heart. To pray without ceasing is to play. Play with the joyful*

abandon of the child, absorbed in the delight of each moment. Let go of obligation and duty. Live for the pure joy of being.[15]

As the Dead Saints testify (from their own experience), and as Saint Francis demonstrates, we can all begin to walk with Christ among the lilies of the field, and find the peace and happiness of Heaven right here and now.

We don't have to wait.

---

1 D.C. Lau 2001. *Tao Te Ching*. (New Bilingual Edition). Hong Kong: Chinese University Press.
2 *Rhea D probable NDE*, #1254, 10.14.07, NDERF.org
3 *Marilyn R NDE*, #2925, 01.08.12, NDERF.org
4 *Anthony M's NDE*, #209, 02.08.03, NDERF.org
5 *Carmel B NDE*, #1920, 05.30.09, NDERF.org
6 *Linda S NDE*, #1864, 02.28.09, NDERF.org
7 *The Canticle of the Creatures* (FAED I, 113-114), Saint Francis of Assisi, Spring 1225 A.D.
8 *Bonnie VB NDE*, #2117, 02.02.10, NDERF.org
9 H.G. Hughes 2015. *Saint Francis of Assisi in a New Light*. See https://www.catholicculture.org/culture/library/view.cfm?recnum=8119.
10 *The Gospel of Thomas*, Gnostic Society Library. The three fragments of Thomas found at Oxyrhynchus apparently date to between 130-250 CE, and each probably represents a separate unique copy of the Gospel. The Nag Hammadi discovery in 1945 which unearthed a complete and well-preserved version of Thomas in Coptic made it possible to definitely identify the Oxyrhynchus texts as fragments from a lost Greek edition of the Gospel." See http://gnosis.org/naghamm/nhl_thomas.htm.
11 *The Gospel of Thomas*, Verse 77. Translated by Thomas O. Lambdin, The Gnostic Society Library, The Nag Hammadi Library, http://gnosis.org/naghamm/nhl_thomas.htm.
12 Ibid. Verse 3.
13 Shirley Maclaine 1983. *Out on a Limb*. New York: Bantam Books.
14 Maria, Charlie and Tyler interview by David Solomon, June, 2014. Printed with permission.
15 *The College of Near Death Experiences*, #282, aleroy.com/board282.htm

8

The Spiritual Journal

~I wonder when the veil revealing Heaven will open wider. Remember, God, this is a science experiment in dying. I am taking notes. ~**Chronicle 821**

Journaling is an ancient technique for recording lessons, communications from God, letters to God, dreams, and visions. Many sacred Scriptures, including the Bible, are largely a collection of spiritual journal entries. Many sacred Scriptures in the Bible, the five Books of Moses recorded by his scribe Joshua, the Psalms, Job, and the prophets are written as journals. Later, in the New Testament, the Gospels and letters written by the Apostle Paul, all record in one way or another the personal relationship with God or with the Master, Jesus of Nazareth.

As we discussed in chapter 5, it is an established ancient belief, when a soul awakens to its spiritual nature and begins seeking, teachers and angels on "the other side" begin to actively help, lead, guide and teach the student through direct contact. The student is assigned a "class" and a teacher or several teachers because we generally need help to learn to listen properly to guidance coming from God, the Inner Teacher within.

It is to this learning process the Earth University Journal is dedicated. Even Rice Paper Teachers, important as they may be, are not meant as distractions from knowing the Inner Teacher and the Light of God within. Every day of our life provides opportunities to learn. We are in a school. We have God, a personal, inner teacher who knows exactly what we need to learn. He is actively participating in our lives right now. He has created the opportunity for the lessons to manifest and he knows what is expected of us in accepting and passing each test. So it is incumbent upon us to get in touch with our Inner Teacher and to begin to recognize our lessons.

In the ancient schools of both the East and West, the student was never told, "this is your lesson." Rather, lessons were built into the daily curriculum. The student might never realize the situation to which he or she had automatically reacted to, was a lesson designed to elicit a different and conscious reaction.

The Journal does not replace a formal Teacher, but rather makes better use of the Inner Teacher and one's relationship with Jesus Christ. It can be used by anyone who accepts the ancient admonition *gnōthi sauton,* Greek for *Know Thyself.*

During my spiritual studies in NYC, I began Journaling. Without practicing this discipline, I would have lost many meaningful dreams, memories and experiences later integrated into *the Dead Saints Chronicles.*

Paul Solomon introduced the journaling method I learned to me and was a formal process called *"The Journal of the Mystery Schools"*—a journal divided into seven sections, each represented by a different color beginning with red and moving through the color spectrum to white. As we saw in the last chapter, the Dead Saints describe gardens we are building within ourselves—a sacred mountain in Heaven through time. In ancient Egypt, masters of a craft, including the pharaohs, would begin building their tombs when they reached a certain stage of mastery. In my own case, I built Akio Botanical Gardens in Washington State. The gardens became my temple, reflecting a vision uniquely me.

When we write our experiences in the journal, we continue building a garden or temple within ourselves. Usually entries are brief, and speaking from experience, in order to turn journal keeping into a daily habit, it is best if entries are brief, concise and clear. The exception to the rule is the Self-Discovery Garden, which becomes, over time, your autobiography.

The Journal's value increases over time. When an entry is made in a specific Garden, the experience is fresh in one's mind. If a similar situation occurs years later, it is easy to find and review that earlier entry. This may enable you to avoid mistakes made earlier or at least clarify a repetitive pattern.

Again, speaking from experience, brief entries are best since keeping a journal is a discipline you may want to continue your entire life. It should not become a burden. That said, there is no right way or wrong way to keep it. Once your relationship with your spiritual journal grows and flowers, you will carry it with you as an intimate friend—one with whom secrets may be safely shared or kept secret for a future reference.

The Gardens

The Journal begins with **The Red Garden**, *Know Thyself*. This becomes our autobiography. One of the rewards of an autobiography is the sheer discipline of writing it. We are forced to face the "why?", "when?", "where?", and "how" of our interactions with others and how others affect us. The autobiography lays out for us the repeating patterns of our lives. Only when these patterns are revealed can we understand and resolve them.

In the next chapter, we will discuss the purpose of a spiritual journal, which is to get a head start on the *Life Review* we all will experience when we die--a perfect playback of EVERY detail of our life from birth to death. This is a feature of most spiritual traditions and is now supported by innumerable Dead Saint testimonials, many from people who, prior to the experience, were not religious or perhaps even atheists.

The remaining six sections of the Spiritual Journal are practical:

The Orange Garden records the events and thoughts of the day.

The Yellow Garden records the people we meet, and our "cast of characters" mean in the movie of our book of life. They play symbolic roles in our dreams, reveries and meditations. The observant gardener/student will find useful lessons enshrined within the ongoing drama.

The Green Garden, records our thoughts and inspirations when we talk to God (by whatever name we apply to Him). We must be truthful and honest, recording our thoughts unfiltered and in detail. Personally, I ask His angels for healing, for help and for guidance in dreams.

The Blue Garden is our Dream Log. When we sleep, whether we remember or not, we attend a non-physical, non-corporeal night school classroom. Every night the soul goes through a process of analyzing and judging its own activities and thoughts. Every incident of the day, every lesson presented and responded to, *prepares the ground for future* *events*. Lessons ignored or badly handled will be repeated. As you grow to understand your dreams and get to know yourself, your dreams will grow beyond the symbolic to the real through approaching-death dreams (ADDs), after-death communications (ADCs), *Words of Knowledge* (psychic/clairvoyant), and prophetic/precognitive revelations.

The Violet Garden is consecrated to our daily lessons, especially lessons that repeat themselves over and over. Those summoning up powerful emotions are particularly significant. *The Dead Saints Chronicles* provide a number of examples of significant lessons to be learned.

The White Garden is the last section of the Spiritual Journal. It is a place at the top of the sacred mountain where we listen to God. We are the student listening to His voice within while watching and heeding His breadcrumbs on the external plane. Of all the Journal Gardens, I feel this section is the most important. We are initiating a daily communication with God who trains our mind to "hear His voice."

Recording Coincidences

My Journal work began in earnest in September 1980, from the very first day I began recording daily entries. There's a magic in articulating both our deepest thoughts along with the mundane events of the day. Unbelievable things happened. Coincidences went far beyond chance. Communications from God became daily occurrences once I started paying attention. I was recording my own personal journey with God.

While I had always believed in God nod coincidences and "God's breadcrumbs," it became clear to me, once I focused on writing the *Chronicles* after June 2013, not only did I notice the breadcrumb trail in greater detail, I noticed the number of breadcrumbs increased—almost daily. When do too many coincidences make it more than chance, the rolling of the dice, or hitting the million to one odds of turning a royal flush?

Are coincidences real? Are we fooling ourselves? Is it the seduction of our all-too-human irrationality?

Professor Jay Koehler, at the Northwestern University School of Law in Chicago, is a recognized expert on probability. He describes a coincidence as "A striking co-occurrence of events that appears to be meaningfully related, but, in fact, are related only by chance." A classic example of coincidence would be, you get to thinking about calling somebody you haven't thought about for years and reach for the phone and—you know where I'm going with this—the phone rings, it's him (or her)!" If we are wise, and taking Professor Koehler's course, we don't tell him we were "thinking" about calling just that person seconds earlier... It is difficult for academics to acknowledge there might just be more going on over and above their laws of probability and chance.

~Coincidence? Last night, I ran into Ben's room and said, "Look son, I found proof of God! 'Dad, what happened?" On Jim Sinclair's website, the top of the page posted this quote on January 30 2015 at 10:34 am. "There are two mistakes one can make along the path of truth –not going all the way, and not starting. ~Buddha

...Two hours later, by chance, I downloaded a book on Kindle: The Fall of a Thousand Suns: Comets, Meteors in History. I opened the first page, and on the top was the quote. "There are two mistakes one can make along the path of truth—not going all the way, and not starting. ~Buddha

*I had never seen this quote before, much less twice within a few hours on the same day. So what are the odds of reading Buddha's quote twice, two hours apart, from two very different sources? Apparently, God's same day coincidences often happen in 2's. Another author, Michael Flipp, wrote an entire book about the coincidence of **2's** called, '2! Signs and Coincidences from God.'*[1]

*The Divine message? Use the comet impact book and economic collapse prophecies of Jim Sinclair in Book III of the Dead Saints Chronicles, the Armageddon Stones. Perhaps, God was saying, "Don't give up." Go the Distance." How many miracles do you need before you will believe? ~**Chronicle 596***

Speaking for myself, a series of astounding coincidences leaves me little choice but to interpret communications from God as real. Scripture says in James 4:8, *Draw nigh to God, and He will draw nigh to you.* The "drawing nigh" part (meaning to close in on) are the breadcrumbs God leaves on the trail for us to notice, which means pay attention! It makes us think, "What are the odds of this? What is the probability of that? Is it of Divine origin? Or is it merely the overlapping of a universal mathematics devoid of consciousness? Can it be the Force of Destiny, or just what Statisticians call the *"Law of Truly Large Numbers?"* The idea is, if you flip a coin long enough, you'll eventually get ten heads in a row and the universe flips a lot of coins.

Hearing God's Voice in Coincidences

In chapter 6, we discussed getting answers to our questions from God in dreams. In this chapter, we write down the same question, but we watch for answers that appear in the world around us.

Are you looking for answers from a booming voice from Heaven, or do you seek to interpret the tapestry laid in the cloth of your life presented to you every day in Earth University? This "still small voice" is referred to *in only one place in Scripture*—after Elijah's dramatic victory over the prophets of Baal:

> *Then He sent an earthquake and a fire, but His voice was in none of them. After all that, the* **Lord spoke to Elijah in a still small voice.**"[2]

In other words, God spoke to Elijah in a whisper—a prompting so quiet Elijah obeyed and *didn't even know why:*

> *And it was so, when Elijah heard it, that he wrapped his face in his mantle, and went out, and stood in the entrance of the cave. And, behold, there came a voice unto him, and said, What doest thou here, Elijah?* [3]

God's "still small voice" quietly directs you every day. He delivers hints like a grand crossword puzzle—to fill in the Across and Down clues, but it is up to you to solve it. The more you pay attention to the whispered clues, the louder the "still small voice"—God's visual breadcrumbs—become.

I have always prayed to hear God's voice. When I could not get answers, I sometimes demanded answers—, which believe it or not, when I did, seemed to work, but not in ways I expected. For example, one day in the early 1980's, I was upset with God because I had prayed for two days and nights to hear God's voice. I literally wanted to be blinded like Saul by a brilliant Light from Heaven or hear a booming Voice from God.

Nothing happened.

In a huff, grabbing only a light blanket and water, I took off out the back door of Hearthfire and began hiking two miles towards the base of the mountain nearby, and began the arduous 2000-foot climb towards the summit. I didn't tell anyone I had taken off by myself. As a former Order of the Arrow Boy Scout and Patrol Leader, I should have known better. I wasn't too concerned about snakes, but the Allegany mountains were chock full of black bears. The danger I courted didn't even enter my mind. I was determined to force God to give me an answer. After spending a couple of hours climbing, the sun had gone down and it was quickly getting dark.

I found a large granite boulder jutting out from the side of the mountain, laid out the blanket, and after an hour fidgeting, I fell asleep. I woke up with the first light of dawn. During the night, I received no dreams, no booming Voice from God, no blinding light, nothing—except for a red fox eying me twenty feet away.

Thank God, it wasn't a black bear! In some cultures, the fox symbolizes a wise and noble creature that delivers a message from beyond the veil from Spirit. Still, the fox was no blinding Light. It was not the booming Voice or a brilliant Light I was hoping for, BUT I AM SURE from God's point of view IT WAS EXACTLY THAT. I am not so dense I didn't recognize that the fox was a not-so-subtle message from God saying, "David, I see you. I hear you."

The Lord is always leaving a still, small voice of breadcrumbs and God nod's. Victor describes his experience:

After making God cry [and I say that in good humor], my life was shown to me in the form of a long road...and it didn't look like a road I'd choose to travel [though I knew I HAD chosen the road]. I saw many of the different places I'd live and people I'd know. Jobs. Experiences. Too much sadness. I didn't want it. But God just kept gently showing me that I was going back. And, way down the road, late in my life, it seemed the trip would become more enjoyable. **God told me to stay true, "follow the clues" and all would be well.**[4]

Statisticians rule out meaningful, God-oriented coincidences. They will never admit to a divine blueprint that brings people, places, and events magically together in a meaningful way. But who anointed the statisticians the rule makers anyway? I believe spiritual people should regard significant coincidences as messages from the Divine. To hear God, usually—but not always—we must believe there is a Higher Power and be willing to listen. The clues are always there, for God is always speaking to us. God speaks when you see a dove sitting on a windowsill, experience an unexpected meeting, receive a call answering a prayer, see a word or phrase you prayed for when you asked God for a sign, hear a long forgotten song with a message, or encounter impossible situations that give you goosebumps. You know it's not a coincidence. There's a gut feeling. You know God is speaking to you.

Recording Rubik's Cube Lessons

The Dead Saints record a very interesting description of how the soul learns our lessons on Earth.

Mary was visiting her dying grandmother a few hours before her own scheduled surgery and was shocked to see how bad her grandma looked. After a short talk with her, Mary had to leave and admit herself for pre-surgical care because the surgeon had to run antibiotics for an hour directly into her blood stream before the surgery.

At this point, she was anxious about her surgery and worried about her Grandma. Time seemed to slow down. Eventually Mary was rolled in for her operation and given anesthesia. Mary found herself out of her body and heard her grandmother's voice. Within a few seconds, she saw her grandmother sitting on the edge of the bed, but instead of her grandmother having an amputated leg, during her near-death experience her grandmother still had both legs. She noticed her hair was thicker and blacker than it had been in the last five or six years, and if she had to guess, she looked like she was in her 40's or possibly 50's. Mary continues describing her conversation with her grandmother during her NDE:

*[Grandmother] proceeded to tell me she was doing great, **but her body was dead**. [Grandma had died during Mary's operation] She also stressed she had limited time with her so basically she was told to "listen up."* Mary's grandmother stated an "all knowing" entered her when her spirit passed out of the body. And, to help her with grieving she was going to give Mary as much information as she felt she could understand, in as much time as she was allowed. Mary did not remember it all, and for fear of being ridiculed, several years passed before she dared talk about it. Here is what her grandmother told her about her experiences during her NDE:

She likened the soul to a 'puzzle cube.' I believe she meant a rubric cube. The cube was the whole soul. Each side was a section of our soul. Each space was a learning experience required for each section of the soul. As she explained it, each section of the soul touched a different dimension, and would continue returning to that dimension until all the spaces of learning were completed. Then that dimensional level would not repeat, and your soul would work on the next section.

Each soul yearns to learn and complete its lessons. Once the "puzzle" of the soul was completed, your whole spirit would remain intact with all the knowledge it collected. [The soul] would not have to return to a vessel and would live in the presence of God forever. It is so much information I can't remember all she said at this time, but I will say she alluded to the fact there were other 'vessels' of learning for our soul other than those here on Earth. The other striking comment [she made] was that she was in contact with my core soul and I would from time to time feel her presence because our 'learning' portion of our soul is connected to the 'core' soul.[5]

In my research for the *Dead Saints Chronicles*, this is one of the most remarkable messages. Grandma dies while Mary is having an NDE on the operation table, and gives her a unique point of view about the compartmentalized lessons of the soul. She is told these lessons can be completed in other worlds and in other dimensions, and her 'core soul' too, would be in touch with her granddaughter from time to time.

The important lesson we should take to heart and not forget in this Afterlife communication is this: Grandma knew she had only a short time to communicate the knowledge she had received upon her death (which we know was permanent) before moving "on" to the Kingdom of Heaven. This particular experience demonstrates there are laws of communication between the living and the dead—a sort of "Afterlife non-interference" rule which shows up from time to time throughout the *Chronicles*.

Moving from Victim to Cause

The Spiritual Journal records the lessons God presents to us every day and to what end? Many of us believe the way we act and think and who we are today, are largely due to external influences; parents, geography, poverty, wealth, IQ, health, or even acts of God. "I am the way I am because of my parents, etc." "I will never get an education. My parents were poor. I don't have good grades. I am not that smart. I am ugly. I am unlovable. I am a burden. I am a failure. I can't do this because..." We use excuses all the time as to why we cannot or do not succeed and this plays out in every area of our lives.

We have been taught to be victims of circumstance, instead of becoming a cause for change in our lives. We do not take responsibility for the thoughts we think, and because we believe we are victims, we do not change. We use guilt and remorse as excuses and point to our failures as evidence. We do this with ourselves, with others, and with God. And sadly, most of us think this way until the moment we die.

So, we ask, to what end? If we are to make a change in our lives, and recognize the mistakes we are making, we must become conscious of what we are thinking and doing. The Spiritual Journal helps us become aware through the art of reflection and observation, our self-talk—what we say to ourselves every day. It records what we see and hear and helps us to correlate *what is real and what is illusion*: What is victim thinking and what is cause thinking; to see repeating patterns of action and thought that do not work for us. To see what helps us grow and become better people. To care about God, others, and ourselves in an organized manner through the act of writing with ink and pen or keyboard. [For more detailed information about the Spiritual Journal: go to www.maryelizabethmarlow.com

According to the Dead Saints, every thought and action builds a garden in your heart and mind on Earth University, and is reflected like a mirror in a garden you build in Heaven. The journal then becomes a record of our apprenticeship in the garden—what we have learned, and its flowering grandeur reflected in Heaven, seen by God and angels in all its glory at the end of our lives.

---

1   Michael Flipp 2012. *2! Signs and Coincidences from God*. Amazon Digital Services, LLC.
2   1 Kings 19:12
3   1 Kings 19:13
4   *V's NDE,* #1866, 03.07.09, NDERF.org
5   *Mary R's ADC* (After Death Communication), #833, 04.23.06, NDERF.org

—— 9 ——
The Life Review

*~**DREAM:** After seeing yesterday the musical, A Christmas Carol, performed at the Virginia Beach Arts Center, I dreamed the following night of three teenagers following me; a girl named Michelle, a tall oriental man, and pretty black girl who looked like Whoopi Goldberg (she was happy and funny). They were following me because they were hungry. I gave in and told them I would feed them all Kentucky Fried Chicken. I somehow knew they represented my past, my present, and my possible future. They followed me into the house and began doing a comedy routine over and over. I told them it was getting a little irritating, "You've got to change up your act, otherwise, nobody is going to listen to you."*

I followed the tall, oriental man into my kitchen, and he stopped to face me. Looking deeply into his eyes, I could see some scaly features to his face, like I get from my chemo and prednisone. Suddenly, he put his hand on top of my head near my brain tumor and began healing me. I could feel the warmth and power of his prayer, and a very real presence of God entered the room. We both were in tears and I looked at him and said, "Why haven't you given your heart completely to God? All you have to do is ask and His presence will enter your heart. He stared at me for a moment and then said, "I am not ready. I still want to play."
*~**Chronicle 908***

NDERF, in a recent study reported almost 23 percent of Dead Saints surveyed had a review of their lives before returning to the body. What did they learn from their dramatic experience, and what can we learn by *beginning the Life Review process in our own Journal work*—before we die on the operating table, or in a car accident, or by a terminal illness or sudden event which does not afford an option to return to life and make amends for our negative actions and thoughts.

Paying attention to God's breadcrumbs—our daily lessons and dreams, interpreting and applying what we have learned about ourselves, and making changes in habits of love, forgiveness and communication—gives us the opportunity to change the direction we are headed *before we die*.

If our daily walk through Earth University is (insofar as possible and practical) devoted to becoming conscious of our thoughts, actions, and emotions, we will be creating the essential conditions for experiencing the celestial realms with their eternal gardens...an opportunity we will all confront soon enough. I hope my own example, as well as the testimonials of the thousands of Dead Saints provide readers with that perspective before you shed your mortal coil and take on the Body of Light.

On July 2, 2013, the day after I came out of surgery (to take a sample for the brain biopsy) I lay there in my hospital bed with nothing to do except ponder my own mortality and look back at what I had done with my life so far. I wondered: Whom had I not forgiven? Who had I not reconciled with? Whom do I need to call to say goodbye to? I'd met many hundreds of people in my life. My ex-wife, my dad, my kids? Was there anyone I'd unwittingly harmed? Whether I was conscious of the fact or not, I was now in the middle of my own Life Review without yet being dead. Those Dead Saints stories? What could I learn from them?

The prospect of the actual, irrevocable Life Review obliged me to examine my own life: every action, every motive, every word and thought directed towards others. Will I be pleased with myself, or ashamed, on the Day I will have to face how my life has affected others?

Overview

The Dead Saints describe the life review as a granular account of their lives. Every minute, every second, every sound of every action and every thought is recorded. The Dead Saint is totally present at his or her life review both psychologically and telepathically. They are not alone. Typically, a council of judges, assessors, and Light Beings, along with God or Jesus Christ, sit through the review with the Saint. They are there to ask questions about the Saint's life. Why did you do this?

Practically all esoteric traditions include some version of the Life Review.

In *Dickens' Christmas Carol* fashion, the deceased (or temporarily deceased in the case of the Dead Saints) can see events from all angles and their consequences, past, present, and future. They experience the Life Review process with the enhanced intelligence of the spiritual mind, the mind that is not limited by the brain and the physical body. They relive the events of their lives with their subtler spiritual senses; touch, taste, smell, hearing, and sight:

> *My senses seemed to all be intact, but there wasn't anything for me to touch. I could smell, but I wasn't breathing-there was no need for air. I could hear, but there were no audible sounds or words being spoken. I perceived myself as having had some sort of form or body, but I couldn't feel anything tangible-skin, hair, nor anything else like we are able to feel while in physical form. There was only my truest, but not purest form of conscious energy. And I was seeing and experiencing all of this through my conscious energy's eye.[1]*

They can see their entire life play out and review it with a 360-degree holographic/Big Screen perspective, recounting details, down to the number of mosquitoes present during the experience. Everything witnessed is more accurate than any memory of the original event. Roger, in his NDE, saw himself reviewing his life. It was like watching an actor in a movie:

> *I went into a dark place with nothing around me, but I wasn't scared. It was peaceful there. I then began to see my whole life unfolding before me as a film being projected on a screen, from babyhood to adult life. It was so real! At the end of the film* (life presentation), *everything went black for a while, almost like in a real movie before they turn on the light. I then understood through this knowledge that I deserved a place in what we call Heaven without knowing what it would be like or what is Heaven! I felt a wonderful feeling of peace, which became stronger and stronger, such a nice feeling.[2]*

Emily's NDE helped improve her husband's attitude about life, each reminding one another, "It's movie time!"

> *Sawyer's revelations about the life review caused me to examine my own life, and each action, each motive, every word and thought directed towards others. Will I be pleased with myself, or ashamed, on the day I experience how my life has*

affected others? Learning about the life review has definitely improved my husband's demeanor. Now, whenever he begins to lose his temper, he wants me to head him off with the words, 'Remember, movie time!' He is dreading the day when he will find out what it is like to be me, listening to his rantings and lectures on various topics. I remind him both of our 'movies' will include joyful scenes as well as sad ones. These days he is trying very hard to insure the second half of his movie will be applause-worthy.[3]

Life Review Theory

Some skeptics theorize it is some sort a DNA download, like downloading information from a hard drive, but it is not only recorded in the cells of your body/brain, it is also viewable from the dimension of the Afterlife in much greater detail. Romy saw "millions of pictures" of her life events during her NDE:

I was surrounded with space as I saw my whole life unfolding. I was watching millions of the pictures of my life's events, like a movie broken down into picture frames. All the little deeds, thoughts and moments upon moments, even the ones I forgot ever happened—were there. It was such a fascinating sight.[4]

It has been said many times when we die, our whole life flashes before our eyes. This is the Life Review. Often the Dead Saints report, Jesus or a Being of Light is there to review our lives with us. Don't be alarmed! He has a great sense of humor! However, you will discover the most extraordinary moments of your life are not framed by money, work, drugs, and alcohol, possessions or self-gratifying behaviors. Indeed, what we consider trivial actions are highlighted as the most significant of our lives. We have a multitude of opportunities to help people and be loving and kind, but in most instances, we chose to ignore these opportunities and instead focus solely on ourselves.

He will ask you many questions. Why did you lie? Why did you pull your sister's hair? Why did you throw rocks at the dog? Why did you pull the neighbor's cats' tail? Why did you bully and insult someone, or tear someone's clothes just for the spite of it? In scenes like these, the Light Beings reiterate when we have done something seriously wrong, or whether we have done some extraordinarily good thing. As they discuss each scene, we must answer why we acted the way we did at that time. When we try to put "a little spin" in our answers to lessen the seriousness of ours actions, they stop and correct us. In scenes where we have done something good, they praise us profoundly.

Romy's NDE shows us our thoughts are recorded and "displayed" before us, as well. It reminds us of Christ's admonition in Matthew

5:28, "But I say unto you, that whosoever looketh on a woman to lust after her hath committed adultery with her already in his heart."

> *I could also see all the thoughts I had all my life. Their 'pictures' were as strong as the pictures that depicted action or words. I was amazed to see that our thoughts are that strong, so real. It looks like they were also threaded on a string of light. I realized everything that happened to me and every single thought I had created an imprint. Also, every single event or thought influenced my life and the lives of those around me...*
>
> *The last moment or picture of my life was myself, rolling down the mountain in a car, with my mother, my brothers and the driver. I was suddenly inside that picture again. I could see how we are all connected. I was connected to everybody in a multi faceted light web, a DNA—like hologram that was in perfect order. Everything connected to everything with delicate threads of light that were the gaps between each moment. It showed my connection to other people, other souls, other incidents, moments past future and present.There was complete order and complete acceptance of everything. Then, there were no more pictures, but a strong sense of motion forwards.[5]*

Dorothy writes about her revelation:

If we understood the awesome power of our thoughts, we would guard them more closely. If we understood the awesome power of our words, we would prefer silence to almost anything negative.[6]

Rick's Life Review contains important questions and perceptions:

> *Then without warning, it happened! [God asked me] 'What have you done with your life? The voice penetrated my very being! I had no answer! Then to my right, I saw what seemed to be like a movie, and I was in it! I saw my mother giving me birth, my childhood and friends! I saw everything from my youth up! I saw everything I had ever done before my eyes! As my life played out before my very eyes, I tried to think of good things I had done. I was raised in church and had been very active in church functions. Yet as I pondered on this, I saw a man in his car who had ran out of gas. I had stopped and given him a lift to a local store about a year ago. I had bought him some gas as he had no money and I helped him get on his way!*
>
> *I thought to myself, 'Why am I seeing this?'*

> *The voice was loud and clear. 'You took no thought to help this soul and asked nothing in return! These actions are the essence of good!'*
>
> *I saw all the people I had hurt as well and was shown how my actions had set in motion the actions of others! I was stunned! I had never thought of my life having an effect on the actions that friends, family, and others I had met would take! I saw the results of all I had done! I was not pleased at all! I looked on until the events ended. Indeed, I had done so little with my life! I had been selfish and cruel in so many ways! I was truly sorry I had done so little.*
>
> *Then again loud and clear I heard the voice speak again. 'You must return!' I did not want to return though. I was content to stay and longed to stay even after the things I had seen and heard.*[7]

Luke 12:2-3 validates the detailed examination we will go through at the end of our lives:

> *Nothing that is hidden that will not be uncovered, and nothing concealed that will not be known. So what will be said in darkness will be heard in the Light, and what you have spoken in the ear, will be proclaimed from the rooftops.*

Butterfly Effect & Spider Webs

Every good or evil thought, word and action from birth to death creates ripples in the universe, like a pebble dropped in a pond, inexorably connecting us. We have all heard about the "Butterfly" effect; that even the fluttering of the wings of a butterfly in India can affect someone far away. In this NDE, Dr. Bell describes the same idea using spider webs:

> *Before making your decision [to go back], you may wish to see your life in review. As I was absorbed in a deep thought of this question, a tiny spot of light appeared suddenly. In the center of the spot, I saw myself, when I was a baby. Then the light spread out in all directions, like a spider spreading silk to build an intricate spider web. I looked closer to the web, and was surprised to find every silk thread was connecting to time as well as the 'cause and effect' of different people and incidents. The threads were inextricably linked to one another. They connected my different stages of life, interweaving and mapping my own web of life.*
>
> *My web was only one of the many others. Each of the individual webs was linked by silk threads, connecting our*

relationships with one another. By that moment in front of me, was a giant nest of webs.[8]

Remorse: Turning Away from the Life Review

Last year, Darrel shared with me an after-death communication (ADC) he had in a dream, about a business associate, Jeremy, who recently died. In the dream, Jeremy was sitting by himself on a bench in an amusement park. It was a colorful place, like a carnival, except nobody was there. Darrel sat next to Jeremy and asked, "What's wrong? You appear sad."

He said, "I am lonely."

"Then, why don't you go through your Life Review?"

Jeremy replied, "I'll do that later."

Most often, it is guilt and remorse that makes the Dead Saint hesitate, rather than enter the Light; an unwillingness to face ourselves and to admit the truth. We do this to ourselves even now while we are alive.

Some spirits who are afraid of the Life Review may walk away from the Light, and become *Earthbound*. Afraid of the self-judgment they know is coming, souls often hang around a familiar home or dwelling, sometimes for hundreds or even thousands of years. In the Afterlife, time does not exist for them. As Virginia experienced in her NDE:

> *Many times other souls could not make the viewing [Life Review] so they would walk away from the Light. Again not feeling worthy. God's goodness over doubt—that is what I was told, to stop doubting myself and know that I am the Light of God.*[9]

Remorse may shackle us to a dark, lonely, Earthbound Afterlife separated from God and the Light, a tragic consequence we will discuss later.

Here Comes the Judge!

Of course, during or just after the Life Review, there is the Judgment of our life—the classic weighing of the heart against the feather of truth.

---

1 *Steve B's NDE*, #441, 07.24.04, NDERF.org
2 *Roger C's NDE*, #253, 04.02.03, NDERF.org
3 Emily L Van Laeys. *Life Review revealed in near-death experience.* Venture Inward (July/August, 1994). p. 51.
4 *Romy NDE*, #3620, 03.09.14, NDERF.org
5 *Romy NDE*, #3620, 03.09.14, NDERF.org
6 Betty J. Eadie 1992. *Embraced By The Light.* Placerville, CA: Gold Leaf Press. p. 58.
7 *Rick R NDE*, #1506, 01.13.08, NDERF.org

8   *Dr. Bell C*, #3401, 07.28.13, NDERF.org
9   *Virginia D NDE*, #2316, 09.11.10, NDERF.org

10

The Judgment

*~**Approaching-Death Dream**: Heading towards a magnificent city at the summit of a small hill. Two round crystal towers made of blue-green sky and clouds rose from the city and towered high above it. I was walking up white steps towards the entrance of the City behind an attorney who was arguing whether he should push for the letter of the law concerning my case. ~**Chronicle 889***

Humans have feared Judgment Day since prophets of old memorialized their experiences and visions on ancient papyrus or clay tablets. For Christians, *The Day* is the day your Book of Life is opened at the end of time, and you stand before God, who reveals all the good and bad deeds you performed during your earthly life. John memorializes Judgment Day in Rev. 21:12-14:

> *And I saw the dead, small and great, stand before God; and the books were opened: and another book was opened, which is the book of life: and the dead were judged out of those things which were written in the books, according to their works. And the sea gave up the dead which were in it; and death and Hell delivered*

up the dead which were in them: and they were judged every man according to their works.

This account holds that the soul dies with the body and sleeps until the end of time when our dead corpses are raised up to stand and be judged before God. Sarah tells us the grave is only for the body, not the soul:

So, I said to Jesus, 'You mean I don't have to go to sleep forever?'
He kind of laughed and said, 'No.'
Jesus told me, 'I was going to live forever and I would never die.
He said, 'This place was my HOME and always had been and I would spend eternity there with them.'
I can't describe the feeling I felt knowing this information.
Some say (religion not revealed) I won't go to Heaven, let alone be with God or Jesus. They say when you die you go into like an eternal sleep state. That your body is your soul and when your body dies your soul dies and you are in this sleep state until Jesus comes to wake you up. That's what they teach anyway.[1]

George further demonstrates sleeping until the end of time is unnecessary:

Here were what I would call angels working with them trying to arouse them and help them realize God is truly a God of the living and that they did not have to lie around sleeping until Gabriel or someone came along blowing on a horn.[2]

Theological Considerations and Complications

Some appear to sleep *in the blackness* until they are reborn. Some are conscious in the Realms of Heaven. Egyptian beliefs about spiritual sleeping surface in Jonathan Cott's biography of Dorothy Eady, *The Search for Omm Sety*, where he writes, "Pharaoh Sety, after he died, looked for me for many ages throughout the realms and could not find me." Omm Sety, in ADC communication with the ancient pharaoh asked him how he eventually found her. He said, "After long ages of suffering, Our Lord Osiris had mercy upon me, and the council summoned me and said that you were 'sleeping in the blackness,' and that one day, you would be re-born."[3]

However, not all sleep. In the Bible, the three apostles, Peter, James and John, even witness the appearance of the prophets Moses and Elijah on the mountain of transfiguration with Jesus (as it is described in the Synoptic Gospels (Matthew 17:1–9, Mark 9:2-8, Luke 9:28–36 and 2 Peter 1:16–18):

After six days Jesus took with him Peter, James and John the brother of James, and led them up a high mountain by themselves. There he was transfigured before them. His face shone like the sun, and his clothes became as white as the Light. Just then there appeared before them Moses and Elijah, talking with Jesus.

This brings up an uncomfortable question. If the dead do not immediately go to Heaven, how could Moses and Elijah have been present and talking to Jesus at the transfiguration if they are asleep waiting for the resurrection? Attempts to explain an early resurrection require a belief that Moses and Elijah did not die. Scripture says Elijah was taken up to Heaven and did not die a physical death. Moses, on the other hand, died in the wilderness before the Israelite people entered into the Promised Land, but the story in Deuteronomy 34:5-7 says God Himself buried Moses. Later, we find out Moses' soul was fought over by the angel Gabriel when Satan tried to take him. Apparently, Moses was not meant to stay dead until the Final Judgment. He was resurrected and has been awake, living in Heaven since that time.

A whole canon of theology has been created in an attempt to reconcile the conflict concerning the Mount of Transfiguration encounter witnessed by Peter, James, and John and the supernatural elements surrounding the Final Judgment. St. Peter believed the experience represented a preview of the Second Coming of Christ. He believed Moses represented the *dead in Christ* who rise to new life, and Elijah represented those who are *alive and remain*, who will be translated to Heaven and eternal life without ever experiencing death in the first place (1 Thessalonians 4:16), which references Christ's promise that "some standing here...shall not taste death till they see the kingdom of God," spoken a few days before the transfiguration (Luke 9:27).

The belief held by many Christians and Muslims is: Moses and Elijah represent evidence that death brings a sleep of unconsciousness until the Final Judgment at the end of time. Why do many believe this theology? The whole crux of the matter is this: There would be no need of a bodily resurrection if everyone immediately went to Heaven to live in Christ's presence at death. Similarly, translation to Heaven would have no special significance because everyone would go to Heaven immediately after they died. Orthodox religion wants you to believe you sleep until the Final Judgment, but overwhelming evidence described by the Dead Saints and scriptural proof of a conscious Moses and Elijah, support an entirely different theology. While some appear to sleep, most souls enter one of the many levels of the Kingdom of

Heaven conscious and awake immediately after their Life Review and Judgment.

There are several other examples of the dead being contacted by the living in the Bible, including Saul's contact with a dead, but *conscious* Samuel. It is interesting to observe how an entire body of theology becomes a universal teaching, even in the face of direct evidence, its beliefs may, in fact, be wrong. I believe the original inspired visions of the prophets, apostles and Saints are true. I also believe the original meaning of some sacred Scriptures over the course of thousands of years and multiple translations and revisions has been lost or changed. If this were not so, why would thousands of Dead Saints return to life and describe a dramatically different reality?

In the end, I believe God is not a God who indiscriminately chooses to awaken whomever he wants before Judgment Day. Thousands of Dead Saints are waking up in Heaven, meeting God and Jesus, and coming back to talk about it.

Now, perhaps, there may be some grand human universal Judgment before our Creator at the "end of time." Who knows? However, until then, I feel you can be sure at the end of your life, this time around, you will be afforded an opportunity to join Jesus, the prophets and friends and family, and have an *awake* conversation with them. It's not an exclusive club. The accumulated evidence from the Dead Saints is clear about this. Offended or outraged members of various dogmatic doctrines may try to use Scripture as evidence against the Dead Saints encounters and testimonies, but I believe, a better approach is to take a closer look at Scripture to understand its deeper meanings.

Readers familiar with the New Testament may wonder about the statement by the Apostle Paul in Hebrews 9:27 "It is appointed unto men to die *once*, then after this the Judgment." This verse is often cited as proof humans die only once. However, if this verse affirms people experience but a single death, this of itself excludes those biblical characters who were "raised from the dead" i.e., experienced death more than once (Jesus excepted). Other Bible Prophets-Enoch, Elijah, and Melchizedek—apparently did not die at all.

The statement by the Apostle Paul (Hebrews 9:27) is also contradicted by the thousands of near-death situations where physical death is medically verified, but the Dead Saint is resuscitated. In the face of such overwhelming evidence, the apparent meaning of "dying once" and then facing the Judgment is difficult to dismiss. When we die, we face the Judgment after we review our Book of Life.

What is the Book of Life?

In our walk through Earth University, our actions and thoughts are daily entries into what Christianity calls our Book of Life. Eastern mystics call this book the "Akashic Record," the record of our thoughts and actions. Every minute and every second of our lives are recorded in this Book of Life.

Mark describes how life is literally written in *The BOOK of LIFE:*

I slowly sank to the bottom of the pool, where I stayed for five or more minutes with a water-filled body. After a short while, I sensed Angels gathering around me; it was peaceful. Then, I was maybe 20 to 30 feet above the pool, looking down at my friend diving into the pool to save me. The Angels took me up to a gathering of clouds. There were a few Romanesque pillars with green ivy, and an archway in the back. I had seven Angels holding me up and four in front of me on the landing. Three were very animated and discussing what to do with me, the fourth angel kept me company.

I looked around and saw very large pure love orbs with silhouettes of human souls - like a chalk outline of a dead body. I looked down at our Earth and it was brown and moving, and alive with all of the souls it takes to make our planet whole; our Earth is alive, as you are. I saw Heaven, a little to my left behind the pillars. It has gold wrought iron fencing with spikes on top. I saw the pearly gates. My three angels, still perplexed as to how to get me back to my body - did not like my response of, 'I don't want to go back down there; it is painful.'

'You Must! Your Mission is Not Yet Complete!'

We communicated telepathically; no lips or mouth movements; all thoughts. Moment by moment you discover how quickly you are gaining knowledge and how easy it is to accept. My Three Angels sought permission from above to show me something. The clouds above their heads lit up as they cringed in fear, as did I.

'Show Him!' was the response. The Angels flew me over to the right of these pillars to what looked like a HUGE 4-Foot Thick Book of LIFE. MY Life. Just as my life had passed before my eyes when I was being drowned, I was now being shown my future life, with as much info as I could remember. Imagine a deck of cards— each card has a scene/event from your life. Now flip those cards in front of your face, and try to remember anything you can from any card you see. That is what I saw with my Book of Life. I gather that Life is written; LITERALLY.[4]

Some Dead Saints see the Book of Life appear as "bar graph" memory files compiled in 3-5 minute lengths. Jo B saw scrolls—"strands of thought" containing huge amounts of information:

> *My mind kept seeing, and attempting to absorb, data that was contained on scrolls. A scroll would unroll and the data implant itself in me. Some of it I could comprehend. Much of it was totally above my head. Gibberish. What was clear to me was the overriding message that humans, as units of consciousness, are capable of experiencing reality in ways far beyond what we typically do. As the data flowed into me, I was stunned and completely intrigued with what little of it I could understand. I could not wait to dive in and begin to unravel the information. A huge sense of purpose and contentment filled me up. Death wasn't such a bad thing after all! Cool.*[5]

According to Anna, this great library is multi-dimensional, and occupied by a team of beings caring for unfinished manuscripts and tablets:

> *My aunt, my father in law, my grandmother was all there, yet the remaining ones weren't relatives I'd known from Earth. They were Light Beings I've known before being born into the Earth. They guided me to a 'library.' I place this word inside quotation marks because it was a multidimensional composition (I cannot even call it a structure). Apparently, I had a 'job' up there and had left it 'briefly' when coming to Earth because I'd needed to experience certain things and learn certain things in order to be able to continue my work. And, BTW, everything I'd learned—languages, subjects, nature observations—while being on Earth, was absolutely useful up there.*
>
> *I'd then floated onto my unfinished manuscript, which looked like some form of tablet except it would only appear by my mind's command. However, the thoughts I had filled into the manuscript, I was in charge of, had a great purpose.*[6]

The Judgment

The Judgment is developed over the course of the Life Review as every thought and action is weighed. Who oversees the Judgment? Is it God? Is it panel of judges or counselors? Or is it simply the Dead Saint judging itself?

The ancient Papyrus from the Book of Dead of Ani, Thebes, Egypt, 19th dynasty, 1275 BC,[7] depicts the Judgment of the dead in the presence of Osiris. This scene from the *Book of the Dead* of Ani reads from left to right. At the left, Ani and his wife enter the Judgment area. In the centre are the scales used for weighing the heart, attended by Anubis, the god of embalming. The process is also observed by Ani's *ba* spirit (the human-headed bird), two birth-goddesses and a male figure representing his destiny. Ani's heart, represented as the hieroglyph for 'heart' (a mammal heart), sits on the left pan of the scales.

It is being weighed against a feather, the symbol of Maat, the principle of order, truth and Cosmic Equilibrium, which in this funerary context means 'what is right.' The ancient Egyptians believed that *the heart* was the seat of the emotions, intellect and character (conscience), and thus represented the positive and negative aspects of the individual's life. If the heart outweighed the feather, the deceased was condemned to non-existence and his heart was consumed by the ferocious Ammit "the Devourer–Eater of the Dead," the strange composite beast, part-crocodile, part-lion, and part-hippopotamus, shown at the right of this scene. However, a papyrus devoted to ensuring the continued existence of the deceased is not likely to depict this happening. Indeed, no such papyrus has ever been discovered.

Once the Judgment was complete, the deceased was declared 'true of voice' or 'justified'— a standard epithet applied to dead individuals in these texts. The whole process is recorded in a Book of Life by the ibis-headed deity *Thoth* (Greek), *Djehuti* in ancient Egyptian. (See the Papyrus of Ani: 12 Deities or *Assessors* (usually 42) supervise the Judgment.)

We find similar "Scales of Judgment" weighing the heart described in Greek, Hebrew, and Christian sacred Scriptures. Paul says in Romans 14:10-12:

> *But why dost thou judge thy brother? Or why dost thou set at naught thy brother? For we shall all stand before the Judgment seat of Christ. For it is written, as I live, saith the Lord, every knee shall bow to me, and every tongue shall confess to God. So then every one of us shall give account of himself to God.*

Paul further explains in Romans 2:28-29 the importance of "what you think in the heart and spirit" is more important than outward appearances:

For he is not a Jew, which is one outwardly; neither is that circumcision, which is outward in the flesh: But he is a Jew, which is one inwardly; and circumcision is that of the heart, in the spirit, and not in the letter; whose praise is not of men, but of God.

The Scales of Judgment: Good and Evil Weighed in the Balance

During David's Life Review, he was asked by beings he recognized, if he had affected more people positively than negatively, again a concept of Judgment Scales:

He cautioned me to be truthful with the group of beings I recognized. These beings showed me my life from the time I picked my parents until the time I died. They asked me if I had affected more souls positively than negatively. I told them negatively, but I did think about lying to them because I knew my future depended on my answer. I wanted to stay in that place I was because of the love I felt there. It felt right like I was home.[8]

Roger compared the Judgment scales to a "bank account" —as though getting good karma points would allow him access to a better place in Heaven:

I was also capable of seeing that the better I made [people] feel and the better the emotions they had because of me would give me some credits (Karma) and that the bad ones would take some of it back, just like in a bank account, but here it was like a Karma account to my knowledge. The more points (karma) I got would give me permission to access a better area or a better place somewhere. It was the knowledge I had then.[9]

Peter experiences the Judgment as a sifting process that will reveal his frequency and vibration:

As this Being, this Light, conjoined me in and with its love, and I returned mine to it, so that both merged together so that neither existed except the two in the one, I knew (it did let me know), that it was 'looking' for something. It was feeling its way through and around me (though I stress it was also in me, or me in it) searching for that upon which 'Judgment' could be made.

I have since having had this experience read of some other accounts of this part of the death process and have read some people actually see images or aspects of their lives played out for them, as if a 'review' was being made. This did not happen to me. Yet, I did know I was being 'judged,' or rather I was participating in a 'Judgment.' I knew this Light, this beautiful Being was 'sifting through me.' Looking for something, gauging something, vibrations, frequencies, taking them into its love, knowing the whole. This did not feel intrusive.

I was happy for this being to 'look at me' in this way. I welcomed it, and loved it. And I knew it was on this that 'Judgment' was based. This is 'Judgment' based on the essence of you within an intimacy that would simply be impossible on any understanding we have in ordinary life. This 'Judgment' has as its basis the answer to a single question which would translate to something quite precise-What is, was, the essence of your love? If you like, in a summative sense of the whole, what vibration, or frequency, did your love resonate at? Wave after wave after wave of love washed through me from this being and I returned this to it. Then there was what I can only describe as something like a pause, it was clear the 'Judgment' was over.[10]

Who Judges Us?

As we discussed in the last chapter, a council of judges along with God and/or Jesus Christ, is present through the Life Review along with the Dead Saint. They are there to gently guide us through the experience and point out the consequence of our actions and where we have erred, or where we have done well. While people may try to lie to his or her self and give an excuse about why they committed a particular act, it is not possible to get away with it during the Judgment. They have no more excuses or lame justifications for their actions. It is all there in plain spiritual sight. They have more than complete telepathic understanding of their actions and their consequences, and understand the truth because they experience it from *inside* the persona of the other person they committed the act against.

It is important to understand that the Being of Light presiding over our Life Review does not slam down a gavel of Judgment against us, but instead brandishes a feather of love—unconditional love—through the entire assessment of our life. *To be clear, it is a Judgment.* However, in the end, if there is any sound of a proverbial Judgment gavel hitting the Judgment Desk of God, it is the sound of our own self-judgment and not the wrath of God or Jesus.

During his Life Review, Carmen was attended by his guide who pointed out in the Book of Life, he had done something very wrong during his time on Earth:

*After the review, I was lead to another marble room where there was a huge open book on a marble table. My guide sat behind the table, and with his index finger pointed in the book, he scanned through the page to see if he found my name on the book. His head lifted up and looked at me, a wave of guilt overwhelmed me. I did something very, very wrong; no one had to judge me. **I judged myself and knew I did wrong.**[11]*

Steve's experience of the Judgment was filled with joy and with pain. Joy when he touched someone's life for good and suffering when he caused pain in the life of another. He had to look at himself and face up to what he had done with his life:

Every aspect of every experience that had occurred from the moment I was born until the moment I departed from the world was made visual before me, and it was done so in a reflective manner. And, adding to the awesome effect, that in our linear time spanned nearly four decades, were the emotional viewpoints of all who were involved in every single instance of my life. It was all so very clear, I was my own critic, my own evaluator. There were many visions where I felt joy and happiness for having touched someone's life in a positive way—helped a person in need—raised a lowly spirit—turned a frown into a smile—made someone laugh when they felt like crying.

But, interlaced with the positive were also many moments where I was utterly grief stricken, feeling shame and sorrow for the negative impact I had had on other lives. I had caused so much unnecessary pain, conflict and strife, and as much as I wanted to, there was no changing what was already done. I saw everything through their eyes, I felt their pain, their emotions, and I experienced their experience and I became very critical because of it holding myself in contempt for having done such horrible things. Part of me wanted to run and hide, but I couldn't. There was no escape. While a higher part [of me] felt compelled to continue and learn from it all, I somehow knew it was for the best.

As the grand finale rolled in front of me, there are no words to describe how I felt near the end when the reflection began to grow dim. I saw before me the lifeless body of a man whose existence had drawn to a conclusion with a consciousness filled with anger, resentment and bitterness because of everything that had transpired just shortly before his departure. That man in the mirror was a reflection of me.[12]

Most of us have not had the stunning lens of an NDE to examine our lives in resplendent, granular detail. We can learn a great deal from these Dead Saint experiences, yet they are somebody else's experiences, not ours. Knowing our lives are being recorded like a movie may help, but most of us do not run around thinking about death or what happens to us when we die.

We are busy living, not dying. (In Zen-speak, we are dying and NOT living!) Death happens "later" to someone else. Whether by disease, or sudden misfortune, death takes us all, prepared or not. If the Judgment were to happen today, how would it play out? The good and the bad, the positive and the negative, the constructive and the destructive? Let's take a different perspective and look at the Afterlife in a different way—through the metaphor of a fallen tree.

---

1 *Sarah W probable NDE*, #3523, 11.23.13, NDERF.org
2 George G. Ritchie, Jr., M.D. 1991. *My Life After Dying, Becoming Alive to Universal Love*. Norfolk, Virginia: Hampton Roads Publishing. p. 24.
3 Jonathan Cott 1987. *The Search for Omm Sety*. Parktown, South Africa: Studio 33 Books, Random House Group, Ltd., UK, p. 167.
4 *Mark NDE*, #1859, 02.22.09, NDERF.org
5 Jo B NDE, #3706, 01.21.14, NDERF.org
6 *Anna A NDE*, #3784, 10.27.14, NDERF.org
7 R.O. Faulkner 1985. *The Ancient Egyptian Book of the Dead,* (revised ed. C. A. R. Andrews). London: The British Museum Press. Compare the ancient Papyrus from the *Book of Dead of Ani*, Thebes, Egypt, 19th dynasty, 1275 BC, with a vignette from the *Book of the Dead* of Hunefer, also in the British Museum.
8 *David O's NDE*, #73, 10.17.01, NDERF.org
9 *Roger C's NDE*, #253, 04.02.03, NDERF.org
10 *Peter N NDE*, #3253, 02.14.13, NDERF.org
11 *Carmen D NDE*, #1902, 05.11.09, NDERF.org
12 *Steve B's NDE*, #441, 07.24.04, NDERF.org

11

We Die in Character

~When it comes time to die, be not like those whose hearts are filled with fear of death. So when their time comes, they weep and pray for a little more time to live their lives over again in a different way. Sing your death Song. And die like a hero going home. ~Chief Aupumut, Mohican Leader

Among practicing Christians and metaphysical students alike, there is a common belief we become different people after we cross over to the other side. Based on the voluminous evidence brought back by the Dead Saints, the state of our consciousness and the personality we presently identify with is what we bring with us into the Afterlife. How we live our lives on Earth, will be how we enter the next world. The old cliché tells us we "can't take it with us." However, this applies only to the material world. We do in fact, take all of our loves and attributes, both positive and negative, with us. (See chapter 17, *Heaven—The Kingdom of Light*.)

Ecclesiastes 11:3 likens us to a fallen tree when we die:

Through all the aeons of eternity. If clouds are full of water, they pour rain on the Earth. Whether a tree falls to the south or to the north, in the place where it falls, there it will lie.

According to an English proverb written in 1678, we see the same sentiment:

As a tree falls, so shall it lie
As a man lives, so shall he die
As a man dies, so shall he be

Described in previous chapters, is the concept of the garden we have all created in our hearts and minds since Creation began. Our gardens grow and ideally become more beautiful each time we return to Earth University to learn one or more of the 12 pillars or lessons (each with their many electives) laid down by the Creator.

In this chapter, I use the fallen Bonsai as metaphor. Unlike the wild tree in the forest, the Bonsai is a product of human actions and human decisions. Thus, if your fallen Bonsai is a product of anger, hate, self-centeredness, obsessions, psychological attachments, aberrations and deformities your heavenly destination will be affected. Even after a successful Life Review and Judgment, Steve witnesses other souls who struggle with actions and negative habits. These became "chains" and prevented them from moving forward:

They, like myself had departed from our physical world for the other side. But, because of their ignorance in refusing to forfeit their negative emotional and physical energies and attachments to the world they were not permitted to continue beyond this point... **'In other words, by use of their own free will they refused to break the chains that bound them to this world.** *And consequently due to that they had to remain* **in this place that some refer to as 'Hell'** *until they came to terms with whatever it was that was holding them back, and then agreed to let go of it.*[1]

Even attachments to our physical bodies can affect our Bonsai character. How do we think we will respond when we die and find ourselves wandering in the Afterlife? Will we be so attached to our physical bodies that upon losing them, we will become enraged...as one Dead Saint found himself?

I tried again and again attempting to use any part of my body, but I seemed to no longer have a body. I became enraged and soon afterward I could see other beings in my same state and they were angry too. I could feel them searching for a place to go, and that they were envious of anyone with a body. I thought to myself, this is Hell, and I said to whoever it was that was watching me that I didn't want to be like that, and suddenly I could feel I was curled up in a fetal position and I could see a tunnel with a Light at the end.[2]

I have noticed this "fallen Bonsai" state in dozens of blogs on GBM brain cancer boards. Good and bad tendencies are amplified during a terminal illness. Unkind, selfish people become more selfish, while normally positive people stay positive. Your Bonsai's shape and personality doesn't change because it fell and died.

Amy's NDE completely illustrates this retention of personality after death. Since she was 17, she had been having trouble with chronic pain brought on by fibromyalgia. It had become a tortured existence-sound sleep was next to impossible to achieve. Often she was able to sleep only in 15-minute increments. She was constantly tired. Her doctor prescribed a medication with terrible side effects. Even in the tiniest amount, her nose would swell and her breathing became too shallow. It was scary and uncomfortable, but it gave her relief from pain. She informed her doctor she believed she was having an allergic reaction to the medication. He chuckled and told her that her body simply needed to 'get used to the meds.' The small dosage was so low it couldn't possibly do anything."

He asked her to take three whole pills. She took a quarter of one to try it out. One night, after a week of brutal pain and no deep sleep, she considered the doctor's prescription of three whole pills and decided to take them all and trust him. She went to bed after taking all three, and within minutes felt herself begin to go numb. Her nasal passages swelled up and soon she could not breathe at all. She struggled to get air in, but could not. She felt encased in her body as if mummified. Unable to call out for help, it only took a few minutes before the struggle was over. She felt a strong vacuum-like suction coming from the top of her head, followed by an absolute sense of relief. She realized there was no longer a need to breathe and lost the feeling of her own physical body.

The next thing she knew she was traveling along with other souls through a tunnel very quickly. It's a long story, but it is a compelling account of the tenacity of our earthly personalities post-death:

The next thing I remember is moving through some kind of a portal along with many others. It felt like I was in some kind of a waiting room situation. With the many others coming through, I was curious, and began to watch them move in. I watched a group of about three teenage boys come through who had an energy and way about them I felt as abrasive. As I was looking at them, it came to me they had died in a car accident where they had all been drunk.

A lot of others came through. I didn't feel the people were either good or bad. It just felt like a room of normal people, unique to themselves. This room or area did not feel very bright to me, and despite the fact I was receiving somehow, information that these people were dead, I hadn't fully accepted that, because everything felt so real and natural. So alive. Nothing felt shocking or strange. I was very curious about what it was all about.

A young woman told me how she had regretted not 'hanging in there.' How it 'would have been better to stay' and work out her issues and continue learning. But she also told me to, 'Tell them how free I feel now.'

...I remember we had congregated into a bigger and brighter room or area where there were many others present. Everyone was so busy talking and getting to know each other. It felt similar to a scene in a high school cafeteria. People even seemed to want to quickly find others they related to or felt at ease with, and there were even little groups that began to form.

At a certain interval, I noticed a man move into the room. He looked at me and I realized he was a kind of teacher or guide for this group. I knew he had died in a truck accident. He had been a truck driver by profession. He was a Latino man. He told me he was not a perfect man, but he had mastered humility. I could feel this when I was with him.

He explained, he had come to help teach the importance of humility to this group of people, because they had been in some ways self-absorbed in their lives, to the degree where this had blocked their own vision and progression. They hadn't been able to learn vital lessons and had aborted their own lives, unwittingly for all I knew. He seemed to be telling me in one way or another, these people had committed suicide—but without using that exact terminology.

This made me wonder, as I hadn't noticed anyone in the room who had hung themselves, intentionally overdosed on drugs, shot themselves, or things like that. I was a bit confused by how the term, 'suicide' could come to me with these people. I came to understand that the casual disregard for life, or flagrant and selfish risks one might take, whether involved in drug use, drunk driving, or any kind of action that could essentially lead to one's own demise is what is considered, in a way, like suicide, at least where I was. When a human takes their own life in desperation, due to emotional or mental imbalances, physical agony, or depression so severe, I understood that as being similar to when a very old person gets so tired of hanging on, that they will themselves to go, simply stop eating and breathing, etc. This is not punished, so to speak, on the Other Side. It is different. It is just the human, willing themselves out of this life cycle. I never witnessed punishment or condemnation.

The teacher continued to offer more information. He explained how in aborting their own lives, these people would have a rest period, but that learning what they needed to learn would be needed and the process would not be easy. I came to understand as much as they were taught and infused with good and helpful information there, and even if they agreed wholeheartedly with what they needed to learn, that learning without a body is like learning to get over an addiction to drugs with no opportunity to do the drugs! Or like learning to love one's own enemy without having enemies to deal with. He explained how he needed to teach this group of people how vital it is to get beyond themselves—how to lose their obsession or fixation with themselves—how they will be stagnant in all progress if they cannot unchain themselves from their own ankles.

He shook his head, smiling slightly, and implied there was still very little he could help them with, without their bodies. His service was to help instill more of a passion for what he had to teach, strong enough that it would leave a seed of Light that might stay with them through their sojourn. I don't know if he taught by talking or just being there as an example. I never experienced him teaching the way we might imagine it done here. I know that just by being in his presence helped me to connect with what he was, though.

When this particular teacher was transmitting information to me, I felt a jolt of sudden anxiety with my next wondering.

I queried, 'Who are these people?'

He came in more clearly, stating telepathically, 'They are deceased. They have died.'

I remember demanding point blank, technically speaking, 'If these people are dead, what am I?!'

I don't know why it took me so long to grasp this fact. (But then again, time wasn't as it is here, so I am not sure it was "long".) He explained gently, 'You are in-between. You are as if in a coma. There will still be life in you. You are not the same.'

With that, I started upward. I wanted out of there, then. As I moved toward the corner of the room to leave, at least a couple of the teenage boys suddenly lunged at me with an energy like, 'She's alive. Touch her!' They were reaching toward me and trying to pull me back toward them. It seemed almost as if they were desiring sexual contact or energy. This of course had me all the more determined, I was leaving.

So I now believe some of the deceased, if not all, still have many earthly or worldly desires. That they go out and arrive, the same human natured beings they were in life. Looking back at that part of my experience, I was astounded by how earthly people can be on the Other Side. One might expect upon entering through death's door, there would be sudden enlightenment—that maybe everyone would realize absolute goodness and choose Light and a fresh start, possibly becoming more angelic and purified, but in that place, everyone came in exactly as they'd been before.[3]

The Swedish philosopher and scientist Emanuel Swedenborg claimed to be able to visit the Afterlife at will. From his Afterlife journeys, he discovered:

A person's strongest love is revealed at death. The love for wisdom and service; or the love of money, evil and corruption. Everyone has a considerable number of loves, but they all go back to their strongest love which a person makes one with —or taken all together —comprise it.[4]

During several of Swedenborg's after-death communications, he would witness people dying and watch their soul journeys in the Afterlife. He stated immediately following death, there is a period of self-discovery where they have "the same face, speech, and spirit and consequently, they have much the same moral and civic life" when they cross over, but eventually (for some, immediately) the social masks worn by people on Earth dissolve away and the true self is revealed. All fear, anger, sadness, and negative emotions vanish.[5]

According to the Dead Saints, the Heaven or Hell we create within us and around us, regardless of religious belief (or unbelief), *our personality, our Bonsai character,* is taken with us into the Afterlife. The loneliness or remorse we create in our minds and hearts is brought with us. Whether born-again Christian, devout practitioner of another faith, atheist or agnostic, it doesn't matter. Our psychological state of mind and heart, not our religion (or lack of it), determines our Afterlife experience. The anger or love in our hearts, the forgiveness or lack thereof we feel, set the stage for the Realms of Heaven (or darkness) we will inescapably experience.

The good news is, if you are reading this, you are not dead yet.

Your Bonsai tree can be pruned and trained in a more becoming direction before it falls. You can become more Christ-like. I experienced a beautiful garden illustration of this concept in a dream I had on October 18, 2015. In the center of my living room, there was a beautiful 12x8 foot desert sand garden bordered on all sides by a shin-high Japanese/Chinese carved, wooden fence and capped with wooden three-inch balls at the corners. On one end of the desert garden, a windswept black pine Bonsai about 18 inches long, flowed partially over the 8-inch-high sand dunes with sharp windswept edges, which were sculpted to look exactly like the Arabian desert. I marveled how it could have been miniaturized to look so picture perfect, as if God sculpted it, not man. It was the most peaceful Bonsai garden I had ever seen. *~Chronicle 858*

The windswept Bonsai tree and the peaceful desert represented me, but the only one who can carve a perfect, peaceful desert is God. The dream became for me a Zen lesson about dying in character peacefully and, no matter what, no matter how we die, *we are loved.*

---

1 *Steve B's NDE*, #441, 07.24.04, NDERF.org
2 *David A probable NDE*, #1411, 12.17.07, NDERF.org
3 *Amy C NDE*, #2386, 10.09.10, NDERF.org
4 Emanuel Swedenborg 2012. *Heaven & Hell*, Swedenborg Foundation Press, USA, p. 493.
5 Ibid. p. 493.

Part II

Afterlife Bonsai

My stepfather Ray visited me in a vivid dream at 3:00 am, the day after he died. Knowing his time was near, I'd been praying that while alive, he would help me put together his Memorial Service. A bright Light illuminated the background behind his face. He was absolutely beaming and appeared thirty years younger. He had this message for me to deliver at his Memorial Service.

'We need to love one another more.'

12

Is our Mission Finished?

*~Delynn talked in her sleep again saying, "ooooh, it's your time!!! Wow!!! I asked her while she was sleep talking, "Whose time?" She said, "Your time." ~**Chronicle 428***

Kiros.

Momento Mori.

The Greek and Latin words for our *appointed time to die.*

Are we resigned to this Mohammedan fate? —to die at a particular moment, on a particular day?[1] The Bible tells us in Psalm 139:16 "All the days ordained for me were written in your book before one of them came to be." So apparently God knows exactly when, where, and how we will die. Does this mean our fate is sealed? Does this mean we have absolutely no control over when we will die? I wondered.

Near-death experiences are classic examples, where we witness a soul's opportunity when they must make a decision to stay in Heaven, or return back to their body here on Earth. Obviously, we only hear the thousands of stories where the Dead Saints decide to return! In nearly every case, those who have had near-death experience are told *"It is not your time,"* and then, they are sent back or sometimes forcibly thrown back into their body.

Recently, my father's longtime friend Dick who died of a heart attack came to my father in a vivid dream a few weeks after he died. In the dream, my father asked Dick why he passed over and Dick replied, "Well, I guess it *was my time*." A strange thing to hear if it was not true. This then, becomes the eternal question. What determines if it is our time to die?

A Dead Saint describes a very interesting situation where Earl is told he must go back, but wonders why his friend Robert has to stay in Heaven:

> *Earl, it's not your time. You have to go back. You have to endure. You must continue with your life.*
>
> *Disappointed, Earl asked, 'Why do I have to continue on? You didn't.'*
>
> *'You still have work to do. I squandered much of my time,' Robert said. 'You still have work to finish. You have to keep on.'*
>
> *Then Earl asked him, 'How will I know when I am finished? Will it be soon?'*
>
> *Robert said simply, 'You will know!'*
>
> *Earl desperately wanted to ask what it was he had left to finish, but he abruptly regained consciousness on the treatment table.*[2]

Earl's discussion with Robert makes me think about my own *Appointed Time*. I know my time is short, but how long do I have left to live? Was it mine to know the hour and day of my death? Could I control when I died? Or was the appointed DAY pre-ordained?

Why Dead Saints Return to Life

My research discovered that there are two primary reasons the Dead Saints return to the land of the living:

First, they are **NOT meant to be dead.** An accident has occurred and either they are not meant to be in the Afterlife, or God has a MISSION for them on Earth; there are things they must learn, people they need to influence, and children and family they need to care for. They are on a Mission from God and their participation on Earth is required:

> *I remember feeling very weak when my eyes rolled back into my head, then suddenly I was standing upright, but not on the ground, it was as if I was floating in a very silent, peaceful space. There was an oval shape of a cloudlike image surrounded in Light*

that became larger and larger in size. I heard a voice saying; 'Tina, it is not your time yet, so don't worry or panic. The voice repeated this statement two or three times and then told me to relax, calm my body and concentrate on opening my eyes.' I then remembered thinking (knowing) it was my angel speaking and comforting me. I felt an extreme sense of peace and stillness.[3]

Secondly, they are **MEANT to be dead**, but they have asked to come back for their own reasons. This means they have stayed beyond their appointed time. Andrew was declared dead on the operating room table for three minutes during brain surgery to correct life-threatening damage to his head. During his NDE, he spoke to his deceased father who had passed away during the accident. His father asked the Lord if he could return Andrew to Earth, but it was Andrew's choice whether to go back or stay in Heaven:

I saw the Light, I followed it. People say 'Don't follow the Light,' but you really don't have a choice. It's either follow the Light, or be stuck there until you wake up—if you do. So I followed. I emerged somewhere outside the Gates of Heaven. I walked up to the nearest Seraph and didn't even get past stating my full name, when the Seraph simply smiled and said, 'Follow me. He wishes to speak with you.' So I did. We walked in through the gates and I was led straight to the chamber where The Lord sat. I seated myself across a desk from Him, and we began conversing...

I remember the Lord said to me, 'Worry not, you will not be kept here. I do not wish to have you home yet, for you have much to live for!' This was in response to my question, 'Am I really "dead" to my life down there?'

The Lord then smiled and my Dad walked in, grinning as he went to stand by the Lord's side. It was his usual mischievous "surprise bearing" smile. It also had a large amount of pride in it.

My Dad simply said, 'I'm home.'

To which I replied, 'Daniel will miss you, and so will I.' Daniel, who was 17 at the time of the accident, is my younger brother.

My Dad simply said, 'Take care of him while you still can.'

To which I said, 'Of course I would.'

The Lord then spoke and said, 'Your father spoke to me earlier and did not wish you to die. I granted his wish...'

I gave my father and the Lord a parting hug. I still remember the hugs well, for when I gave the Lord a hug, he whispered into my ear as I was transported back, 'You will not remember everything we spoke about, but don't worry, you'll remember what you need to know in life when the time is right, and you will remember it all when you cross heaven's threshold once again.' [4]

Mission Possibilities

According to Psalm 139:16 (NIV), God planned our Mission *in a Book* before we were born:

Your eyes saw my unformed body. All the days ordained for me were written in your Book before one of them came to be.

However, the Dead Saints, reveal we may have several possible missions in life, but there is a preferred path God wants us to take. A Dead Saint named "Just" died during a 90 mph head on collision. During his NDE, he discovers he has a job to do, but he will have up to five different paths to choose from:

After the impact, I faded to black. At that point I was in what I call a void. It was dark black empty and wide open. It was the most peaceful and calm felling I ever had. I knew with just one thought I could travel through the void and I was about to shoot myself into it when I heard a voice say, 'Stop. Don't go. It's not your time. You still have a job to do.'

When I turned to see who was talking, it was my mother. She died when I was six months old. I told her I didn't want to live and I wasn't going to go back. That's when she said, 'You can't go yet. You have things to do first.' I didn't care and I turned back to go when she said, 'Look.' When I turned, I saw a woman holding a child. My mother told me this was my wife and child. My mother then told me all the major details of my life up until I die at age 47. [author's note: an atypical future prediction]

Then, she told me that was my path and try to follow it. She also said my choices in life would affect my path. That's when she showed me the major choices I had to make and what would happen as a result. She showed me five different life paths. At that point I was ready to go back to my body and continue my life. [5]

Dot recollects God offering two ways to fulfill her Mission:

In 1987 during the birth of my son, I suddenly went through a tunnel and stood before a Higher Power who is showing us two ways to do a Mission. One He prefers us to do, and the other He isn't crazy about, but seems the main answer He is interested in is, 'Will we do it the way He asks. Yes or no?' [We have] free choice. No one is looking at Him, nor at the other spirits near Him.

'Okay. Yes. I will do as you wish.'

He sends two of the ones on his right with me. So many of the entities near me are telling me I will meet you here and there. Some even said they would be my children in this life. He shows us whom we will be born to, inherited diseases, even our death. I can't remember why and what I'm supposed to be doing though.[6]

Does God Help Us Fulfill Our Mission?

A movie describing this idea came out a few years ago called the *Adjustment Bureau.* Starring Matt Damon, it is a story about the political career of David Norris and the intention of God's Divine Plan to make him president of the United States. Angels (caseworkers) followed him around to make sure he did not stray from the plan, but things went awry when David Norris was determined to marry his girlfriend, Elise. The Adjustment Bureau, a legion of angel/case workers, didn't want him to marry Elise because it would distract him from becoming President. A relationship with Elise was not "written in the plan," and somewhat like a near-death experience, even when the angels made it known he was "destined" to become President and that marrying Elise would not be permitted, he chose to have the relationship with Elise anyway. These fixing angels, or caseworkers, were under the instruction from the "Chairman." He preferred Mr. Norris not to marry Elise, so they kept putting obstacles in front of his path to deter him. They made him spill his coffee to miss a bus, created traffic accidents, but nothing stopped him.

Think about it. When we lose our keys or can't find our cell phone, do those fixing angels who want to gently change our destination without compromising our free will, influence these events? Eventually, David Norris "gets the girl" and the Chairman (God) re-writes the Divine Plan, making everybody happy. It's just a movie and some parts of it are all Hollywood, but I believe it illustrates an important truth described by the Dead Saints.

Charlene describes a "re-write" caused by her Dead Saint experience:

I was told by telepathy that I am done here—if I want to be done here—or I could return. It seemed like I was there for days and days, like in some sort of "holding room." The feeling I got was that they were waiting for my decision. When I told them about my decision, it seemed to take days and days again.

Something that kept coming to mind was something of a 're-write.' *I am not sure what that is. As soon as I said I wanted to return to be here for the ascension, (this is one thing that I didn't forget...out of everything...it was this), all the beings present seemed to be so exuberant. I was told that at first return, I would struggle and it would be difficult, but as I progressed, it would become easier.*[7]

Isabelle remembers from her NDE that the 'plan' needed to be repaired if she didn't return to Earth University:

I knew if I joined these lights I would be one of them forever. I didn't know who they were, or what they did, but I knew that they weren't idle. They had a purpose. The voice reminded me of the vision I had had of my husband and son in funeral clothes. He said, 'if I didn't go back to them, I would disrupt some 'plan.' The plan would be repaired and everything would eventually be okay, so I could go ahead if I wanted.[8]

According to the Dead Saints, your choices become integrated into God's blueprint, which is part of a Divine Plan:

They expressed that I had an important purpose to fulfill for the Earth that was vital to the Divine Plan for our world. *I did not care at the time, and still wanted to move on. Then they showed me an image of my young daughter, insisting that my return was vital to her growth, and I felt the desperate despair she would experience for many years if I did not return. I then agreed to return. They instructed me how to bring myself back.*[9]

Heaven's Captive Audience

Worried about whether you are walking the right path? According to Tim, you have thousands of friends in Heaven watching!

My vision then went totally to the bird's eyes view. I just watched. I remember feeling satisfied and happy, as if I was in a play or something and performed exactly as I was supposed to...but then, I felt as if I was not the only one watching. I felt that I was being watched by tens of thousands of other people.[10]

Return to Life Humor

Cameron's NDE: Occurred during a medically induced coma:

I was in a great white room that was rectangular. I couldn't see any of the walls, floors or ceiling, but my mind just tried to make sense of it all. The room was long, almost tunnel like. Close to the end of this tunnel, there were two men sitting with their legs crossed and face to face with each other. As I approached them, the men stood up. I drew nearer to them. I could see the man looking back at me was Jesus Christ. The other man...I do not know whom he was, but I know he did not like me very much.

The two were bickering about what to do with me. Jesus rose up His hand as if to say stop, and said, 'Hold on for five minutes. We haven't figured out what to do with you yet.' He pointed for me to go to my right or his left. After I followed His instruction, I met Ronald Reagan. I never really liked the man in life. According to my grandmother, he was the Devil. But, I have to tell you, he was one of the nicest guys I'd ever met. We chatted for a while. I asked him about Hinkley and he just laughed. The whole experience with Jesus was telepathic. He did not speak with words, but I heard Him. He was a very strong Shepherd. He appeared like someone from Greece with his haircut from some old movie. The hair looked almost sheered, like that of a sheep. The Jesus that I met had very dark hair and dark complexion, almost Arabic or Greek. You could tell he was from the Mediterranean. He was so strong, nothing like He has been portrayed in movies.[11]

Is Your Mission Finished?

Our life purpose includes a specific Mission God assigned to us before we were born. God reviewed your unique talents and abilities and said, "I've got a *special* job for you to do. It is an assignment so specific, only you are qualified to do it. Imagine the scene from *Mission Impossible*, "Your Mission, should you choose to accept it" is how things were laid out for you. You were given a choice...and since you are here, you can assume that you accepted your Mission.

Your Mission is part of God's Divine Plan and may include several specific people, places or things you are supposed to meet, visit, or do. It may include being at the right place at the right time to meet a specific person; saying a kind word at the right moment; building a company; making friends who touch other friends; writing a book, or becoming President of the United States. A good example is John Kennedy's leadership through the October 14-28, 1962 Cuban Missile Crisis. His decisions likely averted global thermonuclear war. Of course, we will never know, but it is interesting to observe that he was assassinated November 22 the following year. Was he born to accomplish this particular Mission and then depart Earth University? Was his Mission finished? We can only speculate.

Another is Reverend Martin Luther King, Jr., who, the day following his memorable 'I've Been to the Mountaintop' speech, was felled by an assassin's bullet. In that speech, he declares:"

> *...We've got some difficult days ahead. But it doesn't matter with me now. Because I've been to the mountaintop...And I don't mind. Like anybody, I would like to live a long life. Longevity has its place. But I'm not concerned about that now. I just want to do God's will. And He's allowed me to go up to the mountain. And I've looked over. And I've seen the Promised Land. I may not get there with you. But I want you to know tonight, that we, as a people, will get to the Promised Land! ...And so I'm happy, tonight. I'm not worried about anything. I'm not fearing any man. My eyes have seen the glory of the coming of the Lord!"* [12]

Many people regard King's speech as a prescient revelation of his impending fate, a forewarning to his followers that his Mission was over.

You were carefully chosen by God to complete a specific Mission on the world stage of Earth University. Even though you will likely never know your Mission, it is vitally important, no matter how small. Mel describes this situation perfectly:

> *What was my great Mission? I don't have a clue. I'd like to say I grew up and went on to cure cancer or brought about world peace. The truth is, I'm just an average guy. I know after the experience, I got married, joined the military, had kids, and became a cop. My daughters had children and now I'm a grandfather. The experience I had all those years ago continues to grow and dominate my life. It has become more important to me throughout the ensuing years. I now understand a basic human act of kindness amounts to so much more than being president of the United States or a brilliant scientist. I think my earthly job is only a platform to my real job. To accept and spread love. And by love, I mean real love, not some word bandied about in a careless fashion by so many of us. I mean taking the time to care and to show it each and every day. I know I have a long way to go but I no longer fear death. Maybe the greatest missions in life aren't the ones we typically think of?* [13]

The Dead Saints often have to make decisions about returning to life because they have a Mission to finish or job to complete. Often they are reluctant to come back. In fact, many are angry at the prospect of returning to Earth. The Saints are gently reminded they either have a job to complete, children or a spouse to care for—a mission they must finish.

Is the choice to return to the physical body by divine order or is it a free will decision? The pendulum seems to swing equally both ways. The following excerpt from Johanna's NDE is simply amazing in that it involves many souls who weigh in on the need for Johanna to return to Earth or not:

> ***People were milling round, or so it seemed to me, asking what the verdict was.*** *When they were told I was returning, there was uproar, with people saying it wasn't fair and I should stay. I started literally kicking and screaming and saying I wanted to stay there. I didn't want to go back. However, I entered the revolving tunnel once more and hovered again above my body before I floated down and settled back into it.*[14]

This particular soul had earned the right to make a choice to return to Earth, but if she stayed in Heaven, "it would put a kink" in things:

> *A little while afterwards a man stepped out of the crowd. He said He wasn't going to make me leave and I had earned the right to be there, but I put Him in a bind. There were things I was supposed to do, and me, being where I was, put a kink in things. He said what they were, though as I stated before I can't remember the exact conversation. He also said he could get someone else to do these things, but time was short. He also implied my wife and children would miss me. At this point, I felt bad about things. Suffering and misery are two words to describe it though not adequately. He saw my state and asked what was wrong. I told Him I couldn't do these things as I had screwed up. At that point, he smiled and put his hand on my shoulder and said, 'Now is not your time.' And this is the only thing I can say verbatim. My vision returned and the first thing I noticed was this "wet rag" feeling of something under me. I glanced at it and said out loud, 'Oh. It's my body.'*[15]

Denny chose to return to bring Light to the Earth and to be there for his daughter:

> *I sat there as my two personal or guardian angels communicated with the others seated on the circumference of the interior of the dome. The communication was telepathic. I heard the voices, but did not speak. I knew they were talking about me. They were deciding if I should be admitted into the city and then into the heavens, or return to Earth. The general consensus among*

the beings there, including my two guardians, was I should stay. A leader among them stood and asked me directly, 'You have free will, and the choice to stay, or return to Earth is yours.'

I said, 'I have a daughter who must know who I am. And also Earth is in a lot of darkness right now. They need as many people with good heartedness within them alive and on Earth right now. For these reasons, I would like to return and complete my mission.' [16]

Go the Distance

According to the Dead Saints, your decision to attend Earth University comes with an agreement. It is truly a handshake between you and God. It's not that you can't choose to exit the Mission. Of course you can. God chose you and *your participation matters*. Only you can do it. The famous line 'Go the Distance' from the movie, *Field of Dreams*, expresses the common sentiment among the Dead Saints. It is our duty and commitment to God that we battle to stay here on Earth as long as we are able.

So when will death come? The Dead Saints indicate death comes to you when you are *finished* with your mission. Stacy was 36 years old when he blacked out and went into a coma for a full day. Doctors checked him out, releasing him within three hours after he awoke. He remembers an EMT medical staff commenting:

We have a white middle aged male in arrest. Direct us to the nearest emergency room. Stat. I think to myself, 'Hmm, looks like I might be dying. I wonder if I will make it.' Then I am back in my body, open my eyes briefly and ask one EMT, 'Am I going to die?'

He looks at his partner, they exchange a glance and then he says to me, 'Don't worry. You are fine and are not going to die.' I leave my body and return to floating above the ambulance. I think to myself: **'It is not his decision whether I leave or not.'**

The scene below me is bright and vivid with lots of activity. It is as if I am looking through a transparent and translucent membrane [author's note: the veil] at live theater, but I am not emotionally connected to it other than I am curious and interested. All around and above me is a black void. I look over to my right and see a long dark tunnel leading off into infinity. In the farthest reaches of this tunnel, I see a small, singular bright Light. In the front of the tunnel are two figures, my grandparents, both have been dead for many years. A Voice asks me a question. The Voice comes from everywhere, inside me, around me, back in time, forward in time, everywhere.

It says: 'ARE YOU FINISHED?' I instantly comprehend what's being asked. I felt I had all the time there ever was and ever would be to answer. After a while, or a long time, I remembered my wife was back waiting for my return and that we were not finished with our time together.[17]

No matter how you feel in this moment, you are a hero for being here. Mel, a teenager who died in 2007 was told:

I communicated I wanted to stay and could never return to the horrible life on Earth. I was told I had a great mission to fulfill and if I didn't return, nobody else could fulfill it. Whether I was shown, what this was or not, I can't recall. What I do recall, and what I can never forget, is what happened next. I made the decision to return. Angelic beings rose all around me and began to sing a song I couldn't recognize. It sounded spontaneous and improvised and the closest sound I can imagine would be hundreds of the world's best choirs singing perfectly together at the same time. It was the most beautiful and majestic sound I had ever heard. They were praising and honoring me. ME! A teenager from the projects who had dropped out of high school. A kid abandoned by his father and drifting aimlessly. These great Beings were paying tribute to me. **I was virtually lifted up and displayed to these wonderful Beings as a hero.**[18]

How do you know your mission is finished? If you are breathing right now, your mission from God is not over. In the words of Richard Bach, "If we are still here, we have something to do, someone to love, something to smile about, somebody to forgive, that our lives still have meaning and purpose."

~July 27, 2015. I had passed my 26th month of my GBM fight. A visiting Vedic (Hindu) teacher revealed to me there was a high probability of my death occurring sometime between January 23, 2016 and Easter, March 27, 2016. When he made this "prediction," he did not know about the rapid growth of my brain tumor or my prayer to see my daughter Angela graduate high school on June 18, 2016—Chronicle 1102. I didn't tell him, but this "death window" was at least 84 days short of my goal. I suddenly felt like astronaut, Mark Watney, who in the movie the Martian, will die if he is not rescued before he runs out of food. Having consumed his last meal, he is rescued by NASA on Sol 549, before dying of starvation. My rescue—if indeed it is a "rescue"— will

not likely come by clinical trial, chemo, or natural medicine, or by NASA, but through God's Mercy. If my Mission is finished, and I die before then, I will accept it. However, if I can reach Angela's graduation, it will be a miracle glorifying HIM. ~*Chronicle 775*

DREAM: On a vessel navigating in tropical waters bordered by mountains with glaciers down to the shore. (A common Heaven theme: snow covering high mountains down to the shores of tropical waters—a scenario not possible on Earth.) Dream switches to a garden island taken over by terrorists. I advise the terrorists they had better work things out with the islanders soon, because if they did not, the island would be overtaken within six months and everyone would be killed. This dream occurred on September 16, 2015. A premonition, warning of my death window in six months? ~*Chronicle 826*

[Publication Update: February 13, 2016. Growth shown by MRI's taken from July 29 through January 25 2016, show David's brain tumor has grown from 8mm to 22mm in six months. Tumor growth between December 1, 2015 and January 25, 2016 stabilized @ 10% every four weeks]. ~*Chronicle 976*

---

1 "Surely the day of decision is (a day) appointed." (Qur'an 22:7)
2 *Earl NDE*, NDERF.org, unknown numerical reference
3 *Tina R NDE*, #1745, 11.16.08, NDERF.org
4 *Andrew J NDE*, #2758, 07.04.11, NDERF.org
5 *Justin M NDE*, #3605, 02.23.04, NDERF.org
6 *Dot's NDE*, #372, 12.26.04, NDERF.org
7 *Charlene P's NDE*, #1416, 12.28.07, NDERF.org
8 *Isabel R NDE*, #2965, 02.25.12., NDERF.org
9 *Suzy B's NDE*, #1806, 12.17.08, NDERF.org
10 *Tim's NDE* #56, 9.23.00, NDERF.org
11 *Cameron M possible NDE*, #3962, 06.20.15, NDERF.org
12 Martin Luther King, Jr. April 3, 1968. Excerpt from *I've Been to the Mountaintop* speech at the World Headquarters for the Church of God in Christ. Wikipedia.
13 *Mel W NDE*, #990, 01.04.07, NDERF.org
14 *Johanna S NDE*, #3137, 09.09.12, NDERF.org
15 *Larry B NDE*, #1055, 03.22.07, NDERF.org
16 *Denny B's NDE*, #87. 3, 05.13.06, NDERF.org
17 *Stacy S NDE*, #2411, 10.10.10, NDERF.org
18 *Mel W NDE*, #990, 01.04.07, NDERF.org

13
Death Step by Step

~I emailed 15-year survivor of GBM, Cheryl Broyles. Delynn had been keeping tabs with her on Facebook. I sent her a chapter from Book II of the Chronicles, Training Wires of the Soul, for her approval. She and her husband loved it! She suggested I read her own book, Life's Mountains.[1] I read it in one day. Amazing. Keep going Cheryl. Someone should make a bronze statue to honor your determination, stamina and persistence, but your humility won't allow it.
~Chronicle 780

Raymond Moody M.D. Ph.D., a psychiatrist who pioneered work on life after death in 1975 in *Life after Life,*[2] classified 12-18 major elements of the dying process in *Coming Back: A Psychiatrist Explores Past-Life Journeys,* which typically occur during a near-death experience.[3] Moody's division of the different aspects of the NDE, became a reference point for nearly all near-death researchers. After my own intensive investigation, I added several defining Death Elements, expanding them to 23.[4]

Many other near-death researchers have based their own studies on Dr. Moody's work, including Jeffrey Long, M.D., Melvin Morse, M.D,

Bruce Greyson, M.D, Michael Sabom, M.D., Pim van Lommel, M.D., and P.M.H. Atwater.

No two Dead Saint experiences are identical. The 23 Death Elements cannot isolate NDEs as one continuous dying event beginning with Death Element number 1 and ending with number 23. Most often, only a few Death Elements are represented by the NDE, and while most occur generally in order, the experience can start anywhere on the list.

While many Death Elements have already been touched upon already in earlier chapters, this section serves as an overview for all 23 Death Elements and highlights some, which are not dedicated with their own chapter. In most cases, I cite only the first name of the Dead Saint or the title related to their experience. In some instances, where I devote an entire chapter to the Death Element (or Elements), only a summary is written. When available, I cite statistical studies of Death Elements done by NDERF defining the percentage of Dead Saints, described by Jeffrey Long, M.D. as *NDErs*, who experience them.

Death Element #1: Knowledge of Impending Death (Doom)

ER doctors hear this all the time from patients who predict, "I am going to die." And then they simply do just that:

> Tom A's NDE: *I was standing in the hospital hallway when I saw four medical staff working on me. I said aloud, 'I'm dead.' As soon as I said that, I felt a warm feeling wash over me. At no time was I scared, worried or concerned. I felt so much peace and calmness.*[5]

> Priscilla O's NDE: *I was in anaphylactic shock. I knew I was dying; I was in great pain, went blind and then deaf. Then I died.*[6]

Death Element #2: Realization Physical Body is dead

> Kathleen's NDE: *Then I heard the doctors say, 'Oh Lord, we're losing her!' I then felt a pulling whoosh up and then was at the ceiling watching it all! I felt no pain at all. I did, however, feel the fainting sick feeling you get before passing out and I felt light and heard a buzzing noise. I then watched the doctors working on me. He (the doctor) was swearing terribly. I remember thinking, good Lord, He (God) can hear him! I was embarrassed for them all in the ER.*[7]

> Kenneth's NDE: *I really couldn't understand why I was in a state of disembodied consciousness whilst my physical body was clearly dead. It had already become a bluish/grey color.*[8]

Death Element #3: Hearing a Sound or Buzzing

Though not commonly experienced, hearing a sound is often one of the first dying stages *heard*. Sheba heard a 'whooshy sound' during her NDE: *I immediately went into the tunnel... not walking... just floating upright and I could hear a 'whooshy sound'. I again told myself, 'oh, this is the tunnel. I must be dying.' I went further in and then in the far distance I saw the Light. Again, I told myself 'I'm really dying, this is the Light. If I go through there, then I will be in Heaven.*[9]

Richard heard a buzzing sound: *I started to hear a buzzing sound that quickly became very loud. As the sound increased, the hole above me got bigger, the Light got brighter, and I felt myself being pulled up towards it. I felt as if I was being squeezed through an opening that was too small for me. The buzzing sound became a whooshing roar as I entered the hole, with a Doppler-like effect as I passed through it. The sensation was like speeding down a tunnel at light speed, not unlike the "warp" effect you see in movies. I wasn't alone in there, either. I felt the presence of others, but I couldn't see them.*[10]

Death Element #4: Out-of-Body Experiences

The next Death Element, usually the first and most common, is the out-of-body experience (OOBE)—a separation of consciousness from the physical body. Regarding this dying stage, an NDERF survey of 613 NDErs asked, "Did you experience a separation of your consciousness from your body?" 75.4 percent answered "Yes."[11]

A typical OOBE transpires something like the following Dead Saint experience of Michael triggered by substance overdose and seizure:

I floated over the exam table and I saw one doctor and three nurses. I saw a heart monitor, another table, and an oxygen tank. I saw my body with all kinds of tubes coming out of me. I was naked, but the clothes are still there, just underneath my body. I don't know what's going on. I feel a little scared or uncertain about what is going on. Then I floated through the wall and looked down to see my mother and Aunt Barbara. My mom didn't have access to a car and it was close to 1:00 am in the morning, so they were hysterically crying and trying to look through the triangular window in the door to the room I'm in. Now, I float back into the room where they are working on me. All of a sudden,

I was sucked back into my body. During those two seconds I heard a warm, kind, and soothing voice say, 'Go back, not now.' Then swoosh, I was back in my body.[12]

Many OOBE Dead Saint reports describe floating some thirty feet above the body while they often watch dispassionately as the dying process unfolds. Sometimes a "silver cord" is seen connected to the body, which thins as they move farther away. At times, the Earth and other planets in the solar system can be seen from outer space. There is a sense of timelessness and occasionally heavenly music is heard.

Twelve Common Phenomena Associated with an OOBE

There are generally twelve common phenomena affecting consciousness during an OOBE that can be divided into two groups: "effects" and "abilities." When a Dead Saint leaves the physical body, they no longer "think" with a human brain. They are thinking and observing their experience with a mind and a consciousness from an 'outside perspective.' One question you may want to ponder as you read through the OOBE phenomena: If the Dead Saints are observing events without a human brain, with what kind of spiritual mind are they observing and thinking?

OOBE EFFECTS

#1: No Pain

Walter C's NDE: *I could see my physical self was suffering immensely, but my conscious self was experiencing no pain. I felt empathy and overwhelming compassion for my physical self, but the pain evident within that body was not felt by this part of me.*[13]

#2: Profound Feelings of Peace, Quiet, & Incredible Joy

A NDERF survey asked, "Did you have a feeling of peace or pleasantness?" Of the NDErs surveyed, 76.2 percent answered "Yes."[14] The NDERF survey asked another question about the specific emotion of "joy" during an NDE: "Did you have a feeling of joy?" NDErs responded with 52.5 percent selecting, "incredible joy."[15]

Profound peace, quiet, and joy are some of the most common elements of a Dead Saint experience:

Linda Stewart's NDE: *I became aware of a deep sense of peace and warmth that permeated my senses. Confused, because the energy that had enveloped me had a definite presence, I tried to see what was happening and who was carrying me. Who or what cared so deeply for me? I felt peaceful and loved immeasurably. I* knew I was in the arms of a Being who cherished me with perfect love and carried me from the dark void into a new reality.[16]

#3: Perceived Alteration of Time and Space

A NDERF survey asked, "Did you have any sense of altered time and space?" Of the NDErs surveyed 60.5 percent answered "Yes."[17]

Gillian's NDE: *I spent what seemed like a long time—certainly not minutes, hours, or days. More like weeks, months, eons. Time was meaningless.*[18]

Janet's NDE: *Suddenly, my heart started to do what I can only describe as a "shudder." I started to call out to my daughter when my heart stopped. I suddenly realized EVERYTHING had stopped. There was no sound, no movement, nothing. I was standing there taking in this fact, when I looked down & saw my body on the bed, I thought, 'Oh, I'm dead,' like it was a completely ordinary thing. Then I remember thinking, 'I wonder if the rain stopped too,' so I went through the wall & looked around outside...The rain had not just stopped, the raindrops were suspended in mid-air. It was the most awesome sight I'd ever seen. I remember moving around looking at different drops and I found one that was quite large, so I was looking at it closely and was about to touch it when it started to fall. At that same instant I was back on the bed. My heart was beating again and I felt so happy, & realized I was grinning from ear to ear.*[19]

#4: Realization Spiritual-Self is Separate from the Physical Body

Walter C's NDE: *Great understanding came over me, for I knew the "self" existed apart from the physical.*[20]

Sylvia W's NDE: *I was sitting on a kitchen swivel bar stool. I turned to get up and leave and felt myself starting to fall. The next thing I knew I was above the roof of the house. I could see through the roof and lying crumpled on the floor was a female body—about the size of a Barbie doll. My "vision" and "hearing" were very acute. I could see without eyes, hear without ears, and communicate without mouth or other body parts. I knew everything past and present. I felt I was in my natural state and the body was the temporary unnatural state. I was HOME where I belonged, where I wanted to be.*[21]

#5: A Remarkable Detached Point of View

Thomas M's NDE: *Right after the accident when I realized I was floating above a car wreck, I had an altered type of vision because, even though I was above the car, I could "see" inside the car with a sort of "super vision." I saw my body and I saw the body of my friend at the wheel. I had no real emotion to what I was witnessing. There was a calm sense of detachment, and I remember looking at my body as if it were a sweater or a suit I had worn and now had cast off. I remember thinking, 'That was cool being Thomas like it was some fun excursion, this human life.'* [22]

OOBE ABILITIES

#6: External Observer of Events

Walter C's NDE: *Floating above my moving vehicle was an empowering sensation. Moving was effortless; I simply thought myself to be where I wished to be, and there I was. I felt no motion or touch sensations of any kind. As I followed the vehicle, I could see objects on both sides of the road, as though I were in a low-flying plane. My van appeared to be about the size of a quarter, so you can imagine what my peripheral vision was like. The odd thing was I saw objects I had never seen before, set way back from the side roads. The view was complete and accurate to the most, minute detail, even though I never had been down those roads. (After the experience, I drove down those side roads to confirm what I had seen).* [23]

#7: Heightened Awareness / Hyper-Alertness

A NDERF survey asked, "How did your highest level of consciousness and alertness during the experience compare to your normal, everyday consciousness and alertness?" Of the NDErs surveyed, 74.4 percent indicated they had "More consciousness than normal."[24]

Sue D's NDE describes an awareness of her Dad's heart attack in the US during her NDE at age 18 while living in France: *I came out of my body. I could see the family around my bed crying. I was sucked into a tunnel that was incredibly noisy, and was shot out into the Light— the golden Light. Then somebody spoke to me in a loud voice. It was my Dad. He said I had to go back because 'my mission wasn't over yet.' I fell back into my body in the bed with a great sadness... The next morning, I found out my Dad was in the ICU and had had a massive heart attack.*[25]

#8: 360 Degree Vision

Gillian's NDE: *I recall no limits on perception—no binocular vision, but panoramic/spherical/360. It's hard to describe.*[26]

#9: Acute Vision

Marta G's NDE: *I saw detail I would never have seen in "real" life. I could go anywhere, even to the tops of trees, by simply intending to do so. I went out to the dock where the big kids dove off and was surprised to find it empty. I traveled around the lake to view people's back yards, their pets, their sheds, lawn furniture, etc. Later, I walked around the lake into people's back yards looking for specific unusual things I recalled and they were there! I also saw a woman with red hair sticking out from under her bathing cap with white daisies and yellow centers, wearing a black and white bathing suit with a large mole above the strap on her back resuscitating me. I later verified it was she who did so and that was what she was wearing. I was legally blind and for the first time saw leaves on trees, bird's feathers, bird's eyes, details on telephone poles and in people's back yards that were far more acute than 20/20 vision.*[27]

#10: Movement of Spiritual Self Caused by Thought

Jeff's probable NDE: *I became aware I could move around just by thinking about it.*[28]

#11: Increased Intelligence

Barbara E's NDE: *As I settled into the love without condition, I realized more and more how utterly and absolutely intelligent Light was. The sheer level of creativity and intellect was emotionally and psychologically beyond comprehension. I knew that because Light was telepathically melded with me, allowing me to sense at least a minute degree of what was contained within. There was so much thought and information it felt as if zillions of scrolls of data about the true nature of reality just kept unraveling. I was lost and overwhelmed and had no comprehension of what it all meant. Yet, the central message came through loud and clear. Reality is SO much larger, multi-layered and multi-dimensional than we realize. Consciousness is able to experience so much more than what we commonly practice.*[29]

Carmel B's NDE: *Knowledge came in suddenly, from everywhere. The easiest way again to explain is that I was a computer user going into the main frame. My thoughts were much faster and much clearer. My IQ would have been doubled I believe. So not only could I think faster and clearer, I could tolerate knowing more and being told more at the same time.*[30]

#12: Telepathic Ability

One of the most common abilities described by the Dead Saints is telepathy:

Alan M's NDE: *I was met by a being of pure Light, not a human form, but pure point of Light, who communicated with me mind to mind, via some form of telepathy.*[31]

Gillian's NDE: *Communication was non-verbal and instantaneous. It involved relaying entire occurrences, concepts, and events with associated emotions, not just words and sentences.*[32]

Death Element #5: A Black Void or Dark Space

Henry Vaughan, a 17th Century Christian Poet in his Poem, *The Night*, describes finding darkness in God, "There is in God (some say) a deep, but dazzling darkness."[33] The Bible in Job 10:21 says of this darkness, "Before I go whence I shall not return, even to the land of darkness and the shadow of death." Psalm 23:4 describes the darkness we may pass through when we die, "Yea, though I walk through the valley of the shadow of death, I will fear no evil: for thou art with me; thy rod and thy staff they comfort me."

There are hundreds of testimonials from the Dead Saints that describe this initial voyage into the Kingdom of Heaven:

Eben Alexander in his book, *Proof of Heaven*, describes the first phase of his death experience: *Pitch black as it was, it was also brimming with Light.*[34]

Other Dead Saints say the black void is comforting:

Sheila EP's NDE: *I clearly remember experiencing complete comfort; of being totally free from any sort of pain or feelings of bodily sensations at all. I've explained to people many times — that if you could think of your most enjoyable bodily sensation of any time; sex, massage, runner's high, anything pleasurable that has ever been experienced from within your physical body, it could not compare to the experience of total comfort during that state of blackness.*[35]

Other Dead Saints describe they were wrapped in a calming, peaceful velvet blanket, but more importantly, God was in the black void:

Priscilla O's NDE: *I knew right away I had died. It was pitch black, like a total void, and I felt wonderful. I felt so good, I had no pain. I felt light, and as if I had no body. I knew God, or some higher power was* there.[36]

What is the void? It has been described as a "nilism" of black space (not really black, but appears that way) that separates our physical body on the Earth from the Realms of Light through a mechanism called the veil.

Death Element #6: Encountering a Veil

What is the veil? The veil appears to be a thin bubble-thin-like partition separating the physical realm of Earth from the Realms of Light and darkness we know as—Heaven. Sometimes the veil is seen as a tear in the fabric of the black void. Evidently, spirits in Heaven can see through the veil and observe events on the Earth, but we cannot see through it and see events happening in Heaven.[37]

Reina Ji observed: *I see a line of people going through a dark tear in the fabric of the void and a man stares at me. In fact, there are other people milling about on the "floor" who have very puzzled looks on their faces, which are slightly blurred to me. I am puzzled too. I want to go where the other people are going, but again, I am told it is not my time.*[38]

Terry sees the veil as a layer similar to a two-way mirror: *Where I was, it was dark. I was aware there was a layer between me and the scene below, like a two-way mirror, and another opaque layer about ten feet or so above me. Everything between these two layers seemed infinite.*[39]

Barbara describes the veil to be made of a gray semi-sheer twinkling, sparkling illuminated foreign material:

After what seemed to be only a few minutes, an unseen force pulled me from the waiting room into the main part of the tunnel. The main tunnel wasn't as dark as the waiting room and I could see a shimmering shiny veil, which separated me from a boy on one side and an elderly man on the other. The veil was made out of a gray semi sheer twinkling, sparkling illuminated foreign material. My attention was drawn to this veil for most of my journey through this tunnel. I felt mesmerized by it.[40]

Dying Element # 7: Traveling through a Tunnel

A NDERF survey asked, "Did you pass into or through a tunnel or enclosure?" Of NDERs surveyed, 33.8 percent answered "Yes."[41]

In the next phase of dying, the Dead Saint must pass through a tunnel. Not all Saints experience a tunnel. Hindus and Thai Saints, who often, instead, describe bridges or rivers as they cross into the Light, rarely report tunnels.

However, Western Dead Saint testimonials, overwhelmingly describe high-speed transportation through a tunnel before reaching a brilliant Light. The tunnel experience usually follows in sequence when Saints finds themselves out-of-body, or in the Black Void. Their description of the tunnel is remarkably similar to the imaginative wormholes created in the television series *Stargate* and *Contact*. The wormhole is not a transportation method between stars, but a spiritual highway between inter-dimensional realms of the Black Void and the Realms of Light and Heaven.

The interior of the tunnel is described in various colors, lengths, widths, and geometries, but often begins as the Dead Saint departs out of the Black Void. Sometimes, as the Saints would begin the high speed journey through the tunnel, they would experience the lower tunnel realms as "dark and grey," where spirits of the Dead gather in a holding room, preparing to move on to their next destination through the tunnel.

Above the holding room, the Dead Saints from time to time, will pass through a grey zone, a realm of lost souls, who might distract the speeding spirit passing through at light speed. Invisible and Light Beings, or deceased relatives, often referred to as "soul gatherers," assist the dying person as they pass through the tunnel, warning them to keep their eyes straight ahead, and focus on reaching the Light.

Occasionally, the Dead Saint sees images on the walls of the tunnel, beginning to play out his Life Review before reaching the Light at the end of the tunnel. Alan describes a tunnel with two ends—one end leading to Light and the other end terminating in the black void:

I was told one end of this tunnel led to the Light and the other into the dark void. It was explained to me, by this Being of Light, this tunnel had two ends; one into the glorious Light of God, and the other into the darkness of the void.[42]

According to Isabelle, there are rules to traveling through the tunnel:

Then, I was in a dark tunnel. The now "proverbial" Light was at the end of the tunnel, and I was moving toward it. I sensed beings in the darkness surrounding the tunnel. They were crying

> *out to me in anguish. I recognized two of them. They were begging me to help them. I felt so powerful, invincible, that I moved toward them to grab their hands and bring them out of the dark and into the tunnel. A voice told me sternly not to do that. He said, (yes, it was a "he") 'There were rules, and I didn't know them.'*
>
> *I could not take people out of the darkness, but they could drag me into it. He said to keep going straight ahead and that I knew nothing about anything, and shouldn't presume I did or I could get into trouble. I reached the precipice at the end of the tunnel. There were spherical lights as far as I could see. Inside the spheres were searing bright white lines that reminded me of the filaments of an electric light bulb. I remember distinctly thinking I had to find something earthly to compare the insides of the spheres to in case I ever had the chance to tell anyone, and I settled on the filaments inside a light bulb.*[43]

Malla sees multiple tunnels as transition ports for birth and death:

> *For a moment, with my perception enhanced, I was able to view a large part of the European continent all at once. I noticed that there were portals all across the Earth. They were shaped like large transparent circles and they were popping up all over. I knew that these portals were here to let people travel from the physical life to the spirit life and from the spirit life, back to Earth. I knew that when we go through the transition of death that we go through these portals. When we are about to be born to the Earth, these portals are the gates to new life.*[44]

We learn more and more about the details of the Afterlife by piecing together each Dead Saint experience concerning the process of passing over. In this case, Terri describes two tunnels, one blue for two-way traffic between Heaven and Earth and a white tunnel, for one-way traffic to Heaven. Here deceased friends and counselors help them through to their next experience, or if it was not yet their time to die, redirect them back towards Earth:

> *I found myself in a blue tunnel...Eventually, I could see in the distance a point that was a hive of tremendous activity. At this point, the blue tunnel turned into the white tunnel, a very clear line of transition. It was impossible to see into the white tunnel, as there was so much Light pouring out from it. There was also a tremendous feeling of love emanating from this source, and a kind of instant knowledge. You just knew it. The blue tunnel could accommodate two-way traffic, whereas the white tunnel was one*

way for souls leaving the Earth plane. Once you crossed over into the white tunnel, there was no going back.

The Light from this tunnel was so bright that under normal circumstances it would have been blinding, but here it was warm, safe and full of love. As I got closer to the transition point between the blue and white tunnels, the activity became clearer. I could clearly see many, many souls on both sides of the transition point. There were quite a few souls, like myself, coming from the Earth plane. All of these souls were being met by groups of souls who had come from the white tunnel. It was like each soul had its own entourage of souls from the other side to meet them. Some were being welcomed with open arms and carefully guided through the transition point and into the wonderful Light of the white tunnel; some were being greeted with discussions, and some were being turned back toward the Earth plane.[45]

The Light at the End of the Tunnel

Rhea describes arriving at the proverbial Light at the end of the tunnel:

In an instant, I was in a tunnel with a bright Light at the end. I distinctly remember I wasn't moving my feet and wondering how I could be advancing through the tunnel. When I got to the end of the tunnel there was a man in an all-white tunic awaiting me. He never had to speak physically, but I could hear Him and He could hear me he took me by the hand and we walked. I knew Him although I had never seen Him. He loved me, I loved Him and I felt safe with Him.[46]

Death Element #8: The Grand Central Station of Death

The transition to the Afterlife often happens so quickly the soul is often unaware of the change from the physical dimension to another spiritual dimension—primarily because the Body of Light has all of the acute subtler senses you had on Earth—in essence you feel the same...but *different*. Some souls are conscious of the transition, while many others are not. Some cross over awake and aware of the change in dimension, while others "sleep in the blackness," waiting to be awakened, and yet others outright reject they are even dead.

George Ritchie, an army private who had a remarkable NDE in 1943, comments:

> *One of the places we observed deep within this realm seemed to be a receiving station. Beings would arrive here oftentimes in a deep hypnotic sleep. I call it hypnotic because I realized they had put themselves in this state by their beliefs.*[47]

You get the sense from some of the commentary given by the Dead Saints that the recently deceased go through a spiritual processing center with counselors and angels to guide souls through the next realm in Heaven, much like one would find at Grand Central Station in New York City. It is a busy place with lots of commotion and many people—where the crowds of dead humanity are processed like any port entrance to a foreign country. Those who are unwilling to accept their death receive counseling. Some are sent back to Earth because it is not their time. The Grand Central Station observed by Jill is managed by a hotel concierge, a sort of a "passport" control who directs the deceased through to the next realm of Heaven:

> *I was floating down a large hallway, maybe 20x20. There were people there, but I didn't recognize anyone, fading in and out of the cloud walls. I seemed to be floating over the heads of a LOT of people on a level right below me. They were all in white and seemed to be content—I think these were Mormons. As I floated along, I remember one man in particular who was standing off to the left in a bend in the hallway. I asked him where was I? And he kind of chuckled and said, 'Just keep going. Go on down to the front.'*
>
> *So I did. When I got to the end of the hallway, I met a guy that looked like a concierge in a hotel, working behind a desk. He looked up at me with a rather perturbed expression on his face, and he thought, 'What are you doing here?'*
>
> *I said, 'I don't know; I'm just here. This is where the people back there, pointing over my shoulder to those hanging out, told me to come.'*
>
> *He shrugged, furrowed his brow, and thought, 'Well, wait a minute. Let me check something.'*
>
> *While he was checking, I looked behind him and realized we weren't in a tunnel at all; we were in a cave and he was at the entrance. Behind him was a beautiful landscape, a hillside with*

sparkling trees and flowers and a brook-the most beautiful, peaceful place I had ever seen.

...And the next thing I knew I was back outside the gold tunnel. As I was being repelled from the cloud, I could hear the "clerk" say, 'Don't worry.' I hoped he meant, 'Don't worry. You can come back.'[48]

Catholic theologians in the Middle Ages referred to this "place of rest before Heaven" as Purgatory. Their doctrine holds that unbaptized but innocent souls, such as those of infants, virtuous individuals who lived before Jesus Christ was born on Earth, or those who die before baptism, must wait before going to Heaven. They are not subjected to any punishment because they are not guilty of any personal sin. Although they have not received baptism, they still bear original sin. In other Christian denominations, it has been described as an intermediate place or state of confinement in oblivion and neglect. Catholics believe all who die in God's grace, while unpurified, are assured of eternal salvation, but after death undergo purification, to achieve the holiness necessary to enter the joy of Heaven. The tradition of the church, by reference to certain texts of Scripture, speaks of a "cleansing fire" although it is not always called Purgatory.

Anglicans of the Anglo-Catholic tradition generally also hold to this belief. John Wesley, the founder of Methodism, believed in an intermediate state between death and the rebirth of the dead and in the possibility of "continuing to grow in holiness there," but Methodism does not officially affirm this belief and denies the possibility of help by prayer for any who may be in that state.

From my research, there appears to be a cleansing from all that is impure after we are processed through a Purgatorial in-between state that I refer to as the Grand Central Station of Death. The cleansing of impurities, sins and habits we gained from our Earth University experience occur when we don *the Body of Light* (See chapter 16) created for us by God so we can move forward onto Heaven. This place of waiting or rest is certainly verified by the Dead Saints, however, the place is not devoid of Christians, but is a processing center for all who have just died.

Much like the following Dead Saint testimonial, Eugene, a Christian, who briefly died during a head on collision in 1995, describes this Grand Central Station as a large Stadium full of people of every color, religion, and creed. It was a place where souls go to wait before going on toward their final destination: *[Author: Notice the thick "fog" described in Eugene's Dead Saint experience below, a description similar* to the "fog" I see people walk from in my 1975 NDE/Dream in chapter 2].

> [I found myself in] what can be described as Yankee Stadium FULL of people, **and full of fog as thick as pea soup**. I say a stadium because I could hear CROWDS of people all talking at the same time. I couldn't tell what they were saying, just that sound you hear in a crowd. Then I saw her, my Nana. [Deceased Grandmother]. She calmly stepped into view from the fog. She said, 'YOU are NOT supposed to be here!' I remember being happy to see her, but sad she was sending me away. I saw people who had killed themselves and were still unhappy, having learned their problems were not solved by death in this world. I saw people going by, talking to themselves, people crawling on the floor/ground. There was everyone who died! Muslims, Buddhists, Christians...everyone!
>
> **I thought only Christians would be there, but that wasn't what I saw.** I asked Nana what all these people were doing here, and asked where I was. She said I was 'In the middle, a place where souls go to wait!' I asked, 'Wait for what?'
>
> She simply said, 'The destination, the last stop.'[49]

Statistically, on average, about two people die every second—151,600 per day, 55 million per year,[50] so this Grand Central Station of Death must be constantly bustling with the newly dead. Joseph observed this stream of the newly deceased leaving Earth University as they returned to the Light:

> I know I observed a whole lot while I was there but the only thing I can remember actually seeing were "souls" (for lack of a better term)separating from the Light and traveling to the Earth to inhabit human bodies(earthly birth). There were also souls leaving their human bodies (earthly death) and returning to the Light. I didn't see them actually entering or leaving their earthly bodies but I just knew this to be true. They appeared as orbs of Light.
>
> The best way to describe it is blips on a radar screen. There were hundreds if not thousands moving in a constant stream out of the Light and into the Light. I knew as I watched this we existed as part of the Light before we were born as humans. When I came to, I couldn't remember everything I learned there. It was as if trying to recall a movie you saw a year ago. You might remember the gist of it, but you can't recall all of the details. I knew the reason we are here is to love, to learn, to create and to grow, but mostly just to love. It's all about love.[51]

A Confusing Transition

Remember the last time you went to a three-hour *3D IMAX* movie and got so engrossed in the drama, that by the time you left the theater, you couldn't remember where you parked your car, or even what day it was? It took a few moments to reorient yourself from the movie reality to this Earth University reality. Imagine playing the starring role for *seventy years* in your Earth University movie, a movie more real than a *3D IMAX*, and getting lost in its reality when death comes your way? This appears to be the case when the Dead Saints observe the Grand Central Station of Death.

Raina observes souls puzzled and confused after death caused by the sudden change in reality:

> *At first, the man in front of me is approximately 30 feet away from me. He appears to be flooded with white Light in a white suit, bald, with extremely white teeth. He floats me out of formation, then in front of him. He is not in a white suit, but he is "glowing." Inner Light is flowing out all around him. He has extremely blue eyes. I am so happy to see him! I know him and he knows me. I cannot recollect who he is now. I hug him and tell him I miss him. He tells me it is not my time. I disagree!*
>
> *...I see a line of people going through a dark tear in the fabric of the void and a man stares at me. In fact, there are other people milling about on the "floor" who have very puzzled looks on their faces, which are slightly blurred to me. I am puzzled too. I want to go where the other people are going, but again, I am told it is not my time.*[52]

Death Element #9: Perception of an Unearthly Environment and Heavenly Gardens

A NDERF survey asked, "Did you see or visit any beautiful or otherwise distinctive locations, levels, or dimensions?" Of NDERs surveyed, 40.6 percent answered "Yes."[53]

Discussed in detail in chapters 7 and 17, the soul, after the black void and the tunnel, often finds its spirit walking through spectacular garden vistas; trees hundreds of feet high, mountains, waterfalls, meadows, huge flowers without stems, and butterflies. Often the soul observes calm creatures it knew on Earth, such as deer, rabbits and sheep. All life communicates its love for the Creator. A perfectly coordinated palette of neon color illuminates all life. Heavenly music plays. Angels sing. Like Analia and most Dead Saints, Heaven was the most peaceful and joyful experience of their life:

It was a place in the countryside, somewhere I had never been, where the Light was very bright. I was stopped on a totally white road, and on looking either way I could see an infinity of white tulips. I couldn't see the end of this beautiful garden, but it was beautiful! The tulips swayed gently to the rhythm of a warm breeze and the intense perfume of the flowers was very rich. In front, the road continued up to a hill, and the Light shone more brightly here. My clothes were white—extremely white. Someone by my side took my hand. My cousin was with me all dressed in white, as well—20 years ago, she died an angel, at the age of four. She was my friend in those days of eternal infancy. Her smile was so beautiful. She never said to me in words, but I knew what she was saying. She wanted me to come with her to the top of the hill. We began walking looking at each other for a moment, happy. Peace, tranquility and joy. I felt I never wanted to return and live. It's indescribable with words. I was immensely happy and nothing bothered me.[54]

Death Element #10: Meeting Spiritual Beings, Friends, Relatives, and Angels

A NDERF survey asked, "Did you meet any other beings?" Of NDERs surveyed, 53.7 percent answered "Yes."[55]

This Death Element is discussed in detail in chapter 15. In this summary, virtually every Dead Saint experience is with the deceased. Thirty months since my brain tumor was found, I have had 12 after-death communications with deceased loved ones, and only three dreams of the living; my wife Delynn, my daughter Angela, and my father, Ron. How does a debunker explain away that?

The follow Dead Saint account describes meeting two deceased loved ones:

The wall of the hallway began to dissolve behind my Dad. Behind the dissolving wall was a large valley that was very green with a few trees. Further away, I saw large mountains with very blue water in front of them. The sun was behind the mountains. My Dad was smiling with a very bright Light on him. At that time, my Mom walked between Dad and me. She turned to him and said, 'We have to hurry, I don't want to be late.' I then turned to my Dad telling him, 'I can stay here, I want to stay.' My Dad grabbed my upper left arm and turned me around to my right. I saw a rolling countryside with an old farm on it and a well-warn pathway made by animals pulling a wagon. My Dad said, 'You have to go through the gate.' My feet were still on tile flooring. My

Dad placed his hand on my upper back and began to push me through the gateway. As I went through the gate, he told me, 'Tell everyone to be nice to each other.' He seemed sorry for sending me back. I felt someone telling me to tell people to' stop worrying about their pending death because worrying takes life away.' I was pushed and awakened by my wife telling me that I had a heart attack.[56]

Death Element #11: Experiencing a Bright Light / Meeting a Being of Light

A NDERF survey asked, "Did you see a Light?" Of NDERs surveyed 64.6 percent answered "Yes."[57]

Discussed in detail in chapters 15, 17, and 23, this Death Element describes the encounter with a Bright Light, or a Being of Light, God or Jesus. God is seen as Father, Mother, and Triune— the Source of Life and Creation.

As I stood there with my arms out wide, I realized I wasn't alone anymore. I knew I was in the presence of the Creator. The Light had started to get a little brighter and less radiant. I felt the presence of something, something that was way bigger than me. I was in awe of it and the fear I felt was my own shame. I kept telling myself, 'I know I didn't believe; I KNOW I WASN'T worthy.' YET, I felt that The Presence was honored that I was there.[58]

Death Element #12: The Life Review

Discussed in detail in chapter 9, the Life Review usually replays the life of the Dead Saint in granular detail from birth until their NDE:

Samantha H's NDE explains it: *My focus was on what was being shown to me—a sort of film reel that was directly in front of me but up just a bit. It was like watching an immense, very clear TV. I was watching images of every event that had taken place in my life—my entire life all in pictures. The most interesting part of it was that with each picture—with all the pictures (there were more than I could count). I re-experienced the original feelings that had accompanied each one at the time it had actually happened. AND THIS WAS HAPPENING ALL AT THE SAME TIME! Everything was so clear, so vivid!*[59]

Death Element #13: The Judgment

Discussed in detail in chapter 10, the Judgment usually coincides with the Life Review. It is also called a "Hall of Reconciliation"[60] when we face our mission on Earth and all the things we have done and must answer for. A council of judges or assessors (either 7 or 12) along with God or Jesus gently guide a Dead Saint through the experience and point out the consequence of their actions and where they have erred, or where they have done well with the right decisions. The entire Judgment process is unconditionally loving, and in the end appears to be a self-judgment. We judge ourselves with God's help.

Death Element #14: Accessing Special Knowledge

A NDERF survey asked, "Did you have a sense of knowing special knowledge, universal order and/ or purpose?" To this question, 56 percent of NDERs surveyed answered "Yes." Another question asked, "Did you suddenly seem to understand everything?" To this question 31.5 percent responded they seemed to understand everything "about the universe," and 31.3 percent responded they seemed to understand everything about "myself or others."[61]

> Scott H's NDE describes it: *While I was being exposed to a view of the whole universe, I was also exposed to all knowledge of the universe. I knew instinctively the universe is infinite. It goes on for eternity. I didn't see the beginning and the end of the universe because there is no beginning or end. It was certainly far beyond what I could comprehend. It's so large and so perfect and yet, we're able to be so connected to it that we are the universe and it is us.*[62]

Death Element #15: Cities of Light / City of God / Holy City

This Death Element is discussed in detail towards the end of chapter 17. The City of God, also called the Holy City, resides in the higher Realms of Heaven. Described in some Christian encounters much like the City of New Jerusalem described in the Book of Revelation, the City of God houses the Great Throne Room, where Jesus and His angels oversee earthly affairs. Here we read about great libraries of knowledge, administered by a league of angels managing births, deaths, and technical advances on Earth. The City of God spans the breadth and width of a significant portion of the universe and is populated by millions of souls.

Death Element #16: Realms of Bewildered Spirits / Realms of Darkness / Hell

Discussed in detail in chapters 18 and 19, this Death Element describes souls who live on "astral planes" superimposed over the physical Earth plane. However, the darker the soul, the darker the planes of existence they descend until some reach the fiery depths of

"Hell." As souls move between the Earth and the Kingdom of Light through the tunnel, they are usually accompanied by an escort who protects them from the "grey areas" populated by bewildered, sometimes powerfully evil souls who may attempt to mislead them away from the Light toward these darker realms.

Death Element #17: Sensing a Border Where You Cannot Go

A NDERF survey asked, "Did you reach a boundary or limiting physical structure?" Of NDERs surveyed, 31.0 percent answered "Yes."[63]

Every Dead Saint encounters a barrier in the Afterlife they are not allowed to cross. Of course, the Dead Saint testimonials we have on record are from Saints who have reached the proverbial "barrier"—and returned to tell their story. This boundary or point of no return may appear to the Saint as a deep canyon, gorge, river, brook, wall, fence, sunflower field, cornfield, or a traditional pearly gate. The Saint is warned sternly, if the barrier is crossed, their death becomes irreversible.

The barrier to Heaven is described in every religion. In ancient Greece, for instance, it was the River Styx. The dead must cross this river before reaching the Elysian fields of Heaven. The ferryman Charon is believed to have transported the souls of the newly deceased across this river into the underworld. Greek paintings depict the journey across Styx as a perilous voyage, requiring the boatman to fight off lost and angry souls populating the river on its journey to the other side. Some believed that placing a coin in the mouth or over the eyes of the deceased would help pay the toll the ferryman required to cross the river. If someone could not pay the fee, a reference to passing the Judgment, it was said they would never be able to cross the river.

The barriers separating Heaven and Earth University are described in different symbols throughout the *Chronicles*. Gary saw the river as a great divide:

> *I noticed the second this land appears it was separated by a deep canyon. The Guide and I were on one side and this tropical paradise was on the other side. To the degree I could get worried, I was concerned I could feel this place calling my cells to cross the canyon. Actually, it felt more like my atoms were being pulled or attracted to this place. Instinct told me if I cross the crevasse, I could not come back.* **Yet this place called my every being.**
>
> *I wanted to go there very badly, but I knew if I did, I couldn't come back. I thought of how this would impact my sister, my parents, my girlfriend and my friends if I chose to cross. I thought about never being a father or having children. I was only 17 and I*

wanted to experience more of life. So I continued to concentrate on not letting one single atom or cell cross the divide that was before me. Yet, I had this uneasy feeling that I belonged there, that I originated from there. This place was my home and everything came from there, seen and unseen. I really wanted to be there and go there, but I knew there were consequences if I crossed the divide.[64]

The Pearly Gates & the Guards of Heaven

John attempted suicide overdosing on pills and found himself before the pearly gates protected by heavenly guards:

I tried to enter this kingdom or whatever it was. There was a huge gate. Everything was kind of an off-white color (that's what my mind perceived). I was running near the gate and some beings were trying to stop me. I threw a few down, apologized profusely, and started to jump over. I was then pinned to the ground with a power of such that I could not move. Just then, my guardian angel came to me.

Back to the Pearly Gates. He came to me and I said, 'Hey man, you got wings!' He smiled at me. I asked him what was pinning me and that it was really tough. He told me not to look at it, but I did for a second. I had to turn away. He was fearsome, had a few faces some kind of lion, eagle, and such. My feeling was it was the guard to the entrance of Heaven.[65]

A Bridge

I have seen a bridge crossing a river in my own dreams. At times, I attempt to walk towards it or cross it. In this particular Dead Saint experience, Cherie arrives at a bridge she wants to cross. She is in labor under an epidural and feels no pain. There are three men around her bedside: her husband, the gynecologist and the anesthetist. In a bit of humor, she feels little support from them because they are distracted by the soccer world cup event taking place. She knows they all long for the baby to be born quickly so they can go and watch the matches, but the baby would not come. Suddenly, in the midst of her long labor she left her body:

Then I am weightless, all is blue around me; there is a kind of **Light bridge to cross**. *At the other end of the bridge, there is more of the same blue—it's a blue path, and on it there are people dressed in white robes, like monks. Their heads are covered, too. I don't see their faces but I trust them. One of the people parts from the group, looks at me, and waves me away with his hand, telling* me to go back to where I came from. I feel strongly I don't want to. I'd like so much to join them! I feel this is my grandfather (whom I never knew personally; he died when I was 7 months old.) I ask him why he doesn't want me to join them, and he tells me, 'This is not your time. You have something very important to do right now.[66]

A Sun Flower Border

Riki was dreaming when suddenly blackness enveloped her. She moved into a brilliant, white misty Light, with all the accoutements of a mystical near-death experience, including a barrier of sunflowers preventing her from entering Heaven:

> *I also knew I was absolutely **NOT to go beyond that border of sunflowers**. Then, I was back looking at the open space and watching it become smaller until it was gone. When I woke up, I was still overcome from the feelings and wonder of it. I couldn't stop thinking about it, talking about it. I had heard of near-death experiences before, but hadn't really delved into it. Now, I could not get enough stories to read. I was amazed to find all the similarities to my experience! I had thought the border of sunflowers was very odd. I doubted that part a little and tended to leave that out when I told my experience because I thought it sounded weird. Then I read many stories where there was some type of border you were not to go past.[67]*

Cutting the Silver Cord

Perhaps the reason the heavenly hierarchy is so adamant about the Afterlife threshold is because crossing the barrier cuts a cord connecting the physical body to their spiritual body—a cord some call the "silver cord." It has been described by many Dead Saints as being "smooth, very long, very bright" like an elastic cable made of Light, about an inch wide, sparkling like a tinsel on a Christmas tree, and attached to one of several possible locations on the physical body.

The silver cord is our spiritual body's lifeline to our physical body in the same way our umbilical cord is our lifeline to our mother's body during the birth process. During the dying process, as the spirit body leaves the physical body and travels light years into the universe, the silver cord becomes thinner as it is stretched to its limit. If the silver cord is severed, the spirit body is released from being attached to the physical body. It then becomes impossible for the spirit body to ever return to the physical body, making death *"irreversible."*

In the last moments of life, the dying person may see the Angel of Death, or spectral being with a brilliant face personified in ancient and modern myth as the Grim Reaper *(See Grim Reaper ch.15)*. Often depicted carrying a scythe, their mission is to cut the silver cord and take the soul out of the body at the instant of death.

The existence of this silver cord, its severance, and its connection to death is even mentioned in the Bible:

Remember him—before the silver cord is severed, or the golden bowl is broken; before the pitcher is shattered at the spring, or the wheel broken at the well, and the dust returns to the ground it came from, and the spirit returns to God who gave it. (Ecclesiastes 12:6-7)

The two metaphors speak of death. The golden bowl refers to a bowl likely used as an oil light, suspended by a chord. Dying is compared to the breaking of this chord and the crashing of the bowl down to the ground, whereupon it shatters and its light extinguished. Second, death is compared to the breaking of a pitcher and pulley used to draw water at a well. When death ensues, no more water can be drawn.

In my own dreams, the barrier to crossing over into Heaven is symbolized by a deep gorge, separated by a river, or a bridge crossing a river. For you, when you dream about death, it will be different. Each symbol of death is personal to the Dead Saint. I believe the form of the barrier indicates the depth of religious and cultural fear you may feel about crossing over death's door. The decision to turn back from crossing the river separating Heaven and Earth, whether by choice or by heavenly edict, is a decision to return back to the physical body and to life on Earth.

Death Element #18: Coming back to Your Physical Body

A NDERF survey asked, "Were you involved in or aware of a decision regarding your return to the body?" Of NDERs surveyed, 58.5 percent answered "Yes."[68]

Most Dead Saints return to the physical body because they have a mission in life to complete. Some have a choice to return, but many are ordered back into their bodies:

Rick R's NDE: *I heard the voice speak again, 'You must return!' I did not want to return though. I was content to stay and longed to stay even after the things I had seen and heard.*[69]

Shalom G's NDE: *He then went on to indicate I could either stay with HIM or return to Earth. However, if I did not return, many people would miss their connections, in order to complete their* missions and purposes in life. Reluctantly, but with a deeper understanding of my mission, I chose to return to help ALL of my assigned brothers & sisters, on our planet.[70]

Death Element #19: Ineffability—Inability to Put into Words

Information brought back by the Dead Saints comes through telepathic images, which have to be translated by the Saint and put into words. It is a common problem often described throughout the *Chronicles*.

Terri R's NDE: *These are the concepts that are difficult to explain because it wasn't conveyed to me in words. It was an understanding that spoke to me in a way I could relate.*[71]

Death Element #20: Change of Life

Discussed in great detail in chapter 14, this Death Element is the hallmark of a dramatic near-death experience. This Dead Saint describes the joyful, life-changing transformation caused by their NDE:

> When I awoke and tried to understand where I was: I asked myself where I was. I recalled being in a dream state while under. [During Heart Surgery], I recall being on a large promontory in the dark. Way out in front of me was a Light, not bright and not dim.
> I then said, 'Hello?' (no answer)
> 'Hello, anybody out there?' (no answer)
> I then asked, 'Can anybody tell me the meaning of life?'
> Then, I received this EXACT ANSWER telepathically: 'Man has not even scratched the surface to know what life is all about.'
> This answer has changed my life and how I live to this day.[72]

Death Element #21: Elimination of the Fear of Death

Discussed in detail in chapter 3, this Death Element describes the loss of fear in 85-90% of those who leave the physical body during an NDE.

Death Element #22: Corroboration of Events

This Death Element is the Holy Grail of near-death research. Termed "veridical" by researchers, it describes perceptions seen by the dying Saint while out-of-body which can be later proven to coincide with reality. It represents intriguing evidence, which, I believe, will soon validate what religion and the Dead Saints have been saying for thousands of years—the consciousness continues after the death of the physical body in a spiritual body and mind called *the soul*.

In 1997, researchers Kenneth Ring and Sharon Cooper published results from a three-year study of NDE cases of blind people. They reasoned if a blind person was able to report on verifiable events that took place when they were clinically dead, that would mean something real was occurring. In their study, out of 31 individuals they interviewed, 14 were legally blind from birth. Twenty-one had a NDE, the rest had OOBEs only. Their study discovered their experiences conformed to the classic NDE pattern, whether they were born blind or had lost their sight in later life. Ring and Cooper concluded their out-of-body perception of reality does not depend on the senses of the physical body.

There are many such "veridical" cases coming to light in recent years. Maria told her social worker, Kimberly Clark, that during her cardiac arrest, she found herself outside the hospital and spotted a tennis shoe on the ledge of the north side of the third floor of the building. According to Kimberly, "She was able to provide several details regarding its appearance, including the observations one of its laces was stuck underneath the heel and the little toe area was worn. She begged Kimberly to go out on the ledge and try to locate what she had seen while out-of-body." [73]

From the hospital room window, Kimberly could not see the tennis shoe, but investigating Maria's description of the location, she soon found it exactly as Maria had observed it during her NDE. Kimberly later commented, "The only way she could have had such a perspective was if she had been floating right outside and at very close range to the tennis shoe. I retrieved the shoe and brought it back to Maria; it was very concrete evidence for me."[74]

Death Element #23: Supernatural Rescues & Events

Sometimes supernatural rescues and events accompany an NDE. Much like entering Rod Serling's *Twilight Zone,* these phenomena appear to transcend all known laws of time and space. We call them supernatural because we don't understand the science or universal laws under which these events occur. In chapter 7, I described 12-year-old Marilyn's NDE vision of Jesus and Heaven caused by suffocation from a rope tangled around her neck, but her encounter with the Lord didn't end there. The rest of her story defies modern physics and the known laws of science. As Marilyn started to climb the basement stairs to have her mom help her untie a knotted rope, she felt herself fall down and slip into total darkness:

> *I felt someone pick me up in their arms and I was surrounded by Light and I looked in the smiling face of a man*

who said His name was Jesus. He told me not to be frightened. He was here to take me back.

He kissed my forehead, put His hand on the basement door, and said, 'You go back now child it's not your time.' The door opened and he stood me on the floor. I was not able to breath and was gulping in air. My mother and aunt came running and cut the rope off my neck.

My neck was all red and sore and my voice was all hoarse. My mother said how did you get up the stairs like that?

I said, 'I didn't. **The man carried me up.'**

And my mom and aunt said together, 'What man?'

My aunt yelled down stairs, 'Girls, is there a man down there?'

They all said, 'No. There was no man.'

I said, 'There was a man and he did carry me.'

They did not believe me. I went back down in the basement and asked my cousins and sister about the man which they did not see. My sister said she saw me fall and started to come help me, **but she said I disappeared when she got to the stairs. No one saw me being carried**. I had a big cut on my chin where I hit the bottom step when I went into complete blackness. Everyone saw me fall and disappear. No one saw me going up the stairs. [75]

Another supernatural event happened to Valerie, who relocated 8000 miles to Vietnam during a spontaneous OBE/NDE (See #6 of the Seven Near-Death Triggers Table 1, chapter 2):

It was January or February 1968. I was just at the doorway of my apartment, when suddenly I found myself walking in a thickly forested area. Looking around me I realized I was in a jungle following a small group of American soldiers. The two soldiers at the end of the line stopped and turned when I stumbled over a vine and helped me through a thickly wooded area. They did not seem surprised to see me (a civilian) there although they acknowledged my presence.

After walking a short distance with them, I realized I was in Vietnam. I talked with the soldiers quietly as we walked along. Then, I realized a very close friend of mine was the soldier in the lead. (He was the only soldier there I knew.) I excused myself from the companionship of the two soldiers walking with me and started to walk to the front of the line to talk to my friend. (This friend and I were very close in high school and I was glad to see him again.) As I neared the front of the line, another soldier grabbed my arm and restrained me just before I reached him. Just then we heard the click. My friend had stepped on a land mine. The force of the explosion threw me backward against a tree. I screamed as blood splattered my body.

The next instant found me again in the doorway of my apartment. I heard the sound of feet running as my friend and the two boys waiting for me came to see what had happened. They found me standing in the doorway with my hands braced against the door jam on each side. I had blood and dirt splattered on my clothes and face and my right shoulder was painfully swollen and turning black.

...I was wide-awake when it occurred. I was not taking any medication or on any kind of drugs and was not attempting to have any such experience.[76]

Marilyn's disappearance and reappearance as well as Valerie's spontaneous OBE/NDE thousands of miles distant in Vietnam and her return to her apartment with physical traces of blood and dirt on her clothes, reveal laws of teleportation that transcend known laws of time and space. There are many other amazing stories like this scattered in near-death research, and if one looks carefully, these accounts are also found in the New Testament and other religions and myths throughout history.

---

1 Cheryl L. Broyles 2012. *Life's Mountains*. Published with Create Space. Originally published with Xlibris in 2008
2 R.A. Moody Jr., M.D. 1977. *Life after Life*, Covington GA: Mockingbird Books.
3 R.A. Moody and P. Perry 1991. *Coming Back: A Psychiatrist Explores Past-Life Journeys*. New York: Bantam. p.11. See also, R.A. Moody and P. Perry 1988. *The Light Beyond*. New York: Bantam Books. p. 62.
4 Death Element comparison. See Table 2.
5 Tom M NDE, #3929, 04.17.15, NDERF.org
6 *Priscilla O's NDE*, #301, 07.16.03, NDERF.org
7 *Kathleen's NDE*, #213, 03.02.03, NDERF.org
8 *Kenneth F NDE*, #4046, 11.7.15, NDERF.org
9 *Sheba M NDE*, #2382, 09.27.10, NDERF.org
10 *Richard L's NDE*, #578, .03.05.05, NDERF.org
11 Jeffrey Long, M.D. 2010. Jeffrey Long, M.D. with Paul Perry 2010. *Evidence of the Afterlife: The Science of the Near-Death Experience*. New York: HarperCollins. p. 8.
12 *Michael F NDE*, #3949, 06.04.15, NDERF.org
13 *Walter C NDE*, #3199, 03.12.12, NDERF.org
14 Jeffrey Long, M.D. 2010. Jeffrey Long, M.D. with Paul Perry 2010. *Evidence of the Afterlife: The Science of the Near-Death Experience*. New York: HarperCollins. p. 17.
15 Ibid, p. 9.
16 Linda Stewart NDE, *God is Only Love*, #34, aleroy.com/boardh1.htm
17 Jeffrey Long, M.D. 2010. Jeffrey Long, M.D. with Paul Perry 2010. *Evidence of the Afterlife: The Science of the Near-Death Experience*. New York: HarperCollins. p. 13.
18 *Gillian NDE*, #3553, 01.05.14, NDERF.org
19 *Janet S' NDE*, #194, 12.23.02, NDERF.org

20 *Walter C NDE*, #3199, 03.12.12, NDERF.org
21 *Sylvia W's NDE*, #152, 07.30.02, NDERF.org
22 *Thomas M NDE*, #1890, 04.25.09, NDERF.org
23 *Walter C NDE*, #3199, 03.12.12, NDERF.org
24 Jeffrey Long, M.D. 2010. Jeffrey Long, M.D. with Paul Perry 2010. *Evidence of the Afterlife: The Science of the Near-Death Experience*. New York: HarperCollins. p. 8.
25 *Sue D NDE*, #2766, 07.10.11, NDERF.org
26 *Gillian NDE*, #3553, 01.05.14, NDERF.org
27 *Marta G NDE*, #2037, 12.06.09, NDERF.org
28 *Jeff probable NDE*, #2410, 10.10.10, NDERF.org
29 *Barbara E NDE,* # 2821, 09.10.11, NDERF.org
30 *Carmel B NDE's*, #1920, 05.30.09, NDERF.org
31 *Alan M NDE*, #1754, 11.28.08, NDERF.org
32 *Gillian NDE*, #3553, 01.05.14, NDERF.org
33 Henry Vaughan (1621-1695). Poem, *The Night*. John 2.3.
34 Eben Alexander 2012, *Proof of Heaven, A Neurosurgeon's Journey into the Afterlife*. New York: Simon and Schuster Paperbacks. p. 47.
35 *Shiela EP's NDE*, # 3027, 04.22.12, NDERF.org
36 *Priscilla O's NDE*, #301, 07.16.03, NDERF.org
37 Richard Sigmund 2004 & 2010. *My Time in Heaven: A True Story of Dying...And Coming Back*. New Kensington, PA: Whitaker House. p. 19.
38 *Raina Ji NDE*, #1967, 08.30.09, NDERF.org
39 *Terry D NDE,* #1256, 10.14.07, NDERF.org
40 *Barbara W NDE*, #2855, 10.05.11, NDERF.org
41 Jeffrey Long, M.D. 2010. Jeffrey Long, M.D. with Paul Perry 2010. *Evidence of the Afterlife: The Science of the Near-Death Experience*. New York: HarperCollins. p. 9.
42 *Alan M NDE*, #1754, 11.28.08, NDERF.org
43 *Isabel R NDE*, #2965, 02.25.12, NDERF.org
44 *Malla's possible NDE*, #3933, 04.27.15, NDEF.org
45 *Terri's NDE*. Unknown NDERF.org reference.
46 *Rhea D probable NDE*, #1254, 10.14.07, NDERF.org
47 George G. Ritchie, Jr., M.D., Ph.D., 1991. *My Life After Dying, Becoming Alive to Universal Love*. Hampton Roads Publishing. p. 24.
48 *Jill D NDE*, #2922, 12.31.11, NDERF.org
49 *Eugene W NDE*, #2383, 09.27.10, NDERF.org
50 http://www.ecology.com/birth-death-rates/
51 *Joseph S NDE*, #3289, 03.14.13, NDERF.org
52 *Raina Ji NDE*, #1967, 08.30.09, NDERF.org
53 Jeffrey Long, M.D. 2010. Jeffrey Long, M.D. with Paul Perry 2010. *Evidence of the Afterlife: The Science of the Near-Death Experience*. New York: HarperCollins. p. 15.
54 *Analia R probable* NDE, #3920, 04.01.15, NDERF.org
55 Jeffrey Long, M.D. 2010. Jeffrey Long, M.D. with Paul Perry 2010. *Evidence of the Afterlife: The Science of the Near-Death Experience*. New York: HarperCollins. p. 11.
56 *Tom A NDE*, #3929, 04.18.15, NDERF.org
57 Jeffrey Long, M.D. 2010. Jeffrey Long, M.D. with Paul Perry 2010. *Evidence of the Afterlife: The Science of the Near-Death Experience*. New York: HarperCollins. p. 10.
58 *Scott W NDE*, #3885, 02.15.15, NDERF.org
59 Samantha H NDE, #3329, 04.20.13, NDERF.org
60 *Robert N NDE's*, #3337, 01.05.16 & 05.05.13, NDERF.org
61 Jeffrey Long, M.D. 2010. Jeffrey Long, M.D. with Paul Perry 2010. *Evidence of the Afterlife: The Science of the Near-Death Experience*. New York: HarperCollins. pp. 15-16.
62 *Scott H NDE*, #2698, 05.02.11, NDERF.org
63 Jeffrey Long, M.D. 2010. Jeffrey Long, M.D. with Paul Perry 2010. *Evidence of the Afterlife: The Science of the Near-Death Experience*. New York: HarperCollins. p. 16.
64 *Gary D's NDE*, #742, 01.01.06, NDERF.org

65 *John S NDE*, # 1739, 11.01.08, NDERF.org
66 *Cherie J probable NDE*, #2686, 04.25.11, NDERF.org
67 *Riki E NDE*, #2955, 02.13.12, NDERF.org
68   Jeffrey Long, M.D. 2010. Jeffrey Long, M.D. with Paul Perry 2010. *Evidence of the Afterlife: The Science of the Near-Death Experience*. New York: HarperCollins. p. 17.
69 *Rick R NDE*, #1506, 01.13.08, NDERF.org
70 *Shalom G NDE*, #448, 08.09.04, NDERF.org
71 *Teri R NDE*, #2301, 08.10.10, NDERF.org
72 *Guisippi C NDE*, #2862, 10.16.11, NDERF.org
73 Based on an article by Mario Beauregard 2012. Near death, Explained. http://www.salon.com/2012/04/21/near_death_explained/
MARIO BEAUREGARD
74 Based on an article by Mario Beauregard 2012. Near death, Explained. http://www.salon.com/2012/04/21/near_death_explained/
MARIO BEAUREGARD
75 *Marilyn R NDE*, #2925, 01.08.12, NDERF.org
76 *Valerie K Experience*, #1230, 10.14.07, NDERF.org

14
Transformations

~*On December 9 2015, Delynn met, by chance, a stranger named "Jimmy" at a nearby restaurant. She struck up a conversation with him, talked about my book, and our need for a professional head shot for the back cover. Jimmy told her he was a photographer and so they quickly arranged a photo session for 10:00 am the next day at our home. When Jimmy arrived the following morning, he sat opposite from me and asked a few questions about what photos I would like best. During the short conversation, he revealed details about his mother's death six weeks earlier. He noticed I had a small collection of butterflies in our home and a Christmas butterfly ornament near the top of our Christmas tree. Both he and his mother loved butterflies.*

The moment was electric. It was almost as if our meeting were set up so his mother could let him know she was okay. In tears, he placed a candy cane on the Christmas tree, the last one of many placed there by friends and family. It was then he turned to me and said he had a farm in Nashville, Tennessee, called Zenbilly. The obvious divine message to each of us almost shook the room; how strange the Chronicles subtitle, A Zen Journey through the Christian Afterlife, would reflect his farm,

'Zenbilly.' He was an angel sent from God who took the perfect photograph to be used for my book... *~Chronicle 911*

The litmus test for both ancient and contemporary saintly near-death transformations is the absolute KNOWLEDGE of the immortality of the soul and the loss of the fear of death that occurs when the consciousness of the personality separates from the human body.

The transforming effects after a near-death rebirth of the Dead Saint include a far greater capacity to unconditionally love self and others, resulting in an increase in self-confidence. Material gains no longer are a concern. Anxiety levels are reduced as well as suicidal tendencies. There is a greater appreciation for nature and profound sense of connection to all things. The pursuit of knowledge often becomes a central focus in their lives. There is a new feeling of control over their lives because their NDE taught them the power and responsibility of free will. However, the knowledge comes with a sense of urgency to complete their mission—that they have much to do and so little time to do it in. Dead Saints may acquire spiritual gifts and even become interested in the paranormal. Finally, there is often a newfound love for the Being of Light they discovered while out of the body.

Differences apart, my research strongly suggests *all life transforming experiences* are characterized by exposure to a dazzling, unearthly Light, a Light perceived in varying degrees of brilliance and varying exposures and can be divided into four main categories.

#1: Born-Again Transformations: Old Life to New Life
#2: New Faith: Atheist to God-Believer
#3: Spiritual Upgrades & Supernatural Events
#4: Meta-Human[1]

#1: Born-Again Transformations: Old Life to New Life

~MRI at the Hampton VA Medical Center. 45 minutes of boredom. Hope the MRI shows my tumor continues to shrink. We have to a send a copy of the MRI disk to Duke University for the neuro-oncologist to review. And inspirational thought came up while my brain was being irradiated. The Apostle Paul wrote: "I protest by your rejoicing which I have in Christ Jesus our Lord, I die daily."[2] A statement which means to me: To truly live, I must die daily. I must be born-again daily. Why? As the Apostle said, "The good that I would, I do not, and the evil which I would not, I do.[3] ~Chronicle 197

There are two types of *born-again* transformations. One is triggered by an encounter with Christ while conscious and "in the body" and the other by a near-death experience. Both involve the transformation of the heart and a dramatic change in life and lifestyle. The traditional Christian born-again experience is described in John 3:1-7:

> *There was a man of the Pharisees named Nicodemus, a ruler of the Jews. This man came to Jesus by night and said to Him, "Rabbi, we know that You are a teacher come from God; for no one can do these signs that You do unless God is with Him." Jesus answered and said to him, "Most assuredly, I say to you, unless one is born again, he cannot see the kingdom of God." Nicodemus said to Him, "How can a man be born when he is old? Can he enter a second time into his mother's womb and be born?" Jesus answered, "Most assuredly, I say to you, unless one is born of water and the Spirit, he cannot enter the kingdom of God. That which is born of the flesh is flesh, and that which is born of the Spirit is spirit. Do not marvel that I said to you, 'You must be born again.'*

My wife, Delynn, describes a traditional Christian born-again experience she had on October 19, 1986, at the Hilltop Baptist Church in Norman, Oklahoma:

> *I was 21 when my daughter, Leah, was born I had felt a love like no other and felt helpless to know how to raise this newborn and knew I needed someone bigger and higher than myself. The only way I knew to find more about God was to find a church to go. I was not brought up in church so I began my search going to different denominational churches, including Baptist, Lutheran, Catholic, and non-denominational.*
>
> *One Sunday, I decided to attend a small country Baptist church in Oklahoma that was just down the road from my house. Toting my daughter along was difficult sometimes. I was nursing and she was needy. I was a new mom and felt scared to leave her with someone I didn't know. But I still wanted to go. So I took her to the nursery and wanted to nurse her before I went to the service, which I sensed the nursery workers were not happy with me. I felt awkward, but finally decided to leave her with them.*
>
> *Of course, by then I knew the worship service must be over, but I would at least go for a few minutes. When I walked in, there was a thick warm feeling of love in the room. People were singing and the evangelist, Bill Fitzhugh, was preaching. I couldn't hear exactly what people were singing or what he was saying, but my whole being was drawn to the front of the church where there was an altar to pray at. I wanted to KNOW Jesus. I wanted to know*

this love, this joy that was so full in the room. I went to the front and prayed. No one prayed with me, no one said a word. I felt a warmth and a love spread throughout my body like I had never felt before. It was very different from my love experience I had when my daughter was born or any other love.

There was no explaining it. I was changed. I wanted to sing of love, of hope, of strength. I wanted to rejoice constantly. I loved the love I felt. I loved everyone and wanted everyone to know the feeling I was feeling. Of course, my spirit was changed. I knew within myself that I was different. However, my habits were not all changed. I still wanted to do some of the things I knew were not productive for me. I struggled not to cuss. But daily, I wanted to know more about this God of love. Daily, I wanted to sing praises to the God who "set me free." I felt set free. What does that exactly mean? I only know I did not feel judged. I wasn't feeling confused. I wasn't feeling lost. I felt love for everyone around me. I wanted to make all things right with everything and everyone. I felt born-again. I felt NEW. I felt ALIVE. I felt joy unspeakable.

Though not brought up in church I did have a few encounters of sensing God, going to a church, and knowing of Jesus, but what was so different about this than how I felt when I was 7 or 12 or 15 or 20? I only know it was different. I only know it was not a fleeting moment of emotion, or remorse, or searching —it was FOUND. There is Scripture that states, 'It is the Holy Spirit that draws man unto Himself.' I believe this to be true. I believe He was drawing me for years, but until my spirit was totally ready to accept the beautiful gift of Love and Life everlasting, it would not hold.

When I read stories about people who have had NDEs, and how their lives were changed by their encounters with Love and Life, I recognize I felt the same way they did after they returned to life. I felt the whole world was a new place. I felt there was a great hope, and that there was beauty unspeakable. I didn't see Heaven or angels, but I wanted to sing and find more answers about my experience.

And I KNEW... I KNOW... Jesus is LOVE! He brought love to me and woke me up—my true BORN- AGAIN / near-death experience.

After a NDE, Dead Saints report after returning to the body, they feel like a newborn child:

Again I had thought, 'Is this what it is like to die? I thought I was going to see myself at my own funeral and actually be buried while I was in this state. Once again, I slipped into the darkness and felt so at peace with the darkness around me and actually saw the image of a hand through the darkness come at me and my soul turned around and I felt this hand push me away from behind. I truly believe this was my guardian angel. As I was turned away, I found I was falling back at the speed of light. I had re-entered my body and felt as if I was reborn again. My body was taking its first breath and I woke up in a state of shock gasping for air and kicking the paramedics around me. I felt as if my soul had given my body life once again. [4]

Stephanie also felt like a newborn child after her NDE:

All I knew was I know we have the knowledge we don't die and that there is a wonderful peace and knowing when we do. I was distraught and it took me nearly two years to want to live as all I wanted to do was die and couldn't understand why they had sent me back. When I left the hospital, it was amazing I was like a newborn child I could see and feel colors in everything (and even see molecular structures of plants and things). Everything seemed to be vibrating on a different frequency. [5]

Diane who died from cardiac arrest describes death itself as a born-again experience:

I understood death was really a transitional birth. As a baby is born from the mother's womb, it actually has died to its previous life in her womb—the life of water into the life of air. When we die to Earth, we are born-again, this time into the life from whence we originally came. I have a peace most humans do not over death, because I know that is what Christ meant by the words: 'Unless you are born again, you cannot enter into the Kingdom of Heaven.' It has nothing to do with the meaning religion has given it at all. It means it is something we all must do. [6]

From both Christian and Dead Saint experiences, we can easily interpret three meanings to the born-again parable. The first is a spiritual transformation of the heart by the love of Christ. The second is the birth process into the Afterlife when we die. The third is the process of returning to the physical body, after death.

Near-death experiences create a change of the heart and life as well, and are identical in many ways to the traditional Christian born-again experience. Dan, who died in jail of heart failure, describes his life transforming NDE:

> *How does a guy go from a hopeless drug addict to managing a retirement residence, often sitting with and comforting the dying? From being nearly homeless and broke, to running one of God's Homes? I still cannot fathom the amazing transforming power of my NDE. I have not desired drugs or drink since. I do not desire to lie, cheat, or steal. I only desire to live a life of surrender and service to God. I once thought all these things were hogwash. I now spend countless hours reading the word, spiritual books, and meditating. I don't fully understand the implications of this event. I do know my life is defined as-before and after my NDE. It is a mystery.*[7]

Theresa was living with a man who she says was extremely evil. She felt her relationships and her addiction to drugs were killing her. She prayed for God to help her change and give her direction:

> *I admitted myself into St. Joseph Hospital in Marshfield, Wisconsin for medical help withdrawing off Vicodin. Almost immediately, as the Doctor was going to inject some medication to start the withdrawal, I felt a rectangular pain form across my chest. For about a second I thought, wow does pneumonia show up this fast. At that same moment, I said aloud, 'I can't breathe out.' Then, total blackness. I died.*
>
> *I have no recollection of what occurred in that room when I went unconscious. All of the sudden I was surrounded by pure, bright, brilliant, Heaven white. It was white, but not earthly white. Seriously, there are no words that can explain the beauty of colors in Heaven...It was amazing and beautiful. My Savior answered and gave me knowledge that gave me peace about every single thing that had happened to me. Everything. However, He didn't allow me to come back with all of what He revealed to me. What He did is He sent me back with peace in my spirit.*
>
> *Bondages gone. I am a brand new person on the inside. I have been set completely free of my past. I truly believe He knew I was on a one-way ticket to Hell, and because of me crying out to Him, he answered my prayers! That is how much He loves us.*
>
> *I do remember when I woke up. I had scabs under my nose from oxygen. There was a nurse in there that acted surprised that I woke up. The first words she said was, 'You had quite a rough time. You were a very sick girl.'*
>
> *...I did eventually leave the hospital with what I believe a second chance on life. I felt like a brand new baby. Everything felt brand new. My insides were as clean as a whistle.*

When I was with Jesus, I felt more alive than I ever, ever felt on Earth. I remember thinking, I wonder if we are in a sleepwalking awareness level on Earth. Once again, I don't have the correct words to tell you of the alert level...it's simply amazing. The communication between my Savior and myself was all telepathic. I was shooting off questions about my childhood and every bad thing that happened to me. The Lord was coming back with answers that I fully understood and was at complete and utter peace with what He was telling me.[8]

Delynn and I can attest that the manifestation of the Holy Spirit, whether caused by the Spirit of Christ within or the presence of Jesus, can *strike like lightning anytime*. The prevailing Christian belief is you have to be "saved" to experience the movement of the Holy Spirit. Atheists, agnostics, the "unbaptized" and "unsaved" Dead Saints have experienced the Holy Spirit during their near-death encounters with the Being of Light.

The Dead Saints, regardless of their faith, return to life feeling born-again.

#2 New Faith: Atheist to God-Believer

The transformation of an atheist or agnostic into a believer in God, Christ, or a higher power takes more than words or debate. I know. I've tried. In early September 1999, my friend Keith and I were winding our way down coastal highway 101 on the Oregon Coast in our green Altima, enjoying the smell of sea spray from the Pacific Ocean and the majestic view of vertical dolmen rocks rising out of foamy surf. We rolled slowly through every small town looking for antique shops. Keith loved to carefully and painfully investigate them. Our "sideways" trip gave us the opportunity to get to know each other a little better.

He came down to visit us every year from Canada, usually to visit Anna and the kids, because he was their official godfather—a term a bit misplaced for him since he was an avid atheist who did not believe in God or the Afterlife. He was a good-hearted man, but also a man filled with the fear of death. Our conversations inevitably turned spiritual because I was always trying to 'convert' him over to the God side of life.

He would constantly grin at me as if I were the crazy one that having a belief in God was irrational and delusional. I said, "What about those who have come back from the Afterlife?"

He asked, "What proof?"

At that time, I had only casually read a few books about near-death experiences. I brought up several NDEs I could remember that suggested out-of-body experiences were proof of the separation of consciousness. He rejected these too. To him, they were brain-hallucinations, part of the dying process, a gimmick, a trick of the dying mind. We actually got into a big argument, yelling back and forth. It was clear he would never consider the evidence. After the heated exchange, I realized even an Atheist believes in his Atheist faith 100%.

Keith, I have you in mind. I hope years of research and my own experiences, along with convincing testimonies from the Dead Saints, will offer a preponderance of evidence and a glimmer of light that you may perceive in order to lead you to consider the existence of God and reality of Christ. The following Dead Saint testimonials are for you.

Atheist & Agnostic NDEs

Michael Joseph was an atheist who, in his youth, rejected Jesus and all religion. When a 500-pound boulder fell on him and crushed his "biological unit," he found himself in Heaven having a frank conversation with Jesus:

Then it hit me like a ton of bricks. I was DEAD and yet here I was, still alive and fully conscious. How could that be? In that instance, my atheism was wiped away and now I didn't know what to expect. I panicked. I WAS DEAD! Dad was REALLY going to get pissed at me for killing myself. And then the panic went out of the roof when I realized I WAS DEAD!!!!! Dad isn't going to get pissed at me. I'm DEAD! DEEEAAAADDDD!!!! Oh my God, what is going to happen to me?!!! Because I've rejected Jesus, I'm going to Hell! I'm in DEEP DOO DOO! Maybe I shouldn't have been so hasty in rejecting religion. Maybe I should have listened more. Then all that panic was pushed out of me. I can only use the analogy of being bone shivering cold and standing in front of a nice warm fire. All that shivering and cold slowly gets pushed out of you and all your muscles relax as the fire's warmth fills you. I felt this "fire" coming from behind me and I whirled around to see a man with black wavy hair and a black beard, all short cropped and dark well-tanned skin. His eyes were like diamonds sparkling under Light and his robe was like a monk's robe except it was bright white and glowing. I could see it flowing around him with visible eddies and currents. This Being smiled at me and I was instantly filled with love, so much love I felt I would explode from it. I could not contain it. I've never felt so adored. This Being communicated directly with me with thoughts, no words were ever used.

I ended up with a Life Review, and was escorted around "the other side" by a being who was my guardian angel/teacher whom I came to call "professor" but he had an incredible sense of humor. I say "he" with tongue in cheek because "he" was neither a he or a she. I saw what happened to true atheists (apparently I was opened minded enough that I didn't qualify). I got to see various "heavens" and asked to see what "Hell" was like if there was one (and there was, but it was nothing like I expected). I even asked to meet Jesus and apologize only to meet a Man who was nothing like I expected, and was given interesting historical facts I was later able to verify. [9]

Chamisa, an Agnostic before her NDE, admitted her life was changed upon her rebirth into life:

I was in an accident, hemorrhaging badly, and vomiting blood. Taken to surgery, I suddenly became aware of slipping out of my body from my feet through the top of my head as if I were the inside of a Concord grape, and pancaked above the surgical site, as my spirit got out of the way of my body. I could feel this process happen. I watched everything that was going on in a completely detached mode. The tools looked like a carpenter's shop.

I heard the music, the buzz of saws, and I could read the minds and futures of the people there including my own. I saw the reason for my life and what I needed to work out. Physically speaking, I saw through walls. My husband was home chopping wood, red roses waiting in my patient room from my sister in Alaska and my kids were in school and I knew what they were doing. I could instantly read the minds of those in the surgery room and what they would do next. I also knew one of the physicians had cancer and didn't know it. He would die the following year (and did). The other was having a Romeo and Juliet affair that would end up badly (and did). I was in the middle of some kind of hologram. I noticed all my feelings, emotions, personality and knowledge were still with me, and that I carried a large amount of anger toward certain people, especially my parents and the religion they used against me. I'd been an agnostic for years.

Then once having this experience during surgery in an out of my body state, I suddenly observed a Being of Light instantly entering this holographic space and when He came, I was washed with a flood of love and forgiveness for everyone and everything. I even loved the Earth and all its beauty and the animals on the

Earth and "felt" the spiritual process we are all in, and how we are literally tied together as brothers and sisters needing to be unified in love and care.

This experience totally changed my life and the direction of my life.[10]

#3: Spiritual Upgrades

Dead Saints occasionally experience an upgrade in their spiritual abilities after their NDE. One astounding experience occurred at the Fellowship's Joy in Worship service on August 10, 2014.[11] Dr. Mary Hensley was the guest speaker, visiting from Ireland for the first time. I briefly talked with her for a few minutes in the Fellowship foyer, and then she walked into the Sanctuary, took her place at the podium, and began her sermon.

Mary described her near-death experience. It occurred in 1991 when she was only 21. She was hit broadside at 75 mph, her car torn in half. She broke her neck, her spine, broke her ribs, and detached her retina. Then she died-for nearly thirty minutes. During that time, she visited Heaven and came back with some astonishing abilities. Mary disclosed she often saw "dead people" as a youth growing up, but her abilities were given a spiritual "upgrade" after her near-death experience.

During her talk, she described our meeting in the foyer:

"Something happened to me when I talked to one of your pastors, David Solomon. When I entered the doorway, I noticed in a little alcove, some pictures. I remarked to my friend with me and pointed at one of the pictures, 'Oh, I met that man yesterday.' [Pointing to a picture of Paul Solomon]

"No, you didn't."

I said, "Oh, yes I did!"

"Uh, he is not with us anymore."

I nodded, "Oh, yes he is!"

Mary recalled, "This happened to me yesterday when I spoke at Edgar Cayce's ARE. That man walked up to me, hugged me, and said, 'Thank you,' and today thanked me again for Sunday Service. The man I met yesterday was the same man who is here today--Paul Solomon."

Mary went on, "Before the service, David and I were talking about his cancer and death like passing over the toast I ate this morning with butter jam."

She said, "His candor about death is uncommon. Nobody wants to talk about it. We have forgotten as human beings that death is so much a part of the natural process of life."

It was then she realized, "Ahhhh, this is why I had that experience with Paul Solomon and why I am here."

Mary went on, "But what was really interesting is when I met David, I realized why I do what I do. I have dedicated my life to this. This is why I agreed to come back after my near-death experience. Others have asked me, "Aren't you taking all this a bit too seriously?"

"I died. I agreed to come back and do this. Yes, I take it seriously!"

Those who have died and returned often have the experience of having the veil between Heaven and Earth permanently torn, which gives them spiritual, psychic, and prophetic abilities unavailable to the average person. In Mary's case, often there appears to be no difference between seeing the living and the dead, giving her the ability to communicate with those in spirit.

While some of us "average" humans demonstrate the ability to read thoughts, experience after death communications, the Dead Saints who return from the Afterlife, describe increased spiritual abilities of healing, prescient visions such as the birth of children, including their name and genders, received during their NDE.

Healing Gifts

Some Dead Saints come back with profound healing gifts. On June 24, 2014, I met Nigel Mumford,[12] an Episcopalian priest living in Virginia Beach. I was there for a laying on of hands healing session. Before we began, he asked me to talk about my cancer. That's when I told him about the *Chronicles* and my near-death research. His eyes popped open and his mouth dropped. He then told me about two near-death experiences, which changed his life: One from a traumatic injury on the battlefield in 1975 and the other in 2009 from a life-threatening infection. During Nigel's last NDE, he was very close to taking his last breath. The last rites were read. Then, without warning, he began breathing, and he miraculously recovered. It was after his recovery that he discovered his healing abilities had been "upgraded."

We couldn't stop talking. It was as if we were long-lost friends who just had met in this life, but now out of my necessity for healing, here we were. Nigel gave me a healing cloth to apply to my medications, basing it on the ACTS of Peter, where his followers used healing cloths touched by Saint Peter for healing. It has been suggested Peter used the blood on the Sudarium of Christ (burial head cloth) from the crucifixion, as a turban wrapped around his head when he performed healings.

I believe the miracle of my long-term survival is due to his healing prayers, a gift he credits to Christ, who resurrected him from death.

~Update: Delynn and I visited Galilee Church to see Nigel for another laying on of hands healing session on December 17, 2015. Nigel and his wife Lynn had seen us a few weeks earlier on December 5 at our annual Solomon Christmas party where he discovered my brain tumor had dramatically increased in size. My prognosis was grim. We entered his quaint office in the church, filled with photos from his healing ministry travels around the world, served as a heavenly reminder of this man's great faith in the power of God to heal anything. Before we began the healing session, he opened a small box containing a silver wine cup, wine and bread sacraments for serving Holy Eucharist.

He brought out a colorful ceramic plate of Loaves and Fishes I recognized immediately depicting the tiled mosaic floor of The Church of the Multiplication of the Loaves and Fishes in Tabgha, near the Sea of Galilee in Israel—the same identical plate I had brought back from my tour there in 1993. By chance, today also happened to be Nigel's tenth anniversary since the Episcopalian Church ordained him. Strange coincidences aside, from there, we proceeded with communion and he laid his hands on me, commanding the brain tumor to wither and die, just as Christ commanded the fig tree to wither when it provided the Lord with no fruit. Before we left, he suggested I begin a practice daily of placing a Bible over my head in the manner used by St. Barnabas—a healing method depicted in a 1566 painting by Paolo Veronese.
~Chronicle 938

Seeing the Future

Other Saints have the ability to see the future. We briefly touched upon these prophetic gifts in chapter 6, where premonitions come through dreams. In this section, the gift of prophecy comes via a near-death experience.

There are several instances which Dead Saint visions of the future are later fulfilled. Nearly all are personal prophecies about children yet to be born or family members who will die at some time in the future. One such experience was aired on the CNN special, Anderson Cooper 360. Mary Neil, a Wyoming surgeon, drowned in a kayak accident in 1999 on a remote river in southern Chile. Trapped underwater for nearly 30 minutes, she had a remarkable NDE where she describes meeting Jesus. Sitting on a rock, they had a "chat" about returning to Earth to help her husband. During the conversation, Jesus reveals her eldest son will die young. The prophecy was sadly fulfilled ten years later when Mary's son died unexpectedly in a hit and run roadside accident.

While rare, some Dead Saints receive visions of the future on a global scale. Dannion Brinkley in his 1994 New York Times Best Seller, *Saved by the Light,*[13] describes receiving 114 visions of the future during his NDE, which to date, more than 95 appear to have been fulfilled.

My Research has uncovered twenty-five Dead Saint prophecies of the future on a planetary-scale. Repeatedly, the Saints describe something BIG coming soon. They hint decisions made by each of us during the near future are crucial to either a "planet-wide" destruction of our cities and populations, or a gentler transition toward a more "peaceful" planet, heralding a new era, a New Heaven and New Earth. Can we escape the birth of the New Jerusalem and new age unscathed? Will millions perish in a destructive major event? The future they describe, along with ancient prophecies found in the Bible and ancient myths, are reserved for the telling in Book 3 of *The Dead Saints Chronicles, the Armageddon Stones.*

#4: The Meta-Human

*~Those who have had a mystical experience have dropped the scales of darkness that prevent true sight. In that moment, the Saint cries out to God, "I don't know who you are, but I want to get to know you in this moment!" Is the mystical experience triggered by a dark night of the soul? Do we have to get THAT emotional to see the LIGHT? ~****Chronicle 332***

Transformation of the soul by an encounter with a Being of Light sometimes takes a dramatic leap, such as a transcendent Saul to Paul type conversion. This 'mystical-death experience' often eclipses the average spiritual upgrade reported by many Dead Saints, causing the greatest of spiritual transformations. Paul Solomon coined the term *Meta-Human* to describe this type of transformation of the physical mind and heart into the Mind and Heart of Christ.

The Old Testament describes several Meta-Humans who encounter a Light that triggered their transformation. Moses, the Lawgiver of Israel describes his mountain top encounter with a great Light and subsequent metamorphosis in the Sinai desert as if it were a near-death like experience (Exodus 3:2):

And the angel of the Lord appeared unto him in a flame of fire out of the midst of a bush: and he looked, and, behold, the bush burned with fire, and the bush was not consumed.

Hebrew scribes use words such as 'light and flames" to symbolically represent God to describe Moses' startling encounter at the summit of Mt. Horeb (a sacred mountain metaphor). Dead Saints have described this Light as a burning Light, or a great fire they understood to be God:

Well, GOD was there. Or more accurately, a great Fire (Burning Bush) or Light that I was to understand 'represented' or 'stood for' God. (But, in a way, it WAS REALLY God—-this can't be explained, and I sensed it as a paradox, something I just had to accept. It really wasn't an issue, as there was no 'intellectualizing', just raw, naked experience of the Presence of God.[14]

Descriptions of Moses' transformation include "sacredness" described in Exodus 3:2-5, "Do not come near; put off your shoes from your feet, for the place on which you are standing is holy ground." In Exodus 34:30—when Moses came down from the mountain there was a halo of Light around his face:

And when Aaron and all the people of Israel saw Moses, behold, the skin of his face shone.

Following his transformation of heart and mind, Moses reached a higher level of consciousness enabling his renowned supernatural Meta-Human abilities. Forever dramatized by Cecil B. DeMille's, *The Ten Commandments,* Moses became a leader of the Jewish people that changed history.

Biblical Patriarchs, Noah and Enoch, "walked with God" exemplifying this quality of Mind. Jacob dreamed of a ladder set up on the Earth, with angels ascending and descending from Heaven and with the Lord standing above it. (Genesis 28:12-13)

The Apostle Paul in Romans 12:2 also describes the Meta-Human transformation:

And be not conformed to this world: but be ye transformed by the renewing of your mind, that ye may prove what is good, and acceptable, and the perfect will of God.

When the Apostle Paul exhorted us to renew our minds by learning to think with the Higher Mind, the Mind of Christ, rather than our animal brains, he was teaching us about changing our thoughts—how we think and what we say to ourselves—our self-talk. If we learn to plant new seed thoughts of love and forgiveness, rather than anger, doubt and hate, we can begin to transform our minds.

Dead Saints who have encountered the Being of Light, or Jesus Christ, sometimes exhibit qualities and wisdom that make world-changing differences to religion and philosophy in modern times. Both have one common element in their biographies: a mystical-death experience without physical death or physical injury. What makes each of these individuals unique is their initial encounter with the Light, which not only created a superior enhancement of the mind, but also continued to transform their thinking and consciousness, confidence and supernatural abilities, until their eventual physical death.

Paul Solomon (1939-1994)

The son of a Southern Baptist minister, Paul Solomon (born William Bilo Dove), grew up into a family where the ministry was the assumed career. Growing up, he watched his parents seek guidance daily and noted they based decisions on the silent replies they received. God was accessible; the Holy Spirit was an active participant in their everyday lives.

In his childhood, Paul exhibited uncommon abilities that set him apart from the rest of the kids in school. He saw colors around people. He called them "good lights" and "bad lights," depending on how he perceived the individual. He knew what people were thinking and learned early on that most people think one thing and say the opposite. He also knew about events beforehand: He could predict the future, which frustrated and undermined his attempt to be "like everyone else." He could read books just by placing them over his solar plexus.

When he was 12, Paul had a born-again experience during an emotional church prayer meeting at his house. As he recalls:

> *The prayer meeting was going on in our living room and these prayer meetings were something the likes of which you've never encountered. These were all Southern Baptist seminary students, all of them were fiery preacher types who were very serious about what they were doing. They would gather together in our living room and as they would pray, they would get louder and they would get more emotional. They began crying and shouting, laughing and crying at the same time. And the atmosphere became so electric that even in my room, in the dark, without any lights on, I could see, just as clear as day, which terrified me because I was feeling out of sorts with this Presence they were praying to.*

> *So this one night it got so intense, I couldn't stand it. I was crying and I was saying to God, 'I don't want to be alienated from YOU. I want to have a right relationship. I want to be the right kind of person. I don't know what I want, but something's got to happen.' And while I was doing that crying out, it was as if I went to sleep. I know now I didn't fall asleep, but there was a bridge in consciousness where suddenly my bedroom wasn't there. I was out in an open field walking along a road. The field looked as if it had just rained. Everything was fresh and there was this enormous Light that came on the horizon. Then a BEING bigger than the world itself was on that horizon and reaching out to me...and suddenly something inside of me clicked and I ran toward that Being saying, 'You're mine!*
>
> *I recognized God belonged to me from that moment.*
>
> *'YOU'RE MY GOD! I shouted screaming at the top of my lungs.'*
>
> *Suddenly I woke up. I wasn't in the field anymore. I was in my bedroom and I realized I had been screaming at the top of my lungs and I wondered how I was going to explain this to everybody in the house who I thought would rush into the bedroom.*
>
> *Except that didn't happen. My brother was asleep in the next bed and he didn't even hear it, so it didn't affect anybody but me. I sort of sat there going through the experience for a little while until I fell asleep. The next morning, I woke up with an awareness that there was a different relationship between me and my Source and the Universe, and there has never been a time from that moment until this one that I have felt unacceptable or separated from my Source, from God.*

At 14, Paul was ordained. He began his pastoral tasks by ministering to the incarcerated and their families as the youngest Baptist Minister in the Arkansas Prison system. 21 years later in 1972, Paul Solomon had another near-death experience triggered by a hypnosis experiment. His only recollection of the hypnosis session upon awaking was a dream, containing many classic Death Elements:

> *I am approaching the entrance to a tunnel. It is similar to the mouth of a cornucopia because it seems to spiral inward and upward. I can see two figures at the opening. They seem to be waiting for me. One is Merle who was my girlfriend in high school until she died in our senior year. The other is my young friend, Jaida, who remained my secret companion for years following his death when we were seven. They each take me by the hand and lead me through the tunnel. We come out the other side onto a*

grassy hill. As we begin to climb, I see that we are approaching a temple at the top of the hill...The two figures are waiting to take me through the tunnel. As I come out the other side, I find myself in a meadow of wild flowers where a soft breeze blows, and I can hear the sound of a brook. Ahead of me is a mountain. As I climb, I pass through seven-terraced gardens of glorious color. At the top, I enter a temple. The air is rich with music, though I see no one. I see rows and rows of books with names on the bindings. I am in an enormous library.[15]

The encounter with "the Source" as he would later call it, was for Paul Solomon, a life-transforming experience. He found what had begun by accident, he could later duplicate at will. He gave more than 1400 "Source readings" during his lifetime, and later his lectures and classes became the catalyst for a worldwide ministry, before his death on March 4, 1994. (Story expanded in Book II of the *Chronicles, Training Wires of the Soul*)

Edgar Cayce (1877-1945)

Edgar Cayce has been called the "sleeping prophet," the "father of holistic medicine," and the most documented psychic of the 20th century. For more than 40 years of his adult life, Cayce gave over 14,000 psychic "readings" while in an unconscious state, diagnosing illnesses and answering questions about life both ancient and modern. Edgar Cayce's life and work are explored in the classic books, *There Is a River* (1942), by Thomas Sugrue, and Jess Stearn's, *The Sleeping Prophet. (1967)*

Edgar Cayce was a devoted churchgoer and Sunday school teacher. At a young age, Cayce vowed to read the Bible for every year of his life, which he did until the time of his death in 1945.

What is less known about Edgar Cayce is he may have had a near-death experience during his childhood that may have precipitated the onset of his unusual abilities. In 1944, Edgar Cayce told Harmon Bro, a graduate student who was writing a dissertation about Cayce for his graduate studies, that he discovered he had drowned as a young child. Bro, author of, *A Seer out of Season*, writes of Edgar: "He told of how he had drowned while fishing and been pronounced dead in his youth." [16]

Apparently, a hired man passing by pulled him out of a fishing hole and applied simple resuscitation skills that were generally known and brought the boy back to life. The hired man loaded Edgar on a wagon and took him back to his mother. Harmon wrote Edgar's mother was frightened when she heard what had happened and "what he had seen" when he drowned.

The most reasonable conclusion is Edgar Cayce had a near-death experience. After his drowning accident, Cayce demonstrated unusual psychic abilities. He was able to see and talk to his late grandfather's spirit, and often played with "imaginary friends" whom he said were spirits on the other side. He also displayed an uncanny ability to memorize the pages of a book simply by sleeping on it. These gifts labeled the young Cayce as strange, but all Cayce really wanted was to help others, especially children.

Cayce accidentally discovered more about his unusual abilities during a hypnosis experiment in 1901, when he was 24. He had lost his voice due to a cold, and for about a year, he could only speak in rasping whispers. A friend suggested Cayce try hypnosis as a means of helping his condition. The experiment proved to be more than successful. Cayce went into a deep trance and described the condition in his vocal cords, advising, strangely enough, what to do for it. The hypnotist followed the advice—that of suggesting the blood circulation increase to the affected area —and when Cayce awakened he had regained his normal speaking voice. After a number of follow-up sessions, the cure turned out to be a permanent one. He discovered he had the ability to put himself into a sleep-like near-death state by lying down on a couch, closing his eyes, and folding his hands over his stomach.

Cayce's description of going into a hypnotic trance is nearly identical to what has been described in near-death experiences, also containing many Death Elements. Here's a verbatim account of Cayce's waking description of his journey in the trance state, taken from comments he made at a public lecture:

> *I see myself as a tiny dot out of my physical body, which lies inert before me. I find myself oppressed by darkness and there is a feeling of terrific loneliness. Suddenly, I am conscious of a white beam of Light, knowing that I must follow it or be lost.*
>
> *...As I move along this path of Light I gradually become conscious of various levels upon which there is movement. Upon the first levels there are vague, horrible shapes, grotesque forms such as one sees in nightmares. Passing on, there begins to appear on either side misshapen forms of human beings with some part of the body magnified. Again there is change and I become conscious of gray-hooded forms moving downward. Gradually, these become lighter in color.*
>
> *...Then the direction changes and these forms move upward and the color of the robes grows rapidly lighter. Next, there begins to appear on either side vague outlines of houses, walls, trees, etc., but everything is motionless. As I pass on, there is more Light and*

movement in what appear to be normal cities and towns. With the growth of movement, I become conscious of sounds, at first indistinct rumblings, then music, laughter, and singing of birds. There is more and more, Light. The colors become very beautiful, and there is the sound of wonderful music. The houses are left behind; ahead there is only a blending of sound and color. Quite suddenly, I come upon a hall of records. It is a hall without walls, without ceiling, but I am conscious of seeing an old man who hands me a large book, a record of the individual for whom I seek information.[17]

We discussed in this chapter four levels of personal metamorphosis caused by near-death experiences: Born-Again (Old life to New Life), New Faith (Atheist to God-Believer), Spiritual Upgrades and Meta-Human. As we see throughout the *Chronicles*, there are seven valid ways to experience a spiritual transformation of the heart and mind. It's not how you arrive; the goal is just to get there! And you don't need to physically die to do it!

---

1 *Meta-human* is a term coined by Paul Solomon. Also see Paul Solomon 1985. *The Meta-Human, Twice-Born*. Reprinted 2003, Ireland, UK. Paul Solomon Foundation.
2 I Corinthians 15:31
3 Romans 7:19
4 *Jeana B NDE*, #1407,10.17.07, NDERF.org
5 *Stephanie S NDE*, #1417, 10.17.07, NDERF.org
6 *Diane C NDE*, #1369, 12.14.07, NDERF.org
7 P.M.H. Atwater 2007. *The Big Book of Near-Death Experiences*. Charlottesville, VA: Hampton Roads Publishing Co. p. 86.
8 *Theresa C NDE*, #2343, 09.13.10, NDERF.org
9 *Michael Joseph NDE*, #3700, 06.09.14, NDERF.org
10 *Chamisa H NDE*, #2170, 02.25.10, NDERF.org
11 Dr. Mary Hensley, August 10, 2014. Sermon at the Fellowship of the Inner Light. Excerpts taken from You Tube. https://www.youtube.com/watch?v=nbVIp2qq2QQ

12 Notes: Nigel Mumford's conviction to pray for healing came in 1989 when his sister, Julie Sheldon, a ballet dancer with the Royal Ballet in London, was healed by God through the late Canon Jim Glennon. Julie had a very dramatic healing from Dystonia, a severe neurological condition that curled her up into a fetal position and left her very close to death. Nigel and his wife Lynn, were privileged to be a part of creating the healing ministry there for 9 1/2 years. Nigel has relocated his ministry of healing from CT and upstate NY to Virginia Beach.
13 Dannion Brinkley and Paul Perry 1994. *Saved by the Light: The true story of a man who died twice and the profound revelations he received*. New York: Villard Books.
14 *Krikrikit's NDE,* #911, 07.23.06, NDERF.org
15 Paul Solomon Source Reading Excerpt, February 15, 1972. Ireland, UK. Paul Solomon Foundation.
16 Neil Helm, M.A., Scholar in Residence, Atlantic University, 1989. *Did Edgar Cayce Have a Near-Death Experience?* p.426.
17 http://www.neardeathsite.com/cayce9.php

15

You Do Not Die Alone

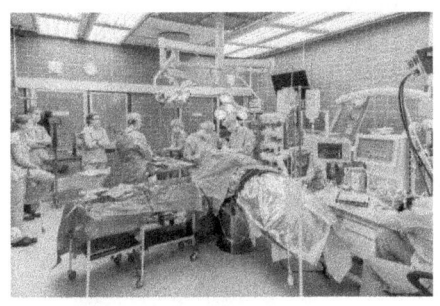

~Dream: While staying overnight near Duke University, I dreamed of receiving a call from an old girlfriend who is still alive. We touch hands palm to palm to symbolically say 'goodbye.' The following morning, Delynn and I received disappointing news. My brain tumor had more than doubled in size from 11mm to 24mm and there were no real treatment options for which I was willing to subject myself. Driving back from Duke to Virginia Beach with a heavy heart, I received a phone call from Kerry, an ex-employee from my company, Fast Transact. I hadn't heard from him in four years. Kerry, hearing about my terminal cancer situation, called to walk me through the "Sinners Prayer." Although I am at peace with my salvation, his call was perfectly timed because I had been debating whether to add a section at the end of chapter 23, called Salvation and Grace. Thank you Kerry for your love and listening to God. I heard you and I thank you. One more wonder ended the day on December 1, 2015: The www.deadsaintschronicles.com website **went live** at 4pm. (*www.deadsaints.org* went live February 2, 2016) *~Chronicle 905*

The hospital room quietly buzzes with oxygen white noise and the droning beep of heart monitors monitoring Grandma. Her daughter has dozed off, but suddenly awakens, and in the dim morning, light notices a figure standing near the dying person. Startled and frightened, they are frozen in awe. Grandma sees the outline of a woman standing at the end of the bed. A smile sweeps over her face in the last few moments of her life. She whispers to her daughter, "It's all true!" and then dies.

That moment of clarity, just before death, is a well-known phenomenon described in Chinese tradition called *Hui Guang Fan Zhao* (*The Light returns*) [1] This is a commonly reported situation where a dying patient would be comatose or confused, but suddenly becomes alert and lucid, often acknowledging loved ones around him/her before dying.

Steve Jobs, co-founder of Apple Computer, passed away in 2011. Just before his passing, his sister reported that, in his last moments, he looked beyond everyone else in the room, and then said, with feeling, "O Wow! O Wow. O Wow," before he died.[2]

My wife's mother Barbara awoke out of her coma, on July 28, Delynn's birthday. With her eyes closed, she said, "I love you." They were her mother's last words before dying a week later. Deathbed visions used to be relatively common because our loved ones died at home. With the advent of modern medicine, many people die heavily sedated in the hospital, with family often separated from the moment of death.

Hospice Care

Many families today, rather than deciding on an institutional setting, are choosing to care for the dying in their own homes with the help of Hospice. Typically, Hospice nurses are called in between six months and six weeks before death. Hospice nurses not only help with medication, but also assist with body washing and showers, and typically work with a Hospice Chaplain who may also visit on a regular schedule.

Depending on the situation, the Hospice nurse will visit your home once or twice a week to check on heartrate, blood pressure, and the rate at which pain or nausea medication is given. As death approaches, they may begin visiting daily to monitor the proper application of pain medication which is usually administered by the caregiver via dropper into the mouth at .5ml every 2-8 hours as needed to keep the patient comfortable.

Hospice is available in most cities throughout the United States. Dannion Brinkley founded the "The Twilight Brigade" one of the largest end-of-life care communities operating as an independent agency within VA hospitals and hospice care facilities across America. It has approximately 5,500 volunteers nationwide that are dedicated to being at the bedside of our nation's dying, especially Veterans.

His motto: "No one need ever to die alone." [3]

End-of-Life / Near-Death Awareness
Dying touches friends, neighbors, coworkers and family, like ripples created when a stone is dropped into a pond. Friends and family begin pouring in to say goodbye. The dying ARE THERE to teach us the ropes about death.

Maggie Callahan, a former hospice nurse, in her excellent book, *Final Gifts*, coined the term **"Near-Death Awareness"** to describe end-of-life observations of dying patients in the few weeks or months preceding death. During this period, a person may have "visions of deceased family or spiritual beings, although they don't necessarily signal death's imminence."[4]

According to Callahan, "It's not uncommon for an onlooker, however wellmeaning, to speak of a dying person as 'out of it' or 'losing it' or 'not quite right anymore.'"[5] Doctors and health-care workers may label these ramblings as "confusion" or "hallucinations." Furthermore, Callahan states, "Family members and caregivers may dismiss what they're hearing as a dying person's dreams and memories. The dreams of a dying person may contain powerful messages. They may describe the dream by saying, "I had a dream, but it wasn't really a dream." [6]

She relates how the dying slip in and out of consciousness, but when awake sometimes recall the grandeur of Heaven:

> *The experience of dying frequently includes glimpses of another world and those waiting in it. Although they provide few details, dying people speak with awe and wonder of the peace and beauty they see in this other place. They tell of talking with, or sensing the presence of, people who we cannot see—perhaps people they have known and loved. They know, often without being told, that they are dying, and may even tell us when their deaths may occur.*[7]

Heidi Telpner, R.N., author of *One Foot in Heaven, Journey of a Hospice Nurse*, describes one patient who had been a flyer in World War II, "I frequently saw and spoke with many of the men from his squadron in his final days." She found it interesting that as they approached death, "men who served in the war commonly visit with deceased friends from their squadron or unit. She concluded that, "Those friends seem to be among the first to make a visit to a dying serviceman, even before deceased relatives arrive."[8]

Most nearing death are mostly concerned for those they are leaving behind. They switch their awareness from the world beyond the veil and then back again to Earth as they prepare to go home.

Death-Bed Visitations
Visitation from angels, deceased friends and family can occur days, weeks, or even months before death. Jacqueline's death-bed experience of her father is chronicled two-weeks before he died. Her Dad, an atheist, is visited by a messenger from God:

> *My late father, Lennie, developed cancer of the left maxilla and was sent to the Royal Brisbane Hospital in Brisbane to have an operation to take out the cancerous parts in his face (internal)...He said at some time during the operation he was above his body looking down on it and knew he was dead. He said the next instant he was sucked through black space, the blackest he could ever imagine, and then he was standing outside this golden tunnel. Inside the tunnel 'was a holy man standing with the whitest brightest long robe on.' He had long hair and Dad knew this man to be very holy.*

Dad also knew he could not go in the tunnel until it shone bright gold. Dad said he wanted to go in because he could feel the love and peace all around him. He said he did not know how he knew the man was holy, or if he could only enter when the tunnel shone bright gold, but he knew. When the tunnel did not shine bright gold the man inside the tunnel said, 'You have to go back we are not ready for you. When we are ready, we will come and get you.'

The next thing Dad remembers is waking up in his body in recovery. The experience bothered Dad. He could not forget what had happened to him. He knew it was not his imagination or a hallucination. It was real to him. Dad being an atheist could not fathom it. He was sent back to our hometown in Blackwater to die because he had secondary cancer in the bones.

One day while in Blackwater Hospital, he had a visitation from an Angel whom identified himself to Dad as a messenger from God at 12 noon. The Angel's feet did not touch the ground. He told Dad, 'I have a message for you from God. In order for you to get to Heaven, you have to follow these instructions. Dad did not tell me all the instructions, but one he did tell me was that he had to read the Bible every day until he died, and if he did not understand it, to get a pastor to help him.

I nursed at a hospital in Rockhampton, so I had Dad transferred to our Hospital because it had an oncology ward, because I knew Dad needed to be near his family. About two weeks before he died, he told us he would not be here in two weeks.

My sister asked him, 'Where are you going Dad?

He said, 'I will be dead.'

He said, 'This night another young guy named Danny died.'

Danny had melanoma and was in the bed opposite Dad. Dad relayed to me what happened just prior to Danny taking his last breath. Dad saw two large angels enter the room and stand on either side of the bed not touching the ground. Dad heard Danny take his last breath and then Danny with the two angels stood at the foot of Dad's bed. One of the angels said to Dad, 'We will be back for you in two-weeks' time. Dad died exactly two-weeks to the day Danny died.*

He told me, 'When he saw Danny's soul, he was happy and rejuvenated.' Another thing Dad told me was not be afraid of death as it is like walking through a door. My father went from being a person who believed in nothing to being saved by Almighty God. For that, I am so grateful and privileged to have been a witness to His saving Grace.[9]

Dying is Letting Go

Jeffrey Long, M.D., writes about Kathleen's death-bed vision as "an exceptional experience of transitioning with her dying grandfather into the Afterlife. These types of experiences, along with shared NDEs, are among the strongest evidence that what happens in NDEs is what happens at the time of permanent, irreversible death:" You will need a Kleenex for this one:

The ambulance had gotten there and I told them that they did not need to do anything to help my grandfather. I just wanted him to be taken to the hospital so that he did not die in the house as my grandmother could not have handled him dying there. I went with him to the hospital in the ambulance and into the emergency room. We were put in a multibed room and the curtain was drawn. As I watched my grandfather struggle to breathe, I realized that as a Catholic, he could not say his final words to God. So I started to pray, asking God to let me be his voice so my grandfather could tell God whatever he needed to.

I wasn't really sure this would work or what would happen, but it just seemed to be the thing to do. As I started to pray, I asked God to allow my grandfather to use my voice to confess to Him his sins and to ask God for his blessing. I began telling my grandfather that it was okay to let go and God would take care of him and to go towards God. When I felt like I was being pulled toward a great bright Light—not a harsh Light—but a Light filled with warmth and peace, I remember feeling and seeing my grandfather's hand in mine, and him telling me he was scared and he needed me with him.

It was bizarre as I was not dead or dying, but I was having this feeling as if my spirit body was being pulled toward the Light at the same time as my grandfather's. The Light got brighter and then enveloped us. We were standing in a place that was illuminated, but not with regular light or lamps or candles. There were other people there, but I could not make out who they were nor was I frightened or surprised to see them. My grandfather was on my left and we were still holding hands. I could sense/feel the presence of something/someone else coming toward us with a brighter Light about them than where we were.

There were no footsteps heard, but I saw and felt this person/entity coming closer. When he arrived next to us, I realized that this was Jesus and he was talking to my grandfather, and I was answering him for my grandfather. I felt my grandfather's fear leave him and Jesus outstretched His hands to take my grandfather's hand in His. At the very moment God/Jesus took my grandfather's hand, I felt God touch my hand. Suddenly I felt and knew this tremendous sense of peace and forgiveness and universality...

I remember being thanked by my grandfather and God, realizing I couldn't stay, but not wanting to let this place go. It was okay. Then, I was being whooshed backwards away from the Light and found myself back in the room with my grandfather's body.

I knew he was dead and in Heaven. During the time, I had no sensation of being in the hospital nor did I hear the hospital noises, or sense smells or people. I remember feeling speechless. Moments later, my mother and grandmother walked into the room and I told them my grandfather was gone.[10]

Cutting the cord between life and death is part of the dying process of letting go. It is a journey in which you are never alone. When a loved one is within a few months to a few weeks of crossing over, the veil between Heaven and Earth begins to thin. Deceased family and friends begin to appear, unseen by the living. A one-sided conversation ensues. You may think they are hallucinating from medication or reliving old memories. It's all part of the dying experience.

Visits by Family and Friends before Death
Molly experiences family and friends during her NDE after having cardiac arrest during surgery:

I saw so many people I knew throughout my life. My grandmother was the one who greeted me. She said, 'Hello Molly,' and I felt love from her. She said for me to put this little angel costume on and, 'I'll show you around to everyone.' So we went flying.

I saw my uncle Stan who owned a bar I used to work at. He was into a lot of drugs and drinking so we were not sure if he killed himself or someone killed him. My mom found him in his garage with the garage door down and car on. It could have been a killing from someone we knew. He was so happy to see me and wanted to show me his restaurant I worked at. When we flew in, it was like an old fashion ice cream parlor with tons of candy like Willy Wonka and the chocolate factory. It was so cool it never leaves my brain. I told my mom he had a bruise or brown spot on his forehead. A year later my mom said that to his daughter. She was in shock because she was the only one who knew he had that on his forehead.

Then, I saw my sister's best friend who hung herself at age 20. She too was so happy. Then I saw a neighbor I did not know was dead. I used to babysit for him. Then I saw my grandfather who said, 'Hello, hello.'

I asked him, 'Why hello two times?'

He said, 'One for you and one for your mother.'

Then we came to the church. Grandma took me to the most beautiful church I have ever seen. First, I saw an angel crying up where the singers would sing. I felt her pain. I flew to her and it was me crying. Then, I saw the three large angels. I was mad because they would not let me sit with them. They said I had to go back because there are things I need to do. I was so upset I had to go back.[11]

Escort Angels Help Guide the Soul Home

Donna in 1974 was given general anesthesia for a common but invasive medical procedure, and near the end of the operation the doctor made a terrible mistake. He cut an artery and she lost massive amounts of blood, too much blood to sustain life. For a short time, her heart stopped beating and her brain ceased to function. As her body lay dying on the operating table, she rose up and surveyed the situation:

> *I looked down at my spiritual body to make sure it was still intact, and what I saw surprised me. There were two cherubs, stark naked except for tiny loincloths, and every bit as cute as the putti in Raphael's paintings.*
>
> *'We are Escort Angels,' said one of the twins, with the noble pride of a royal servant. 'We have come to take you home.'*
>
> *Suddenly, the white Light was much brighter. The cherubs positioned themselves on either side of me, near my waist, and we drifted to the corner of the ceiling. I was fully prepared for take off, but my head hit the wall. I repeated the motion again and again, each time expecting the wall to give way, but it didn't budge.*
>
> *The cherub on the left flew close to my face. 'You have forgotten,' he said. 'There is something you must do before you can leave.'*
>
> *I struggled with my memories, trying to figure out what I was supposed to do. Finally, it came to me. 'Oh, that's right. I forgot to look at the body.'*

My eyes zoomed in on the woman lying on the bed below us. She was 25 years-old and in perfect health, except for the loss of blood and spirit. Like a seasoned mechanic inspecting a car, I knew I could fix her.

'This isn't serious enough,' I said more to myself than the cherubs. And in a split second I was back in my body.

I plunged headfirst into the navel, and it was like diving into wet concrete. My body had become stiff, and I had to twist and turn to make my spirit fit. After settling in, I looked up at the ceiling. The cherubs were waiting for proof I was all right. I made eye contact with one of them, and then they flew through the same wall that had prevented my escape. Tears brushed my cheeks. What have I done? I could have left with them. Right now I could be on my way home, but once again I'm trapped in a world of limitations.[12]

Meeting the Angel of Death

An ancient personification of the Angel of Death is the "Grim Reaper." All religions describe him. While descriptions vary somewhat, the basic entity is the same— a tall figure appearing male, wearing a long monk's robe tied by rope at the waist, sometimes with a sickle or scythe. A skeleton-like face is occasionally reported, but more often, there is no discernable face and no visible extremities.

Steve's NDE during an auto accident in 2006 encountered the Grim Reaper whose face shone like a 'thousand suns':

On 12/12/2006 a school bus ran a red light and t-boned my 2005 Chevy Avalanche. I was conscious during the accident (everything went into slow motion) and was coherent enough to talk to OnStar and describe the location of the accident as well as the extent of my injuries (a cut above my left eye, whip lash, three broken ribs, contusions on my lungs, and a torn rotator cuff). I was sitting very still I didn't want to move for fear of being paralyzed. I was sitting in the truck with my left eye closed, (because of the blood and also because I was covered in glass) while they used the Jaws of Life to pry the door open.

While this was happening I felt confused. How could I be standing where the house should be? Why am I standing when I was sitting in the truck? How could I see myself being worked on? Then I turned to my right (facing forward) and **I saw the Grim Reaper***, the dark robe, the sickle, no face, but where the face should be, was just blackness, blacker than anything I'd ever seen before in my life. It was as if you could take the brightest Light you could find (the sun, or even 1000 suns and shined it in there and it would just swallow it up. Then I heard a voice in my head say either 'come with me, or come to me' and as I stared into the blackness, I started to go.*

As I was going, the scene behind me (the truck and paramedics) was fading away at the same time all my senses were fading and the pain was fading. I then realized it was death wanting to take me and I thought of my 14-year-old son and my wife. I then told the Reaper... [expletive] 'I'M NOT GOING ANYWHERE!' Then I was back sitting in the truck and one of the paramedics was saying, 'come on stay with me.' After that, they extracted me and took me to the hospital.[13]

The Grim Reaper and its universal depiction as a harbinger of death is rarely reported in near-death experiences, or when loved ones are near the moment of death. Most see the bright Light, rise above their bodies, see some sort of tunnel, and communicate with various entities, but there are few reports of seeing this particular shrouded figure.

According to the Midrash,[14] the Angel of Death was created by God on the first day.[15] His dwelling is in Heaven. "Over all people have I surrendered thee the power," said God to the Angel of Death, "Only not over this one which has received freedom from death through the Law." It is said of the Angel of Death is full of eyes. In the hour of death, he stands at the head of the departing one with a drawn sword, to which clings a drop of gall. As soon as the dying man sees Death, he is seized with a convulsion and opens his mouth, whereupon Death throws the drop into it. This drop causes his death; he turns putrid, and his face becomes yellow. A drop of gall caused the expression "the taste of death" originated in the idea death.[16]

The term *Angel of Death* can be found in nearly every culture in various forms. However, there are many accounts of angels, both good and bad, specifically found in Christianity, Judaism and Islam. The book of Genesis recounts the deaths of the first-born of Egypt that many people believe were also delivered by an Angel of Death under the direction of God.

The thought of an angel that brings death is an ominous one indeed, and it is a small wonder such a figure might be associated with an evil nature given many people's fears about what happens after life ends. The Islamic and Jewish faiths are bit more specific about naming a death angel. Islam speaks of Azrael, while Judaism has no less than 14 death angels.

Carolina had a dream ADC (after-death communication) about the Angel of Death warning her about her health:

When I was a child, I was hospitalized with Anorexia Nervosa. I had been in a depressed state again recently, and had even mentioned to family members I'd be better off dead. A few nights ago, while I was sleeping, I was extremely aware I was dreaming. There was this middleaged man with me. I said to him, 'Wow, I know I'm dreaming, but I can say whatever I feel and I have total control of my dream.' [Author's note:

lucid dreaming. See chapter.6, Dreams: Night School]

The man said, 'It takes practice.'

After this, I asked if he was my spirit Guide.

He replied, 'No.'

Then my voice started to fade as if I was beginning to wake up, but I asked him, 'Who are you then?'

The man said in a serious voice, 'The Angel of Death.'

I was so frightened I thought it was my time to go. I began to regret all the times I said I wish I were dead. He also warned me about my health. Soon as I awakened, I remembered every detail of my out of body experience. It was indeed a spiritual awakening.[17]

The Angel of Death may be a personification of our fears about death, and a portent about the possibility of death in our near future. Perhaps, our fear of death determines the appearance of God's angel.

Several years before, I had a dream about the Grim Reaper before my brain cancer occurred. In the dream, the Grim Reaper was chasing me in a black, late 1940's Hearse. He was "after me," but I was able to hide and get away from him. Certainly, we would prefer Jesus, a beautiful angel, friends or family to be the soul escort who will take us to our heavenly home. In Christian, Jewish and religious literature there are other books that describe God's heavenly angels, each angel with a specific job to carry out. The Angel of Death is listed as an angel under God's command. He may be the most despised and feared of all angels, but if required, he may be the one to alert us our journey home may occur sooner than we think.

Death Protocols
At the time of death, we are given the choice to remain on Earth until our bodies are buried or cremated. Betty Eadie, a #1 NY Times Best Selling author, writes in *Embraced by the Light*:

Most spirits remain on Earth for a short time and comfort their loved ones, as families are subject to much more grief than the departed. Sometimes spirits remain longer if their loved ones are in despair.[18]

Some spirits move directly on to a realm or level in the Kingdom of Heaven in which they are most comfortable. However, extended grief, can sometimes bind the departed to Earth and prevent them from moving on. There are also times when the transition for a loved one may have been difficult or unwanted. Those who die atheists or those bonded to the appetites of the physical, may find themselves Earthbound.

Prayer then becomes important to help both the living and the dead to help release their attachments and their grief, so both can go on living.

*~Delynn sat up in the middle of the night sound asleep and look up into the corner of the room near the ceiling and exclaimed loudly, "Oh, my God, how beautiful!" She was so excited. Then she said, "We are one." Then she laid back down still asleep. I didn't see anything, (how typical) but I feel an angel visited our bedroom that night. ~***Chronicle 311***

~I prayed aloud, "God I need reassurance you are out there, that you hear me."

*John, a friend living in New York, called me out of the blue two hours later, "David, how are you doing?" I hadn't heard from John in over 30 years. We had a great call. Brought John up to date about my medical condition. He said, "Let God finish writing your book." God heard the cry of my heart. ~***Chronicle 333***

16
The Body of Light

~On January 20, 2015, **(Chronicle 586)** I wrote in my journal: *Faith first brings evidence of Christ. Evidence first, never brings faith, because there is always doubt. An amazing corollary about belief and faith showed up on NDERF, on November 18 2015. "Seek not to understand that you may believe, but seek to believe so that you may understand.*[1] *Both revelations remind us of Hebrews 11:1 "Now faith is the substance of things hoped for and the evidence of things unseen.* ~**Chronicle 890**

When you die, you no longer have a physical brain. You have a mind, an intelligence, independent from the physical body that survives and retains its personality. Your mind, however, is free of the restraints of the physical body. Oxygen, sugar, and genetics do not play a part in limiting your ability to think. You are not only smarter, your thoughts are exponentially sharper and faster.

The Body of Light

Your mind will be contained within a new Body of Light that mirrors many of the senses you had on Earth, including a subtler sense of sight (360-degree sight instead of 180 degrees) touch, taste, smell, and hearing, and a sixth sense of telepathy that can absorb massive amounts of information, images and thoughts simultaneously.

Let's talk for a moment about the Body of Light. We know from our NDE studies that the gift of receiving a new spiritual body occurs soon after death. Dead Saints report thinking and observing events with a 'spiritual mind' contained within a 'spiritual body.' St. Paul describes this immortal, incorruptible body (I Corinthians 15: 51-52):

Behold, I tell you a mystery. We shall all indeed rise again: but we shall not all be changed. In a moment, in the twinkling of an eye, at the last trumpet: for the trumpet shall sound, and the dead shall rise again incorruptible: and we shall be changed.

My interpretation of the Apostle Paul's description of a spiritual, immortal, "glorified" body born from a natural physical body is entirely consistent with testimonies from the Dead Saints. At the moment of death, in the twinkling of an eye, we are changed. That which is corrupted, the flesh, is given a Body of Light—an incorruptible, immortal body.

Most Dead Saints describe donning a Body of Light soon after death. However, there are points of contention: Is the immortal, "incorruptible" Body of Light "donned" if the mind of the departing soul is in distress and does not attend the Judgment?

Egyptian Beliefs about the Body of Light

Ancient Egyptians describe aspects of the Body of Light and a "name"—definitions which may help define St. Paul's "incorruptible" body, Dead Saint descriptions of the "Body of Light," and the dilemma of a soul who doesn't attend or pass the Judgment:

> ➤ **The ba**: *The Astral Spirit.* A Spiritual Body which can roam beyond the veil at night and can visit with the deceased and stands before the Judgment council at death. It is connected with a silver cord which is released when the physical body dies. This is not the Body of Light or St. Paul's "incorruptible" body. Souls who refuse to stand before the Judgment will remain in the astral world as an "astral spirit" who co-exists with the physical Earth plane. (See chapter 18, *Ghosts, Apparitions, & Earthbound Spirits*)

> ***The akh***: *The Immortal Spirit.* Equivalent to St. Paul's "incorruptible" body and the Dead Saint's "Body of Light." According to the ancient Egyptians, it will be awarded *after the Judgment.*

> ***The name***: *The name* of your Immortal spirit. Revelation 2:17: *...To him that overcomes will I give to eat of the hidden manna, and will give him a white stone, and in the stone a new name written, which no man knows saving he that receives it.*

I believe the answer is self-evident. If a soul does not continue onto the Light and face the Judgment, they will not receive an "incorruptible" glorified Body of Light described by St. Paul and the Dead Saints, nor given a "new name." The soul and mind will remain encapsulated as an astral spirit with its old Earth University personality and desires.

Body of Light Abilities

Bill expands our understanding of what we feel, see, taste, smell and touch in the Afterlife, a world that reflects our human understanding of our five senses, but on a much higher, more enhanced level:

When I died on the operating table for the first time, I didn't realize I was dead. There was no out of body experience, no tunnels, no Light at the end of the tunnel, no spirits, nothing. I was out of my body and just popped into the most beautiful place I have ever seen. Light is not visual there. The senses are all-encompassing impressions flooded into my being all at once. The experience is so intense that it is hard to explain, because it doesn't follow a logical sequence and it is totally wrapped up in emotion. Words are far too limited to explain, but I'm doing my best to try to say what happened.

The senses are extremely heightened and don't really work like they do here. Words are completely inadequate, because all the senses are wrapped up in each other. We have the largest vocabulary on Earth based on describing events in terms of what we see. Although I felt the experience, I can best describe it in terms of vision.

The grass was so green it hurt to look at it, and it felt so good! I could even taste the grass by feeling it, it tasted like watermelon. Walking on the grass was wonderful – it was an incredible feeling. The best way I can describe it was, 'OH MY GOD! WOW!!!' The sense of smell was not with the nose. It was more like it permeated through my cheekbones under my eye, like smelling through the sinuses.[2]

Feeling Whole Without a Physical Body

Sue answers perhaps one of our deep fears about the Afterlife. How will we feel without a physical body?

I was experiencing some sort of free fall during all of this, however, it is hard to pin point any direction I was travelling in because, well, there was no direction. 'It is hard for me to imagine now, even after experiencing it personally, how it could be one would FEEL so much, yet only have awareness mentally with no physical. From this, alone I can assure you after death you will feel completely as you do now, whole, even without a body.[3]

The Appearance of the Body of Light

Dead Saints describe donning a new "glorified" body during their NDE that generally looks like a human body, but in many ways different:

I had a body with arms and legs resembling the physical body on Earth, but yet somehow very different. This new spiritual body was translucently white, but then again, it wasn't. It's so hard to describe. It "glowed" or "radiated" such Light. It was not subject to gravity of the laws of physics I had known while on Earth. If I wanted to go somewhere, I didn't use my legs to get there. I simply thought of where I wanted to go, and there I was. I could not "speak" or "hear" like the physical body, but I could "speak" and "hear" just the same. It was like telepathy. I could "hear" everything "speak" and I could do the same. I "knew what the people on Earth below were thinking and feeling without even being near to them. I automatically "knew" things and accepted this without fear or hesitation: it was normal for this new dimension I was now in.[4]

The appearance of the Body of Light sometimes does not necessarily appear human, but may appear spherical, oval, or look like a round pulsing loci of Light. Dirk describes people wearing white gowns of a very fine fabric:

Everything had an extra dimension to things. Everything looked more real. I remember taking note of how people looked— and the only explanation I have is I was able to see complete around [360 degrees]. When we see people normally, we only get to see what they want to reveal. This was like seeing people for who they are—as God sees them all at once. Also the white gowns were part of people; it wasn't like they had put clothing on as a separate fabric, but it was an extension of who they were—like the robe of salvation, or the gown of righteousness, from Scripture. They all looked young, but were not young in age, just freed from the decay and curse of death. Fully alive.[5]

The Creation of the Body of Light

On July 30th, 1994, Mira drove her white 560 LS Mercedes convertible about 400 miles with her secretary from San Francisco for a couple of meetings with some clients. After about 10 minutes on the road, a car with two young boys, driving in the left lane, suddenly swerved to the right and impacted her Mercedes head on. The next thing she knew a white stream of Light swept through her body, filling her with electric white Light. Mira describes the creation of a "Light Body" while flying fast through a dark void:

I saw with complete amazement, a very interesting transference starting to happen, as a string of atoms started flowing out from within the left side of my electric body, disappearing upwards into nowhere. And almost as if from thin air, a much finer frequency of atoms, seemed to be appearing from the right side and were entering through my right side into this same electric Light body. I was watching and experiencing at the same time again, with no sense of duality, as my entire Being was totally emptied and refueled and re-programmed, with this ethereal, orderly, interchange of atoms.

I saw the new entry was of a vastly different energy constitution and seemed to have a much more expansive and delicate DNA energy, with a new wave of very lightweight, subtle cellular frequencies, as they spiraled in, expanding and changing the previous electric body formation. And again, all the above was happening very fast and yet...taking an eternity. Enfolded in the comforting wrap of Pure Divine Love during this cellular 'exchange,' it seemed as though I, as the one who had arrived here, was gradually disappearing with the atoms leaving this electric Light body, and almost as if, another 'me' was birthing through the newer, finer atoms entering into this Light form. It seemed as if my whole Being was cleansed and purified, making it ready for its next role in God's divine drama.[6]

The Body of Light is a vehicle for our minds to traverse the immensity of the Afterlife universe faster than the speed of light. While we no longer have a physical body with its physical DNA, we have a subtler spiritual body composed of "Light DNA" that mirrors our former Earth body and contains all the memories and experiences of our earthly life. The Body of Light sees, feels, hears, smells, and tastes. It is smarter, sharper, and thinks exponentially faster than you think or I can imagine, and is just the beginning of the miracles God has promised you and me when we die.

---

1 *Sharon NDE*, #4055, 11.18.15, NDERF.org
2 *Bill W NDE*, #180, 10.29.02, NDERF.org
3 *Sue C NDE*, #2927, 01.18.12, NDERF.org
4 *Katie W NDE*, #4029, 10.11.15, NDERF.org
5 *Pastor Dirk W's NDE*, #525, 11.24.04, NDERF.org
6 *Mira S NDE*, #3898, 03.08.15, NDERF.org

17
Heaven—The Kingdom of Light

"Let nothing stand between you and the Light...When you travel to the celestial city, carry no letter of introduction. When you know, ask to see God... ~Henry David Thoreau

Many Christians remain skeptical of *Near-Heaven* experiences because so few Dead Saints experience Judgment or hell-like conditions. Instead, the Saints describe all manner of people, even non-Christians in Heaven, overcome with a profound, life-changing encounter of God's unconditional love.

How can this be so? Because God, the Living One, knows your heart. Jesus Christ knows your heart, Christian or non-Christian, saved or unsaved, baptized or unbaptized.

Throughout the *Chronicles*, I have conveyed from Scripture and from the Dead Saints, guidelines for entering one of the many levels of

Heaven. You must be joyous and lighthearted. You must be peaceful and loving, and innocent like a child.

The mansion (or level) of Heaven that you enter is determined by the magnitude or depth of unconditional love that you attain while in the physical. The depth of one's love is expressed by the purity of one's heart—the extent to which the heart is free of all fear and inflamed by faith, unconditional love and universal kindness. Your heart, not the religion you profess, is the REAL you that you present to God when you pass over—a reflection of the ancient Biblical saying in Proverbs 23:7, "So as a man thinketh in his heart so is he."

While many Dead Saints see Heaven as a "place" with gardens, people and buildings, Teri's revelation about "Heaven" is different. She sees Heaven as a "frequency" we attain:

> *Being in the presence of White Light was "Heaven." It was more than the greatest feeling I had ever experienced or dreamed was possible. Having that feeling again became what I wanted to strive for, not going to a place. The feeling, the energy I was experiencing became "the place."*
>
> *...I knew somehow, I had to raise my vibration and become more loving in order to experience this* ***indescribable love on a permanent basis***. *These are the concepts that are difficult to explain because it wasn't conveyed to me in words. It was an understanding that spoke to me in a way I could relate to. But it was never conveyed as Judgment or with the intention of creating fear of punishment. This White Light wasn't capable of anything but Love, because that was truly the essence, 100% the vibration of what it was.*
>
> *...I learned, Heaven isn't a place you are admitted to, but it is a frequency you attain.*[1]

In *Saved by the Light*, Dannion Brinkley, describes beings below him who shimmered at a slower frequency than his own. Just looking at them caused him discomfort by slowing down his vibration. Conversely, watching beings above him caused him similar discomfort because he would begin vibrating faster, *"like drinking too much coffee."*[2]

A corollary of the Law of Frequency and Vibration is something I call "reality bubbles" —a bubble that has a particular frequency/vibration that encapsulates our consciousness and beliefs —it reflects the reality we believe in. Bubbles of a higher or lower vibration attract or repel one another. Our reality bubbles can expand beyond our immediate environment, to encompass our neighborhood, city, county, nation, world or...Universe. Higher frequency bubbles can see into lower frequency bubbles, but not vice versa.

This same idea is also reflected in Edgar Cayce's well-known quote about Heaven, "You don't go to Heaven. *You grow up to Heaven.*"

The Transition to Heaven

Robert's heart attack in August 2005, precipitated his awe-inspiring visit to Heaven:

> *The transition [to Heaven] did not feel odd in anyway. I must admit there was some apprehension because of the unknown but that slowly passed too. An intensity of different feeling began to rush over me all at once.*
>
> *The first feeling was a feeling of intense peace. It was so calm and serene with an incredible amount of tranquility. Never on Earth had I had anything at all feel so incredible with calmness and peace. The intensity of these feelings was so intense that you realize that they are not from life on Earth in any form.*
>
> *All of my earthly worries, thoughts, fears, opinions, were gone. It was as if my entire 47 plus years on Earth did not exist. The intensity of the tranquility was so incredible and overwhelming that you were willing to give your soul to GOD and accept the transition to Heaven without questioning a single thing. This is what the love of GOD can portray; complete and total release of your soul and you will put your soul into the hands of GOD without question.*
>
> *There was no fear in what I was experiencing, no fear on where I was going, and what to expect when I arrived there. I knew it would all be just fine when I arrived at my final destination. The feelings I was having were not happening in any chronological order, but happening in sync and it wasn't overwhelming.*
>
> *Then there was warmth. It was as if I was wrapped in a blanket that came out of an oven. It wasn't too hot or too cold. It was simply perfect. It was so incredible and comforting; any anxiety remaining in your soul was expelled out of you. It was as if you were being held in the loving arms of an Angel with their wings wrapped around you to keep you warm and to insure you are secure. The love of GOD is far reaching and His love is warmth and that is what you feel. You are the child of GOD coming home and home should be a warm and welcoming place, which Heaven is.*
>
> *...You can travel to all areas of heaven with just a desire to be there. You can enjoy the climates you are attracted too. You can visit whom you like and you can see the greatness of the musicians*

and artists that passed before you and who are now in Heaven. Imagine being able to learn the nuances of Pablo Picasso's painting style, or perhaps Van Gogh's unique style being done in front of you. If painting isn't your thing can you imagine being able to sit and listen to Stevie Ray Vaughn and B.B. King play guitar together. Perhaps, you would rather listen to an Italian operatic tenor, Luciano Pavarotti. Could you ever imagine you would be able to sit with Frank Sinatra and Dean Martin and listen to them just break into song? In Heaven, it is all possible and that is the love of Heaven and what the grace of GOD provides.

Then there was the love. This is a very difficult feeling to describe. Try to remember the first time you saw your child or met your significant other. You know what I am talking about. That feeling of first time love that is so positive and so powerful. Now take that feeling and multiply it thousands of times over. It is a love you can never imagine being possible on Earth. This is difficult to explain, but I suppose the best way to explain it would be that GOD took your soul and held you close to His bosom and gently brushed His hand over you and said in a soft, soothing, yet powerful voice, 'You are safe. I have you and you are home with me. Welcome home my child.' [3]

Family Reunions

Our hope is we will be reunited with departed friends and family in Heaven. There is no way to explain how we will truly be together again. The reunion may or may not be as father and son, husband and wife, or as a dear friend. When we descend to Earth University and occupy a physical body, it's as if our souls are part of a Body of Light that has been split, and then when we return to the Kingdom of Heaven, we suddenly come back together again as a single Body of Light, united yet separate, and we share together what we have learned.

Robert continues his walk through Heaven, describing the joy of reuniting with loved ones:

As my vision began to clear, I saw numerous faces all happy and smiling. It felt as if I was being held by so many different souls. Each of which were welcoming me back home. It was difficult to recognize who they were; they were all young as if in their twenties or early thirties. But, their faces started to become familiar once again. I began to recognize them and I knew who they were and the level of happiness that was felt can't be explained in earthly terms. There is no possible way to explain this and how it felt.

I saw my aunts and uncles that passed on before me. I saw my grandparents and others I knew that went before I did. I knew I was safe and I was meant to be there. Then, I saw my Father and we made the connection that so many years on Earth have taken away. It was as if it was yesterday and not over 38 earthly years since his death. My Grandparents were there and Grandma Lucia had that same smile of love and harmony she always had. Grandpa Pete was younger and more resilient. They all were younger than my memories held. They all appeared to be in their late 20's or 30's. Does it have something to do about that age as being in the 'prime' of our lives?

As I looked around to familiarize myself with Heaven, off in the near distance, I saw incredible towers and buildings all glistening with inviting incredible colors. The skies were brilliant with various colors from blues to purples. The grass fields were vast and the trees were magnificent. It is GOD's creation and it is all in perfect harmony. All the areas of Earth seem to be in Heaven, but it isn't like Earth. It is better and it is as perfect as GOD originally created it.

There was so much to explore and to see and so many other souls to meet and talk to. I wanted to familiarize myself with Heaven (home) once again and move freely from place to place and explore its great halls and draw in its knowledge. I felt content where I was and in no hurry to explore. I was with those that had meant the most to me on Earth and I wanted to stay in their presence for as long as I needed to. We were all one in GOD's design and our souls were there to reconnect. [4]

The Mansions of Heaven

Concerning Heaven, Emanuel Swedenborg writes, "*All of Heaven is differentiated into communities on the basis of differences in the quality of love.*"[5] They consist of all those who have lived in the goodness of love according to their own spiritual life on Earth. Heaven is a place of peace, harmony, pure Love and Light, and it is bigger, more multi-dimensional than you can possibly imagine. It is a celestial universe filled with many kingdoms.

Jesus said in John 14:2, "In my Father's house are many mansions: if it were not so, I would have told you. I go to prepare a place for you." Jesus was saying, after your arrival in Heaven, you have a mansion to live in especially prepared for you. Other translations describe these mansions as rooms, dwelling places, or homes. On a grander scale, these Afterlife dwelling places are cities, universities, and at its highest level, the City of God. But how many dwelling places of Heaven are there?

Barbara had an encounter with Jesus when she collapsed from a serious bout with the flu when she was 21. In a remarkable question and answer session with Jesus, she describes Heaven thousands of grey layers and dimensions comprising the 'in-between worlds' before Heaven is reached. At first, Jesus tries to explain the complexity of where she is, but Barbara asks the Lord to simplify it so she could understand:

> *I looked around and noticed a white figure to my left side. There was no mistaking who this figure was. It was my Lord Jesus. As I stared at Him, I sensed there was another world above us. I knew this was where God was and I was not allowed to view any part of His world. I felt a familiar connection between God, Jesus and myself. It was Love that connected us. We were all the same and yet we were different. After my Life Review He told me I had to return back to Earth. I knew He was right but I wanted to stay here because there was so much unconditional love and besides I had so many questions to ask Him. He told me I could ask Him questions before returning to Earth.*
>
> *My Questions: [To Jesus]*
> *First Question: Where am I and what is this place?*
> *Reply: At first, I thought He was speaking in a foreign language. I said, 'God please, I am a simple person, put it in simple words.'*
> *He then replied, 'Think of this as the Tunnel of Grays; Dark to Light; Hell to Heaven. All the different shades of GRAY are the in-between worlds. If you took a stack of CD's and piled them from the floor (Dark) to the ceiling (Light) this would represent the tunnel, I was now in.*
> *God showed me a panorama view of the tunnel.*
> *Second question: How far away is the Earth from the floor?*
> *Reply: About 12 inches.*
> *Third Question: If I decided not to back to Earth, where would I go?*
> *Reply: About 24 inches from the ceiling.*[6]

I took away several pieces of wisdom from Barbara's very interesting NDE. First, Earth is only 24 inches from the floor, the dark realm of Hell. The different shades of gray are in-between worlds represented by CDs. Imagine, if you stacked CD's from the floor to the ceiling; it would take a minimum 2000 CDs to reach a ten-foot ceiling, the highest point of Heaven. 24 inches from the floor is about 400 CDs. 12 inches from the ceiling is about 200 CD's.

I believe Jesus was attempting to demonstrate to Barbara, not only where she was and where she was going, but just how diverse, complex, and multi-dimensional the Kingdom of Heaven truly is. The Zen realization here is an answer to one of our Afterlife questions: It is not if we survive, it is where we are going and how far we will be from the ceiling when we arrive!

Heaven Has a Mansion Designed Just for You

Heaven is a place God personally created just for us, more beautiful than we can imagine. Our spiritual eyes perceive sound and color on wavelengths far beyond any we ever experienced on Earth. The greenest grass is greener. Stately forests are taller. Impossibly high waterfalls flow from dizzying heights, and gentle waves crash quietly below on tropical beaches of white talcum powder sands. Green meadows and wildflowers spread as far as we can see. The air is filled with sweet aromas. Flowers of every imaginable size and color dominate the landscape. Trees grow hundreds, if not thousands of feet tall.

The sounds of play dominate Heaven. We hear children's laughter and watch them dance and play games with new soul arrivals. Beautiful music is heard everywhere. Angel's songs praising God. There is no pain, no sadness, no gravity, no time, and no sun, because God's Light brightens the skies with a golden blue Light that casts no shadows. Heaven will seemingly have infinite dimensions and scope, holding us breathless (an Afterlife joke!). In Heaven, time is relative. Your moment in Heaven may be days, weeks, years, or a thousand years. It may be forever.

However, you will come to the realization that still there is much work to do.

The Dead Saints describe Heaven as a world familiar to them. American Indians describe their happy hunting grounds and beautiful prairie lands they roamed during their life on Earth. Egyptians describe Heaven, or *Amenti,* landscaped with colorful painted temples, lush gardens, pyramids, and surrounded by family and friends.

Heaven will be familiar to us. We will realize with a great sigh of relief we are still ourselves. We will retain our blessed uniqueness and our thinking habits. Miraculously, our new spiritual body has made us whole, healthy and young again. We will appear to others in Heaven at the age we were happiest. We are the creator of our reality; clothes, hairstyle, and appearance.

Amanda had been writing in her journal, posing a question to her dead brother Chris. "What is Heaven like?"—and then fell asleep. She then dreamed about her mother and her sisters who were talking about her brother Chris who died several months before. Suddenly, Chris appears next to her mother in the dream:

He was laughing right along with his family, as if he had been listening in and now decided to make his presence known. Megan cried out to her brother, 'Chris!' He assured the family in the dream it was really him. Megan wasn't so sure, so she took her hand and placed it on his arm. Despite the fact that he was still somewhat transparent, Chris's arm felt solid to the touch. Megan realized this was her chance.

'Chris,' she said breathlessly, 'Tell me about Heaven.'

His face glowed. 'It's awesome and beautiful beyond words. And the people are themselves. They still look like themselves, and they have their own personalities.' Megan and her sisters exchanged glances. 'So, Brooke will still be Brooke? And Amanda will still be Amanda?'

'Exactly!' Chris said. 'And everyone has jobs. Not like the jobs here, where people are often bored or unhappy. Everyone loves their jobs there. In Some ways it's like Earth, but everyone is happier.'[7]

Many Activities in Heaven

Heaven is a busy place. Apparently, we keep on going to school and attend classes, and we all have jobs we like! There appear to be many levels of people doing activities they love. Ana describes this idyllic scene:

There were teenagers, people of middle age, and people just growing old. I saw harmony, serenity, and happiness. People smiled and I felt strengthened. The voices were clear harmonious and fluent; the communication flowed in a natural manner. The atmosphere was total peace, and completely full of love. There was also a fountain surrounded by flowers of every color, in the center of a large garden. The water cascaded in different rhythms forming images and its sound was in harmony and was amazing. People were sitting around talking and smiling at one another. They didn't talk with sounds from the mouth. It was as if just with the mind, they could say everything and I could hear them. There were people leaning in the garden reading a book, or just enjoying the sun. The countryside was fantastic. I continued being carried along on this journey.

...I went on a bit further towards a layer of branches, but this time I could see a large group of old people. The elderly people smiled, they looked strong and vigorous. Many were sitting and talking, but without saying anything, just enjoying the countryside. They were in the middle of flower-filled gardens, trees of various species, and rivers flowing with clean fresh water. They walked along paths and shared stories.[8]

Heavenly Universities

My mother lost her older brother Roy to cancer in 1995. Before Roy died, Mom was worried for him because he was angry with God, a God he didn't even believe in. A few months after his death, Roy appeared to mom in a dream, looking about 20 years old, sporting a very cool Elvis Presley hairdo like the one he used to do in his youth. He was carrying a laptop and was beaming. In the background, Mom could hear Andre Bocelli singing, *It's time to say goodbye*. He said, "I'm learning a lot of new things over here." Mom noted Roy was not only happier, "the real interesting thing is Roy never used computers while alive."

Therefore, our education in the Afterlife seems to continue. Linda adds more color describing heavenly universities:

> I was greeted by a Light Being, although I don't remember flying into a Light as such. I knew this soul and was guided around the place. I was shown rooms and doorways mostly, which contained other souls learning things and preparing for their return to Earth or wherever their next journey was to be.
>
> I also saw souls who I would call angels or higher Beings. They were helping Earthlings with many problems even medical discoveries. I was taken to many different levels by this friend and learned anything is possible in this place. I can't remember most of the levels as each one seemed more complex than the last, but I do remember the lower levels, so to speak. I'm sure I was taken to higher places, but I am not to remember these places as my life here would be affected. I think there may be about seven or possibly more but I have a basic memory of about three or four.[9]

Pets in Heaven?

For all you pet lovers...yes! Mary encountered animals in Heaven during her NDE caused by a severe head injury from a criminal attack:

> Horses and dogs were playing together and when they stopped, they seemed to stare a hole through me and then went back to playing. I was told they were checking to see if I was the person they were waiting for that they had loved while on Earth.[10]

Rev. Robert's NDE showed him even dogs go to Heaven:

There was a brief darkness, a sensation of going through a dark void of some sort then I was in another place. I saw dogs playing in a grass-covered field and I was with them. I have always loved dogs. I think they were dogs that I once had as an adult or child. I'm a minister and I don't really believe 'all dogs go to Heaven,' but there they were![11]

Soul Reconciliation

Many of us have gone through divorce or have had disputes with friends and family, which seem irreconcilable. According to Robert, we have a chance to get Afterlife counseling in Heaven:

The reality is simple: If your soul was hurt on Earth by another, you do not automatically forget that pain and it simply goes away in Heaven and we all sing Kumbaya together. Some souls do not mesh in Heaven as they do not mesh here on Earth.

There is no anger in Heaven. There is no hate. There is no violence, but that does not mean there are no misunderstandings. Does that mean that that particular soul does not want to see you or talk to you? No, not at all. You can have the opportunity to sit with that soul and other higher-level angels to find a solution to the challenges you two may have. You can discuss and ask questions about why they may have done certain things that affected you in a dramatic way. Perhaps, there is an explanation we did not see on Earth that would make sense now that we are in Heaven again. This may sound strange but you must remember we are not perfect and we must grow our souls to become close to GOD and to achieve a high status in Heaven. We have lifetimes upon lifetimes to learn and to grow. Unfortunately, there are times when we are not able to secure this meeting since the other soul has chosen to return to Earth to relearn or learn a new task.[12]

Encounters with God

When I was 12, I dreamed of a picture of a Father God I thought existed as a Renaissance Painting in our Family Bible. You know, one of those big, heavy Bibles with dozens of color renaissance paintings, mixed among pages of sacred Scripture. Later on, I realized my dream memory of God had a face that resembled the negative photo image similar to the face of Christ on the Shroud of Turin. He had a long, grey bushy beard. His hair was slightly curly and fell 12 inches over his shoulders. He was tall—at least six foot. He wore a long, dark black-silver robe tied about the waist with a white rope. Most notably, God had two dark black/grey ¾" x 3" x 14" inch stone tablets stacked on one another, balanced on the top of his head, bound together by tight twine near the ends.

When I awoke, I looked for God's image in every Bible I could find. I never found it.

I can't tell you what my "vision" of God meant, or if my dream image has any relationship to the classic Jewish and Christian anthropomorphic image of a Father God described by the Prophet Daniel called the "Ancient of Days." In his vision, he creates a picture of an ancient, or venerable, Person who sits on a flaming throne with wheels of fire, His hair and clothing white as snow. (Dan 7:9)

Perhaps we must ask ourselves: Why would the Creator, who can shape the universe with His thoughts, need such simple tools as hands? The only way we can create is with our human hands, so we imagine God with hands. Could it be that the confusion and strife over the nature of God is caused by syntax, translations, and interpretations? Yet, God is also described by the Dead Saints as Father, Mother, Light, Love, and Triune, yet one consciousness who is the Source of all that is.

Cristeal describes God's beauty in Heaven:

The Light kept coming closer until it enveloped me. I was surrounded by waterfalls of Light, by rivers of Light, by oceans of Light that were all around me. I reached out and touched the Light with my hand (which grew out of the spherical me, especially for that purpose) and I was reassured. It was like touching a mother's breast.

I asked the Light, 'What's happening here? What's going on?'

The Light parted, like stage curtains in front of me, and I saw a panoramic vista of buildings and parks and trees and flowers and beauty and so many things I could not comprehend or understand.

'Where am I?'

And the Light answered me, not in words but in thought-concepts.

'Now you are at the moment of beholding the Imperial Heaven, the heart of God, the great Master Awareness that overflows to create all that is.'[13]

A Feminine God?

In another NDE, Corey sees Jesus and then describes a feminine aspect of God:

The entire time I was with my family, I could feel their love-like a warm feeling all over me. I suddenly felt like I was on a moving platform and I saw Jesus! I knew instantly who he was, although he didn't tell me. He was dressed in a white robe. His presence felt warm and I could feel love coming off Him. Jesus said I should go back to the living and live my life. Jesus vanished and God appeared to me. She was bright and I felt her love immediately (and, yes, God is a female). She looked like the sun, with love coming off her in rays. (It's hard to explain, but she reminded me of a painting of the sun I had seen when I was very young, with Light shining from the center of her body). She hugged me and then suddenly she was gone. I saw images of my father flying in a plane. I then saw gates, and as I walked toward them, they opened and I walked through them. I remember seeing an "M" on a window and then I found out I was in the hospital.[14]

A Triune God

DREAM: *I dreamed of a nuclear fallout sign when I was 18 during my tour in the USAF. I discovered recently scientists chose the nuclear symbol, unaware that it was an ancient symbol representing the "Godhead" similar to the Christian Triquetra, a three-part interlocking fish symbol symbolizing the Christian trinity.* ~**Chronicle 604**

Ancient tradition describes God in three forms; "Water, Air and Light." Masonic tradition defines the Trinity as 'Living Waters, Breath of God, and Light of the World." In traditional Christianity; Father, Son and Holy Spirit. Dead Saint encounters with God add more details to the Triune definition. Ron sees the Trinity as three Spirits, separate but ONE:

I came to understand this Trinity is not God, exactly. They are more like the Godhead. They are the omnipresent embodiment of the Impartial Force. The Force they mastered is not a composite, but a self-sustaining whole. It is the "first cause." It knows no good or evil. It is neutral. Though tangible and pervasive, the Ultimate Force is not a Being, but a principle.

...It is perfect love--unconditional and universal. To describe it is difficult, because to describe it is to give it structure and anything structured cannot be unbounded or infinite. So we err every time we try to define God within the parameters of our

structured minds, using structured words and structured thoughts to imagine structured beings.

...To describe God as a Trinity or entity, however, misses the mark. God is a Spirit, and should be worshiped like a Spirit. It is the benevolent force of love in our souls and has little to do with our physical appearance.[15]

Ancient Ones

The Dead Saints encounter many beings in Heaven. In this experience, William encounters ancient ones who work as guardians, but who are not angels or unearthly mystical beings, but prophets, teachers, leaders and apostles of old:

My last NDE was not one single trip but actually seven trips. I would leave my body, not only to escape the tremendous pain I was in, but to also to continue those things I was being instructed in on the other side. During this time, I was surrounded by those I call the ancient ones...not so much in accordance to their earthly age, but to their eternal celestial age.

The ancient ones, are men and women who had been chosen, from the beginning, before the creation of this world, in the counsel of Heaven to be servants of our heavenly Father and our Lord, Jesus Christ, during the lifetime they chose to be upon this Earth. The ancient ones are the prophets, teachers, apostles and leaders of old and the not so distant past. Yes, as I just mentioned, I was guided to the tunnel of Light by my guardian angels. What is really amazing about our guardian angels is we choose them. I also came to realize one of the things we know, from pre-existence, is we will have our guardian angels that will work with the Holy Ghost to lead and guide us. We don't always listen, but they are there still the same. As I mentioned, we choose them, and they us.[16]

Heavenly Angels

Humanity has encountered angels since the beginning of time. Taken from the Greek, *angelos*, meaning messenger, the Bible records over three hundred angelic references. They are spiritual beings of heavenly residence, employed by God as the ministers of His will. The Dead Saints describe many types of these angels during their heavenly journeys. The following excerpt from Bobby describes a fascinating account about these heavenly beings:

Next, I was at the top of an assembly, similar to an arena. There stood the choir of angels. I was so very excited. The sound was loud and beautiful. I can still hear it in my head, though it cannot be described with words in my vocabulary. The music was like incredible streams of notes and chords that cannot be heard by the human ear. The appearance of the angels was hard to describe because they barely had shape to them and their bodies did not look like human bodies. There was a very vague line that defined their substance, almost like pillars of energy contained by a thin line of light. I don't recall distinguishing features like noses, hair, or anything else like what humans have. However, the angelic mouths were soft o's as they emitted beautiful music. Their eyes had no definitive description of color but they did look identical to each other. Their eyes all gazed at the center of this stage where this bright Light shined. This was GOD. The choir lined left to right and for as far as the eye could see.

I remember someone else to my right, a guide perhaps? It was male. I say this based on the feeling and understanding that it was male. I recall being extremely excited and in awe. I said something to the effect of, 'Do I get to sing too?' and the guide saying, 'Oh, no. You cannot sing with them.'

I said, 'Their eyes! Look at their eyes!' I seemed to be trying to get their attention, but the guide lovingly said, 'Yes. They NEVER take their eyes off HIM.'

'Never?' I asked.

'Never,' he replied.[17]

Many Dead Saints describe great halls and libraries in Heaven where angels keep track of everything happening on Earth: births, deaths, animals, plants, water, and scientific advances people are making. Siobhan was catapulted through a white tunnel and found himself in one of these great halls that looked like the Parthenon in Athens, Greece:

I went inside and saw the beautiful, white marble flooring. I went down a long hallway and there was a room with thousands of scrolls. I pulled one out to read it. It was writing that I've never seen before. Then the writing disappeared in front of me. I then looked over my shoulder and there was a man standing in the doorway with a stern look on his face! I got scared and took off running. That's the last thing I remember. I woke up in the hospital in a lot of pain. I was getting zapped with a defibrillator.[18]

The City of God

Jean describes her visit to the City of God in 1981. She woke up lying in her hospital bed, unable to breathe. Every joint in her body was in excruciating pain. Jean knew she was in trouble. In the days that followed, her heart stopped beating four times. During this time, she had experienced an amazing journey to Heaven:

> *I found myself in a city and was told this was the City of God. I was shown other parts of the city as well...where souls were working with people on Earth...scientists, the arts, and more. There is always a push there to "inspire" those on Earth to create beneficial things for mankind in every area. There was so much more too. But, more than anything this place was filled with love...love of mankind, love of everyone on Earth, and of the Earth itself. Communications were transparent there. Thoughts shared as in a conversation here. The people I saw were all working happily so and in great joy.*
>
> *This city had many different places, all geared to a different need. There was a place of rest where souls could recover from traumatic lives on Earth. There were working places where souls could help mankind and others grow and be more. There were libraries and theaters and schools. And there was also the Temple of God. I was taken into this large hall and before me were beings of pure Light. One was sitting directly in front of me on a chair or throne. These beings did not have human shape but were more like pure energy of Light. I found myself prostrating before them in awe. The love that emanated from them, particularly the one in the center, was overwhelming. I definitely did not feel their equal, but did feel this great, great honor to be there. I was embraced by this entity in the center and told, 'You have done well, my Child, and I am pleased.' The love that came flowing through me and the approval made me weep.*
>
> *Was this God? Was this the ultimate? I really don't know. I just know I was and am so much less than this Being and those who were nearby. Yet, the love was so wondrous to have too. I found myself, upon returning wanting to just be worthy of that love.*[19]

In closing this chapter about Heaven, even the visions of the Dead Saints and those of Scripture likely pale in comparison to the real majesty of these mystical celestial realms. According to the Dead Saints, the Kingdom of Heaven is not a gated community. Heaven is like "a kid opening Christmas presents multiplied by millions," says one Dead Saint.[20] No peeking!

1 *Teri R NDE,* #2301, 08.10.10, NDERF.org
2 Dannion Brinkley with Paul Perry 1994. *Saved by the Light.* New York: Villard Books. p. 10.
3 *Robert N NDE's*, #3337, 01.05.16 & 05.05.13, NDERF.org
4 *Robert N NDE's*, #3337, 01.05.16 & 05.05.13, NDERF.org
5 Emanuel Swedenborg 2012. *Heaven & Hell.* USA: Swedenborg Foundation Press. p. 280.
6 *Barbara W NDE*, #2855, 10.15.11, NDERF.org
7 James L. Garlow and Keith Wall 2010. *Encountering Heaven and the Afterlife.* Bloomington, Minnesota: Bethany House Publishers. pp.156-157.
8 *Ana Celicia G NDE*, #3891, 02.25.15, NDERF.org
9 *Linda G NDE*, #1653, 07.20.08, NDERF.org
10 *Mary R NDE*, #1716, 10.12.08, NDERF.org
11 *Rev. Dr. Robert J NDE*, #3915, 03.18.15, NDERF.org
12 *Robert N NDE's.* #3337, 01.05.16 & 05.05.13, NDERF.org
13 *Cristeal B NDE*, #3131, 09.02.12, NDERF.org
14 *Corey L NDE*, #3293, 03.14.13, NDERF.org
15 *Ron K's NDE*, #724, 12.04.05, NDERF.org
16 *William C's NDE*, #119, 04.29.02, NDERF.org
17 *Bobby HR NDE*, #3932, 04.23.15, NDERF.org
18 *Siobhan B Probable NDE*, #3980, 07.26.15, NDERF.org
19 *Jean R's NDE*, #2932, 01.18.12, NDERF. org
20 *Anthony A NDE*, #3264, 02.09.13, NDERF.org

18

Ghosts, Apparitions & Earthbound Spirits

Dream: I saw two homeless men on a city street sidewalk attempting to suck water from a potted plant through ½-inch straws. The dirt they were trying to draw water from was bone dry. In the next scene in the dream, I saw the same two men in a conference room full of people going through the same routine, attempting to suck water through large straws from the same, bone-dry potted plant. Shocked, I asked the taller man 'Can I get you some water?' He nodded yes.

I filled a glass pitcher of clear water and poured it into a cranberry juice glass bottle I thought was empty. No matter how much I emptied the cranberry juice bottle, when I poured the clear water, it colored the water a red cranberry juice color. Handing him the juice bottle, it became apparent to everyone in the room, he was not a destitute homeless man at all. Like a veil falling away, he revealed Himself to be a King. I wondered, 'How could someone so great become a beggar?' Then I began to cry realizing He was Christ in disguise. ~**Chronicle 927**

This is a subject of perennial interest to many people on many levels—from the merely curious to cheap—thrill seekers to avid debunkers (posing as "scientific" researchers) to serious researchers looking into paranormal phenomena and genuinely spiritual realms.

Over the centuries myriads of books have been written on the subject of ghosts, Earthbound spirits and all manner of strange, disembodied phenomena. However, from the perspective of the Dead Saints, none has been written. Given their frequent encounters with such spectral apparitions in their life-altering journeys into the Afterlife, it is perhaps they more than others who are best qualified to speak with authority on the matter.

The Internet has made it possible for the first time to systematically collect, collate and explore large numbers of NDE testimonies looking for commonalities regarding the subject. Earlier investigations, however well-intentioned and intelligently devised, were hampered by the subjectivity of both the data and the providers of the data, along with its unavoidable unrepeatable nature. It was next to impossible to establish verifiable connections. Now, the Dead Saint testimonies take much of the guesswork out of the study. A common event links them all: all have died, (most can provide medical records to prove it); all have returned to life from the dead with their individual stories out of which come common themes, one of which concerns ghosts, apparitions and Earthbound spirits.

It is not so much the conclusions reached are very original. Rather, they re-inforce and elaborate upon very ancient teachings, including the spiritual guidelines laid down in nearly every religion, warning us like a parent admonishing a child, not to dabble with summoning up spirits in the Afterlife. For when we do so, we play with a fire we do not understand. The advice of religion has always been to seek God within for answers. If God, then, wants to send a spirit, or grandfather Tom, or an angel to communicate with us directly or in a dream, then and only then, is that acceptable.

The Dead Saints confirm that the ghostly entities they so often encounter in the Afterlife are indeed lost souls who never reach Death's Grand Central Station to prepare for the Life Review and Judgment—so they can move on. It is complicated. What we see, in our normal state, in the spiritual dimension is only the tip of the iceberg. We are playing in a very big universe with "powers and principalities"[1] we are only beginning to understand. It behooves us to beware.

Meanwhile, modern science, with no such qualms, tries an end run around the priests and psychics, attempting to communicate with spirits using electronic equipment to detect changes in magnetic, infrared, and room temperature when "spirits" are present. The SyFy channel's popular *"Ghost Hunters"* has produced convincing data regarding the existence of ghosts using sensitive equipment to detect (and sometimes literally "see" or "hear") ghosts.

All across America, amateur investigative teams are creeping through people's homes at night, trying to rid them of paranormal pests. Bill Wilkens, who created paranormalsocieties.com, a national online database of ghost-hunting teams across the United States, says 4,413 ghost-hunting teams are registered on his site, and 200 more have asked to be added.

John Zaffis, a paranormal investigator for 38 years (dubbed the "Godfather of the Paranormal") who hosts the television show *Haunted Collector* claims he's been attacked by hostile entities.

"I've been scratched, I've been burned. I've seen people levitate. I've seen people's eyes change, and I've seen people thrown around," he says. "That changes how you look at things." Noah Voss, a paranormal investigator for 25 years who sells ghost-hunting equipment at GetGhostGear.com, says the job requires not just nerve, but sensitivity as well. People share experiences with him they don't reveal even to their spouses.

Stephen LaChance, founder of the Missouri Paranormal Research and an "extreme" haunting specialist says, "Novice teams will try to provoke spirits, and the next thing you know *these things follow them home,"* he says. "About two years ago, we had more investigative teams calling us to help them than individual families. It was crazy." LaChance talks about his work as if were a ministry and sees their work as a way to help people in distress.

What is not made clear to their mass audiences is how dangerous this work can be. That the release of the movie '*Ouija*' is pitched to naive teenagers on the premise that contacting the dead through "Ouija Boards" or devices that can digitally record the voices of the dead, is "fun," disturbs me. It opens the uninitiated, untrained, and unprotected to spirits who are, at the least, no more evolved than those who summon them up and who are often spiteful and angry. What is promoted as "fun," could (and has) led to a number of dangerous situations – such as possession, spiritual attack, a haunted home.

There is a good reason a veil separates the living from the dead and separates the first Realms of Light from darkness in Earth University.

Superimposed Existence

The Dead Saints suggest the lower realms hold many mysteries. Dr. Ritchie describes in his book, *My Life after Dying*, how he went with the Son of God who revealed how the physical reality of the Earth is superimposed within dimensions of the "astral plane." According to Ritchie, these beings are not typically aware of our existence, just as we are not aware of them, including their structures and cities. He says beings there segregate themselves into "neighborhoods" according to "ethnic and moral" standards just as we do here on Earth. Birds of a feather stick together—because as he says, "It is too threatening to be with beings with whom you know disagree with you."[2]

Superimposed Astral/Earth dynamics are further revealed during a June 2015 interview I had with Margaret. During her NDE as a young toddler, she conveyed to me one distinct memory of how unseen beings co-exist on Earth:

> *I was on the brink of death. My family members (who were practicing Roman Catholics) had the village pastor perform final rites (called Extreme Unction at the time; now known as "Anointing of the Sick"). I experienced an initial period of darkness. I assume this was when I first fell unconscious...At some point I became aware there were two beings in the room with me. Although they seemed very solid, to my young self, they were VERY tall and appeared to be made of almost transparent pure white energy. They caressed me, and one sat with me at all times on the side of my bed while the other stationed himself beside the door to my room like a guard. I was aware at all times of both the 'real' world and the plane the beings of Light inhabited. In fact, the two worlds seemed to be super-imposed on one another. At times, I could see my parents in the room with the priest and he would sit on the chair right on top of one of my guardians. This astonished and upset my young self by its ignorance and rudeness, and from that time I developed a dislike and distrust of him and authority (especially religious authorities) that I have not been able to shake.*[3]

How these "astral" planes border the Realms of Heaven is an open investigation. From Dead Saint descriptions, these realms are diverse and multi-dimensional—all the way 'up' to the City of God.

Are Ghosts Real?

Henry had one question that was answered during his NDE. He asked, "Are ghosts real?" The answer he was given:

> *Yes, in the human body there are two forms of spiritual being. One is the "soul" which is the spiritual being that has a symbiotic relationship with the physical body. The second is the being created by the "biology" of the human body. This Being is intelligent and is basically the personality of the individual. Its purpose is to provide for the human needs of food, hunger,*

survival, and procreation. This concept is very similar to Freud's "Id, Ego and Superego," the division of mind and personality. The soul provides us with all the things of the individual that separates us from the Animal Kingdom. This is the ability to reason, use logic, or feel awe when seeing a sunset. The soul is the creative side of humankind. The second being is more our animal side and drives us to accomplish or pursue things to satisfy our needs and wants.

When we die, the soul separates and proceeds to the other side (Forgive me for simplifying everything). The entity of the body also dies taking with it the strong emotions, "baggage," and drives of human beings. This is a natural part of the dying process. However, sometimes under violent or sudden death this other/being, for lack of a better word, doesn't have a chance to die. Instead, it remains behind as the drive, emotions, and motivation of our spirit. This body being, without the guidance of the soul is basically just a shell. It wanders about with no goals or purpose.

It often repeats acts it has done before because memories are the only "guidance" it has. In time, this being's energy dissipates and nothing is left. But that process can take a long time. Hence, we have a "ghost" that haunts a house or person. A ghost has the center of its existence when it was with its human body and soul. Here on Earth it remains until it eventually vanishes. The ghost can be communicated with and guided, yet has no real will of its own, but only that of habit.[4]

Hafer noticed shadows of people walking like Zombies without purpose, a description indicative of ghosts:

> *I sensed I was in some kind of cave or dark tunnel, and towards the back a small Light appeared that grew larger to the degree my own light grew. It got nearer, as if it were a reflection of where I should go. In the darkness there were many shadows of people around me walking without feeling or purpose. (Like Zombies) I saw on my right a being who didn't show me his face and I thought it was my dead Grandfather because of the suit of English cashmere, his cane and hat, he wore when he was alive. He indicated to me that I shouldn't try to speak with those people because they would pay me no mind. They were in their own unconscious dream walking like robots. This made me sad and feel compassionate towards them. I decided to continue on my way towards the Light at the back of the tunnel and came out upon a very beautiful little beach where there were many ranges of colors I have not seen on Earth.[5]*

Ghosts are Memories, Spirits are real

Dead Saints have often reported spirits of those who are Earthbound are not typically the spirit of Grandma hanging around the house, because she is, for whatever reason just "hanging around." Spirits (not ghosts) often appear to be angry, hateful, and filled with guilt and remorse. When a "ghost hunter" or Ouija Board curiosity attempts contact, they find dark spirits in this type of emotional space. Of course, there will be the occasional "friendly spirit," who is afraid to face the Light, or some souls who have committed suicide and are so remorseful they cannot face the Life Review and Judgment, and for this reason, they have not gone through the tunnel, which deposits the soul into the Grand Central Station of Death in preparation to enter Heaven. It is why, I believe, there is the admonishment by Holy Scripture, not to attempt to contact spirits. Why? Bad things can happen.

On the other hand, there are mediums who appear to have the ability to receive communication from "normal" spirits, mothers, sisters, brothers, uncles and aunts who have gone onto the heavenly planes, but have the ability to reach down to this world to telepathically communicate with a medium to pass on information.

The Bible itself contains stories of ghosts or spirits. Some have expressed their confusion stemming from the teachings of their church, which claim, "Communicating with spirits is impossible...because when one dies, they are either in Heaven or Hell."

According to the Dead Saints, this is not necessarily the case. The spirit realm and physical realm do co-exist, yet, are on different planes. It is believed some ghosts may not be people on the other side; they could be residual energy or thoughts left over from traumatic or emotional past events, or ghosts in forms mentioned in the Bible.

One of the first verses many will recognize is I Samuel 28:13-15, where Saul has a medium, the witch of Endor, calls up the prophet Samuel from the other side of the grave:

"And Samuel said to Saul, why hast thou troubled me, to bring me up?"

The Scripture is very clear this was the spirit of Samuel and as Samuel had died and crossed over to the other side, that would make him a spirit.

This medium, the witch of Endor, who Saul used, saw many people on the other side, when she was calling up Samuel. One should also note in this verse, Samuel had maintained his form of an old man wearing a mantle, just like many documented ghost sightings of apparitions, which report the ghost to be dressed in period dress from their own time here on Earth.

So was Samuel a ghost, an after-image of the true prophet? Alternatively, was it really his spirit called down from Heaven? The first question to ask is how did this first human king of Israel, selected by God, get to a point where he would use the services of a witch?

There is major debate among Biblical scholars whether this was really the ghost of Samuel or some type of "familiar" or demon. The Hebrew word for medium, is *belowb*, which means, possessing a familiar spirit or Spirit Guide. Throughout Scripture, there are numerous warnings about what God thought about such people and warned others not to consult them. "Do not go for advice to people who consult the spirits of the dead, (Leviticus 19:31, see also 20:6) and "Any man or woman who consults the spirits of the dead shall be stoned to death." (Leviticus 20:27)

Why were the Old Testament Patriarchs so harsh? In what way is it dangerous to religion? Saul's experience shows mediums, or any one of us, can contact people on the other side. Nevertheless, Saul himself prohibited necromancy and divinations; departed souls could appear to the living *only with permission from God*. This may be the key; it is safe to listen to "spirits" from the other side of the veil only when God sends them to speak to us.

Earthbound Spirits: A Unique NDE Perspective

Spirits can attach themselves to houses, buildings, ships, and even lighthouses. They create their own "reality bubble" within the astral world, creating their own furniture and surroundings within a structure on Earth. It also appears sometimes these souls are so protective of their own "space" they haunt homes on Earth to deliberately drive out its physical occupants.

This actually happened to my mother in 1981, when an angry, hateful woman, who screamed at her "Get out of my house", attacked her in a dream! Mom and Dad lived in this 70-year-old gift shop with an attached apartment, along Hwy 11, in the Shenandoah Valley for six months. The dream attacks continued for several months, until they finally gave in, and moved out the house and back to Virginia Beach.

Another story of a soul creating a "reality bubble" could be taken right from the plot of the movie, *The Sixth Sense,* where a fatally wounded psychiatrist (played by Bruce Willis) continues to visit his widowed wife, and during his "day job," counsels an emotionally disturbed teen who can see the dead. He has no memory (or refuses to remember) of his dying, because the kid responds and communicates with him as he did in everyday life on Earth when he was alive.

Thinking he is still living, the psychiatrist tries to communicate with his wife in the same way, but wonders why she does not hear or notice him.

An interview I conducted with Daniel in 2014 describes a similar situation. During his NDE, Daniel had a casual conversation with a deceased friend who was a former narcotics police officer in Brazil. He had been shot and killed during a police blitz many years earlier:

> We talked for a long time remembering our childhood. He told me his family needed financial help. He left a wife and children. He told me he was thinking of working nights as a Security Guard after finishing his day work as a police officer. I was amazed by this. I interrupted him, 'How can you say that? You are already dead!' I stared at him. He didn't accept it, moved his head, and said, 'No,' you just dreamed I had an accident and died. The truth is that it didn't happen.'
>
> No matter how I tried to convince him he was dead, he refused to believe it.[6]

Why Do Spirits Become Earthbound?

A Dead Saint story reveals why spirits become Earthbound:

> Then, I saw [the Light] coming from beside the white table next to the head of the bed. It continued to brighten as I watched. It brightened to such an extent that had it been any ordinary light I would most certainly have been blinded. The next moment there flooded directly into my mind the words 'Stand Up. You are now in the presence of the Son of God' —whereupon out of the Light stepped what I could only describe as the most magnificent Being I have ever known.
>
> ... I suddenly found myself on the move again. This time we didn't bother about doors. It was straight up through the hospital roof. Then we flew at incredible speeds across the surface of the Earth, however there was no wind to slow us. After a few moments, I found myself approaching a city beside a huge expanse of water. In the city, all the streets and offices were unbelievably crowded. I could see people passing through other people like they weren't there. We walked into a factory and I saw assembly line workers who were putting together lawnmowers and enjoying a coffee break, while behind them a woman pleaded for a drag of their cigarettes as through she wanted it more than anything in the world.

When one of the workers clearly blind and deaf to the women behind him actually took a cigarette out of his packet and began to smoke it, the woman repeatedly snatched at it, but it was as if she was clawing at thin air. I came to the conclusion those people must be ghosts (spirits). Even though they were dead, they remained chained to the material world by the very things they had deemed most important during their lifetimes— their jobs, their cigarette smoking, and their material possessions...

Earthbound ghosts [spirits] destroyed by hatred, lust, and destructive thought patterns, find whatever they think, however fleetingly or unwittingly, becomes instantly apparent to all those who are around them— more complete than words could have expressed and much faster than sound waves could have carried it.

In addition, the thought that is most commonly communicated amongst Earthbound spirits were usually selfish thoughts, and this by its very act, kept them Earthbound. The Being of Light, it seemed, felt only compassion for these unfortunate souls, but he knew it was their will, not his, that kept them there.

I felt like Scrooge in "The Christmas Carol," having this wise Being accompany me back to the hospital for the final time. I wanted to start my life again afresh when I would care far more about other people and not just myself. No longer would money and possessions be my supreme objective, but I would live my life with a desire to make other people happy.[7]

There is a difference between the Realms of Light where deceased loved ones communicate love and deliver God's messages and the astral realm of Earthbound Spirits who are filled with hatred, envy and destructive habits and attachments. Losing these addictions is evidently, critical while still attending Earth University. It clears a path to the Kingdoms of Light, and away from the lower, darker realms, our topic of discussion in the next chapter.

---

1 Apostle Paul, "For our struggle is not against flesh and blood, but against the rulers, against the authorities, against the powers of this dark world and against the spiritual forces of evil in the heavenly realms." (Ephesians 6:12)
2 George G. Ritchie, Jr., M.D. 1991. *My Life After Dying, Becoming Alive to Universal Love.* Norfolk, Virginia: Hampton Roads Publishing. p. 23
3 Margaret W Interview with David Solomon, June 20, 2015. Reprinted with permission.
4 *Henry W NDE*, #1634, 06.22.08, NDERF.org
5 *Hafur Experience*, #1609, 01.19.08, NDERF.org
6 Interview with Daniel R. with David Solomon. August 10, 2014. Printed with permission.
7 *A New Hope NDE*, #270, aleroy.com/board270.htm

19
Tragedy, Evil, & Hell

~ After a finger pruning two-hour soak in the hot tub at the Atlantis Resort, we got to know everyone—their jobs, where they lived, and why they were visiting such a lovely tropical place. Sometime after dusk, it came my turn to talk about my life. I was still bald from radiation and never liked to mention my illness, but it came out anyway—the story about cancer and the Dead Saints Chronicles, which quickly became the hot topic of discussion. A businessman in the hot tub named "Marc" began telling Delynn and me about an experience when he was stabbed on a New York City street while on his way to a business meeting sometime during the 1980's. A man nearby in the midst of a drug deal saw him stabbed and ran over to help him after the assailant ran away. Blood was everywhere. The drug dealer flagged down a cab, dragged him in, and together they rushed to the hospital, an act that ultimately saved Marc's life. He later discovered the dramatic event caused the drug dealer to give up drugs and later he became a paramedic. After Marc told the story, no one spoke for several minutes. Like my cancer, tragedy is sometimes part of God's plan. ~Chronicle 176

In her best-selling book, *Finding Me: A Decade of Darkness, a Life Reclaimed*, Michelle Knight describes her kidnapping in 2002 by a Cleveland school bus driver. Trapped in a small cell along with two other kidnapped girls chained together in the room next to her,

Michelle was tortured, beaten and raped for a decade. In 2012, during her capture, she ingested mustard given to her on a hotdog, and nearly died of anaphylactic shock from an allergic reaction. After five days, her body bloated and in excruciating pain, she tells her co-captor Gina, "*I can't take it anymore.*" The next moment, she finds herself in total darkness, only to open her eyes to see a bright Light, brighter than any light she had ever seen on Earth. She heard a deep voice say, "*Michelle, it's not your time.*"[1] The next voice she heard was Gina, reviving her.

Her probable near-death experience convinced Michelle: *God is real.*

Upon her return to life, and subsequent escape and release, Michelle wrote about the tragedy, and has been an inspiration to millions...eventually forgiving her assailant.

If she had died, or if she did not have the horrible experience, she had, perhaps she would not have become the example of the power of forgiveness for millions. The horribly uncomfortable question is: Did God plan this for Michelle, or was she the victim of absolute evil?

When I first introduced this concept to my wife Delynn, she looked at me in angry disbelief, "Are you [expletive] serious?" Anyone who has lost a child to murder, rape or tragedy, despite their religious beliefs may react this way, and feel justified to react that way. Born-again Christian or not!

The testimonies of the Dead Saints give comfort and thought to this spiritual dilemma. It is a wrangling that drives some to become agnostic or atheist. Why would a loving God allow some people to be born into a good life of luxury, love and goodness, and others a life of poverty, pain, torture and evil? Is the universe a dartboard for being born into a life of wealth or poverty? Is God a God of Chaos or a God of Order?

Amy considered the same question during her NDE:

> *All of my life, I had felt confusion and dismay at what I believed was lack of order. When I saw suffering that I deemed, unnecessary, sadness, or anything I couldn't make sense of, I'd been riddled with a painful impression of Chaos. I was flabbergasted the God I so fervently believed in, and was taught to trust, could do no better than what I beheld in my everyday life. It tore at my soul and I prayed daily and sometimes for hours and hours, begging for an answer that could provide some kind of a reckoning for my confusion.*[2]

Religions have all sorts of explanations for the reasons behind tragedy like "good karma" and "bad karma," or some even pawn it off, as "It's just God's will."

They ask the question, "How can a loving God be part of such suffering? How do you explain evil in a world where God is supposed to be all-Loving?" Scripture and the Dead Saints teach us we are eternal beings. Life is a flash, a moment in our eternal existence. The manner in which a soul chooses to suffer is a part of the drama, the play or movie God, the Creator, and we plan in his blueprint set out for this life.

Indeed, despite their profound differences, many Christians (though perhaps not all) and many atheists can presumably agree concerning this:

If a young girl should be brutally raped and murdered and this should be the end of the story for the child, then a supremely powerful, benevolent, and just God would not exist. An atheist may seriously doubt *any* future compensation would suffice to justify a Supreme Being's decision to permit such an evil in the first place. The point even many Christians would concede, apart from an Afterlife, such an evil would constitute overwhelming evidence against the existence of God. In addition, some might even concede such an evil would be logically or metaphysically inconsistent with His existence as well.

So, how can we find answers to murder, rape, and tragic accidents in the NDE?

Rather than arguing for either side of the dilemma, please carefully read the testimonies of the Dead Saints. I believe these testimonies give another perspective in our search for one of the greatest dilemmas in life...a perspective not easy to hear.

Why Do Bad Things Happen?

According to the Dead Saints, tragedy is often planned into our Earth University curriculum before we are born. However, is tragedy all pre-planned, pre-ordained before we are born as part of our mission, or are we sometimes victims of tragedy by souls who use their free will to commit evil acts that were not planned? It is clear from Dead Saint testimonies that unplanned events...accidents...occur. Perhaps if nothing bad ever happened to us we would all be the same. Could we be like metal in a forge that has to be heated and struck repeatedly to make a useful tool from it? In addition, to be an effective tool for God, the Saints believe some of us choose to enter this life with a very difficult class schedule with some of the lessons appearing from our earthly perspective, horrific.

Therefore, while we may experience pain and sorrow on Earth, it is only a second in the grand scheme of things. We have an eternity to live. When we leave this life of pain, the trauma is forgotten and put in its proper perspective as part of the learning process.

Why Do We Have So Much Pain On Earth?

John attempted to take his own life. He discovered God had been with him throughout his life and he had come to Earth to learn how to love and forgive:

> *It was then I asked God why there had been so much pain in my life, and where had he been while I was suffering and so afraid? He then told me to hold my hand while He showed me something. I don't know exactly how to describe what happened next. The only way I know how to describe it as follows: have you ever seen a pond where, as matter decays on the bottom of the pond bubbles rise to the surface?*
>
> *Well, as God held my hand I could see great chunks of memories, many of which I had repressed as they were so painful, come floating up in front of me. I saw myself as a boy getting physically and emotionally abused by my father. I saw myself in grade school, being mocked and ridiculed by other boys and girls, for I had been a loner and an object of ridicule. I saw myself suffering at the hands of nuns and teachers who only knew how to humiliate and denigrate me. The memories were terrible, and watching them I felt so much sorrow and compassion for me as a child.*
>
> *He then told me to look closely, and it was then I could see a Light around my body during every one of the events. I could feel God's love for me as a little boy and He told me He had always been right next to me, and He had never left my side. I was overwhelmed by His love for me at this point, it was completely overwhelming. It was then everyone who had ever hurt me, from my childhood all the way to some of the personalities in the monastery I was having trouble dealing with what I saw, and they too had a Light around their bodies.*
>
> **I could see we were all wounded children**, *and the reason we were here was to love and forgive one another, and to help one another through this spiritual journey.*[3]

Thomas says Jesus can take away our pain. It is left behind when we die, but the lessons we learn from pain are eternal:

> *I remember asking [God] questions and receiving answers. The first question I asked was very impertinent. 'Why is there so much pain down there?' (Meaning on Earth). The answer was laughter. So much joyful laughter like a mother laughing at the amazing questions only a small child can ask. The laughter was*

followed with something like: 'Don't you know I have the power to take away all the pain? **I can rewind the universe and start all over again with one simple wish. The pain is left behind on Earth. It does not travel with us, but the lessons we learn from it are eternal.'** *I immediately accepted this without a doubt.*[4]

Sylvia says it's all part of the school—even the abusive stuff:

I knew I got this body because my mother and father had this little baby and all their close spirit (family friends) were used up. The baby was going to be a very weak, sick female body, but it was what I needed to experience, what I (the spirit) needed in order to grow spiritually. It was like taking a college class you hated, (like calculus), but you knew you had to get a passing grade in it in order to graduate. So I reluctantly agreed to take this body that belonged to a family I had never been with before. I also knew I had been in a previous body that was a huge mean man who abused women and children. I needed to experience what it felt like to be a small, sickly woman. I understood why the body was dyslexic. Now, that was a real challenge back in the 40-50s when you were humiliated and punished because you didn't know right from left. And (it is) why I chose nursing, and every time I tried to quit and go into another profession, I was pulled back. Everything was clear.[5]

Dead Saint 'C' says people will hurt you, but loved ones and angels can't interfere. It's a universal non-interference law. It is something we have to go through:

She told me to explain why she couldn't stop the people who were hurting me, from hurting me, but as she explained it, I knew the pain I was enduring hurt her, too. She was completely empathetic. I knew she (and the others with her) would always be with me. She explained while they couldn't stop what was happening, they would always be there to witness what was happening. I knew I would always have contact with someone who would understand completely what I had been through.

She wanted me to know that because they are not of this realm, it takes sensitivity to connect with them. They cannot directly affect what happens here **(she couldn't intervene to stop the abuse)***, but they can communicate and affect people (or animals, etc.) in this realm. Then we can, in turn, affect the world around us. It's a little difficult to explain the concept! Like I said,* *it was something I kind of just understood. It came from her—she was explaining it, but not in words.*[6]

What Is the Purpose of Evil?

There is probably no subject in all religious thought so hard to deal with as Evil. Theologians and philosophers of all persuasions have wrestled with accounting for its origins, the fact it exists at all, what defines evil in the first place, and a host of other intractable associated, but legitimate problems.

The great, primal, unavoidable question for theologians is this, "How can we account for the existence of evil within a Cosmos created by a supreme, omniscient, omnipotent, holy and benevolent God?" How can a Loving Creator God for no reason other than to suit "His all Knowing Will" rain tragedy and misfortune down upon the heads of the apparently guiltless and good fortune upon the heads of the certifiably malevolent without discernible rhyme or reason?

It's an ongoing argument between God and Satan in the Book of Job. It's a theological dilemma that can be, has been, and no doubt will be hotly debated to the end of time. Proverbs 16:4 says, "The LORD has made everything for its own purpose, even the wicked for the day of evil."

The prophet Amos specifies Evil is "of God," and poses a rhetorical question whose obvious answer would be blasphemous to the orthodoxy: "Shall there be evil in a city, and the Lord hath not done it?" (Amos 3: 6) and in Isaiah 45:7, "I form Light and create darkness; I make peace and create evil; I, the Lord, do all these things."

All major religions attempt in vain to answer definitively the question of Good and evil; Love and fear; Light and darkness; Heaven and Hell. In Christianity, Jesus is the embodiment of ultimate Good; Satan the embodiment of evil. In the East, the idea is expressed through Yin and Yang: duality, polarity, opposites—positive/negative. Every philosophy—religious or secular; every tradition sophisticated or mythical, addresses the dilemma to its own satisfaction, but seldom, if ever to the satisfaction of those not sharing that particular tradition.

Rather than trying to resolve the historically unresolvable myself, I feel it might be useful to see what the Dead Saints have to say about the matter...in those infrequent NDE testimonies where the question is addressed.

While perhaps no more satisfactory or definitive intellectually than any other explanation, they have, in my opinion, one huge advantage over practically anything previously written. They are personal and experiential, rather than abstract and theoretical. Speaking for myself, I would rather follow a recipe for fried eggs, written by someone who has actually fried an egg, than by someone who has not.

Carol describes the purpose for good and evil:

> I understood all good and bad happens for a purpose. That God wants the Devil to understand God is so good not even with all the bad the Devil does, God cannot do any harm to him [the Devil]. When the Devil understands such great love, this whole world or system of things will come to an end and everyone will experience this other world people like me try so poorly to describe. I understood God is everywhere because matter obscures that which scientists look for so diligently. The smallest tiniest part of all matter is God, too.[7]

Encountering Evil Spirits During an NDE

Dead Saints who encounter evil (shadow beings) when they are out of the body are not common. Most near-death researchers estimate "distressing" or "hellish" NDEs occur in a percentage in "the mid and high teens."[8] So while these dark and scary experiences seem uncommon, there are accounts to which we should pay attention. Evil takes advantage of fear, guilt, and ignorance at the time of death—situations we describe throughout this chapter.

On October 20, 2012, Kenneth had a heart condition known as atrial fibrillation, an irregular pulse, which required a procedure called 'cardioversion.' This is a process designed to shock the heart back into normal rhythm by means of administering an electric shock, but instead of restarting Kenneth's heart, the procedure killed him. His remarkable NDE describes him following his own body to the morgue where doctors prepare to do an autopsy on him. What Kenneth saw when he was out of his body, raises questions that should interest people of all faiths (or no faith):

[Author's note: Kenneth W's corpse was photographed in the morgue on October, 20, 2012, and posted on NDERF along with his NDE, but was removed within hours by their webmaster for obvious sensitivity reasons.]

> I really couldn't understand why I was in a state of disembodied consciousness whilst my physical body was clearly dead. It had already become a bluish/grey color. I could think reasonably clearly, but I feared for what would happen once my

body had been dissected for medical study. Would I be abandoned as a kind of spiritual wisp, a nothingness? Ostensibly dead, I was now an artifact and not a person. Clean, I was wheeled into another room down the corridor. Here, I was put on a sort of giant set of weighing scales, used for cadavers.

...I was squeezed in with other dead bodies, some covered in sheets and others naked. There didn't seem to be much space, as I was laid over a couple of old men, both with grey beards and obese; one completely bald and the other with a torso covered in tattoos - ugh! In the morgue, the presence of what I took to be the astral bodies of the dead people there was quite palpable. I got the feeling of welcome, and once again, other emotions such as shock and outrage, and resentment at being plucked from the living world.

I got the sense, more and more, of something very sinister lurking over me. I would describe this as a spiritual presence both malignant and at the same time seductive. I had the feeling it wanted to absorb me, and enfold me in an embrace that would end up in my oblivion. Something in me, as I floated in my non-physical state, wanted to surrender to this blackness and lose myself in it forever. But another voice seemed to be saying, 'Be careful! Don't!' I could liken it to the pull of gravity as the presence seemed to be pulling me closer and closer into its embrace.

I heard the mortician drone on about the tissue samples he intended to take, and felt the lines being drawn on my torso with marker pen to indicate where I would be dissected. But as I was about to be sliced, one of the attendees noticed a trickle of saliva dribble from my mouth. At first, the mortician refused to accept there were signs of life, and wanted to press on with cutting me open. He said my corpse was still fresh, and would provide valuable medical data. Lying there, my naked body was the source of much discussion, but luckily, instruments began to show a barely discernible pulse. I was brought back to life largely with the help of heart massage and a defibrillator.[9]

I struggled whether to include this Dead Saint experience in the *Chronicles*, but alas, while rare, there are more Dead Saint encounters like Kenneth's describing encounters with evil presences when out of the body. Three other NDEs describe such a situation right after death. Annette had a conscious (awake) after-death communication (ADC) with a man who had died seven days previously in a truck roll accident:

> *He had a demon-like creature on his right with its hand on his shoulder and an angel on his left, right in my living room. He was terrified. I immediately went into this deep prayer, I don't know for how long, and when the moment broke and I looked up he smiled, the angel grabbed him around the waist and flew off with him the demon thing hissed and snapped at me for a moment and flew off the other way. I know it sounds unbelievable but it is so true.*[10]

Deborah was facing off with "demons" when she cried out for God's help. Notice there is a hierarchy in Heaven:

> *[God] had a stern message for me concerning the chain of command. There was God, all of the angels, good and bad but somehow equal and somehow all loved by God. Then, there was Jesus, and I had a vision of His throne and his knees and somehow we were placed somewhere below his feet. I accepted all this knowledge happily without question. Then, I was told by the power of Jesus I could leave the demons and return to my body. Suddenly, I was facing the demons again and in my mind I repeated the information I was just given.*
>
> *Then I had to say it to the demons, 'By the power and authority of Jesus let me return to my body.' The demons gave me a total look of surprise and then I was back in my body.*[11]

Atana was being watched by "shadows" when she died:

> *Reaction to insulin. Low blood sugar. Unconscious. I cannot move or speak. Seeing myself bathing in bright Light, surrounded by 12 beings in white garments. I was in the middle of the circle, and also saw shadow people in the corner of my back yard. They were told they cannot come near me because I have done 108 good things in my life time.*[12]

The '108' things Atana had done in her life, perhaps representing all the good actions and thoughts of her life, more likely is symbolic and should not be taken literally.

Dead Saint "TO" was bitten by a Black Widow spider three times on the arm. She was found by her husband not breathing and without a pulse. She also reports "shadow beings" trying to wrap themselves around her:

> *As I opened my eyes, I saw the foot of the sofa was about 5 feet below me. I was ready to ask my husband to call 911...but decided against it...and then decided to pray. I WANTED to take [the*

Light] in..to go to it...but I DIDN'T because I knew what it meant. What I know it meant was, if I went with that Light, I'd be taken from this Earth. I cried inside and asked God to please spare me and give me a second chance at life. Before I was presented with the Light/Presence, I first went through a period of seeing and feeling several strange shadows kind of wrapping themselves around me and over me...suffocating almost. It was very frightening. This is when I began to beg God's forgiveness and mercy--for I suspected these "shadow beings" may have meant I would not be able to go to God... but that some horrible alternative would take over.[13]

Is Hell Real?

The fiery descriptions of the lower, dark realms stand in stark contrast to the brilliant Light of Heaven. Called *Gehenna* in Greek, and translated as *Hell* in English, it is a place of torment, hate, anger, resentment, and remorse. Traditionally, Hell serves as a prison for evildoers; it is punishment for those who repudiated God; a kingdom ruled by Satan, and the personification of evil.

But the hypothetical concept of Hell presents a real ethical/theological problem to several religions where the idea of a dark realm existing for the eternal punishment of damned souls is seen as inconsistent with a belief in an Omni-benevolent, loving, Creator God.

Some religions describe a plane of existence that can be likened to Hell, but they are not considered permanent or eternal. They are considered only an intermediary state brought about by a soul's evil actions while living on Earth. While some people believe Hell was created as a fantasy to scare people into good behavior, a dark reality should not be easily dismissed. The British novelist, and Christian apologist, C.S Lewis writes, "There are two equal and opposite errors into which our race can fall about devils. One is to disbelieve in their existence. The other is to believe, and to feel an excessive and unhealthy interest in them. They themselves are equally pleased by both errors and hail a materialist or magician with the same delight."[14]

Dead Saint Experiences of Hell

Dr. Ritchie describes in his book, *My Life after Dying*, how he went with the Son of God who took him on a tour of Hell:

There was no fire and brimstone here; not boxed-in canyons, but something a thousand times worse from my point of view. Here was a place totally devoid of love. This was HELL...There were beings arguing over some religious or political point, trying to kill the ones who did not agree with them.[15]

George observed remorse and the unwillingness to be accountable for our thoughts and actions is another slippery slope we must be aware of as we ponder our Afterlife destination:

I briefly "saw" both what would be considered Heaven and its counterpart. The terrible torment of those in "Hell" was far worse than the fire and brimstone crowd preach. It was something akin to spending eternity with those who would harm others in the same fashion as yourself, or conversely eternal loneliness for those who would, for lack of a better phrase, "fleece" others. The strange thing about the dark place was it was a place (and no place at the same time) you went to because of yourself. No one sent you there but yourself, and by the same token, only you could get yourself out.

Eternity seemed to be more of how you wished it. While Hell was well populated with millions of souls, it only made a very small dent in the total population of the Afterlife. I was struck by the accuracy of the Robin Williams movie, "What Dreams May Come," I saw just a couple of months later. Although not the best movie, its portrayal of the Afterlife is closer than anything I've ever been able to articulate.[16]

I believe all have a chance at redemption, even those living in the darker realms. The Dead Saints describe angels waiting for souls lost in Hell to look up with a desire to return to the Light, to God. Jean witnesses such an event:

Though I was also shown a much darker place too...where people did not seem to know they had moved out of their bodies and continually fought each other for material things. Material possessions were their focus, and all the actions were self-based there. But above them were also a legion of beings...waiting. Whenever someone looked up and asked God for help, they were whisked away to another place, a place more peaceful and tuned to God and God's love. But many seemed lost in this place, never looking up and never asking for help.[17]

NDEs of Hell often become a trigger for the soul to change its ways. It doesn't mean, as one Dead Saint declares, change is forced upon a soul, but it has another opportunity, another "mop and bucket" placed in the path they can pick up and to learn the lesson of love. It is an experience to remind the soul to turn towards the Light and to turn towards love. Nearly all who record hellish NDEs do just that. Of course, we do not hear about those who do not.

---

1 Michelle Knight with Michelle Buford 2014. *Finding Me, a Decade of Darkness, a Life Reclaimed*. Philadelphia, PA: Weinstein Books, Perseus Books Group. p. 204.
2 *Amy C NDE*, #2382, 10.09.10, NDERF.org
3 *John K NDE*, #3628, 03.26.14, NDERF.org
4 *Thomas M NDE*, #1890, 04.25.09, NDERF.org
5 *Sylvia W's NDE*, #152, 07.30.02, NDERF.org
6 *CS's NDE*, #428, 06.13.04, NDERF.org
7 *Carol M NDE,* #1616, 04.29.08, NDERF.org
8 Holden, Janice Minor, Ed.D. Greyson, Bruce M.D., and James, Debbie. RN/MSN, 2009. *The Handbook of Near-Death Experiences, Thirty Years of Investigation*. Santa Barbara, CA: Denver, CO. Oxford, England: Praeger Publishers, an imprint of ABC-CLIO, LLC. p. 81.

9 *Kenneth F NDE*, #4046,11.07.15, NDERF.org
10 *Annette W probable NDE*, #2379, 09.26.10, NDERF.org
11 *Deborah NDE*, #1150, 09.16.07, NDERF.org
12 *Atana NDE*, #1790,12.15.08, NDERF.org
13 *TO's NDE, #83,* 12.09.01, NDERF.org
14 C.S. Lewis 1942, 1961, 1996. *The Screwtape Letters* (New York: Touchstone), 61, Lewis, ix.
15 George G. Ritchie, Jr., M.D. 1991. *My Life After Dying, Becoming Alive to Universal Love*. Norfolk, Virginia: Hampton Roads Publishing. pp 24-25.
16 *Edward B's NDE*, #252, 04.02.03, NDERF.org
17 *Jean R NDE*, #2932, 01.18.12, NDERF.org

Part III

Bonsai Secrets

According to St. Paul, we see reality through a glass darkly. Our "perfect understanding" is still "yet to come" until we see the truth "face to face"—in Heaven or during a near-death experience. It is why, I believe, considering the translation problems encountered by early Christian scribes, we should weigh all Scripture carefully in our heart. None of us wants to doubt a single word we read in the Holy Book. Walking down this path is a no-win situation. If we begin doubting the words, where do we stop? I am sure many reading this paragraph are nodding in agreement. Still, I would like to find out why people, when they read some of the words in the Bible, feel conflicted in their hearts as to their true meaning. Bearing this convoluted and difficult, scholarly/theological discussion in mind, it is very interesting to see what the Dead Saints have to say on the matter.

20

The Governing Laws of Religion Are Not Absolute

"With every approach to knowledge guarded by the formidable array of experts and bibliographies, the aspirant must possess sharp wits and unnaturally developed skepticism if he is not to fall victim to one or other of the rival schools of dogma, secular and ecclesiastical, which, though mutually exclusive, unite instinctively to frustrate any attempt to avoid altogether the established orthodoxies, defined by Einstein as a "collection of prejudices which are fed to us with a porridge spoon before our eighteenth year." ~John Mitchell, City of Revelation

A few months after I began writing the *Chronicles*, I fell asleep early one night and within an hour woke up with the words, *"The Governing Laws of Religion are not absolute."* In my mind, that phrase was the Word of God. I had no conscious role in creating it. It fell and alighted in my mind like a bird from above. It was a straightforward, direct statement about religion that piqued my curiosity. And since I didn't rationally "create" the sentence, I wondered. Are the laws governing religion absolute? Without error? Infallible?

In my search for an answer among Scripture and the testimonies brought back by the Dead Saints, it became clear to me: **THAT MOST**, if not all, of our world religions (especially in the West) have been *self-*

shackled to the words of their own scriptures and self-sentenced to a lightless prison of self-righteous judgment about sin, morality, salvation and the Kingdom.

It's a heavy subject for any writer to tackle, much less handle in one chapter. A good starting point for understanding the words of religion, their laws, and whether they are absolute, is to take a quick look at how the words in the Bible became cemented in tradition.

~New Year's Eve 2013. Another day. Another year. Any wise words? The Dead Saint experiences seem altogether wholly consistent with a Biblical worldview with few exceptions. It's the few exceptions that make the Chronicles interesting. **~Chronicle 201**

The Old Testament

Originally, the Old Testament, which included the five books of Moses (*in Greek, Pentateuch*-five scrolls), the Prophets, and Apocrypha, were Divine revelations, both written and oral, given by God through Moses, some of them at Mount Sinai and others at the Tabernacle. All of the teachings were written down by Moses, or his scribe Joshua, and passed down orally in an unbroken chain from generation to generation, until its contents were committed to papyrus around 700BC (Archeological evidence discovered in 2004, suggests before the Babylonian captivity).

Painstaking care was taken in making written copies of the Old Testament, which is reflected in a statement in Psalm 18:30, "*The word of the Lord is tried*" pointing to the extreme caution taken with every word, letter, and mark of the Holy Texts preserved during the copying process (counting words and letters to insure accuracy).

The Hebrew priests memorized the Torah word for word. When the Old Testament was eventually written, the text appeared as one continuous set of consonants known as the "*Word of God*" with no breaks or vowels to separate words, and thus could only be read by priests who had memorized every word. To the uneducated, the unbroken document was incomprehensible.

In 278 B.C, Ptolemy II, the grandson of Alexander the Great, acquired a copy of the Torah for the great, new Library of Alexandria, but initially, was unable to find willing translators for the ancient, Hebrew script. According to tradition, Ptolemy eventually succeeded in convincing 72 Jewish scholars (six from each of the 12 tribes of Israel) to travel from Israel to Egypt to provide a translation from Hebrew into *Koine Greek*, the common dialect at the time. To guarantee accuracy, it was stipulated that the translators were to be kept in separate cells and deprived of the ability to communicate and compare notes.

Given the ancient obsession with secrecy, it might seem odd the Jewish priests would be willing to make public their Holy Text. According to a legend recorded in the *Letter of Aristeas,*[1] not only was the translation (on the island of Pharos) accomplished in just 72 days, astonishingly, each of the translations matched perfectly. According to tradition, Ptolemy was able to place the Greek translation of the Torah (called the Septuagint) in an honored place in the Library of Alexandra. Within the century following the writing of the Septuagint, the remaining 53 books of the Old Testament, included 14 Apocrypha, were translated separately into Greek.

It is assumed, under the direction of the High Priest Eleazar, the Hebrew scholars were *willing* to complete the Greek translation because the Hebrew Torah preserved its secrets in each Hebrew character-secrets that could not be translated into Greek.[2] What could be translated, was already memorized using three separate codes[3] to assign symbols to concepts:

Firstly, *Gematria*, a system by which all words have a numerical value which corresponds to the inherent numerical value of the 22 Hebrew letters, a code in which any word can be substituted for any other word of the same numerical value in order to disguise its meaning (both Hebrew and Greek letters have numerical value); and secondly, *Notarikon* (or Notariqon) derived from the Latin word notarius, meaning to write or interpret words according to their first or last letters, so the interpretation is based on abbreviations; and thirdly, *the Mazzaroth*, a system encoding the astronomical sciences, or study of the planets, stars, and zodiac (for example, Enoch was 365 years old when he was translated to Heaven—an obvious reference to the number of days in a year).

Unless you had the keys to the three systems of translation, you could never understand the deeper meaning of the five books of Moses, the Torah (The Law and history), the literal, written word, the Mishnah (knowledge), the symbolic interpretation of history, and the Qabalah (spiritual wisdom)—the ability to use the heart, not the mind, to interpret the Law, and apply that knowledge for spiritual growth.

This elaborate symbolic triple code written in Greek in the Old Testament, subsequently became the basis for the Latin Vulgate translated by St. Jerome in 382 A.D. for the Catholic Church, (the only authorized version of the Bible allowed to be read by priests and the public for nearly a thousand years). It was believed the Latin Vulgate-only view was necessary because of differences, errors, or corruptions in the Hebrew and Greek manuscripts.[4]

John Wycliffe, the German Gutenberg Bible in 1455, the Tyndale Bible in 1523, and eventually the familiar 1611 King English version of the Bible translated the first complete English version of the Bible in 1382.

Allowing for the immense tangled—and legendary—complexities involved in rendering the Old Testament from Hebrew into Greek, Latin and then English, it should be absolutely clear the veracity of the *Word of God* in the Old Testament is problematic at best, without even taking into account the numerous deeper symbolic codes embedded within Scripture.

The New Testament

During the first one-hundred years of Christianity, there was no Christian Bible. Different versions of Christ's story were read aloud to Christian congregations (who were only 15% literate at the time)[5] and passed from one to another. By the third century, some thirty Gospels circulated through Christendom including the Gospels of Phillip, Mary Magdalene, Thomas, and Judas-discovered in the Nag Hammadi Library, a collection of 13 ancient codices containing over fifty texts discovered in Upper Egypt in 1945. All were ultimately proven authentic and dated to the late second century by modern archeologists.

St. Irenaeus,[6] Bishop of Lugdunum in Gaul, (today Lyon, France) was an early Church Father whose writings were formative in the early development of Christian theology. In 170 A.D., he examined all the known gospels in circulation and condensed these into the four familiar Gospels of the Apostles Matthew, Mark, Luke and John:

> *The heretics boast that they have many more gospels than there really are. But really they don't have any gospels that aren't full of blasphemy. There actually are only four authentic gospels. And this is obviously true because there are four corners of the universe and there are four principal winds, and therefore there can be only four gospels that are authentic. These, besides, are written by Jesus' true followers.*[7]

Most scholars believe all of the apostles died long before their Gospels were committed to writing, as their stories were anonymous. From the Catholic encyclopedia, "It... appears that the titles [the authors] to the Gospels are not traceable to the Evangelists themselves."[8] Later editors added the attributions, they were not originally signed by their putative authors. If this is true, can anyone believe the words recorded in the Gospels attributed to Matthew, Mark, Luke and John are the exact, infallible words of Christ.

Citations of early 2nd century Latin and Greek fathers are made to appear as if they support one another, but in reality, the opposite is true:

> *In the first two centuries nearly all the various readings of the New Testament came into existence; the majority of them by deliberate alteration of text, many for the sake of style, and several in the interests of dogma...Often readings were rejected as falsification of heretics, but often the heretics were right in their counter complaint...every province, every order, every monastery, has a tradition of its own.*[9]

In his best-selling book, *Misquoting Jesus*, author Bart Ehrman notes the lack of original authentic New Testament documents:

> *Not only do we not have the originals, we do not even have the first copies of the originals, or copies of the copies of the copies of the originals. What we have are copies made later – much later. And in most instances, they are copies made **many centuries** later. And these copies all differ from one another in many thousands of places.*[10]

Church historian, Origen Adamantius,[11] in the early third century, describes the copies of the Gospels at his disposal:

> *The differences among the manuscripts have become great, either through the negligence of some copyists or through the perverse audacity of others; they either neglect to check over what they have transcribed, or, in the process of checking, they make additions or deletions as they please.*[12]

Richard Simon, a Hebrew Scholar, who published in 1689, *A Critical History of the Text of the New Testament,* argued all manuscripts embody textual alterations, especially the Greek ones:

> *There would not be at this day any Copy even of the New Testament, either Greek, Latin, Syriack or Arabick, that might be truly called authentick, because there is not one, in whatsoever language it be written, that is absolutely except from Additions. I might also avouch, that the Greek Transcribers have taken a very great liberty in writing their Copies.*[13]

The point of Simon's research was to show that while the books of the New Testament provide a foundation for Faith, the books themselves have been subject to interpretation and change as the Catholic Church handed them down over the centuries:

> *Although the Scriptures are a sure Rule on which our Faith is founded, yet this Rule is not altogether sufficient of itself; it is necessary to know, besides this, what are the Apostolical Traditions; and we cannot learn from them but from the Apostolic Churches, who have preserved the true sense of the Scriptures.*[14]

According to Greek and Hebrew scholars, there are some 200,000 to 400,000 variants, possibly more, of New Testament manuscripts known today. As one Greek professor states:

> *There are more variations among our manuscripts as there are words in the New Testament.*[15]

The Word of God in the New Testament (except for the *Book of Revelation*) is not so much a problem of trying to fathom complex variations in translation and hidden meanings of the Old Testament. Rather, it is a problem of verifying the authenticity of Greek and Latin documents which claim to accurately record the words, the life, the death of Jesus Christ, and the acts of the Apostles. Early Greek documents that comprise the 27 books of the New Testament do not have the same degree of perfection as ascribed to the Septuagint. There are no (legendary) 72 scholars to verify the word-for-word translation of Hebrew into Greek. Instead, thousands of Greek and Latin documents which have been altered, changed, and added to in many thousands of places, creating a firestorm of controversy about their word-for-word veracity, or for that matter, their veracity at all.

Even if we can verify them, most of us cannot read the ancient languages to understand the subtle differences in meaning. Bart Ehrman writes in *Misquoting Jesus*:

> *If the full meaning of the words of scripture can be grasped only by studying Greek (and Hebrew), doesn't this mean that most Christians, who don't read ancient languages, will never have access to what God wants them to know? And doesn't this make the doctrine of inspiration a doctrine only for the scholarly elite who have the intellectual skills and leisure to learn the languages and study the texts by reading them in the original? What good does it do to say the words are inspired by God if most people have absolutely no access to these words, but only a more or less clumsy renderings of these words into a language, such as English, that has nothing to do with the original words?* [16]

As a Christian, it is difficult for me to accept such conclusions along with the weight of historical facts, but most Greek and Hebrew scholars will not deny them. They point out most textual differences are minor, but debate (and sometimes turn a blind eye) to certain alterations that completely change the meaning of pivotal, theological concepts. Unavoidable and unresolvable translation problems further complicate and muddy the waters.

As we expand in later pages, subsequent theological changes to mainstream Christian beliefs were ratified at the Fifth Council of Constantinople convoked by Emperor Justinian in 543 A.D. Many Christians are unaware how much of the Bible we read today was determined by Church politics in those early centuries. Today, within the Church, the general belief is the Holy Spirit saw to it the integrity of the *Word of God* remained pure and inerrant. The Catholic Encyclopedia states:

> *These Books are Sacred and Canonical, because they contain Revelation without error, and because, written by the Inspiration of the Holy Ghost, they have God as their author.*[17]

Within this framework of history, how can the laws governing morality, sin, Heaven and salvation, and the words, which govern them, be absolute? If we do not have the original documents, how do we know the Word of God is the Word of God? The argument then follows: Can Scripture be inerrant when the early Christians were rarely, if ever, unanimous in any of their writings?

The Apostle wrote about dilemma of "partial knowledge" in 1 Corinthians 13: 9-12:

> *For we know in part, and we prophesy in part. But when that which is perfect is come, then that which is in part shall be done away. When I was a child, I spoke as a child, I understood as a child, I thought as a child: but when I became a man, I put away childish things. For now, we see through a glass, darkly; but then face to face: now I know in part; but then shall I know even as also I am known.*

According to St. Paul, (I am paraphrasing): *we see reality through a glass darkly. Our "perfect understanding" is still "yet to come" until we see the truth "face to face"—in Heaven or during a near-death experience.* It is why, I believe, considering the translation problems encountered by early Christian scribes, we should weigh all Scripture carefully in our heart. None of us wants to doubt a single word we read in the Holy Book. Walking down this path is a no-win situation. If we begin doubting the words, where do we stop?

I am sure many reading this paragraph are nodding in agreement. Still, I would like to find out why people, when they read some of the words in the Bible, feel conflicted in their hearts as to their true meaning. Bearing this convoluted and difficult, scholarly/theological discussion in mind, it is very interesting to see what the Dead Saints have to say on the matter.

Dead Saint Commentaries about the Bible

Nilda never understood the Bible. Yet, during her NDE, Jesus insisted she would learn that the BIBLE IS SUFFICIENT:

> *[Jesus] told me, 'You had been searching a great deal, studying and reading too much, but not what you should have read. Why didn't you read it?*
> *I asked Him, 'What hadn't I read? And He replied, 'The Bible. All that you should know is there. It is sufficient.'*
> *I said, 'I tried to read it, but I didn't understand it. It is too complex for me.'*
> *He said, 'Now you are going to understand.'*[18]

The Bible is sufficient. It has everything we need to grow spiritually. However, if we don't understand it, the Word of God can become an obstacle or used as a judgment gavel. It is why I believe Dead Saint "commentaries" from the Afterlife are so important. Their holy experiences help bring clarity and understanding to the Bible.

Scott didn't find any conflict with his NDE and the Bible:

> *What amazes me is how much of the Bible is correct as a base for understanding God. I didn't find any conflict within the Bible and my near-death experience. Instead, it helped me better benefit from the experience by giving it additional meaning. It was such a relief and a good feeling to know something mankind has placed on that level is truly meaningful. One of the things I mulled over is the age-old debate over evolution or creation, but it is really quite simple. This is what I meant when I said things are unbelievably simple, but yet mankind tries to complicate things, for whatever reason. Maybe we're not involved enough yet, but it isn't really hard to understand that God created evolution, so therefore you have both. At some point, science and religion meet.*[19]

During Diane's NDE, she gained a new understanding of the Bible:

> *I had read the Bible before my NDE and can't say I understood it or appreciated it, but during my experience, I had a revelation about it. I read it again after my experience and I understood it completely, no longer through a glass darkly. And not anything like I learned in Bible study. Actually the Bible*

helped me put my experience into words. It's all there. You just have to read from a different level of consciousness to see it. I realized a lot of it was about what people back then learned through their own near-death experiences. People haven't stopped having them, we're just more vocal about it today. **Back then, others thought people who claimed to have mystical experiences were Saints.** *Today they call us nut cases or try to explain it away scientifically so we don't cast doubt on their long held beliefs based on a wrong worldview.*[20]

Anne Marie felt closer to the Bible after her NDE:

One day I felt compelled to find a Bible I had been given shortly before my NDE. I had never really read it, wasn't interested, and thought it confusing. On that day, I opened it blindly to whatever page fell open. The page spoke of the wisdom of God, and how the spiritually immature can read and hear God's word, but are unable to understand. As I read, the words seemed to be absorbed literally into me, as though I recognized them and knew them somehow. I read for hours, feeling spiritually fed and renewed.

Now, I feel close to God when I read the Bible daily and interact with other believers. Religious organizations will always have conflicts and leaders who are stubborn and rigid. They are human and imperfect, but many people gain a Christ-centered life through organized religion. I was given a short cut, but didn't recognize it as that until the past eight or nine years. I don't want to waste any more precious time. No one has all the answers, but if we allow ourselves to be led by His spirit, truth will always be evident.[21]

What is perhaps the most striking common feature of the NDE as it relates to religion is that people who weren't openly religious, or not religious at all, prior to their experience, return as unshakeable believers, with a keen living appreciation for the spiritual, invisible realm. In other words, the Kingdom is not reserved only for the religious—as much as the more extreme adherents of every religion would like to us believe.

The Dead Saints come back from their NDEs often focused upon a common, reiterated theme: true religion resides not in doctrines, dogma and denominations, but in our ability to love. The Saints have learned through personal experience that God is infinite, magnanimous, a Being or Presence greater than any single religious institution. That said, people who were Christian tend to stay Christian. People of other faiths tend to remain in them as well, albeit with a heightened appreciation of their core values.

Sometimes, if they were members of some fundamentalist denomination preaching a vindictive, judgmental doctrine, they will make a quick exit and look for a place committed to a loving God corresponding to the God of their own near-death experience. Still, others will consider any institutionalized religion too structured and constricting and will find their way to some alternative, spiritually oriented discipline better suited to their personal needs, beliefs and experiences.

Interpreting the Word of God through a New Perspective

Linda describes how her understanding of Christianity changed after her NDE:

> *My journey to understand God began in the rugged environment of a Texas childhood that was filled with "rattlesnakes, tornadoes, and hellfire-and-damnation." My early concept of God was molded by the pervasive, extremist religious community of the Bible belt exemplified by the Southern Baptist Religion practiced by my parents. The wrathful, vengeful God, as taught by my religion, instilled in me a deep fear of God, death and the Afterlife... 'My lifelong search for a loving God and release from the paralyzing fear of death culminated in a brief journey to Heaven after a debilitating illness. The near-death experience transformed me, showing God is only a loving God, who does not judge and punish. I came to understand the Oneness of all existence which permeates my life with peace and the unfaltering knowledge of God's goodness... It was not a belief, perception or understanding, but my recognition of Christ came from my new perspective of Spirit.*[22]

This Zen-like recognition came from a new understanding of Spirit, not from words written on paper.

Defining God

The revelations of the Dead Saints put all religions into a bright, fresh perspective. That perspective, I believe, requires us to define in words (as best we can) "Who and what is God?"

John says in 1 John 4:8: "He that loveth not knoweth not God; for **God is Love.**" 1 John 1:5 helps expand the definition: "This then is the message which we have heard of Him, and declare unto you, **that God is Light**, and in Him is no darkness at all." In Job 33:4 the ancient

Patriarch says, "The spirit of God hath made me, and the breath of the Almighty hath **given me life**."

Therefore, from a Biblical point of view, "God is Love, Light, and Life" are simple definitions most Christians and, I believe, most religions are capable of agreeing with. This Creator "God" force empowers all matter, all flesh, and all life. It is described by the Dead Saints as a brilliant, dazzling Light, which would blind us if we saw it with our physical eyes on Earth.

The Dead Saints report there is a "Light that casts no shadow," a Light that is synonymous with unconditional Love, Life, and God, the origin of all creation, and in Christianity—Jesus Christ.

Paul Solomon related principles of this spiritual Light to physics:

> *The light we see on Earth can be measured in photons. Even from a strictly scientific point view, light is real. At the apparent opposite end of the light spectrum is darkness. Unlike light, however, darkness is not a "something." Darkness is the absence of light. The absence of light is "no thing," and we equate it with Fear, Death, and the Anti-Christ (Satan). In physics, there is no such thing as a "unit of darkness." [Author's note: Theoretical physics describes anti-matter; an opposite charge to matter, but it is not the same analogy here].*
>
> *Darkness cannot be measured. Therefore, darkness is not real, not in any physical sense. It appears real, but it is not. It is an illusion. While darkness may serve us well as a point of reference for a source of Light, because darkness has no substance, it has absolutely no power or defense against the Light. The presence of Light simply reveals that darkness does not, in reality, exist.*[23]

Using this principle, we can understand fear is not real. Only Love is real. Only Light is real. Sherree describes the brilliant Light she saw during her NDE:

> *All I remember is seeing a bright Light that was 1,000 times brighter than the sun and the feeling I had as the rays shone down on me of peace, love, serenity, like I was safe, I was home, and I belonged. It was awesome!* [24]

Clara experienced the Light as God:

> *I then consciously let go of the struggle for life and was immediately with the Light. Outside of the physical world entirely; outside of time and space. Seeing not with eyes, but sensing? Enveloped in the Light. I felt unconditional love, peace*

and joy to an extent that can never be felt or experienced here. I was one with the Light. I was whole. I was home. No bad or evil exist there. There is no pain, no hunger, no thirst, no suffering, no struggle, no baggage, no illness, etc. I sensed there were many and we were all one, one with each other and one with the Light in perfect, Holy Communion with the Light. I felt such awe and love and peace and joy. I call the Light God. I love that Light with all my heart and soul.[25]

Linda experienced God as Christ:

The Light moved over and through me, washing every hidden place of my heart, removing all hurt and fear, transforming my very being into a song of joy. I had thought the love I felt from Christ was complete; yet, the Light toward which we were soaring was the fulfillment of my search, the loving Source of all that exists, the God of truth and unconditional love, the origin of creation.[26]

The Logos, the Word, & the Light

In John 1:1-5, The Evangelist prefaces his Gospel with an introduction about the Word, the Light, and the Divine Nature within us:

In the beginning was the Word, and the Word was with God, and the Word was God. The same was in the beginning with God. All things were made by Him; and without Him was not any thing made that was made. In Him was Life; and the Life was the Light of men. And the Light shineth in darkness; and the darkness comprehended it not.

During my Seminary studies, Paul Solomon interpreted the first chapter John in a manner similar to many Dead Saint testimonials I have read. He interprets the (Greek Logos) or Word, as the "expression" or Christ, so John 1:1-5 could be paraphrased:

In the beginning, God expressed Himself, and the expression of God is Love, and Love is God expressing Himself. The Love that is God expressing Himself was with God when all things were made. Love made all things, and all things are made of Love. In Love is Life, and without Love, there is not Life. It is Love that gives Light and consciousness to all who are born. Love shines out in darkness as the Source of Life and awareness, though there are some who do not know it.

Paul's paraphrase of John 1:12 concludes:

A gift to those who become aware that it is Love that gives Life and Light is the ability to know themselves to be the Sons and Daughters of God." In essence, we are all capable of becoming the True Light, the Sons and Daughters of Light, by accepting Christ as the ruler of our heart, mind, and body.

The Divine Nature Vs Our Animal Nature

When we start trying to be "religious," we often start trying to force our animal nature to behave as though it is not a beast. Our animal nature is naturally "afraid." It is fearful. But rejecting the animal within is not a path that works, or that can work. A central problem with most organized religions is they deny, even vilify our human, animal nature. Organized religion often rejects the beast and its nature. However, if we reject an animal, we will have trouble living with that animal. If we don't accept it exactly as it is, even love it, it will rebel to our peril.

We may try to so discipline our mind and body that we obey the "rules," including ancient, hallowed rules that are nevertheless contrary to our nature. The result is a self-incarcerated, cornered, angry being always ready to explode.

Religions can, and do, have that effect on us. They demand a code of behavior that almost invariably conflicts with our natural desires, yearnings, and appetites. However, there is a divine nature, a consciousness, a spark of life within separating us from our animal nature. This is the uniqueness of humanity! All other beasts, as far as we know, have a nature born of animal, born of the earth and it follows that nature. Unless humanity intervenes, it acts according to its nature. There is nothing wrong with a tiger killing a deer—that is its nature.

There is nothing wrong for us to experience our animal nature in its totality—desires, emotions, expressions. What is wrong is to identify wholly with that animal nature, our beast, as if it were our *only* real nature. According to Amy, she learned exactly this lesson:

I learned we are here to learn how to Love, Divinely. To become masters of ourselves. To rule our own lower, or denser aspects of self and to bring these forward and upward within, to our highest possibility.[27]

Areliala's NDE describes how we can learn to overcome our denser self, and identify with the Word, the Logos, allowing us to graduate Earth University with flying colors:

> *There was a man or a being that was male who explained things after I had to leave my husband. He explained WE create our own dilemmas as a species. The object is not to create dilemmas, not to get around it, but to go through it as though it doesn't exist. Our Earth reality is only an illusion. In other words, this reality is a false sense of power we buy into.*[28]

Dealing with the Governing Laws of Judgment, Punishment and Damnation

Institutionalized religions are commonly replete with governing laws relying upon Scripture as their basis for Judgment. In the process God (by whatever name) gets polarized into a wrathful Being verses a loving Being, a God of damnation and punishment vs. a God of love, mercy and forgiveness.

John W. Price in *Revealing Heaven,* writes about Robert, a former Fundamentalist preacher whose transforming NDE cost him his pastoral career. Robert told Price, "I used to tell people to read Jonathan Edwards' 1741 Sermon, *Sinners in the Hands of an Angry God,*[29] a puritanical, fundamentalist approach to the Bible. Then one day, Robert had an NDE while in a coma. He left his, floated away and went into what looked like a dark womb, lit up inside by a ball of yellow Light:

> *I believe I went into the womb of some nature to be healed. It was like my hard drive just got completely erased, and I came back to relearn.*[30]

According to Price, "He rested in a peaceful state that seemed like five-minutes." When Robert woke up from his NDE, he immediately knew he had believed a "lie that hurt thousands of people. People would fill the churches up to hear this [lie]. I had a very charismatic personality. It seemed the less I preached in love, the more busy I stayed." [31]

Price describes Robert's return to his church to share his NDE with the congregation: "When he returned to the pulpit, he shared the new insight about a loving and forgiving God. The congregation melted away; his income went down to nothing except for his loving wife, who liked what he had become. I know of three preachers with similar backgrounds who lost their congregations when they switched to talk about a loving God.[32]

Robert eventually lost his church and his career. He didn't want to teach about the God of Fear anymore, and now uplifts the God of Love, pastoring the dying through Hospice.

Preachers (of all religions) committed to serving an "angry God" turn the Deity into a Being inspiring only fear. Their congregations are given long lists of dos and don'ts designed to curtail and control their base animal nature. These harsh, rigid sects ban drinking, feasting, dancing, music, card playing, and especially sex. Indeed, anything fun or gratifying to the senses is reviled as a temptation to sin.

I feel it is the attempt to *control* our base *animal nature* in order to avoid "sin" that has created the angry God; the judgmental, punitive God who overshadows us in the living of our daily lives.

Steve, after his NDE, understands this angry God fabrication or "myth":

There is a myth that has been circulating for centuries, and just for the record, I used to be one who put stock in this myth. If we are not all good little people and follow God's word and seek salvation, in the Afterlife, he will condemn us to eternal hellfire and damnation. Contrary to this very popular belief it isn't a wonderful and loving God who condemns us by any means, but rather by the use of our own free will, we choose to—in a sense condemn ourselves.[33]

Sometimes Dead Saint experiences shed new light on harsh Christian beliefs, changing their spiritual perspective. Bette was a Sunday school teacher in a fundamental church. After her NDE, she realized nothing was as if she had always believed:

I became metaphysical overnight. It was like osmosis. There were no books. Nothing was even whispered like my 'knowing.'[34]

The Belief in Punishment

As far back as 3,500 years ago, patriarchs, priests, and even leaders of nations established punishments based on the laws governing the religion of their day. Judaism meted out harsh sentences for breaking any of the Ten Commandments. Those who broke the Sabbath or committed adultery faced death by stoning. Some Fundamentalist Muslim countries and sects, even today, continue with this literal adherence to Sharia Law (even harsher than Mosaic Law), but adding beheading to the list of preferred punishments—even as more civilized, advanced, largely secular societies have abandoned such practices.

The historical record reveals virtually all past societies worldwide found ways to twist their specific laws of religion to justify wars of conquest, and subjection, enslavement or decimation of the conquered peoples.

Today, some of the governing laws of religions have begun to change. Orthodox Christianity and Judaism at least no longer stone sinners to death—even though the failure to do so is technically a violation of the words of sacred Scripture. As though in compensation, Fundamentalist factions of these religions have re-employed the same harsh, ancient language to condemn individuals for their views on sexual preference, abortion, marriage, divorce, and suicide, judgments which supposedly determine their Afterlife destination.

Do we worship a God of severity, punishment and hate or a God of love, kindness, and mercy? In reading thousands of Dead Saint testimonies, I have never read one, no matter his or her sin, who encountered a wrathful God. EVER.

Sin and the Law of Zen Archery

The meaning of the word "sin" has come a long way from its origins. The principal word in Hebrew translated, as sin is the word *chatta'ah* and its derivatives *chata* and *chet*. The word *chatta'ah* means to sin, miss the way, go wrong, or incur guilt. The sense of the Hebrew word includes both willfully going against what one knows is right and accidentally going against the Divine order of things. The second most common word for sin in the Old Testament is the word *pesha*. This word is most commonly translated as *transgression*, but it is also translated as trespass or sin. The word *pesha* has a connotation of breaking a rule that has been established.

There are other Hebrew words translated as sin as well, but the common Greek word for sin used in the New Testament is *hamartia*.[35] This word derives from a technical word used in archery. It comes from the ancient story of King David written in Isaiah and means, literally, to "miss the mark." Sin simply means failing to hit the target. It means being less than perfect. It doesn't mean the sinner is a criminal, or evil. It just means more practice is needed to get it right.

Scripture tells us David was a man after God's own heart. In spite of David's "sins," God considered David a friend. In Psalms 27:11, David asked God to "teach him," using the Hebrew verb *yara*, a verb about shooting arrows, but also the root word for *Torah*. David wasn't asking God for archery lessons, so why does he choose this verb and how does it relate to sin? David was asking God to "teach him" to become a better person using the metaphor of archery. If you practice daily, God says your aim will get better and better, until one day you may finally shout, "Bull's eye!"

From the perspective of Zen, however, there is no target to hit. We are the target. The same metaphor is used in the movie *The Matrix*, when Neo realizes he doesn't need to bend the spoon, that he *IS* the spoon.

Religion gives us rules as guidelines for living a holy life, not nails to crucify others and ourselves. Repeatedly we discover in stories of the Dead Saints we are judged by love, and when we look more closely at the Bible, this begins to make more sense. Pre-marital sex, homosexuality, eating pork, and shellfish, charging interest on loans, and violating the Sabbath, are among the many restrictions that were a part of the Old Testament Law Code.

However, Romans 10:4 says, "For Christ is the end of the law for righteousness to everyone that believeth." Hebrews 8:13 says, "A new covenant, he hath made the first old. Now that which decayeth and waxeth old is ready to vanish away." Since Christ fulfilled the law, love overcomes it, and that is all that really matters.

A Dead Saint's Point of View of Sin

I have included a few Afterlife commentaries on what are considered sins by the noisiest of the self-appointed religious: abortion, divorce and suicide. The few testimonials I draw from are not exhaustive, but are a small sampling for a much larger study that needs to be done.

Abortion

Is the decision to have an abortion wrong? What do the Dead Saints say about it? Randy describes her own guilt about her abortion:

> *I started to feel a panic about whether or not I would go to Hell for having had an abortion. The Light communicated to me I was completely loved and the difficulty of the human condition was totally understood. I was told 'EVERYTHING IS COMPLETELY ALRIGHT.' I can't communicate the intense and all-encompassing nature of that statement, but it completely washed away every single fear I ever had.*[36]

Mary had experienced life-long guilt about aborting her fetus at age 21:

> *As I had an abortion when I was 21, several years before (& incidentally, THAT is the experience that truly shook up my life and put me on a different course), I expressed my never-ending guilt for having taken away the life of my unborn being. Instantly, I focused on what seemed like a star, a bright Light, and I knew*

that that was the soul of that being. It was irrelevant whether it was a male or female. I put forward my feeling of sorrow and guilt and was in turn washed over by a feeling of complete forgiveness - unlike any earthly forgiveness.[37]

What happens to the spirits of the aborted, or those who die at birth? Mary reports aborted babies, and those who die at birth, continue growing in Heaven:

> Then I saw babies as far as the eye could see and then some. They were **'our precious abortion babies'** said the angel. But when I told him they were all different ages, he told me, 'You don't stay a baby, but will grow to about 34 or 36 [years of age they would have been in Earth years]' [38]

If a woman can extend her belief system, I believe she can communicate with the incoming soul about her ethical dilemma. She should watch her dreams. They may carry a message about the importance of her choice. Again, setting an absolute rule of right and wrong doesn't solve a woman's dilemma about abortion. Nor does a decision to abort condemn her to Hell, or keep her from entering the Kingdom.

Divorce

Bolette describes an NDE where she is told a divorce would happen later in her life:

> I was told I would be divorced from my husband later on, because we couldn't go on together, my former husband and me. That we both had something else to do and I should look at it as a joyful thing for me. It would give me joy and much freedom to be divorced, but it wasn't to happen just yet. I should forgive my then-husband and his actions and attitude. I should with joy and gratitude go on with my life after, even though he would hurt me deeply, because it was required for me to let go of him. [39]

Sylvia in her NDE wondered why she didn't feel married to her husband:

> I searched for many years for the answers of "why I didn't feel married to my husband, after this near-death experience, and also as to why my two small sons didn't seem like they belonged to me. I visited many churches, talked to many pastors, went to several doctors but none could give me even the remotest clue. God pointed [her] to a story in the King James Version of the Bible

about the woman who had many husbands who passed away and the disciples asked the Lord to whom would she be a wife to once in Heaven? His reply was 'to none of these.'[40]

Robert sees his ex-wife during his NDE:

I instantly knew the Light was pure goodness and love, like nothing I had ever felt before or since. I noticed some people near me and walked over to them. One was my mother and another was my first wife...they would be watching over me and we would all be together again. Before I could respond, I opened my eyes and found myself lying on the ground.[41]

Suicide

In all cases, I have read and researched, God responds to suicides in a loving, non-condemning manner. From the viewpoint of the Dead Saints, suicide is not condoned, but neither is it condemned However; there are repercussions to acts of rash suicide. However, most suicides are not born of well thought out endings. Most are rash acts born of desperation to escape the mental and the emotional agony of witnessing or experiencing pain. It is this type of suicide, the deliberate aborting of the Earth University Mission, I am addressing.

I believe there is a root cause to the belief that leaving through suicide is a mistake or a sin. The evidence brought forth by the Dead Saints indicates we made a commitment before we were born to complete our Mission on Earth. I also believe those who commit rash acts of suicide do not understand the repercussions of withdrawing from Earth University before their appointed time. For example, 13-year-old Lisa, decided to commit suicide by drowning. Choosing this path was in a way, an intentional act of disobedience:

I felt a presence with me, and I knew this presence was our Creator. Through thought, He presented me with a question, 'Do you really want to hurt your family like this.'

This Presence asked me through thought. He did not stop me, but wanted me to weigh the price of my decision to allow myself to cross the line and die, or to choose life. I argued no one seemed to care whether I lived or died anyway, so what was the point of life? Then I was reminded of my sister and mother— and how much grief my death would cause them. That alone almost made me want to get up from the water right there, but I still stubbornly remained floating and tried to see what would happen if I did die.

With this intention I had, I felt God showed me if I did decide to go against what I knew He wanted for me at that time to know

> that I would be causing a great disobedience in my life and I could actually FEEL this friction of disobedience—that I was really pushing things.
>
> This felt very uncomfortable so I decided then to get up out of the water mainly for that reason alone even though I also knew I didn't want my mother to suffer any grief over me...I realized this was a supernatural experience I was permitted as a type of lesson about suicide's repercussions.[42]

We see another example through Nicole's NDE when she saw the consequences that would occur from suicide:

> [Then] either a Seraphim or God Himself, flew right over my sleeping body (my spirit returned to my body, and waited to be collected by angels) and said, in the most loving of voice. 'I can't take you now honey, I'm sorry.'
>
> ...I also heard the same voice, God, who said, 'I'm sorry doll, but sometimes when people attempt suicide, and it's not their time to go, they end up in situations just to pass time away, until it's time for that lifetime to end. And sometimes they end up in situations such as this. This is what happens.'
>
> The voice was so soothing, so loving. I knew this was a time to learn.[43]

The Dead Saints teach if you choose suicide to depart Earth University before your scheduled "Graduation,"— your appointed time of death— you may have to repeat your classes all over again. Bummer.

Observing Dark Marks Within a Soul

So, then, isn't there a consequence to making mistakes? Committing sin? Missing the mark? Who serves up justice when evil kills, rapes, pillages, and steals? Who judges the just and the unjust? Does it mean we have no rules to live by? How will love guide us to rightfully approach mistakes in ourselves and in others? Certainly, the Word of God can guide us, but in the end it is the Divine spark of God within, the Word, the Christ, who becomes our conscience and helps us decide what is good and what is not.

Drawing from the Dead Saints, justice comes swiftly at the end of life during the Life Review, of this there is no doubt. There are consequences for the decisions and actions we take. Decisions and actions which create fear, hate, anger, pain, and imbalance are evil and must be paid for. Decisions and actions, which create love, joy and balance, are rewarded. They glorify God and the Light.

One of the more interesting finds in my research show how wrong decisions and actions affect us. Lucia observed black marks on a soul who had done many "bad things":

All of a sudden, I was standing at the head of my body, looking to my left. I did not see my body (that I can remember) but my vantage point was from there. To my left, the head nurse started screaming I was having a severe allergic reaction. She started running towards the cot and then tripped over someone's I.V. I remained calm, watching this like I had no stake in this. Like a scientist observes something under his microscope.

The next thing I remember I was flying at some high speed through a tube. It was bright colors of purples, reds, and blues. Then, I found myself in a tunnel. Everything I saw from here on was in shades of blacks, whites, grays, silver. I was walking. Something from my left side reached out towards me. Someone on my right side slapped the "hand" away. It fell to the floor of the tunnel. I turned & helped it back up. I took its hands & positioned them back to the walls of the tunnel. I knew the one on my right was my guardian angel/guide, who was protecting me. The one on my left was a soul who had done a lot of "bad" things & was terrified of going into the Light. I could see marks on this soul. They appeared almost like veins on its "body."

The soul was lit from within and these black marks were all over it.[44]

Is Any Religion the "Right" Religion?

While this book is mainly focused upon the Western Christian religion, I have included a few testimonials from the Dead Saints who refer to other religions. Jean says each religion has something valuable to teach:

[The nurse] came to my room and talked to me soothingly, while she took my blood pressure. It was 0/30 and thus, my long journey through near death began.

...I found myself in a city and was told this was the City of God. I was at a water fountain with a man in a long white linen robe tied around the waist with a cord. He told me I could ask any question I wanted and said he would take me on a tour. Because I had been raised at a time where Catholics said to even go into another Christian church was a mortal sin, and Lutherans said those Catholics were going to go Hell, because they had statuary in their churches and prayed to the Saints.

I had a very pressing question [to ask God].

The first question I asked was, 'What is the right religion?'

I was told, 'They all are. Each religion is a pathway trying to reach the same place.' I was shown a mountain, with each religious group trying to reach the top, separated from each other by distance, but each one was trying to get to the same place. I was then told people choose to be born into whichever religion or group that will help them achieve the lessons they are sent here to learn.[45]

Alexander's NDE encounter describes the reason for many religions:

Religion was created to teach humans the basic laws of Nature or God. *God being the intelligent Being he is, understood humans in different Societies, needed different instructional manuals (so to speak). i.e. French, English, Spanish, Hebrew, Islam, Chinese, etc. God knew you can't explain to a Jew in Chinese why he should not eat pork. I felt the fighting between religious groups was very distasteful, and man was using religion for his own personal gains of power. Massive power in the hands of a few seemed to be one of the major issues of my enlightenment. This is what came across to me while in the Light.*[46]

A Few Concluding Thoughts Regarding the Governing Laws of Religion Are Not Absolute

First: Wise men who wrote the Old and New Testaments knew any concept communicated in words, is only analogous/approximate to reality, which means the communication, the *written word is symbolic and of itself is not the truth.* Put another way: At the very heart of sacred teachings and sacred Scripture are paradoxes. Nothing is mysterious we can see, because it can be explained. The mysterious concepts are those we have to use points of reference/analogies to define. The only way we can reveal their meaning is to describe what they are not. That is, by its very nature, paradoxical, and without grasping the paradox the teaching doesn't work.

Second: the Spirit of the Law transcends the Letter of the Law. If indeed, the *Word of God* contains inaccuracies, if they are fallible due to mistranslation and error, it is up to us to have a close relationship with the Spirit of God, so we might know the Truth, and make our judgments accordingly.

Third: Throughout *the Chronicles*, we find different religions use different names for the **Creator God, our Source of Life and consciousness.** A prayer in April 2015, read before a large audience at

Westminster Abbey in England, acknowledged all faiths who believe in a Creator God who gives life and breath to all things:

> *We may quibble over conflicting doctrines and cavil over contradictory revelations, but if St. Paul can address a meeting of the Areopagus[47] (the Greek worship of the unknown God) and exhort the incipient virtue in the ignorance of Athenian religiosity, whether you call the Creator of the universe 'God', 'Jehovah', 'YHWH', 'I Am' or 'Allah,' you are acknowledging (in mirrors darkly) the One who does not live in temples built by human hands, and the One who gives everyone life and breath and everything else.*

> *[author's note: As Hebrew and Arabic are closely related Semitic languages, it is commonly accepted that Allah (root, ilāh) and the Biblical Elohim are cognate derivations of same origin, as is Eloah, a Hebrew word which is used (e.g. in the Book of Job) to mean '(the) God' and also 'god or gods' as is the case of Elohim.]*

Finally, perhaps Cynthia and Amy's face-to-face encounters with God sum up the laws governing the "right religion" required to enter Heaven:

Cynthia at age 12 asked God during her NDE:

> *'Is there just one religion that will make it into Heaven?'*
> *He said, 'All who believe and have faith, even those who don't outwardly think they do. It depends on their hearts.'* [48]

Amy at age 17 asked God about religion:

> *I'd also wondered at religion while I was there, and I quickly received the knowing that this wasn't important in the way I imagined it was prior to my NDE: That one's religion, no matter which they joined or didn't join on Earth, was what was written in their own heart. It was about who the person was, not what label they wore or who or what they worshipped or believed in.*[49]

Wisdom from the mouths of babes.

---

1 Wikipedia. The legendary story describes seventy or seventy-two Jewish scholars who were asked by the Greek King of Egypt Ptolemy II Philadelphus to translate the Torah from Biblical Hebrew into Greek, for inclusion in the Library of Alexandria. This legend is first found in the pseudepigraphic Letter of Aristeas to his brother Philocrates, and is repeated, with embellishments, by Philo of Alexandria, Josephus, and by various later sources, including St. Augustine. A version of the legend is found in the Tractate Megillah of the Babylonian Talmud: King Ptolemy once gathered 72 Elders. He placed them in 72 chambers, each of them in a

separate one, without revealing to them why they were summoned. He entered each one's room and said: "Write for me the Torah of Moshe, your teacher." God put it in the heart of each one to translate identically as all the others did. Philo of Alexandria, who relied extensively on the Septuagint, says the number of scholars was chosen by selecting six scholars from each of the 12 tribes of Israel.

2 Stan Tenen 2011. *The Alphabet That Changed the World: How Genesis Preserves a Science of Consciousness in Geometry and Gesture.* Berkley, California: North Atlantic Books (Penguin Random House).

3 Paul Solomon 1982. *Trail of the Mystery Schools.* 8 CD's. Ireland, UK. Paul Solomon Foundation. www.paulsolomon.com.

4 William Fulke's English translation of the New Testament from the Latin Vulgate in 1589, pointed out the controversy over the Hebrew and Greek translations was a Roman Catholic view, not his, "The question is whether the original text, in Hebrew or in Greek, has been so corrupted, either by the carelessness of copyists or by the malice of the Jews and heretics, that it can no longer be held as the judge of controversies and the norm by which all versions without exception are to be judged. The Roman Catholics affirm this, we deny it." See also William Fulke, D.D. Master of Pembroke Hall, Cambridge. *A Defence of the Sincere and True Translations of the Holy Scriptures into the English Tongue, Against the cavils of George Martin.* Printed at University Press, 1843. pp.113-114.

5 For literacy rates among Jews in antiquity, see Catherine Hezser, *Jewish Literacy in Roman Palestine* (Turbingen: Mohr/Siebeck, 2001)

6 Wikipedia. Irenaeus pointed to Scripture as a proof of orthodox Christianity against heresies, classifying as Scripture not only the Old Testament, but most of the books now known as the New Testament, while excluding many works, a large number by Gnostics, who flourished in the 2nd century and claimed scriptural authority. Often times, Irenaeus, as a student of Polycarp, who was a direct disciple of the Apostle John, believed he was interpreting scriptures in the same hermeneutic as the Apostles. This connection to Christ was important to Irenaeus because both he and the Gnostics based their arguments on Scripture. Irenaeus argued since he could trace his authority to Christ and the Gnostics could not, his interpretation of Scripture was correct.

7 St. Irenaeus 170 A.D. *Against Heresies.*

8 Catholic Encyclopedia, vol. VI, 655-656; 132, *Gnostic Gospels.*

9 *Bible in the Church*, the Encyclopedia of Religion and Ethics. See also, E. Christopher Reyes 2014. *In His Name, Vol. IVC, Who wrote the Gospels?* North America and International: Trafford Publishing. p.16.

10 Bart D. Ehrman 2005. *Misquoting Jesus: The Story Behind Who Changed the Bible and Why.* San Francisco: Harper Collins/HarperOne. p. 80.

11 Wikipedia. Origen, or Origen Adamantius (c.185-c.254) was a scholar and theologian. According to tradition, he was an Egyptian who taught in Alexandria, reviving the Catechetical School where Clement had taught. The patriarch of Alexandria at first supported Origen but later expelled him for being ordained without the patriarch's permission. He relocated to Caesarea Maritima and died there after being tortured during a persecution. Using his knowledge of Hebrew, he produced a corrected Septuagint. He wrote commentaries on all the books of the Bible.

12 Commentary on Matthew 15:14, as quoted in Bruce M. Metzgre 1968. "*Explicit References in the Works of Origin to Variant Readings in New Testament Manuscripts,*" in Biblical and Patristic Studies in Memory of Robert Pierce Casey, ed. J. Neville Birdsall and Robert W. Thompson. Freidburg: Herder. pp. 78-79.

13 Richard Simon 1689. *A Critical History of the Text of the New Testament.* London: R. Taylor, pt. I. p. 65.

14 Ibid. p. 31.

15 Bart D. Ehrman 2005. *Misquoting Jesus: The Story Behind Who Changed the Bible and Why.* San Francisco: Harper Collins. p. 89.

16 Bart D. Ehrman 2005. *Misquoting Jesus: The Story Behind Who Changed the Bible and Why.* San Francisco: Harper Collins. p. 7.

17 *Catholic Encyclopedia*, vol. VI, p 543, Note: This 1546 Dogma of the Infallible Church was reaffirmed by the Sacred Vatican Council in 1870 C.E., and again by Pope Leo XIII, in his Encyclical Prov. Deus in 1893.
18   *Nilda P NDE*, #2662, 04.05.11, NDERF.org
19 *Scott H NDE,* #2698, 05.02.11, NDERF.org
20 *Diane G's NDE*, #175, 10.13.02, NDERF.org
21 *Anna Marie F's NDE*, #251, 04.02.03, NDERF.org
22 *Linda S probable NDE*, #1011, 02.03.07, NDERF.org
23 Paul Solomon 1984 lecture, *The Physics of Light and Darkness*. Excerpted from David Solomon's Journal notes.
24 *Sheree F NDE*, #3093, 07.28.12, NDERF.org
25 *Cara A NDE*, #2433, 10.11.10, NDERF.org
26 *Linda S probable NDE*, #1011, 02.03.07, NDERF.org
27 *Amy C NDE*, #2382, 10.09.10, NDERF.org
28 *Areliala's NDE*, #146, 07.07.02, NDERF.org
29 John W. Price 2013. *Revealing Heaven, The Christian Case for Near-Death Experiences*. New York: HarperCollins. p. 140.
30 Ibid. p.140.
31 John W. Price 2013. *Revealing Heaven, The Christian Case for Near-Death Experiences*. New York: HarperCollins Ibid. p.141.
32 Ibid. p. 141.
33 *Steve B's NDE*, #441, 07.24.04, NDERF.org
34 Bette's NDE, #59,12.03.00, NDERF.org
35 Hamartia is also used in Christian theology because of its use in the Septuagint and New Testament. The Hebrew (chatá) and its Greek equivalent (àµaptía/hamartia) both mean "missing the mark" or "off the mark."
36 *Nancy H's NDE*, #368, 01.18.04, NDERF.org
37 *Mary E's NDE*, #311, 08.29.03, NDERF.org
38 *Mary R NDE*, #1716, 10.12.08, NDERF.org
39 *Bolette L NDE*, #3379, 06.20.13, NDERF.org
40 *Sylvia R NDE*, #2079, 01.02.10, NDERF.org
41 *Robert L NDE*, #2029, 12.06.09, NDERF.org
42 *Lisa A NDE*, #1619, 03.01.11, NDERF.org
43 *Nicoles' NDE*, #330, 11.04.03, NDERF.org
44 *Lucia L NDE*, #937, 09.07.06, NDERF.org
45 *Jean R NDE*, # 2932, 01.18.12, NDERF.org
46 *Richard H's NDE*, #730, 12.25.05, NDERF.org
47 Acts 17:22-23 "People of Athens, I see you are very religious. As I was going through your city and looking at the things you worship, I found an altar with the words, "To an Unknown God." You worship this God, but you don't really know Him. So I want to tell you about Him."
48 *Cynthia H NDE*, #2626, 03.02.11, NDERF.org
49 *Amy C NDE,* #2386, 10.09.10, NDERF.org

21
Pre-Existence

Before I formed thee in the belly I knew thee; and before thou camest forth out of the womb I sanctified thee, and I ordained thee a prophet unto the nations.
~Jeremiah 1:5

Most Christian theologians today maintain the soul is created with the physical body at conception. Our personal consciousness did not precede it. However, dozens of Dead Saints dispute this. They claim to remember existing long before taking on a physical body, with some accounts claiming memories going back billions of years.

Many Bible passages may also be interpreted as evidence for pre-existence. This is true, especially in the light of irrefutable facts drawn from Church history with its voluminous detailed records of the many bitter theological disputes over doctrinal issues such as Pre-existence.

My years of research into NDEs and related topics (seldom if ever taken into consideration by Churchmen) has convinced me pre-existence is not only possible, but also probable. Dead Saint

Testimonies regarding memories experienced prior to physical birth, while not common, shine light on this very important doctrine:

Dawn was told gently, 'You must go, my child.' She had to leave Heaven and be born:

> *I remember being within a golden city full of the brightest white Light, and the Light was love, and I also was a part of that Light and Love, like a large ocean of Light and Love with countless others. Then I was pulled away and became separate. Example: 'like the ocean, and then take a dropper and pull out of the ocean one single drop. I am still the ocean, but now a separate single drop. I was carried away by a compassionate father figure. I will be so bold and say [it was] Jesus Christ, and He was also Light and there is no physical form. I was held and carried away as if flying at great speed until we were into the heavenly stars, just as you see when you look up. I was then placed on top of a very small planet looking place, all that was there was this rocky dirt path that started from the very top and spiraled all the way around this planet till the bottom.*
>
> *I became of physical form the moment I was placed there atop this path. I cried to Him as if He my father, 'No! Please, I don't want to leave!' like a child when a parent drops a small child off somewhere (like school) and they desperately don't want their parent to leave.*
>
> *I was in a long white robe with a golden rope of some sort tied loosely around my waist. I also had a very large staff taller than myself. I definitely did not want to go. I was extremely crushed and broken hearted and pleaded I didn't want to leave. The Light being Jesus was very bright and hovered way above me like a bright star. I remember my tears and sadness.*
>
> *He said to me in a male voice telepathically, 'You must go my child.' He said it with all the love and compassion in the universe.*[1]

Barbara's ADC (after-death communication) describes choices she needed to make to be born:

> *Beings without shape or form needed to discuss with me my future parents. I was given a choice of three. The first was a lovely older couple, without children, very good people. I immediately felt these were the ones but I guess they felt I had "my right" to CHOOSE so they told me about two other couples and I indicated 'No, no, I want **this** couple. I knew my future father must be sickly*

and they needed a compassionate, mild child and I would be that for them—the best I could be.

I wanted to be this for them and not to send anyone else in my stead because they were such good people and I didn't want another "being" to inflict any harm or hurt to them. Then came "the discussion" on what sex I was to be. I did NOT want to be a female. I wanted to be a male because I did not want to go through the loss of children who would die in childbirth or at an early age. I evidently went through such great sorrows regarding that. I was told I really had no choice in the matter because the being I had to help in this lifetime, which I agreed to help (evidently, I already knew this "person" and was in full agreement to go to Earth to "straighten out"), I loved very dearly.

This "person" was going to be a male. I agreed to my being a female with the promise I would never have children and go through what evidently I once did, and with the promise no matter how hard I tried to get pregnant, do NOT allow me to become so. Thus, it was totally agreed upon. I knew I had to find this MALE and help him get through life. (He must have been in a lot of trouble and they wanted him to redeem himself). I went to put my non-existent feet end into the tube at the right to get ready to go and then everything went black and I wasn't "there" any longer.[2]

Anna's NDE. She was excited to be human again:

I had a difficult birth with my first child —she was induced and the birth lasted almost two days. When I finally got into the delivery room, things started to go wrong. I heard them talking about tachycardia, and then something about my oxygen level and fetal problems. I wanted to stay and help, do what I could to make things go right with the birth, but I was suddenly out of my body and somewhere else.

It wasn't a bad place, just filled with people in line and very dark. There was a clicking sound all around us. I asked what the sound was, and why we were in a line. The "person," a Light in charge, told me we were in line to be born and this would show us what was coming and how it would all end. The clicking happened every time someone was born, and when it was our turn we would get a flash of our lives, and then live out our lives and then come back home. I was so excited. I was going to be a human. I was going to be real. I was going to get married and have a family and do all kinds of wonderful things!

> *Finally, it was my turn, and I stepped into the world, and I saw everything that was going to happen with me, the good and the bad, the child that was just being born, and the choice I could make about living and raising her or stopping now... and then the bad things were shown and I was asked to choose.*
>
> *Of course, I'd been so excited to have a chance to choose life. Everyone agreed with that choice. I was shown the future lifetime, and I could see the end coming, but all I could think of was, when it ends, I want another chance, another go-around, because it was so wonderful. The clicking stopped. I was brought back to consciousness and so far, life has progressed pretty much as it was told to me.[3]*

Lining Up to Be Born

David's Dead Saint experience is unique because, as he is waiting in line, he hesitates, and someone else takes his place. He subsequently decides to enter a different womb:

> *And suddenly I could feel I was curled up in a fetal position and I could see a tunnel with a Light at the end. I somehow knew I was in a woman's [birth canal], about to be born. I also somehow was told by the one watching me that I will forget everything and learn all over again, and there was no guarantee that I'll be okay. I thought to myself, 'This is what it must be like for angels who don't have any experience. They're like children and could easily be fooled, or hurt.'*
>
> *So I refused. Suddenly another being took my place in the womb. Then I saw children laughing and playing, teenagers talking with each other, and young people going through experiences and learning from them, becoming old and calming down from their worries and finding peace, which made them happy. I said, 'This is what I want. A life in a human body with the ability to taste, touch and feel, smell, and see, and especially the knowledge between good and bad, to live, and have an advantage over the other two states of being.'*
>
> *Then I awoke in the hospital.[4]*

God Prepares a Physical Body for Us

A curious topic brought up repeatedly by the Dead Saints describes our "Ancestors," our parents, their parents, a family tree reaching far back in time, who provided the DNA that helped create the physical body we inhabit today. I believe this is why we see the importance in the Old and New Testaments devoted to the long lineage of Jesus, son of David.

The remarkable NDE of Laura below, in an epic discussion with Jesus Christ, further strengthens the importance of our genetic family tree going back through ancient history:

> *I died to the world but I had not lost consciousness for even a second. I was still "me" and still alive. Then I was with HIM [Jesus Christ] ...enveloped in such a Great Light and love it defies description. And there, I rested in Joy, Bliss and Grace! He spoke to me telling me, it was not my time and I needed to return to my body, to complete my life's Mission, but there was still more for me to understand.*
>
> *The focus again fell on my infant son and hundreds, if not thousands, of my ancestors. I was aware of Light surrounding many of them—they stood out. I felt tremendous love from them. [I noticed] He said, 'Your ancestors.'*
>
> *'All of these beings came together in your behalf to make you uniquely you.' I realized in Earth words He was referring to my DNA.*
>
> *'You wanted to go to Earth to learn, to progress, and to contribute to Creation. All these spirits came together to help you do that!'*
>
> *The focus then was back to my baby.*
>
> *'In All of Creation, He said, your infant son chose you to be his mother! None Other!' Together, He said, "You made a Covenant to fill these roles in each other's Earth Life. This Covenant is and was a very Sacred Covenant not to be taken LIGHTLY!' Suddenly, I could not wait to return to Earth. It was not my time and I needed to return. From that instant I agreed to come back.*[5]

The Importance of DNA

Scott's Grandmother revealed during his NDE the importance of DNA not only in humans, but also in all life forms throughout the universe:

> *The universe was full, absolutely full of strings of Light and energy. They were pulsing. They were moving. We were in it, a part of it and it a part of us. DNA stretched for eons; memories, connected, intertwined, but all moving according to the Light. I could see molecules, atoms connecting, intersecting, building and becoming new life forms and consciousnesses. Galaxies, stars, fish, trees, air, water, and man are all patterned forms, built from all over the universe. Then we were back in the field, but it didn't stop*

there. I looked at my grandmother and the Light. Everything opened up, illumination poured through me, out of me and in me. It can't be changed, or threatened. It can't be manipulated, or colored. There are no Illusions or fairy tales about it...

Each is at its own time, in its own evolution, doing its own reality, living its own consciousness. We are part of it and it a part of us. We truly have nothing to fear. We are really loved. There is a power so great, it can only be called God.[6]

Souls Created Billions of Years Ago?

The Big Bang theory confidently holds the Universe as being created some 13.66 billion years ago. When Tony experienced his NDE in a car accident, he tells of awaking to the memory of knowing God even prior to the Big Bang:

I felt the presence of another person next to me. I was not disturbed by this, as I felt familiar with Him (God). I guess it was a "him." This was not expressed either way. I remember turning to this person and trying to look into his eyes. I couldn't really focus on his face, and it was almost painful to look. I turned back to the events that were happening. I was watching them load me into the ambulance. I was having a conversation and laughing with this person. I looked again at Him and I knew that I knew Him really well. I recognized I knew Him before I came in here, into this body. I felt happy being with Him. The more I looked at Him, the more I saw how long I knew Him.

I actually remembered knowing Him even before this universe was created. I could actually see this. I looked and looked and I couldn't see any time I didn't know Him, and I could see long before any of this stuff came into creation.

He called me by a different name I recognized. It wasn't like a sound, but rather a feeling I recognized as me. I felt as though He was my oldest friend.[7]

(Note: Pre-existence, a state or condition PRIOR to manifestation, is an element common to many ancient esoteric traditions. It is extremely unlikely that many, or even any, Dead Saints were familiar with such a concept.)

An idea totally foreign to Christian theology, Dead Saint Chantel feels she was a co-creator with God when He created the Solar System (estimated 4.66 billion years ago by astronomers):

I realized then that I was dying. I watched as I expired my last breath...I found myself floating, like in a cloud...All of a sudden, I noticed movement to my left. It was a Light coming towards me. As I looked at it, I noticed that this Light was a being, a Being of Light! As this Being of Light was approaching me, I started experiencing all kinds of images in my mind. At first I thought he/she was communicating with me telepathically, but then I realized, all these images were memories, my memories. I was remembering who I really am. (It was like an amnesiac who regains his/her memory). I had total recall of who I really was.

I was this old, old being, who had always existed.

I was wise and loving. I remember knowing everything. Not so much from an intellectual point of view. I knew what it was like to be a flower, to be an animal, to be an insect. All the knowledge of the universe was inside my being. I no longer felt as a separate individual. I felt as if I was part of a collective consciousness. I sensed billions and billons of beings and we were all One. The feeling of oneness on the other side is amazing!

And then, I remember distinctively how we created the solar system. I was part of this collective consciousness who had "willed" it into being. I remembered we had done so for the purpose of experiencing mortality. It was so important to my soul to come to Earth and experience mortality. I then remembered asking to be born.[8]

From my own point of view, I can only imagine as this intense Big Bang Creation of planets, stars, galaxies, and nebulas unfolded and expanded throughout all space and time, you and I sat on the other side of the veil, where time has no meaning, and watched the fireworks in awe and wonder. For those of us destined for Earth, we watched 10 billion years go by before our own Sun and circulating gases began to coalesce into planets. We observed comets impacting the Earth adding water and amino acids enough to fill oceans and enough gases sufficient for an atmosphere. From one-celled creatures to the first species of humans, we watched as life gradually developed.

Could it be we watched Creation unfold? Does the Bible hint of this possibility?

Ephesians 1:3-4 and Job 38:7 references an occasion where *all the sons of God shouted for joy when the foundations of the Earth were laid.*

Psalm 139:15-16 states:

My frame was not hidden from you when I was made in the secret place. When I was woven together in the depths of the Earth, your eyes saw my unformed body. All the days ordained for me were written in your book before one of them came to be.

John 17:24 indicates we were loved before the world was made:

Father, I will that they also whom that hast given me be with me where I am; that they may behold my glory, which thou hast given me: for thou lovedst me before the foundation of the world.

However, if we were created before the beginning of the Universe, how and why did we end up getting stuck in our mortal bodies on Earth? I believe the answer lies in the cosmology allegorically described in Genesis. After God created Eden, He formed Man from the dust of the Earth, and soon after, God took a rib closest to Adam's heart and formed the woman, Eve "The Mother of all Living."

The story goes on to say a serpent, hiding among the branches of the Tree of the Knowledge of Good and Evil, tempts Eve to eat of the forbidden fruit—Creation. God had specifically warned Adam and Eve "not to touch it, or eat the fruit thereof or they would surely die. However, the serpent argued otherwise. "You will not die," he said. "For God knows that in the day you eat thereof, then your eyes shall be opened, and you will be as gods knowing good and evil." Eve saw the fruit would make her wise so "She took the fruit thereof and did eat." She gave it to her husband Adam, and "he did eat." Apparently, the eating of the fruit of the tree made them aware and ashamed of their nakedness, so they covered themselves with fig leaves and hid from the face of God. God asked them, "Where are you?" Adam took the heat but blamed it on the woman. "Lord, the woman did beguile me, and I did eat."

What does this all mean? If we interpret the story of Genesis from a Dead Saints' point of view, the original Garden of Eden was a heavenly place, our original "spiritual home" cited and described many times throughout the *Chronicles*.

According to Linda, it is our true spiritual home:

I had reached my true home. I turned to Christ and said, 'This is beautiful. I am HOME. This is where I want to be... [It is where] I want to stay.'[9]

In the heavenly Garden of Eden, we were naked and unashamed. We were co-creators with God. Death did not exist. We could eat of every fruit in the Garden, but we were forbidden to eat of the Tree of Knowledge of Good and Evil, lest our "eyes be opened." The Tree of the

Knowledge of Good and Evil represents the state of duality, of the qualities and pairs of opposites inherent in Nature, of false discrimination, of separation (from God and all things), and ultimately of suffering and of death itself. By contrast, the Tree of Life symbolizes our undivided state of unity. Dan describes this heightened state of oneness as a "Being" connecting all existence during his mystical-death experience:

> *I lifted up the skin of Creation and saw that every living thing in Creation was an expression of this Being, connected to this Being, indivisible and One. Every person, plant, animal, insect, microbe, drew its very existence from this Being. Without this Being, if Creation existed at all, it would be filled with lifeless, empty rocks. Within this realization, I was shown how everything is interconnected, from the Beginning to the End. From the largest galactic cluster spinning around the hub of Creation, to the smallest quantum fluctuation, [I saw] how everyone and everything has a place and a reason.*[10]

The decision to partake of the fruit of the Tree of Knowledge precipitated our fall from purity and innocence and, through our involvement with flesh; we lost our ability to remain eternally in the Kingdom. Our choice to enter physical form is symbolized by the serpent. By "touching and tasting" of its fruit we "put on animal skins," and became entrapped in flesh. Because of living in a physical, mortal body, we are required to "die" to be released from it.

God curses the serpent "above all cattle and above every beast in the field" and commands the creature to "grovel in the dust" for as long as it lives. From that moment on, the serpent, the woman and her offspring would be enemies. "He shall strike you on your head, and you [woman] will strike him at his heel."

The tragic *Curse of the Serpent*, a "striking of the heel and the head," is symbolized in various religions as a serpent swallowing its tail and is called *Ouroboros*. It represents the cycle of birth and death in the physical world, a curse etched into Christian theology as *"original sin."*

Early Christian Gnostic sects sought to overcome the curse of the serpent by becoming living Christs—beings capable of surmounting and ultimately conquering the addictive round of desire to once again identify with and experience the universal Light and harmony of the "One" represented by the Tree of Life—the Christ.

We see this sentiment reflected in the Gospel of Philip:

> *It is not possible for anyone to see anything of the things that actually exist unless he becomes like them.... You saw Christ, you became Christ.*[11]

W. R. Inge in *Christian Mysticism* says that early Gnostics believed "literalist Christianity" only preached the outer mysteries for "people in a hurry."[12] He believed their teachings revealed inner mysteries of Jesus of Nazareth that went beyond "blind faith." Early church fathers, Clement, honored as a Saint by the Catholic Church, and Origen Adamantius, wrote volumes about the Gnostics whom they called "true Christians."[13] According to Freke and Gandy in *The Jesus Mysteries*, their writings, "Do not paint a traditional picture of strange and insignificant heretics on the fringes of Christianity as tradition would have us believe."[14]

The Christian Gnostic belief is identical with testimonies returned to us by the Dead Saints. Overcoming the curse of suffering and death involves an awareness that the 'Kingdom of the Father', or in Dead Saints' terms, 'the Light', exists in and around all things. It was a goal to which all Gnostics aspired, and failure in achieving this goal symbolically meant being trapped within the coils of the cosmic dragon.

Is it heresy to believe that Christ lives, both in everything and beyond? To ignore such a belief is to deny the very Source of Life that lives within us. Conversely, to accept the challenge of the quest for Eternal Life requires that we follow the laws of salvation and grace as laid down by Christ as Jesus. However, as we shall see in the next chapter, there are a few more stones to be turned before the path becomes clear.

---

1 *Dawn's Pre-birth Experience*, #140, aleroy.com/board140
2 *Barbara's ADC*, #312, 03.12.03, http://www.adcrf.org/barbara_s's_adc.htm.
3 *Anne S's NDE*, #852, 05.13.06, NDERF.org
4 *David A probable NDE*, #1411, 12.17.07, NDERF.org
5 *Laura M NDE*, #2995, 03.31.12, NDERF.org
6 *Scott W NDE*, #3885, 02.15.15, NDERF.org
7 *Tony D's NDE*, #215, 03.02.03, NDERF.org
8 *Chantel L NDE*, #3155, 10.06.12, NDERF.org
9 Linda Stewart's NDE, *God is Only Love*, #34, aleroy.com/boardh1.htm
10 *Dan Ta's NDE*, #527, 11.21.04, NDERF.org
11 *The Gospel of Philip* translated by Wesley W. Wisenberg, The Gnostic Society Library, The Gnostic Society Nag Hammadi Library. http://gnosis.org/naghamm/gop.html. From the Gnostic Society Library website regarding the Gospel of Philip: "Now over fifty years since being unearthed and more than two decades after final translation and publication in English

as The Nag Hammadi Library, 7 their importance has become astoundingly clear: These thirteen papyrus codices containing fifty-two sacred texts are representatives of the long lost "Gnostic Gospels", a last extant testament of what orthodox Christianity perceived to be its most dangerous and insidious challenge, the feared opponent that the Church Fathers had reviled under many different names, but most commonly as Gnosticism. The discovery of the Nag Hammadi texts has fundamentally revised our understanding of both Gnosticism and the early Christian church."

12   W.R. Inge 1899. *Christian Mysticism*. London: Methuen. p. 86. Quoted in Freke and Gandy, *The Jesus Mysteries*, p. 90.

13   Clement, *Stromata*, 7.1. "The Gnostic alone is truly pious…the true Christian is the Gnostic." See J. Stevenson and W.H.C Frend 1957. *A New Euesbius, SPCK Church History. Documents illustrating the History of the Church to AD 337*. First Edition published 1957. Revised Second Edition published 1987. Authors.814ff. Also Quoted in Freke and Gandy, *The Jesus Mysteries*. p. 90.

14   Freke, Timothy and Peter Gandy 1999. *The Jesus Mysteries*. Three Rivers Press, Crown Publishing Group. p. 90.

―― 22 ――

An Uncomfortable Possibility

~I will never convince Delynn we have lived a previous existence. It's not something I can prove and I don't need to prove. I just know if I had never met her this time around, the Chronicles might never have been written. ~Chronicle 231

In a survey by the Pew Forum in 2009, 22% of American Christians expressed a belief in reincarnation.[1] Dozens of Dead Saint encounters describe past lives. Before we discuss their experiences, I want to share with you a few paragraphs about how I was introduced to reincarnation during my youth.

My mother was always a deeply spiritual person. Her parents were alcoholics, and did not attend church, but through it all, she found a deep love for God. Her beliefs were later influenced by Jess Stearn's story about Edgar Cayce, *the Sleeping Prophet*, which referenced Cayce's views about reincarnation, beliefs that Mom outright initially rejected because she didn't think it was fair. She thought, "Why should I suffer in this life, for something that happened in a past life for which I have no memory?"

For Mom, finding answers to the reincarnation dilemma was a journey. Her search led her to read everything she could about it. It was fortuitous Dad was relocated to Norfolk, Virginia two years later in 1971 to finish out his Navy Career near the headquarters of the ARE (Edgar Cayce Foundation) in Virginia Beach.

After the move, Mom and Dad looked for a church for the family to attend. She interviewed several pastors with a specific question. Did her mother go to Hell if she died "unsaved?" Four pastors at various churches said, "Yes." One pastor at the United Church of Christ said, "I don't know." The pastor was Tracy Floyd. It was the honest answer she was looking for, and so for five years beginning in 1972, our family attended the United Church of Christ every Sunday to hear Reverend Tracy Floyd preach.

Mom quietly carried her 'reincarnation' beliefs to church, careful not to talk to anyone about them, but sometimes shared her thoughts with me. She encouraged me to spend time studying at the ARE, whose spiritual and metaphysical library is one of the largest in the US. It was not long before I passionately took on Mom's beliefs about reincarnation and brought the debate to our youth group, looking for example cases in the Bible that might prove or disprove it. Of course, Tracy never preached about reincarnation, nor would he, being raised a Southern Baptist. He never really entered the debate, but I know I piqued his interest along with a few friends in our Youth Group.

When I was 27, after Mom divorced Dad, and after she lost her second husband in a tragic accident two years after they were married, Mom met my stepfather Ray in 1986. Before they married, they discussed their religious beliefs. Ray was a staunch Southern Baptist, and Mom an unconventional Christian who believed in reincarnation. She debated with Ray everything she knew and believed about her faith, but she could never convince him about living past lives. Ray and Mom agreed to disagree. Ray ended their debate saying, "I don't believe in this "recyclist" theology, but I've never known anybody who has a stronger faith in God." Equally yoked by their strong faith, they remained happily married for 29 years, until his death in June 2015.

During this time, after much prayer, meditation and research, Mom suddenly realized reincarnation wasn't a punishment at all for past life mistakes. She came to view it as "a reaping and bringing into balance that which we have sown."

Reincarnation explains a "great many things" about why we have certain talents, or pursue particular careers, but my belief in Rebirth hasn't changed anything in my life. I've not made choices (I am aware of) because of it. If I have made choices, like building Akio Botanical Gardens, it was because it was something I loved to do. Why did I love it? Perhaps, a past life would explain it.

Maybe I'm a bit wiser now, but where reincarnation used to be passionately important to me, now it's settled into a backstage theology. I never think much about it anymore. I believe Jesus taught it, and the apostles believed in it, but it was not the focus of his teaching. Jesus came to preach about practicing the PATH (see chapter 24, *the 13th Path*) of Love and Forgiveness, which leads us out of the cycle of death and rebirth, so we can attain eternal life.

In the end, it doesn't matter whether you believe in reincarnation or not. If it is true, and if your spiritual evolution is not finished after this life, you'll take a break in Heaven, and then decide to be born again for a new adventure on Earth. On the other hand, God might send you on a special Mission back to Earth. Perhaps you've already volunteered once or twice!

For most Christians today, accepting the *"uncomfortable possibility"* of reincarnation is an uphill battle. Try to keep an open mind. It's a hot button issue in the Bible. Let's first start there.

Reincarnation in the Bible?

In chapter 10, *The Judgment*, we discussed the Jewish and Christian belief that flesh one day will cover our bones and reanimate our dead corpses. If taken at face value, the belief seems to say our dead bodies will reanimate, not that our souls will reincarnate in new bodies. This theology is reiterated in Job 19:25-26:

> *For I know that my redeemer liveth, and that He shall stand at the latter day upon the Earth: And though after my skin worms destroy this body, yet in my flesh shall I see God.*

ALL Biblical translations of Job 19:26 describe he will 'stand at the latter day upon the Earth, after worms destroy his body' and 'in his flesh' he will see God. We can only assume he meant seeing God in the person of Jesus of Nazareth born over 500 years later in Bethlehem, Israel. [2] But how could Job see God in the flesh *unless his soul was born again in a physical body?*

It seems clear Job believed even though his body was destroyed by worms, *in his flesh*, he would one day see God. To accomplish this, he would have to be reborn again in the flesh to see his Redeemer. He was not speaking about a gruesome night of the resurrection of the dead at the end of time on Judgment Day!

He was talking about reincarnation of the soul. Shocking? Is it the truth?

The Bible affirms reincarnation in several well-known instances—which are difficult to interpret in any other way. The concept of specific spiritual qualities transferring from one life to another is obvious in the New Testament: The Jews expect the reincarnation of their great prophets (King David will return as the Messiah; Elijah will be reborn as John the Baptist.). Jews believed their latter-day prophets had already been reborn in times past. The Jewish sect called Samarians believed Adam reincarnated as Noah, then as Abraham, then Moses. So later Jews expected the Messiah to be a reincarnation of King David.

Reincarnation of the old prophets was also on the minds of the Jews at the time of Jesus. In fact, followers of Jesus thought He was a reincarnated prophet. How else to regard the following passage in Matthew 16:13-14?

When Jesus came into coasts of Cesera Philippi, he asked disciples, saying, 'Whom do men say I, the Son of Man, am?' And they said, 'Some say that thou art John the Baptist, some, Elias (Elijah) and others, Jeremias, or one of the prophets.'

Herod, who was in command of Jerusalem under the Romans, also speculated Jesus might have been one of the old prophets. When Jesus proclaimed he was the Jewish Messiah, his followers were confused, since the scriptures predicted the prophet Elias (or Elijah in Greek) would return and precede the coming of the Messiah. The disciples pointed out in Matthew 17:10-13:

Why then say the scribes that Elias must come first? And Jesus answered and said unto them, Elias truly shall first come, and restore all things. But I say unto you, That Elias is come already, and they knew him not. Then the disciples understood that He spake unto them of John the Baptist.

In Matthew 11:14-15, Jesus unequivocally states John the Baptist is the reincarnation of the prophet Elias:

Among them that are born of women there hath not risen a greater than John the Baptist. And if ye will receive it, this is Elias. He that hath ears to hear, let him hear.

Reincarnation is alluded to in John 9:34 in which the disciples ask Jesus why a man was born blind. The disciples asked, "Which did sin, this man or his parents?"

This passage implies the blind man had a previous incarnation where he had the opportunity to commit a sin whose karmic consequence would be blindness. Without reincarnation, how could the blind man commit a sin responsible for his handicap at birth? Jesus didn't dispute the reasoning of the disciples, though he stated the blindness was so the "Grace of God" could be made manifest.

So why isn't reincarnation taught or at least addressed in church?

To understand why, we must go back to ca. 250 A.D, when Origen, one of Christianity's early theologians, wrote about the pre-existence of the soul and the concept of reincarnation. This was nothing new and/or heretical. His writings, based on early Christian Gospels (which numbered about 30 at the time along with hundreds of early parchments) merely elaborated upon the common, predominant Christian beliefs.

Father Origen taught the soul's very source was God and the soul's purpose was to become one with God through lessons learned in successive lives through what Origen termed the "transmigration of the soul." He taught Christ came to show we could become like Him, *and thus escape the cycle of birth and death as taught by other world religions.*

While vehemently argued against by modern Christian apologists, it is clear Origen's belief in pre-existence and the transmigration of the soul was common among many Christian sects, including the Gnostics. Sages who adhere to the doctrine of reincarnation included Simon Magus, known as the father of Gnosticism. His second century contemporary, Basilides of Alexandria, taught his followers that Gnosis (knowledge) was the climax of many lives of effort and taught that 'men suffer from their deeds in former lives,' indicating a Gnostic version of Karma. Theodotus, a follower of the Gnostic master Valentinus, taught that an element of Gnosis was understanding 'what rebirth really is.'" [3]

Reincarnation is revealed to the Apostle Paul, who in the *Valentinian Apocalypse of Paul*, takes a "mystical voyage through the heavenly realms. He witnesses a murderer punished by angels and who is then cast down to Earth to inhabit a new body." [4] Further, in the *Secret Book of John*, where "Jesus explains to the Apostle John that human souls are recycled by Jehovah, constantly thrown into 'forgetfulness' and 'prisons' (the physical body). When John asks him how a soul can become liberated from the Ouroboros, Jesus answers: 'This soul needs to follow another soul in whom the Spirit of life dwells, because she is saved through the Spirit. Then she will never be thrust into flesh again.'"[5]

Beliefs in pre-existence and reincarnation persisted through Constantine's attempts to unify the Christian church during the convening of the Council of Nicaea in 325 A.D. He was no theologian, nor did Constantine really care to any degree what basis would be used to forge the unity he desired. The purpose of the meeting was to resolve controversy within the Church over issues concerning the Trinity (Father, Son, and Holy Ghost) and *"homoousios,"* the concept that God the Son and God the Father were *made of one substance*. No decisions were made by the council regarding pre-existence or reincarnation during this third century convention.

Church Politics Rewrites Mainstream Christian Belief

Fast forward to the sixth century A.D.

The Emperor Justinian and Pope Vigilius disagreed on whether or not the teachings of Father Origen should be condemned as heresy. The Pope supported Origen's teaching as consistent with the teachings of Jesus, the Messiah. Emperor Justinian wanted Origen's works condemned and destroyed, but Pope Vigilius refused to sign a papal decree condemning the concept of pre-existence of the soul and Rebirth. There was a political reason why the Emperor was opposed. He reasoned, if only Christ had come from God, and *God made brand new souls at the time of conception,* then only the Holy Church could bring these souls to God. Justinian had the disobedient Pope arrested and sentenced to jail, but en route, Vigilius escaped, leaving Origen's writings officially still uncondemned. [6]

In 543 A.D., Justinian convoked the Fifth General Council of the Church, but with only six bishops of Vigilius' Western Church attending, 159 bishops of the Eastern (Justinian-controlled) council produced 14 new anathemas against "heresy." The very first one condemned the concept that souls pre-existed with God:

If anyone asserts the fabulous preexistence of souls, and shall assert the monstrous restoration which follows from it: let him be anathema.[7]

Their one-sided vote, ratified in 553 A.D., decided for all future Christian generations that pre-existence and reincarnation minimized Christian salvation. Additional anathemas stated that the "monstrous" theology was in conflict with the resurrection of the physical body (reanimation of dead bones on Judgment Day). The council invalidated the teaching because of 'speculative use of Scripture', finally ruling it out based simply on the idea that "we didn't remember past lives."[8] Even though these events are historical facts, contemporary Christianity treats the "heretical" doctrine as though Jesus never taught it or that early Christians ever believed it.

While it is understandable in today's evangelical environment to label everything not following standard Christian teaching as cultish, pagan, or of the Devil, I believe, despite historical evidence to the contrary, we should look both to science and testimonies of the Dead Saints to weigh in on the matter.

Tabula Rasa or Rebirth?

Western religions contend when a soul enters a human body it is a *Tabula Rasa,* (a "scraped tablet" in Latin, or as we call it a "clean slate.") The assumption that we are at birth a tabula rasa is likewise an axiomatic problem of modern science.

However, there are glaring apparent exceptions to the tabula rasa assumption. Chief among them: The child prodigy. Chief among prodigies was Wolfgang Amadeus Mozart whose life is well documented. He showed prodigious ability from earliest childhood. He was brilliant on keyboard and violin; he was composing from the age of five and performing before European royalty. There are thousands of such Mozart-like examples that seem otherwise inexplicable except as "memories" and special skills brought forward from another life into this life. And the examples proliferate thanks to the internet. Scarcely a week goes by without some new musical, sports or intellectual prodigy in the limelight. Even for us average humans, many of us, at some point in our lives, gravitate to fields of expertise and interests that cannot be explained by our education, social conditioning or genetics or any combination thereof. When it does occur, we know we have come "home." Where did this love of and talent for music, art, science, math, or sports come from, if not from a previous life?

No matter if secular science dismisses and derides the notion, popular interest persists and even intensifies. The mainstream media, normally groveling before the secular directives of the day, grows rebellious when it is advised to ignore anything that smacks of the supernatural and the unscientific. This is especially true when popular interest is rampant, there is money to be made, ratings to be achieved, and while the unwelcomed evidence keeps on getting better and better, it reaches the point of unavoidability.

Children Who Remember Past Lives

In *Life before Life* by Jim B. Tucker, M.D., St. Martin's Press, and *Return to Life, Extraordinary Cases of Children who remember Past Lives,* these two works present powerful evidence for reincarnation. Case after verifiable case is presented in documenting the incontrovertibility of reincarnation as a fact of human existence.

Here is just one particular poignant story related by Dr. Tucker, the remarkable tale of 5-year-old Ryan, raised in a conventional Christian household.

Ryan's mother, Cindi, grew up in a Baptist church. Her husband was the son of a Church of Christ minister. They had never been taught anything about reincarnation. Nothing was out of the ordinary in the family. Cindi was a county clerk deputy; her husband was a police officer.

When Ryan was four, he began talking to his mother about going to Hollywood. Often he would plead for Cindi to take him to see his "other" family home, and when she didn't make the trip, he would cry. Ryan did other things that may have been recollections of a past life. She recalls when Ryan was playing, he would often shout "action!" and begin to direct imaginary movies. His parents didn't take this play-acting very seriously, until he began having nightmares about an inability to breathe; he would grab his chest in sleep. Ryan told his mother when he was living in Hollywood, he felt his heart explode and then he died.

One night Ryan began to tell Cindi in detail what it was like to die. He described encountering an "awesome" bright Light—and related to her we will go to the Light when we die. He said "everyone comes back" and he knew Cindi before. He claimed he chose her to be his mother. Cindi picked up some old books about Hollywood, and showed them to Ryan. When they began to look through the books together, he saw the photograph of Rita Hayworth. He said he knew her and she used to make an iced drink called "Coke floats."

Cindi came across another picture from a 1932 movie called *Night after Night*. Ryan got excited again and said, *"Hey mama, that's George. We did a picture together. And mama, that guy's me. I found me."* The photograph was a picture of six men from the 1930's and 1940's, but Cindi couldn't identify the man in the picture Ryan said was himself. Ryan subsequently identified other famous actors, including Marilyn Monroe, whom he called "The Mary lady." He recalled a memory when he had been at a party and made a move to talk to her. He laughed and said, "One of the studio guys punched me in the eye" before he could reach her. Ryan said he liked being Ryan but he liked living in Hollywood too, living in a big house with a swimming pool outside, and making films.

Like some of the Dead Saint experiences discussed earlier in the chapter, Ryan also seemed to remember life before he was born. He described events during Cindi's pregnancy he could never have known anything about. He said, "I saw it all from Heaven." The family never identified who Ryan thought he was. He later began to forget about his previous life in Hollywood, which made him sad, but gradually he forgot the personality of his previous life experience, and became just Ryan.

Are Birthmarks Evidence of Previous Lives?

Dr. Tucker, following leads provided by earlier researchers, in *Life before Life*, researched children with large birthmarks who claimed to remember previous lives. He theorizes if the mind has lived before, part of its personality survives and can still enter the fetus to be reborn, transferring its memory into the fetus, affecting to some extent physical appearance, IQ, talents, memories and birthmarks. In his research, he discovered most previous life memories came to the surface between ages two and four.

Dr. Tucker worked with Dr. Ian Stevenson, who earlier theorized birthmarks were evidence of the mind carrying over traumatic memories of a major wound to the body. He documented cases where children remembered where the deadly instrument or weapon impacted their body in a previous life, which manifested on their bodies in this life in a skin lesion or birthmark where the trauma occurred. Dr. Stevenson noted, "The fatal wound does not always produce the most significant birthmark, so a factor other than the severity of the wound must be involved."[9] Presumably, the development of a birthmark involves the mental or emotional trauma surrounding the death in a previous existence. So why are not more people born with birthmarks provoked by previous-life emotional traumas?

Dr. Stevenson cites evidence of the power of the mind in *Reincarnation and Biology*. In his study of birthmark cases, he suggests it may be an effect similar to stigmata wounds exhibited by unusually devout individuals that correspond to the crucifixion wounds of Jesus, as described in the Bible or paintings. St. Francis of Assisi may have been the first recorded stigmatic, but since his time more than 350 cases have been documented.

Dr. Stevenson reports that stigmata cases were initially thought to be miracles. Yet they were often observed in individuals who could hardly be described as 'saintly,' even though in many cases they were reported to be engaged in intense religious practice. They have come to be regarded as psychosomatic in origin."[10] He concluded a believer's mental image of Jesus' wounds produced very specific changes to the skin to match their mental image.

This actually happened to David Berry, a good friend and teacher who taught with Paul Solomon. He recounted a class on Good Friday in 1979, where eight students developed stigmata marks, bleeding wounds Christ received during the Crucifixion. One of the classmates, Jane, a Catholic, prayed to experience Easter as our Lord experienced it and discovered the palms of her hands were bleeding. The rest of the class who saw her wounds, all woke up on Easter Sunday with swollen, non-bleeding scabs on their palms. Some were very painful and lasted several days before disappearing. Berry was shocked. Nothing like this had ever happened to him before.

Carmel's NDE cites this psychosomatic phenomenon: our physical body (our DNA) records past and present thoughts:

> *I became extremely aware the body is completely a recording system for memories and events from not only this life, but past lives where there is unfinished business.*[11]

There are literally dozens of references to reincarnation that could be lifted from the pages of my near-death research. Several Dead Saints remember Jesus explaining the concept of reincarnation to them during their NDE. Cathleen, John and Cara's NDE recollections are typical.

Cathleen walked with Jesus during her NDE, and asked him several pointed questions about whether we live one life or many:

> *He (Jesus) asked me if I was now aware that I was dead.*
> *I said, 'Well, yes. I guess I know I'm dead.'*
> *I asked Him, 'Please tell me.'*
> *He took me to the entrance of a hall. We stood and looked down this long hall and there were millions and millions of doorways leading off this hall. He made me aware there were many choices available to me and that that choice was the very answer to the question I had asked. The choice was up to ME. He made me understand I could choose to stay where I was, I could choose to walk down the hall and pick a door. He made me aware picking a door would be my exit out of Heaven and I would be born again out of the womb of some woman somewhere on Earth.*
>
> *I asked Him, 'But how do I know what door to pick?'*
>
> *His reply was merely that the door I picked is my choice. He could not reveal what that life would be like. It would be a mystery.*
>
> *I asked Him, 'Do we HAVE to pick another door and live over and over?' That in itself would be Hell to me because what I had experienced, in large part, was very sad and distressful. He told me some people choose to go back again and again. He doesn't want them to. He wants them to stay with Him, but He understands my feelings. He explained when we choose to leave Him He removes all memories of previous lives because He doesn't want us distressed.*
>
> *He means for life to be a good thing for all of us. He then reiterated all my choices and again infused me with His love.*
>
> *He then asked, 'Now, why would you want to leave me?' I don't remember responding.*
>
> *He asked, 'Now, how do you feel about being dead?'*
>
> *I said, 'It really didn't bother me that much, but my only regret was I hadn't had the chance to say good-bye to my parents.'*

The very next thing I became aware of, amazingly, remarkably, astoundingly, was that once again, I was in my old body without realizing I had made my choice.[12]

John's NDE occurred in 1994 when he was 18. His health troubles began when a lung collapsed and he was hospitalized. The doctors could find no apparent reason for the event other than he had a history of cold infections and asthma. About a month later, during sleep, he was dreaming he was on top of a cliff and fell. The moment he landed, he felt he had stopped breathing. That is when he realized, he had died and his NDE began. He discovered he had lived as a well-known musician:

I asked, 'Am I dead?'

I didn't even question if it was Jesus because I just knew it was Him. I felt peace and love in the presence of the Light / shape of Him.

I asked Him at that point, 'My name isn't Jim. Why was I called that?'

And Jesus replied, 'A mistake was made and it isn't my time.'

In that second or for that second I assumed they had called the wrong person up, but then something compelled me to ask, 'Is there reincarnation? And if so, was I reincarnated and who was I?'

Jesus responded to me, 'That there is and I was reincarnated, but that's not what's important.'

I then asked if I was an [undisclosed famous musician]?

[While it is] something I perceive of as weird now, because, I had very little knowledge of Him before the NDE. Looking back now, it seemed like the thoughts were put in my conscience to ask Jesus, so He could respond.

He responded, **'Yes, but it wasn't important, because reincarnation isn't as we perceive it.**[13]

Cara's NDE is interesting, not only because she realizes she has reincarnated several times, but that she didn't believe or disbelieve in reincarnation. Like many other Dead Saints, Cara sees our planet as a school:

There were no limitations such as space or time in the spirit world. I was aware of the big picture regarding the past, present and future. I was aware the Earth School experience was one part of my evolution.

There was a review of my life in this body, and also my past lives. I was the judge as to the benefit and value of each experience. They all seemed very interconnected, and yet separate. There was a focus to each life experience, and all the experiences contributed to an end result. I didn't want to come back to the Earth School, and after some deliberation with the other beings of energy, including the God Being, or large mass of energy, we decided coming back would serve the greater good. I had a choice, and yet the choice seemed to be made in unity with the other beings. I also knew if I didn't come back at this time, in this body, I would return to the Earth School in another body, to finish what I was here to do. Before the experience, I didn't believe or disbelieve in reincarnation. Now, I am sure I have had many reincarnations.[14]

An amazing Dead Saint experience was reported by a boy involved in an inner tube accident. While the following account seems very simple in content, it is filled with tons of information about the Afterlife we rarely see or hear about:

I'm not sure about the whole reincarnation thing, but it certainly opened my mind. Not only did I feel they had been human in the past, but I felt they expected to be human again. Like a part of a natural life cycle where being born and dying are just transitions between different forms of our existence.

I believe with all my heart we carry certain things like love and giving between these realms. Most all of what we feel is important as a human is of no importance in the other realm. They are excited to be human again as they can do things like having a family. They also really like the excitement of being in human form as it comes with struggles, challenges, danger, risk, unpredictability, etc. They miss things like making love, music, art, etc. Many of our core values are the same.

They have a high regard for humans who are humble, giving and tough. For these reasons, the souls of firefighters, single moms and the like rank high. They like those who protect others and fight to survive.

They are non-judgmental and quick to forgive as they know the temptations humans face and know they will face them again themselves. I really love life in a way I am sure I would not have, were it not for this experience. If everyone could have a glimpse of this realm, the world would be a much better place for humans... no killing, violence, etc.[15]

Earth University exams?

One possible reason for reincarnation is failing your Earth University exams. The exams are comprised of very specific lessons, tests and trials we were born to overcome. Ramon's probable NDE reflects this challenge:

> Next, I wanted to go through the door of Light, and he told me I could not, I had to go back, so I let myself return for my daughter Melissa. On coming back, before re-entering my body, I stopped in that place people speak of where there is peace and tranquillity, next to the Light that emerges as if from a tunnel. It was there I thought I was going crazy, as I was surrounded by thousands and thousands of energies (spirits) like myself, all moving towards the place I was coming back from.
>
> I went over to the left and came upon another very big group of energies, and from these one detached himself and went down on his knees as if begging forgiveness from me, though I did not recognize him (though later I did). From this immense gathering of energy is born a long line of energies (spirits) going towards and delivering themselves to where the Light ended. When I approached this line, I did not like the feeling there, it was like the feeling of having studied hard for an exam, and then failing it despite all the study. I looked again at the place where I first arrived, and could still see thousands and thousands of energies appearing and disappearing, going towards the place from where I was returning. I wanted to go on looking because I wanted to understand what that place was, but then I felt myself being called, and I entered through my head down as far as my feet.[16]

We learn lessons faster here than we will learn them in the Afterlife. The knowledge we gain on Earth will help us move higher in the Realms of Heaven. We see this with JB's NDE:

> I needed to get the Word in me while on Earth because I couldn't approach God in the great Throne Room until a certain level of knowledge was attained [on Earth] or I would learn it there [in Heaven] which would slow down my journey there.[17]

Learning lessons (*the Word*) while we inhabit a physical body infuses this knowledge into our DNA, both physically and on a spiritual level—knowledge that is passed on to future generations enrolled in Earth University.

Evolution was the theme of a 2006 dream I had during a rapid phase of growth at my company, Fast Transact. In the dream, I found myself in a 1960's High School classroom, with the old style wood top desks that opened up and a dark green chalkboard with a script and standard alphabet over it at the front of the classroom. Two angels (I knew they were angels, but I don't believe they had wings) stood on either side of the chalkboard and had drawn pictures of homo-sapiens evolving from Neanderthal to Modern Man. Underneath and below *Neanderthal Man,* the one angel wrote *Retail Man.*

On the other side of the chalkboard was a picture of Modern man in suit and tie carrying a briefcase. Underneath *Modern Man* the angel wrote *Internet Man.* Between Neanderthal Man and Modern Man they wrote the word *"EVOLVE."* While I later made the dream into a successful advertisement for our company to solicit Internet merchants, the dream wasn't just talking about business.

Pass or fail, our purpose for being born into Earth University is to evolve. Some Dead Saints see us in a 'childing' stage of spiritual evolution where we grow for billions of years to become like the Being Jesus referred to as 'My Father'—a thought provoking statement to say the least.

---

1 Pew Forum on Religion and Public Life, *U.S. Religious Landscape Survey, Summary of Key Findings,* http://www.pewforum.org/2009/12/09/many-americans-mix-multiple-faiths/
[2] Wikipedia: Ascribed by Jewish tradition to Moses, it is generally agreed by scholars that the book comes from the period between the 7th and 4th centuries BCE, with the 6th century as the most likely date. The anonymous author was almost certainly an Israelite, although he has set his story outside Israel, in southern Edom or northern Arabia, and makes allusion to places as far apart as Mesopotamia and Egypt. According to the 6th-century prophet Ezekiel, Job was a man of antiquity renowned for his righteousness.
3 http://www.examiner.com/article/do-gnostics-believe-reincarnation
4 Ibid. web article.
5 Ibid. web article.
6 Based on an Article by: Walter Semkiw, M.D., from *Born Again and the Revolutionaries.* Charlottesville, VA.: Hampton Roads Publishing.
7 (The Anathemas against Origen), attached to the decrees of the Fifth Ecumenical Council, A.D. 545, in Nicene and Post-Nicene Fathers, 2d ser., 14: 318).
8 http://www.near-death.com/reincarnation/history/bible.html.
9 Jim B Tucker M.D., 2008. *Life before Life.* New York: St Martin's Press. p. 70.
10 Ibid. p. 67.
11 *Carmel B NDE's,* #1920, 05.30.09, NDERF.org
12 *Cathleen C NDE,* #1734,11.01.08, NDERF.org
13 *John C's NDE,* #275, 04.17.03, NDERF.org
14 *Cara NDE,* #1645, 07.06.08, NDERF.org
15 *Ken W NDE,* #2139, 02.25.10, NDERF.org
16 *Ramon probable NDE,* #3099, 08.09.12, NDERF.org
17 *JB NDE,* #1307, 11.10.07, NDERF.org

23
Jesus, Planetary Headmaster

~As Headmaster of Earth University, I don't believe Jesus is overly concerned one way or another where you choose to worship. If your place of worship serves Love and kindness, then that serves Him. I have never read about a Dead Saint meeting Jesus in Heaven and Jesus tries to convert the Saint from his or her religion. How ironic. If salvation is through Christianity alone, shouldn't the Dead Saints typically report Jesus urging them to accept Him as their Lord and Savior and attend church every Sunday? That's not what is happening. Meeting Jesus changes the life of the Dead Saint forever. No religion is required. Post resuscitation, some embrace their old church with renewed faith. Some walk away from the church (if it doesn't reflect the Love of Christ they experienced in the Afterlife). Some find a new church. And some even become Taoists or Buddhists. The Dead Saints are not looking for a prison of religion after meeting an infinite God. They are looking to recreate the peace, the Light, and the unconditional Love they felt when they met God or Jesus in the Afterlife. ~*Chronicle 193*

Why are so many Dead Saints of all faiths seeing Jesus during their near-death experience? Since Earth University is a school, and every school requires a Headmaster, it seems, regardless of our faith, its Headmaster is Jesus Christ. Bridget describes the Lord's work:

> *That is when I recognized he (Jesus) was a part of the greater Light and in a way a custodian of our planet, kind of like He was assigned to it, it was his to "rule" and watch over, to guide and protect and to love and nurture.*[1]

The Dead Saints who are sent back to Earth describe Jesus as a gentle, but "strict father." He is a Dad who forces them to go to their first day of school despite their tantrums and crying. David hinted at Jesus' responsibility to guide our spiritual development and evolution:

> *Jesus is the being who is entrusted by God to ensure souls evolve. He was told Jesus is of the highest in vibration than any other soul. He said God holds Jesus in the highest of favor because He was the best example of what humans need to do.*[2]

We have read numerous Dead Saint encounters where Jesus is present at their Life Review—observing, watching and questioning in an attempt to arrive at a decision whether to return to Earth University or not. It appears to not matter whether the Dead Saint is Atheist, Christian, or of another faith.

Jesus is there anyway.

The Historical Jesus & the Mystical Christ

Many books have been written in an attempt to portray Jesus of Nazareth as a conjectural or putative Christ, who never existed as a historical figure. Mythologists, such as Joseph Campbell and others, point out that many of the stories of Jesus of Nazareth are so similar to perennial tales ascribed to god-men like Osiris in ancient Egypt and Dionysus in Greece, that early church Fathers, including Justin Martyr, Tellurian, and St. Irenaeus, were understandably disturbed by these "heresies," assigning these tales to the realm of "diabolical mimicry," accusing the Devil of "plagiarism by anticipation," a thesis that describes how Satan, "Deviously copied the true story of Jesus before it actually happened in an attempt to mislead the gullible."[3]

While I DO NOT support the author's final conclusions, we can see from research below done by Freke and Gandy in *the Jesus Mysteries*, why early church fathers were "unsettled" by ancient pagan stories of Osiris/Dionysus "Christ-like" motifs describing similar stories found in the Gospels (*list quoted from the Jesus Mysteries*):

> ➢ "He is God made flesh, the Savior, and the "Son of God."
> ➢ His father is God and His Mother is a mortal Virgin.

> He is born in a cave or humbled in a cowshed on December 25 before three shepherds.
> He offers His followers to be born-again through the rites of baptism.
> He miraculously turns water into wine at a wedding ceremony.
> He rides triumphantly into town on a donkey while people wave palm branch leaves to honor Him.
> He dies at Eastertime as a sacrifice for the sins of the world.
> After His death he descends into Hell, then on the third day, he rises from the dead and then ascends into Heaven in glory.
> His followers await His return as the Judge during the Last Days.
> His death and resurrection are celebrated by a ritual meal of bread and wine, which symbolize His body and blood."[4]

Viewed impartially, it *appears* the Apostles adapted some of these ancient pagan stories into their Gospels. Indeed, newer religions commonly adapted themselves to ancient archetypes and motifs. It is likely the Gospel writers absorbed some of the stories handed down from Egypt and Greece, but does that invalidate or minimize the meaning of the life of Jesus of Nazareth?

Not in my opinion.

Aside from millions of Christian (and non-Christian) encounters with the Love of Christ changing hearts and lives, as well as Dead Saint encounters with Jesus described throughout the *Chronicles*, I believe it is important we find an answer to this all-important question. Blaming the Devil does not explain why these ancient pagan stories exist and why they are so similar to stories told by the Apostles in the Gospels.

Without getting into a long dialogue about pagan history and stories about possible manifestations of the Christ before Jesus of Nazareth, there is a simple answer where Paul Solomon sheds some light on this theological dilemma:

There are several challenges in revealing the mystical side of Jesus' life, because the story of Christ begins before the world, and even further back to Creation itself, and ends with the crucifixion, resurrection, and ascension of the historical man, Jesus of Nazareth.

There is a quality of Being, born of God, who is God's child, who is a power, a consciousness who is the Christ. Speaking of the

"Christ," we are not speaking of a historical person. Yet, telling the story of the mystical Christ is best done by telling the story about the life of an individual, the historical man, Jesus of Nazareth...

In reading ancient Egyptian, Greek, and Christian literature about god-men, the stories are told as if the stories were about historical beings. The academic approach is always that the stories were mythical, that the individuals never really existed, or the stories were exaggerated and distorted. And where historians have found similar or identical stories in different cultures, coming from different periods of history, and identifying different historical men as "living" this particular life, the academics assumed, one was copying from another—that these universal myths and legends are symbolic, not literal, not real—written to fit an imposed pattern or belief. But there is another important possibility to consider.

There have been great teachers from time to time in history who used words well, but there is another way of teaching that is accomplished by those spectacular beings who can plan and dictate the circumstances of their own birth and choose to live their life in such a way that the story of their life becomes their teaching. So it is with the life and the story of Jesus of Nazareth. It just happens when we read the story of the historical man, we simultaneously read the story of the mystical Christ. The two become inseparable. They are one."[5]

Believing in a Mystical Savior Versus a Historical Savior

Paul Solomon expands the mythical / historical Christ debate from a "Savior" perspective. He writes in *the Meta-Human: Twice-Born*:

There are those who believe that the Christ we should invite to become the Lord and Ruler of our life should be the historical Jesus. Others say that Jesus demonstrated the Christ and is an example of a teacher rather than a mystical Savior. The argument even becomes bitter around the statement said by Jesus, 'I am the way, the truth, and the life. No man cometh to the Father, but by me.' The idea that this one Being could establish Himself personally as the only way to the Father was thought by some to be the absolute limit of dogma and even ego...[6]

Jesus presented Himself as a Rabbi who taught Judaism consistently up until the time of His death, later through His disciples who continued to teach in the Synagogues. Jesus always taught the one principle tenant and watchword of Judaism: 'Hear, oh Israel: The Lord thy God, the Lord is one.'[7] In this context of *one God, Jesus presented Himself as one with God and declared the only way to live in total harmony, or to express limitlessly, (to enter the Kingdom of Heaven) is to be one with Him and to be one with God. He could not possibly teach "at-one-ment with God" and be an example of it, and not be one with God and with Himself, the Christ.* [8]

The moment Jesus declared before the Jews, "I and My Father are one,"[9] they picked up stones to throw against Him. Jesus said, "Many good works have I showed you from my Father. For which of those works do ye stone me?"

The Jews holding the stones responded, "We are not stoning you for any good work," they replied, "but for blasphemy, because you, a mere man, claim to be God."

Jesus answered them, "Is it not written in your Law, 'I have said you are "gods"' (Psalm 82:6) If he (the Psalmist) called them 'gods,' to whom the word of God came—and Scripture cannot be set aside—what about the one whom the Father set apart as His very own and sent into the world? Why then do you accuse me of blasphemy because I said, 'I am God's Son'? Do not believe me unless I do the works of my Father. But if I do them, even though you do not believe me, believe the works, that you may know and understand that the Father is in me, and I in the Father."[10]

Paul Solomon goes on to answer more questions about Jesus:

Does that make Jesus any less than God? *Certainly not. You can't be any more God than one with God.*

Does this mean Jesus is any different from you and me? *It means He is very different unless you and I have so completely lost separate identity as to be totally one with God.*

Wasn't Jesus born the Son of God from birth? *Yes, but so were you. According to His teaching, Jesus said, 'Don't you know who you are? I have said, 'Ye are gods and children of God.' Jesus Christ was described by the Apostle Paul as 'The first fruits of them that slept.'*[11] *Jesus was the first to rise from the dead—the first to become equal to His Father in Heaven.*

Can I ask the historical Jesus to be the Lord of my life? *Why not? If you call on the historical Jesus Christ, you are calling on the one who is supposed to be the same as the consciousness of God. If you seek your 'Higher Mind,' you seek the expression of God that is the Source of your Mind. They are one and the same.*

What if I do not believe in the historical Jesus, but want to identify with the Christ inside me, my Higher-Self. Can I experience transformation of my mind, heart, and life this way? I do not believe Jesus has an ego problem. If He is in charge of your thoughts, your life, your actions; if unconditional Love is the ruler of your life, then you have accepted Him whether you are attracted to the historical account of Jesus of Nazareth or not."[12]

Committing to a historical or mythical Jesus is not an issue of religion. It is about your life being transformed by LOVE. Regardless of your approach to Christ, if it is sincere, I believe you will run into Jesus of Nazareth—the historical MAN—the Being of Light...anyway.

Definitions of Christ

The Dead Saints see Jesus as our Big Brother. The Son of God. The Living One. The Living God. The Great 'I Am':

Are you Jesus? I am the Great I AM. I come to you the way you want to see me. There is a golden thread in all religions and practices. I am the Blanket and you are the thread of it.[13]

One distinctive reference stands out among all other names for the personification of Christ in The Dead Saint Chronicles— the Son of God:

The very next moment the absolute impossible happened; a tiny pinprick of Light at the side of the bed began to grow brighter and brighter. At first not noticing the pinprick of Light, I thought it was a tiny night Light that was the room's only illumination that was getting brighter.

But then I saw it was coming from beside the white bedside table at the head of the bed. It continued to brighten as I watched. It brightened to such an extent that had it been any ordinary Light I would most certainly have been blinded.

The next moment, there flooded directly into my mind the words, 'Stand Up...you are now in the presence of the Son of God,' whereupon out of the Light stepped what I could only describe as the most magnificent Being I have ever known.

Thankful at last for a little company in this strange situation, I joked, 'That's it! Just like that...I am with the Son of God...Isn't there a reception area or something before we meet?

I felt a presence of Power and pure Love that was older than time but yet more modern than anyone I have ever met.[14]

Christianity refers to Jesus in John 3:16 as "The only Begotten Son of God," but a more accurate translation is "The unique Son of God"—a Greek term meaning *one of a kind*. What made Jesus unique as a historical man is that He lived His life so perfectly to become identified with God the Father, the *Living One, Living Love*. In I Corinthians 15:20 Paul says, "But now is Christ risen from the dead, and become the *first fruits* of them that slept."

While Jesus was the first to overcome death, we have been tasked as Sons and Daughters of God, to be part of a royal lineage to follow His example.

A Royal Lineage

Julie's NDE describes our relationship with Jesus as our Brother. Other Dead Saint testimonies describe Him as Big Brother, or our Great Grandfather, and insist we are children of the most High God, a Royal lineage with the same spiritual blood running through us:

I looked at Jesus and asked if that was the way to Heaven. He smiled and said, 'Yes.' I then asked 'Can I go there right now?'

Jesus said 'Yes, you may go. God is ready for you anytime you are ready to go home.'

I said, 'Yes, I'm ready.'

At that point I said, 'I want my husband to go with me.' Jesus smiled that forever patient loving smile of His and said, 'God is not ready for Hugo yet. He can't go with you.'

So I looked at Jesus and said, 'I don't want to go to Heaven without my husband, so I'm not going.'

We then walked over next to the river, then Jesus took both my hands turning my palms upward. While holding my hands He said, 'I want you to remember something. **You are of a royal lineage***. You are a child of God, The Most High God. You live in the world, but are not of the world. Your rightful place is in Heaven with the Father.'*

I said 'Yes, I understand.' The whole while He was telling me this I felt like I was the most precious, most loved, most beloved person in existence.

Next I asked, 'Just what is your relationship to me?'

Jesus said, 'I am your brother.'

I said, 'I know that's what the Bible says, so it's true?'

Jesus said, 'Yes, I am your brother. We have the same blood running through our veins. *I will never leave you or* *forsake you. I will always be there for you. Never ever forget who you are.' I just stood there looking around us for a while. He then said, 'Now go back to your bed and wake up.'* [15]

What Does Jesus Look Like?

The Dead Saints record dozens of after-death sightings of Jesus and describe His appearance. There are a few common denominators, a 2000-year-old robe clothing tied with a sash or rope, sandals, long brown hair, and blue/gray eyes—but it is never exactly the same. Even in my own dreams, Jesus fits the same stereotype described by the Dead Saints.

Chamisa found a pencil drawing of Jesus after her NDE that looked like the Jesus she saw during her experience:

> *A Holy Being so filled with Love and forgiveness. I searched afterwards, to find a picture of what I saw. I finally found a pencil drawing by Frances Hook of Jesus with the children. That is the closest image of a Holy Being to what I saw although I'd never seen that particular picture before my NDE experience.*[16]

Jean reported nearly an identical response from Jesus:

> *The Light turned a magnificent blue and rolled toward me like an ocean wave. It was not really close to me, but nevertheless I could see the image of Jesus within the blue wave. Love poured out upon me, like warm water. Jesus looked just like He did on the poster in my Sunday school class. I had the thought that if I had been a Buddhist, perhaps he would look like Buddha, and I was told, 'That is right. God appears in a familiar form.'*[17]

So does this mean Jesus and Buddha are interchangeable? Yes, and No. Jesus is still the Man who is Love personified, *the unique Son of God*, the Being who sits at the right hand of the Father, and will appear this way to those who see Him that way. However, if a Buddhist dies and sees Buddha, there is no conflict. God appears to the faithful in familiar form.

A Chronicle of Christ

A day after the one-year anniversary of leaving Akio Botanical Gardens, November 13, 2014, Jesus came to me in a dream:

~I was traveling with a group of people who saw a man they thought was Jesus. I asked them if they had seen Jesus perform any miracles to

prove He was Jesus. They said, 'No.' He seemed like an "average Joe" kind of guy.

"Jesus" invited me to fly with Him in His small, burgundy-blood red, beat up Cessna.

I said, 'Sure!'

I climbed in and sat in the left side passenger seat behind Jesus. (I assume we were flying in a 4-seater Cessna) When we got up into the air, I climbed into the co-pilots seat. He showed me how to turn the aircraft to the right and, in many ways, was instructing me. Jesus said the small plane was used to get back and forth from country towns to Washington, D.C. (symbolic representation of the City of God or Holy City in Heaven). Jesus wanted me to fly the Cessna, but I asked Him to be my Instructor Pilot.

I joked with Him, 'It's what the piloting rules require!' I knew I could fly the plane, but I didn't know when and how to communicate with the flight control tower for takeoff and landing. (I have had one other approaching-death dream (ADD) about flying a Cessna to a tropical place, but was nervous because I didn't know how to communicate with the flight control tower).

It was getting late and we needed to sleep. We landed the Cessna on the side of the road near a town with a small farm with garden supplies. We picked up two 50# bags of grass seed, each containing millions of seeds. I began looking for a hotel or restaurant for Jesus and me to stay overnight. I found a simple bed and breakfast, but before we could check in, we were approached by a couple of Secret Service agents who were returning items—keys—they believed were stolen from me.

I remember thinking, 'What nice guys! They were so honest to return them!'

Immediately afterward, we checked into our room, and instead of carrying luggage, I dragged in the two heavy bags of grass seed! Jesus laid down on a big king-sized bed, and covered Himself with an old granny-style thin white cover. I laid on top of it and slept at His feet.

The Secret Service agents stood watch over Jesus and me during our overnight stay. They had "ear communication" devices and seemed to be on-guard...as if they were protecting us. (Symbolic of God's warrior angels?)

The next day, during our flight back to the US capitol, we were going to open the plane doors and spread the millions of grass seeds over the land. **~Chronicle 518**

Fifty days later *(symbolic of the Biblical Jubilee Year and the forgiveness of debt?)*[18] on January 1, 2015, I had another dream of Jesus. He simply said to me:

David, cherish the time you have left. ~**Chronicle 558**

Will the Real Jesus Standup?

Jesus was the most important person in my life as a young man, but I knew in my heart, something was missing in our understanding of Jesus in the Church. My explosive encounter with Jesus—in the form of a Bag lady in New York in 1981 and a similar, more powerful experience in October, 2011 (chapter 2)—are reminders that anyone who has touched his powerful Presence, never, ever forgets. It is indelible, permanent, and life changing.

I take a risk of alienating some non-Christian groups and individuals, as well as some orthodox Christian groups who are very passionate about their beliefs and what they believe is the "right" (and only) pathway to knowing God. However, since the *Chronicles* will make at least a small contribution towards our knowledge about Heaven and Jesus Christ, I will tell the truth as I see it.

My near-death research and my own experience taught me that Jesus is not interested in being worshipped. Instead, He wants us to strive to become a carbon copy, a Xerox, a perfect Bonsai representing His life. He has no need to be called Jesus or even to be recognized as Jesus of Nazareth, or even to be called by His Aramaic birth name, Yeshua.[19] He has no interest in building large, ornate churches or temples to honor Him. I believe His wish for all Christians and non-Christians, and even those who do not believe in Him or in God, is to find a way to experience unconditional LOVE by touching His Holy Presence *within and without.*

How can we do this?

Experiencing Jesus Christ is not the same as believing in Jesus...though believing in Him prepares the ground for the experience. Without that belief, the experience of Christ may be less likely to happen, but by no means uncommon as non-Christians and even atheists have discovered in mystical experiences throughout history.

Often, children grow up believing in Jesus, only to reject the belief as teenagers or in early adulthood. He is put on the back burner for years, and then suddenly, in some extreme life crisis, the early belief will resurface, but this time as an experience. It happens neither through studying nor through some deliberate effort to re-establish the earlier belief. It is a life crisis, challenging them to find the power capable of dealing with their challenging difficulties, which opens the doorway for the new birth or born-again experience. An authentic encounter with the presence of Love, circumcises hate, anger, guilt and fear from the heart. While the process of going through the words of salvation is often an emotional experience, not all who do so are circumcised. An encounter with Christ rarely happens in a Sunday school church service where somebody is telling us how sinful we are, and what we must do to be saved.

So how do we invoke the power of Christ? Do we look for the historical Jesus in church? Or do we look for the Christ inside ourselves? Do we look for His Spirit in the lilies of the field, or do we look for His Presence in the eyes of a man freezing in the dead of winter? Dead Saint transformations describe, in Zen-like fashion, the realization that Christ's Love dwells in our own heart. His spiritual blood runs through our veins. He is always there as our Inner Teacher, waiting to help, guide and instruct. We just need to let Him in.

Researching my Bible Class journal notes, I found a great lecture from Paul Solomon where he paraphrases Jesus' swan song to His 12 apostles in the 14th chapter of John:

Jesus systematically through His lifetime took one law of nature at a time; mineral life, plant life, animal life, human life, and ultimately the weather, one at a time and proved all these things would obey Him. And they obeyed Him because of His teaching.

He said, 'When you live in harmony with the Law—in absolute obedience of the Law, then the Law obeys you. You then become Master of all that is. But as long as I walk among you, then you are going to say, 'He can do all of these things, but we cannot.'

But Jesus said, 'I do not these things of myself, but the Father that is in Me, He does the works.' Jesus wanted us to understand this: 'If I am in the Father and the Father is in me, then He is doing the work. And if you are in me and I am in the Father, then that makes you and the Father one.' None of the apostles understood what Jesus was talking about at the time. The only way Jesus could get His point across was to die. And when He died, Jesus overcame the last adversary—-death. And in overcoming death, He raised Himself up an incorruptible, spiritual body and said, "You can do this too.

Jesus came to show us how to love and how to forgive. We are made of the same Light as Jesus Christ. As Sons and Daughters of God, we are a part of God's Royal Lineage. We can become one with Him. It is our commission from Him to do so, so we might better serve the Father. I believe the greatest testimony of Jesus Christ was his humility and honesty, and yet it is these very remarks that our Christian church sometimes likes to take away from Jesus. I mean it in this way:

First, we take away His humility by suggesting He was the only one who ever could accomplish the things he accomplished—that no other person could match what He did in the flesh. We take away His humility when we do, because Jesus didn't say He was the only one who could do great works. In fact, He said quite the opposite. In John 14:12 Jesus said:

Verily, verily, I say unto you, He that believeth in me, the works that I do shall he do also; and greater works than these shall he do; because I go unto my Father.

Here is His humility and His honesty. Jesus created the challenge for all who believe in Him to do 'greater works'—healing, service, compassion, empathy, peace, saving the lost and even saving the world.

I believe this was core to Jesus' teaching. He showed us this when He asked Peter to have faith to walk on water. When Peter realized what he was doing, he began to sink into the water's stormy depths. Jesus admonished Him, "Oh, Peter, where is your faith?" The faith that has the power to move mountains.

Jesus Christ overcame death itself, and bore on His shoulders the cross of humanity, taking responsibility for every mistake and (every sin), any soul has ever committed or will commit for eternity. His life continues after His death and ascension when He was born-again into the hearts of his Apostles, disciples and Saints....and you.

There are at least a hundred authentic Dead Saint close encounters with Jesus Christ in the referenced in the NDERF archives. Sadly, I only have enough space to tell you a few of these face-to-face meetings. It is my hope these remarkable stories will help to inform you of the Man, the Personality, the Humor, the Love, the Light, and the Power He IS.

Dead Saint Encounters with Jesus

You may wonder, "Is Jesus real?" Regardless of our belief, since His crucifixion two thousand years ago, Jesus has continued to appear to the living, in waking or dream states, and to those temporarily dead—the Dead Saints. During my research for Dead Saint direct encounters with Jesus, I catalogued a fairly complete library of several—dozen, unique, fascinating, sometimes breathtaking accounts of Christ. Every account validated a very real, approachable Jesus.

Irene didn't believe in Jesus Christ—until she was hit by a van while studying in medical school:

Everything around me was dark. I sensed that a figure approached in front of me. By some method, I received the impression I was unworthy of being there… Then, I saw the figure of a man who stood over a sort of stream. The water seemed to be made of the Light of liquid neon. I saw His feet, shod in some sort of sandals and [I saw] His attire. All was dazzling in Him. He seemed to be made of Light. I felt extremely good in His Presence; full of an unconditional [and] absolute Love.

I knew inside of me He was Jesus Christ (and I didn't believe in Him). I was surprised.

I said, 'But you exist…!'

He said, 'Live.' His voice sounded warm and sweet, but I didn't want to return.[20]

Shalom, a conservative Jew, died during an operation, when his heart stopped. This was his second NDE and he was shown his "Book of Life:"

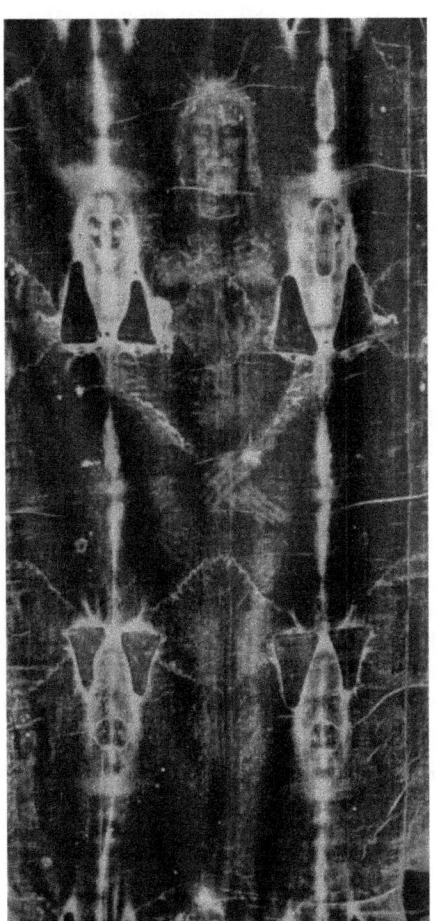

Then, suddenly I saw & sensed a very special man, standing over to the left of where I was standing. My heart recognized HIM before my eyes did.

I immediately walked over to Him & asked, 'Are You the Being, called JESUS?'

And with a warm soft, sense of Love & Laughter, He replied back, 'I am called by many names, however because of your background you can call me BIG BROTHER, and I will call you, My Little Prince of Peace'… He then went on to indicate I could either stay with HIM or return to Earth. However, if I did not return, many people would miss their connections, in order to complete their missions and purposes in life. Reluctantly, but with a deeper understanding of my Mission...I chose to return to help ALL of my assigned brothers & sisters, on our planet. JESUS instructed me I was to do this, "Without greed or ego getting in the way, I was to connect doctors, attorneys, priests, rabbis and peoples of ALL faiths, young and old alike, to help one another.

...I was told to BE PATIENT. 'Heal yourself through forgiveness, love, prayer & meditation.' Then I was sent back to my body on the operating table. I was born and raised in a conservative Jewish Family, the Great Grandson of the Chief Rabbi of Moscow. I went to Catholic High School, and studied Chinese Buddhism. My name "Shalom," which means Peace.[21]

John's encounter with Jesus got my attention. It described Jesus looking like the image on the Shroud of Turin:

I AM THE ALPHA AND OMEGA THE BEGINNING AND END."
At that moment then, I saw a Light come from the right side of me, and it was at a far distance, it got closer and closer until it immersed me in Light, and all I could see was Light and feel warmth... **'Then at that moment the Light took the shape of what appeared to me to be an outline of Jesus, similar to what the Shroud of Turin would look like.**[22]

When John mentioned the appearance of Jesus looking similar to the Shroud of Turin, I decided to dig deeper into the latest research. I discovered that the Carbon-14 dating didn't settle the issue at all. Nobel laureate Willard Frank Libby who invented and perfected the C-14 archeological dating process, stated he was against the tests, due to the likely contamination of the holy Cloth. A January 20, 2005 paper in the professional journal *ThermoChimica Acta* by Dr. Ray Rogers has shown conclusively that the sample cut from the Shroud in 1988 was taken from an area of the cloth that was re-woven during the Middle Ages thus, *"the radiocarbon date was not valid for determining the true age of the shroud."*[23]

J. Michael Fischer, in an article adapted from John C. Iannone, writes about new chemical evidence discovered in 2014, dating the Shroud to the 1st Century A.D. In *The Shroud of Turin, Evidence it is authentic?* Fischer writes about three new tests applied to the fibers of the Shroud: two chemical and one mechanical. "The chemical tests were done with Fourier Transform Infrared Spectroscopy (FTIR) and Raman spectroscopy, examining the relationship between age and a spectral property of ancient flax textiles. The mechanical test measured several micro-mechanical characteristics of flax fibers, such as tensile strength.

The results were compared to similar tests on samples of cloth from between 3250 BC and 2000 AD whose dates are accurately known."[24]

Fischer explains, "The tests on fibers from the Shroud of Turin produced the following dates: FTIR = 300 BC +/- 400 years; Raman spectroscopy = 200 BC +/- 500 years; and multi-parametric mechanical = 400 AD +/- 400 years. All the dates have a 95% certainty. The average of all three dates is 33 B.C.+/-250 years. The collective uncertainty is less than the individual test uncertainties)."[25]

Iannone and Fischer's reporting of the 2014 fiber tests on the Shroud came from years of groundbreaking research from Italian scientist and renowned Shroud researcher Giulio Fanti, an Associate Professor in the Department of Industrial Engineering at the University of Padua in Italy. In June 2015, Fianti and co-author Pierandrea Malfi released *The Shroud of Turin: First Century after Christ!*[26] which reveals details of the fiber tests as well as numismatic analysis performed on Byzantine gold coins showing clearly the facial image of the Shroud of Turin—600 years before the faulty 1988 Carbon-14 tests dated the Shroud fibers to a range of 1260-1390 A.D. It is clear the 1988 testing was off by more than 12 centuries!

The new chemical and mechanical tests use an infrared light beam and the red laser of the Raman spectroscope to "excite the various energy levels of the molecules" in the fiber of the Cloth, resulting in reflections that make it possible "to evaluate the concentration of particular substances contained in the cellulose of the linen fibers." According to Fianti, because cellulose degrades over time, *"it is therefore possible to determine a correlation with the age of the fabric."* [27]

So we are likely looking at a much older cloth, dating back to the time of Christ, but is it the true burial shroud of Jesus of Nazareth? According to exhaustive research done by a pathologist, the image on the Shroud appears to be of a crucified man, but is he crucified man Jesus Christ? [28] In 1979, chemist Piero Ugolotti was examining the negative photo images of the Shroud and noticed marks near the face of the Shroud he later identified to be Greek and Latin letters. He brought his work to Aldo Masteroni, professor of ancient literature at the Catholic University of the Sacred Heart of Milan, who immediately identified the Latin and Greek letters, and more—Hebraic writing.[29]

In 1994-95, Marcel Alonso and Èric de Bazelaire, two members of the Centre International d' Études sur le Linceul de Turin in Paris, went to a team of experts in signal analysis, Andre Marion and his colleague Anne-Laurie Courage at the Institute d'Optique.[30] They identified at least five separate words from the jumbled, faint images, including the Greek words (T)iber(iou)—referencing *Tiberius*, the Roman emperor at the time of Christ's crucifixion, and (I)esou(s)

Nnazarennos, or Jesus Christ.[31] The text also mentions the man who was wrapped in the shroud had been condemned to death—in effect a "burial certificate" for Jesus Christ.

What caused these words to be imprinted on the Shroud?

In November 2009, Barbara Frale expanded Alonso and Bazelaire's original research of the faint Hebrew, Greek and Latin letters found in sequence on the facial image on the Shroud. She says the date of the "death certificate" was in accord with the Gospel records:

> *In the year 16 of the reign of the Emperor Tiberius Jesus the Nazarene, taken down in the early evening after having been condemned to death by a Roman judge because he was found guilty by a Hebrew authority, is hereby sent for burial with the obligation of being consigned to his family only after one full year....*
>
> *Barbara Frale continues: "The 'extractor mortis,' the centurion charged with ensuring the execution of the condemned, had drawn strips of glue onto the cloth and wrote the name of the deceased with a red liquid. When the resurrection occurred, the faint writing was indelibly imprinted on the Shroud. Since Tiberius became emperor after the death of Octavian Augustus in 14 A.D., the 16th year of his reign would be within the span of the years A.D. 30 to 31.[32]*

Another discovery added to the excitement surrounding the image captions. In 1991, M. Moroni in a white paper writes of the work of J. Jackson and G. Tamburelli who expanded the work of an original discovery of a coin symbol found on the Shroud made in 1980 by Father Filas, of Loyola University in Chicago and Michael Marx, a coin specialist. The two researchers found images of "two roundish bodies in relief" in the eye-socket area of the Shroud. It gave them a premise for considering that "coins were placed over the eyes" of the crucified man after death.

"The coins, (Leptons of Pontius Pilate. In Greek meaning "mite"— Mark 12:42-44), we have found out, had an irregular diameter with a maximum axis of 16mm. In addition to the imprint of a 'staff' in the shape of 'a question mark' reversed. Applying radiographic experiments carried out on a skull, and by using coins of that period, we also confirm that only a certain kind of small coin laid on the eyes can reach the medialis hollow of the [crucified man's] skull.

Also, the discovery of two skulls, both with two small coins, of Christ's time at Jericho, lead us to the irrefutable conclusion that on the Shroud cloth, a decal of a coin really was imprinted which portrayed a 'staff' or LITUUS—the symbol existing uniquely on very rare coins minted by Pontius Pilate in 29-30 A.D." [33]

Of course, it is interesting to note scholars traditionally assign 29, 30, or 31 A.D. as one of the years Jesus Christ was crucified.

How were Images of a Crucified Man Imprinted on the Cloth?

The theory is the transformation of Christ's physical body left an indelible "positive" image on the Shroud, an image of a crucified man that has captivated the faithful for centuries. The images are scorch-like, yet not created by heat, and are a purely surface phenomenon limited to the crowns of the top fibers of the Cloth. The Shroud is clearly not a painting; no evidence of pigments or media has been found. Researchers know the blood was on the Cloth before the image was created.

So how was this image (not made by human hands) imprinted on the Cloth? Dr. Thomas Phillips (nuclear physicist at Duke University and formerly with the High Energy Labs at Harvard) says, "A potential milliburst of radiation (a neutron flux) could be consistent with the moment of resurrection. Such a milliburst might cause the purely surface phenomenon of the scorch-like (scorch-by-light) images, and possibly add Carbon-14 to the Cloth."[34]

As Dr. Phillips points out: "*We never had a resurrection to study.*"

Dr. John Jackson, Director of the Turin Shroud Center of Colorado in Colorado Springs, proposed a new theory about how the image of Christ was imprinted on the Shroud:

"First, the intensity of the images correlated directly to the distance between the body and the enveloping cloth. Second, gravity was a significant factor in producing the image. It appears the physical body of Jesus converted into Light, becoming transparent to its physical surroundings and causing the cloth to collapse and fall vertically onto the table. These findings support the idea the image on the Shroud was made by a sudden blast of high-energy radiation. They also refute the possibility of forgery, since lasers were obviously not available in medieval times."[35]

Dead Saint Sees the Marks of a Crucified Jesus

The Dead Saints have found several instances of seeing the marks of crucifixion on the glorified body of Jesus during their NDE. The following example depicts this.

Micki died and saw herself floating over her dead body. She was pulled through a tunnel, with the Light at the end getting brighter and brighter:

> *After a while, I was suddenly standing in front of this beautiful wrought iron Victorian gate, covered with the largest and most brilliant colored flowers I had ever seen, but just before I entered, a voice in my mind spoke to me, I turned to look to my left and there stood Jesus Christ, I* **could see His nail prints in His hands and feet but they were not in His hands, they were more in His wrist area and angles out as though they were torn from His weight.**[36]

Micki noted in her NDE the nail prints were in the wrist area, not the palms, *as depicted by the Shroud of Turin.*

Dead Saint Witnesses the Crucifixion

A few Saints transcend time and space, witnessing the crucifixion and death of Jesus on the cross during their NDE, including Vinni who appears to be the Centurion stabbing Jesus with His spear:

> *One thing I will never forget is that love I saw in His [Jesus'] eyes, I felt accepted, like I couldn't do anything that would stop His love for me. I began to question Him about some things. He transferred me to a time during the Crucifixion. I remember being in the crowd yelling for Him to be crucified. I could smell the blood and I could smell death. I remember as He hung on the cross. I remember stabbing Him with my spear, but He was already dead! I didn't cry.*
>
> *I didn't regret my sins. I just remember stabbing Him. I don't know if this was a vision He was showing me, but I remember telling Him we "killed" you. You died. I saw you die. He looked at me and said, 'Yes, but I arose on the third day remember?'*
>
> *I said, 'Yeah, you did.' It was at this time I knew they were sending me back, and I asked Him, 'Do I have to go back?'*
>
> *He smiled and said, 'Yes.'*
>
> *He didn't say anything about me having a job to do or anything like that... just you're going back.*[37]

Jesus Appears Outdoors Under Moonlight Conditions

Kenneth Vincent has uncovered a multitude of Jesus appearances; visits with Christians, non-Christians, atheists and agnostics, and published his findings in *The Journal of Near-Death Experiences*. In this encounter, a woman and her husband-to-be shared a vision of Jesus while they were walking in the moonlight:

Then the figure emerged, a most brilliant sight. We were both speechless, but not afraid, it was so beautiful. The figure, Jesus Christ, glided onto the center of the road while we were on rough pavement. We still remember every detail, but our views on religion have deepened; although, still, we are not too religious.[38]

Jesus visited hundreds of people after his death and resurrection two thousand years ago. It is clear, His appearances continue unabated to this day.

Planetary Headmaster

Regardless of our faith, from the Dead Saint evidence I have collected, it appears Jesus is Headmaster of our school, Earth University. He is responsible for our spiritual evolution. It is His job. He was a historical figure. He is not a myth. He left indelible evidence of his spiritual resurrection on the Shroud of Turin, and I believe, as the prophet declared in Isaiah 52:13-14, will be proven authentic:

Even as many were amazed at Him, so marred was His look beyond that of man, and His appearance like that of mortals—so that He will startle many nations. Because of Him, kings shall stand speechless; for those who have not been told shall see, those who have not heard shall ponder it.

He wants us to know, "**He is real.**"[39] It is the reason why the after-death appearances of Jesus in the Gospels resemble the modern ones. It is because He is still walking here among us, talking to Dead Saints in the Afterlife, and visiting many in broad daylight comforting those in need.

He wants us to know all mistakes are redeemable. All can be forgiven. That salvation—being saved—is about letting go of fear, hate, anger and pain; that he can help us release our burdens, our fears of Judgment and our fears of death.

Salvation & Grace

In closing this chapter, it is important I share with you one of the major driving forces behind the early development and writing of the *Chronicles*.

When I was 13, I listened while our pastor, Tracey Floyd, preached at the United Church of Christ. His Sermon was about salvation and grace. After he spoke, I remember wondering, "What will happen to all the other souls who do not receive the gift of salvation? I had difficulty in believing only the saved are redeemed from death and will go to Heaven, leaving 4.8 billion people lost in eternal darkness or damned to a place called Hell. Those same people are born just as human as Christians. It is not their fault they were born in families of other faiths who do not know the Lord!

So I wrote Billy Graham and asked how this could be? I received a form letter back which basically said, *"You cannot be saved by good works alone but only by the blood of Jesus Christ,"* referencing Ephesians 2:8–9: "Before being saved our works are done in the flesh and cannot please God; our most righteous deeds fall far short of God's glory. (Romans 3:20 and Isaiah 64:6). We can be saved only because God is gracious and merciful and has designed a way for us to be declared righteous when we are not." (Psalm 86:5; Ephesians 2:4)

Other religions have different approaches to dealing with immortality, Heaven and death. Christianity is unique in presenting Jesus Christ as Savior. His Grace is the only means of lifting the Judgment of Original Sin against us—a precise formula of salvation, eternal life and immortality. These cannot be received through "good works alone."

Evangelical Christians who hang on to the "believe or perish" scenario point to John 3:13-17 as further evidence:

> *And no man hath ascended up to Heaven, but He that came down from Heaven, even the Son of man which is in Heaven. And as Moses lifted up the serpent in the wilderness, even so must the Son of man be lifted up: That whosoever believeth in Him should not perish, but have eternal life. For God so loved the world, that he gave His only begotten Son, that whosoever believeth in Him should not perish, but have everlasting life. For God sent not His Son into the world to condemn the world; but that the world through Him might be saved.*

According to John 3:13-17, no one has ascended to Heaven except Jesus Christ, and the only way we can inherit Eternal Life and enter Heaven is to believe in Him. Conversely, why would Jesus Christ threaten destruction if we didn't believe in Him?

For me, it was important to understand the true meaning of Christ's words. Researching further, I found whenever the Bible used the word *perish* in the New Testament, the original Greek word is *apollumi*. It means *to be destroyed*. This definition has created fear in the church for a long time, which I believe, is manipulative at worst and misguided at best.

There is another definition of a*pollumi* with Biblical precedent. It also means *to lose*, or to be lost. *Apollumi* is the same word Jesus uses when He said in Matthew 15:24, "I was sent only to the lost (*apollumi*) sheep of Israel," and in Luke 15:4-7, "Does he not leave the ninety-nine in the open country and go after the lost (*apollumi*) sheep until he finds it? And when he finds it, he joyfully puts it on His shoulders and goes home. Then He calls His friends and neighbors together and says, "Rejoice with me; I have found my lost (*apollumi*) sheep."

The Dead Saints agree. If a soul has gone astray and becomes lost, as Rob was told in his NDE, they will be found: *All is forgiven. All spirit is eternal. All can be redeemed.*[40]

Still, the theological "good works" dilemma facing 4.8 billion non-Christians haunted me. For 42 years, the question was a constant prayer of my heart. Finally, an answer came. On August 14, 2015, I woke up with an astonishing dream:

~I saw a giant cubed, seven level mansion covering the whole Earth with Christ as its overseer. It was called Salvation Mansion and Jesus' blood ran through its walls providing its power. All souls past, present and future lived in this Mansion (shaped like a cube). All had been invited to its grand ballroom to dance. They entered the ballroom through one of 12 doors, three on each side. They came up to the first floor to the ballroom, dressed up to the hilt, and danced and danced and danced. The ballroom was packed with everyone, dressed in fancy gowns and regalia of every color, smiling, laughing, and having fun.

*They were all good people who had done good works. I knew they were already saved because salvation was available to everyone who lived in the Mansion, even those who were not invited to the ball. Whoever plugged into the power in the walls of the Salvation Mansion were automatically forgiven. At the back of the ballroom, was an elevator that would take the ballroom dancers to higher levels of "eternal life," but very few chose to go up. ~****Chronicle 424***

I asked God to help me interpret the dream, which I did in the following manner: I woke up understanding why "good works" alone are not sufficient to reach the Heaven of "Eternal Life."

It is because there are many different heavens.

Christ's Mansion is Earth University and the seven heavens over it are the many mansions within our Father's house described by Jesus Christ. The first floor of the Mansion is the *first level of Heaven* filled with the good ballroom dancers, honest people who have done good works on Earth. As James 2:24 says, "Ye see then how that by works a man is justified, and not by faith only." Their good works are weighed and counted during the Judgment at the end of their life. If good outweighs evil, a soul will *at least* enter the first level of Heaven. When evil outweighs good, the soul is sent to "lower" darker planes or existences often referred to as Hell or "outer darkness."

The opportunity of "salvation" illustrated in the dream is available to all who "dance" in the Mansion of Earth University. The good people still carry the burden of mistakes (sin) they have made in their life, which makes them fall short of "God's glory." My dream showed me the ballroom dancers can "plug" into Grace anytime to remove the burden of their sins, which affect the depth, and vibration of Live in their heart, but most of these souls—both Christians and non-Christians—do not notice and even ignore the opportunity. Once they "plug" into Grace, they have additional opportunity to grow by going up the elevator to God's higher Realms of Heaven.

This includes born-again Christians who still feel their post conversion "mistakes" will bar them from entry into the Heaven of "Eternal Life." Christ can still remove the dark marks of sin anytime in Heaven and on Earth, while one works on becoming an example of unconditional love and forgiveness.

While my belief about good works, salvation and Heaven is different from traditional Christian teachings, *it does not conflict with Scripture.* The Truth is: 4.8 billion non-Christians will not perish. The "bad guys" will be sent or resigned to darker, lower realms discussed in chapter 19, *Tragedy, Evil, and Hell.* Good souls will enter at least the first level of Heaven when they die. Perhaps, it is why the Dead Saints find both the "unsaved" and the "saved" in the Realms of Heaven they see. One thing is clear. They describe a path to Heaven open to *all who believe and have faith*; a path ruled by "the condition of the heart"—a quality of character defined by love, integrity, honesty, and goodness. It is who we are, not the religion we profess or the words we say. John says in Revelation 3:20, "Behold, I stand at the door, and knock: if any man hears my voice, and open the door, I will come in to Him, and will sup with Him, and he with me."

Ponder in your heart: That which is closest to the truth can be used as the most dangerous untruth. ~Chronicle 965

---

1 *Bridget F NDE*, #1654, 07.21.08, NDERF.org
2 http://www.near-death.com/experiences/notable/david-oakford.html
[3] Freke, Timothy and Peter Gandy 1999. *The Jesus Mysteries.* Three Rivers Press, Crown Publishing Group. pp. 6-7.
[4] Ibid. p.5.
5 Paul Solomon, in a Seminary Come Alive Bible class in 1984, talked about the controversy and differences between the mystical Christ and the historical Jesus. Quoted from transcripts, Paul Solomon 1982. *A Closer Walk with Jesus.* 8 CD's. Ireland, UK: Paul Solomon Foundation.www.paulsolomon.com.
6 Paul Solomon 2003. *The Meta-Human, Twice-Born. Ireland, UK. Paul Solomon Foundation.* Originally published by the Master's Press, 1985. p. 27.
7 Deuteronomy 6:4.
8 Paul Solomon 2003. *The Meta-Human, Twice-Born. Ireland, UK. Paul Solomon Foundation.* Originally published by the Master's Press, 1985. p. 27.
9 (NIV) John 10:29
10 (NIV) John 10:31-39
11 I Corinthians 15:20
12 Ibid. p.27.
13 *Nicholas P's NDE*, #676, 09.03.05, NDERF.org
14 *A New Hope NDE*, #270, aleroy.com/board270.htm
15 *Julie H NDE*, #3228, 01.15.13, NDERF.org
16 *Chamisa H NDE*, #2170, 02.26.10, NDERF.org
17 *Jean K NDE*, #2555, 01.01.11, NDERF.org
18 The Jubilee year is the year at the end of seven cycles of Shmita (Sabbatical years). On the following (50th) year, the Jubilee, according to Leviticus 25;8-13, occurred on the Day of Atonement: slaves and prisoners were freed, debts were forgiven, and the mercies of God were particularly manifest. The entire year was considered Holy.
19 Yeshua is the Hebrew name, and its English spelling is "Joshua." Iesous is the Greek transliteration of the Hebrew name, and its English spelling is "Jesus." Thus, the names "Joshua" and "Jesus" are essentially the same; both are English pronunciations of the Hebrew and Greek names for Jesus.
20 *Irene A NDE*, #1231, 10.14.07, NDERF.org
21 *Shalom G's NDE*, #448, .08.09.04, NDERF.org
22 *John C's NDE*, #275, 04.17.03, NDERF.org
23 Raymond N. Rogers September 2004. Abstract. *Thermochimica Acta* 425 (2005) 189–194.
24 http://www.newgeology.us/presentation24.html. Based on the Article, *The Shroud of Turin, Evidence it is authentic*? J Michael Fischer, adapted from the original article by John C. Iannone.
25 Ibid. web article.
26 Giulio Fanti and Pierandrea Malfi 2015. The Shroud of Turin: First Century after Christ! Singapore: Pan Stanford. p.197.
27 Shaver Parker, Jr. May 06, 2013. The Daily News: *Science Shines New Light on Shroud of Turin's Age. While questions have been raised about his methodology, an Italian researcher's novel use of test procedures suggests the shroud is indeed 2,000 years old.* http://www.ncregister.com/daily-news/science-shines-new-light-on-shroud-of-turins-age/#ixzz3zyPZwF4
28 Numerous surgeons and pathologists have studied the Crucifixion wounds on the Shroud

(including Dr. Frederick Zugibe (Medical Examiner-Rockland, New York), Dr. Robert Bucklin (Medical Examiner-Las Vegas, Nevada), Dr. Herman Moedder (Germany), the late Dr. Pierre Barbet (France), and Dr. David Willis (England)
29 Barbara Frale 2012. *The Templars and the Shroud of Christ.* Skyhorse Publishing. p.196.
30 Ibid. p. 202. See also, Marion and Courage, *Nouvelles dècouvertes*, forward by Christian Imbert (director in chief, Institute d'Optique and of l'Ecole Superieure d'Optique d'Orsay), pp. 7-10.
31 Ibid. pp. 202-204
32 Barbara Frale April 2004. Abstract. *The Chinon chart: Papal absolution to the last Templar, Master Jacques de Molay.* Journal of Medieval History, 30,.2, pp. 109–134.
33 Stephen E. Jones July 9, 2009. *The Shroud of Turin. My commentary on Shroud of Turin related matters.* http://theshroudofturin.blogspot.com/2009/07/re-there-is-compelling-evidence-it-is.html. See also, Moroni, M., 1991, *Pontius Pilate's Coin on the Right Eye of the Man in the Holy Shroud, in the Light of the New Archaeological Findings,* in Berard, A., ed., 1991, "*History, Science, Theology and the Shroud*," Symposium Proceedings. St. Louis Missouri, June 22-23, 1991, The Man in the Shroud Committee of Amarillo, Texas: Amarillo TX, p.286.
34 Based on the Article, *The Shroud of Turin, Evidence it is authentic,* J Michael Fischer, adapted from the original article by John C. Iannone.
35 Based on the Article, *The Shroud of Turin, Evidence it is authentic,* J Michael Fischer, adapted from the original article by John C. Iannone.
36 *Micki P's NDE,* #328, 11.02.03, NDERF.org
37 *Vinnie G NDE,* #1094, 04.23.07, NDERF.org
38   Ken R. Vincent Ed.D. 2005. Journal of Near-Death Studies. Abstract, *Resurrection Appearances of Jesus as After-Death Communication.* Houston, TX. Excerpts taken from (Maxwell & Tschudin. pp. 77–78), p. 142.
39 *John F's NDE,* #61, 12.03.00, NDERF.org
40 *Rob D NDE,* #1216, 10.06.07, NDERF.org

24

The 13th Path

Approaching-Death Dream: A wolf bites off the roots of one of my Bonsai trees, killing it. As I traveled down the road, I passed by a Japanese maple nursery. A Bonsai master lived in a house on the nursery grounds, and I stopped in to see him. I noticed everything in his home was in perfect order. Nothing was out of place. I told him I had taught

Bonsai, but he spoke almost no English. Soon, several other Bonsai teachers came in. We were all excited because it was so unusual to get so many Bonsai teachers together to share our love for the art. I then saw the remaining Bonsai tree the wolf hadn't killed. I looked closely at the top third of the tree, and noticed I had wrapped copper wire too tightly around the main trunk, choking off its circulation. The bark was falling off. The tree was rotting and dying. It would only be a short time before the top of the tree would break off. ~Chronicle 865

In Japanese gardens, pathways are composed of stone and gravel, and when we walk on them, they make a crunching sound. The sound makes us conscious of our footsteps and surroundings.

Our life is a "Zen journey." We picked up a walking stick and began stepping on these granite stones. Our experiences, our lessons, and our classes have been closely monitored by our Inner Teacher, the Christ, and our Planetary Headmaster. His servants—Rice Paper Teachers, professors, teaching assistants, family, friends and angels—have left a trail of breadcrumbs to help us pass the syllabus designed for us before we were born. These lessons derived from the 12 pillars of Life, help us evolve and grow so we can accomplish our Mission and graduate Earth University with our intended Bachelor, Masters or Doctorate—with honours.

The story of Jesus Christ and the 12 apostles, describes the 12 paths of Earth University with Jesus standing as its central pillar, a 13th path to God. The Book of Revelation reflects this same philosophy. It describes a Virgin woman in Heaven, crowned with 12 stars, the Sun and Moon beneath her feet, preparing to birth a child, a 13th archetype, known in mythology and legend as *The Redeemer*. The 12 is repeated again (Revelation 21:12-14) describing the New Jerusalem coming down from Heaven—its 12 gates looking like pearls, with 12 angels representing the 12 tribes of the children of Israel and its 12 foundations representing the 12 apostles of the Lamb (Christ).

At the *centre* of the Holy City, in the midst of the street on either side of a river, is the Tree of Life, which bears 12 manner of fruits every month (Revelation 22:1-2). Here again, the Tree of Life stands at the *centre* of New Jerusalem and represents the Christ, a 13th archetype, who declares, "I am the Way, the Truth, and the Life."

This ancient teaching, impressing itself in modern times, describes the mysterious importance of the 13th path. In previous chapters, we referred to the 12 paths as part of the Tree of Knowledge of good and evil—a path of birth, death, reincarnation; a path represented by a serpent swallowing its tail: a path of evolution, but also a *path described as a curse*. Yet, in Revelation 22:3, for those who overcome,

"**There shall be no more curse, but the throne of God and of the Lamb shall be in it and His servants shall serve Him.**" The curse of death and rebirth will end. Revelation 21:4 promises when this occurs, there will be an end to all sorrows:

And God shall wipe away all tears from their eyes; and there shall be no more death, neither sorrow, nor crying, neither shall there be any more pain: for the former things are passed away.

In Revelation 21:22-25:

And I saw no temple therein, for the Lord God Almighty and the Lamb are the temple of it. And the city had no need of the sun, neither of the moon, to shine upon it, for the glory of God did lighten it, and the Lamb is the Light thereof. And the nations of them which are saved shall walk in the Light of it, and the kings of the Earth do bring their glory and honour into it. And the gates of it shall not be shut at all by day—for there shall be no night there.

The Dead Saints describe Heaven as a place with no tears, no sorrow, no pain, no sun, and no moon. There is no contradiction between Scripture and the Dead Saint experience. They consider the City of God in Heaven, the New Jerusalem, our heavenly Home. However, both the Apostle John and the Dead Saints believe the City of God will someday descend from Heaven and manifest on this physical Earth. When will this occur?

When we begin walking the 13th path—the path of redemption, love and forgiveness.

Walking the 13th Path

How do we walk the 13th path and bring down the Holy City to Earth? To reiterate, the 13th path doesn't deny the 12 paths. They are *fruit from the Tree of Life for the healing of the nations*, (overcoming), but offers a faster way to evolve through the lessons of the 12.

One powerful mystical-death experience describes the 13th path. It happened in 1995 to Afshin Javid, an ex-Hezbollah Iranian extremist who was captured carrying 300 passports across the Syrian border and jailed. During his incarceration, Afshin had a dramatic encounter with Jesus, an experience foreign to his religious beliefs at the time. Afshin was a fervent, Islamic Shiite. He prayed five times or more a day and read the Qur'an cover to cover every ten days. Then one day during his jail term, Afshin felt a "spirit" enter the room. It frightened him. He tried to use every tool Islam had taught him and prayed in the name of Allah, "I rebuke you!" He used all of these prayers, but nothing helped:

In that moment, I was totally desperate. I felt like this spirit was choking the life out of me—that I was dying.

I then cried out to the heavens saying, 'God, help me!'

Immediately, I heard a voice as clear as day saying, 'Great is the name of Jesus.' I felt like a man drowning. 'When you are thrown a rope, you never question the color of the rope. You just grab on.... So I did.'

I cried, 'If you are really true, show yourself!' I wonder to this day, 'Why did I word it that way? Why didn't I just say, Jesus help me?' I didn't know why, but that's the way it came out. And before I was finished with the sentence, everything went back to normal.

Now, this was not my conversion to becoming a Christian; it was only the beginning of my confusion. I thought, 'Why would Jesus help a Muslim?' I would have been a martyr for Allah, and would have walked on mines and sacrificed my life. I thought I had done everything I could do to fight the infidels.

So the question came back, 'Why would Jesus help a Muslim?' Over and over I said to myself, 'I believe in Mohammad the last prophet. I believe in Allah.'

This supernatural encounter confused Afshin. He desperately needed an answer. He demanded God to show him the right path. There are verses in the Qur'an, which say the ways of Allah are many, and no matter what part of the mountain we climb, we always arrive at the same mountaintop. Afshin thought, *'Maybe God has a specific purpose for me?'* Frantic, he decided he was going too fast, and prayed to find an answer. From the bottom of his heart and with all his strength Afshin asked God, *'What is it that you want me to do? Which way do you want me to follow?*

I wrestled and demanded of God every waking moment for two weeks the simple question, 'What do you want me to do?' And every waking moment, I fasted, prayed, and then fell asleep with the haunting question, repeating over and over in my mind. For two weeks no answer came. Then out of sheer frustration, I shouted, 'Then forget it God! I am over it. I don't even know if you really exist! I feel like I've wasted my entire life. I have been afraid all my life. I've tried to do everything that would please you.' I felt if Allah could see my heart, God would know I truly loved him. Still, I wondered, 'Does it really matter what I called God? And if it does matter, why isn't He responding after praying for two weeks?

Then, in that precise moment, I felt the power of God fill the room. In Islam, the greatest sin you can commit, and you cannot be forgiven, is to doubt God. I thought I had done that. In Islam, God never visits human beings. I thought I could never be forgiven for that because God's presence was in the room, a great holiness, which pressed the weight of my sin upon me.

I knew God was just and I expected to be killed—wiped from the face of the Earth for my doubt. I truly believed I had no chance to live, and I cried because I literally did not want to die. The Being before me was so holy, and I felt so wicked. I retreated into the corner of the jail cell, buried my head in my hands, and cried out, 'God forgive me!'

As I was crying, I felt a touch on my shoulder, 'I forgive you.' And in that very instant, I physically felt like I was forgiven. In Islam, you cannot be forgiven until the Day of Judgment. That's why there are no verses in the Qur'an that say Mohammad is in Heaven (Al- 'Akhirah). He must wait his turn like all the other people for the day of Qi amah (Qur'an 4:141), the Day of Resurrection at the end of time, where the people will be divided, some will enter Jannah (paradise) and some will enter Jahannam (hell-fire) during the Judgment (Yaumud-Din).

So Afshin wondered, 'Who is this God who says... 'I forgive you and I am forgiven?'

I asked, 'Who are you?'

Then I heard the words, 'I am the Way, the Truth, and the Life.'

The moment I heard it, I knew they were of great importance, but I had absolutely no idea what it meant. I had no clue who God was, so I asked again, 'What is your name?'

And I heard, 'Jesus Christ. The Living God.' The moment He spoke those words, 'It was as if every single bone was taken out of my body, and I just fell down to the ground and started weeping.'

Standing before the Presence of Jesus Christ, Afshin just wept:

18 years have gone by and I cannot forget his Love and his Mercy. I cannot forget what happened to me that day.[1] (I highly recommend you watch the 9-minute You Tube of Afshin's testimonial)

When we stand in the Holy Presence of God, our soul becomes ecstatic. There is a tendency to prostrate, even as I did in my post NDE dream before Christ when I was 16 and in my living room in October 2011 during my *Near-Death Lightning* experience. John, in Revelation

1:17, describes this same moment, "And when I saw Him, I fell at His feet like a dead man."

Afshin's mystical-death experience of Jesus was not a conversion through words of religion or doctrine. Christ responded to Afshin's sincere desire to be forgiven. Crying out to the universe, Jesus appeared to him and forgave him. He showed Afshin that love and mercy, rather than hatred and anger, are the truth.

Bridget observed the actual process of forgiveness when she met Christ in her near-death experience:

> *At this point, a Being made of Light came to my side. I neither was raised religious nor was I baptized. I could be wrong but, it felt like what people call Christ. It was not the Christ we see in paintings or pictures. It was not the Christ we hear about from the Evangelicals. It was not America's Christ or any other representation of Christ I have come across. This was a Being so pure, so benevolent, and so non-judgmental I could barely comprehend the level of compassion this Being possessed in the small yet brilliant Light it was. Not until He touched me, said, 'I'll take that, it's for me', took the beam from me, and touched me, was I even able to fathom this amazing Love.* **His Light seemed to go dim for an "instant" and the beam disappeared. Then He said, 'you are forgiven.'** [2]

Bridget and Afshin are two dramatic examples of Christ's forgiveness. A cry out for God's help begins filtering Grace into our soul, but going forward, we must remain *mindful* of our actions, our thoughts, and our lessons we have yet to overcome.

The Secret of Eternal Life

Experiencing Christ's forgiveness is the beginning of our journey. Jesus' words of salvation are redemptive. However, we *must also learn to forgive others*. Robyn discovered this secret when her husband brutally assaulted her with an intent to kill. Her husband had stabbed her repeatedly in the bathroom, covering her white blouse and blue skirt with blood, threatened to pour gasoline over her and set her on fire. The situation reached a fatal moment, when her husband told her to lay down on the floor, so he could kill her, and said:

> *You're dead, [expletive], no matter what. During that hour, he had already told me exactly what he was going to do to me. Besides telling me he was going to cut off my nose and breasts, his final plan was to light me on fire with gasoline. I knew he had a 5-gallon can in the garage. During the hour I had been praying,*

> 'Please Dear God, let this cup pass from me. No one is coming to save me, no one heard me scream, no one.'
> ...It was at this point I "knew" I was in two places at the same time. I left my body and passed through a tunnel of Light which took me to a door of brilliant Light. The door opened. I knelt down (and saw I was dressed in a dark robe of some sort). As I knelt, I looked up to see Jesus in front of me nailed to the cross, He looked down directly into my eyes. I've never seen eyes like those before or since. As he looked into my eyes, I asked Him, without speaking words, 'What do I do?'
> He answered without speaking words, 'Forgive him.' As He "said" the words, it was done. The forgiveness happened in that very instant.
> I was returned fully to my body in the bathroom but everything had changed, and I knew this. While I was "gone", my husband had continued shaving my head so now there was only one inch left to shave. I opened my mouth and started to speak...using words I did not consciously choose or have any control over whatsoever. The first words that came out of my mouth were 'The water will make everything okay.'
> When I said the word "water", I noticed he put the razorblade down and seemed to almost go into a trance. He stared at himself in the mirror as if waiting for my next words. I repeated again, 'Everything's okay. The water will heal everything.'

Her husband continued staring into the mirror, waiting. She then instructed him to take off his clothes and get into the shower:

> ...I felt surrounded by a protective force that was explosive. It felt as if the universe itself was trying to fit into that small bathroom and the air inside the room became alive with a profound life force - I could actually see particles of some sort in the air surrounding me and the walls appeared to be pulsating and expanding. Something was happening outside of myself that made me a witness. Jesus' words evoked a power I became a part of, but it did not emanate from me. As an individual human being, at that moment I did not exist, but rather I was one with the spiritual force that was enveloping me. I knew even with the horror of what was still happening to me in that room that a power beyond myself was in control and I had surrendered to it by forgiving my husband.
> The act of forgiveness was the key that unlocked the door, and it was my surrendering to it that allowed me to be the empty vessel, so its power could be made manifest. The healing words

that came out of my mouth were not my words. I spoke them, but they were coming from somewhere else. "I" did not exist. There was only Love, pure love, and it was all-powerful.

*...As the words kept coming out of my mouth, I felt as if my veins were being injected with a substance. I can only describe it this way—the substance felt like liquid thought going into my veins and coursing throughout my entire body so the only thought I consciously had was 'Love is the greatest power in the universe.***

...At the time this all happened to me, I was reading more about Buddhism than Christianity. I had not grown up in a family with religion and so had taken it upon myself to read the entire New Testament several years before this happened. However, the majority of my reading was about Eastern philosophies since I was a teenager. So it's more than interesting that it was Jesus, not Buddha, who appeared to me in that hour of need to save me. I believe the message of forgiveness had to come directly from the Source, and that was Christ. Still, I'm at a loss for words to explain it.[3]

Robyn wrote after her NDE: "He planned to pour gasoline over me, but instead I poured water over him...and all was healed. Jesus proved to me that His words are as alive today as they were 2000 years ago when he said, "Forgive him, for he knows not what he does."

How has this concept of forgiveness affected her since? "I taught my three sons to forgive so when their father got out of prison they would be able to communicate with him from a place of peace." Robyn's experience taught her, "Forgiveness releases us from the burden of judgment." Saint John Gualbert, who founded the mountaintop Abbey of Vallambrosa in 1073 A.D., has a motto about forgiveness I think we all should remember, "He who cannot forgive others destroys a bridge over which he must himself pass, for every man has need of forgiveness."

Redemption happens in many ways. It happens when we experience the forgiveness of Christ, when we forgive others, and when we forgive ourselves. People of all faiths carry the weight of self-judgment. Many Christians have been conditioned by the concept of 'original sin' to expect recrimination, judgment and punishment for their sins when they die, but are shocked to find no judgment and only unqualified acceptance and forgiveness from the Being of Light.

In chapter 5, we talked about how our lack of alrightness (the ability to love ourselves) drives how we communicate, think and act. Our successful ability to love others stems from our own success of loving ourselves. How do we find the experience of loving ourselves, so we don't give people the power to hurt us anymore? How do we learn to feel alright and gain confidence in ourselves? Lao Tzu describes the importance of alrightness:

> *Because one believes in oneself, one doesn't try to convince others. Because one is content with oneself, one doesn't need others' approval. Because one accepts oneself, the whole world accepts him or her.*[4]

A transformational experience of love helps us walk the 13th path. Barry didn't remember anything about his attackers. They had ambushed and beaten him after a rodeo and he woke up in the hospital. After the doctors began working on him, Barry blacked out and had an exceptional NDE that taught him God loves us no matter what:

> *I was off, outside somewhere. I was so mad at God for letting this happen. I cursed, yelled, screamed, and said 'What is this be good to your fellow man crap?'*
>
> *I screamed, 'How could you (God) betray and ambush me like this? I do all of this good stuff and look what you give me. You are a lying double-crossing [expletive].' I yelled, kicked, punched, and swore as best I could. I was screaming and crying and mad I couldn't curse better.*
>
> *Then, as all of this is happening, I felt what was like, a warm hand come down and just cradle me. I screamed louder, kicked, and hit, and the hand just held me. It exuded the most perfect Love and warmth and softness, and absolutely no judgment. But my rage continued, because now I had something to fight against. I screamed my lungs out and kicked and hit, and from out of the hand came a voice. It said, in the softest, nicest, most honest, beautiful, trustworthy voice, 'Barry, all you need to know is I love you absolutely, no matter what.'*
>
> *That made me even madder. I yelled and cried, and cursed, and cried, and hit, and cried, for what seemed like a long time. I challenged the voice and said, 'Oh yeah. What if I was a pedophile, a murderer, or a wife beater? Then, would you still love me?... You liar!'*
>
> *The voice just kept saying, 'None of that matters. All you need to know is that I love you, absolutely no matter what.'*
>
> *After what seemed a long time of this, I finally wore out and just fell down and cried, and cried, and cried. And the hand with the perfect Love, far softer and more perfect than ever experienced*

here on Earth, just held me and kept saying, 'All you really need to know is that I love you absolutely, no matter what.'

I just gave up. And as He held me, I felt a Love and a trustworthiness that would be like the best friend you could ever have in the world. And I thought if it is true, what He told me, then I can do anything I want and God will see it as OK. And, feeling the most beautiful Friend in the world, who will never leave me, then I will never do anything this Friend would ever be ashamed or embarrassed for me doing. I will do whatever I think He will like. For Him.[5]

We Are Precious to God

Stephanie's NDE: It was not like I went anywhere, but more like a realm opened up right where I was... I was looking into this blue vastness when a beautiful Being appeared. He looked a little like Jesus, but at the time, it wasn't important who he was. He was all Love, the kind of love that has everything in it (not the sappy sentimental kind). Everything in it meaning it was solid, supportive, permanent, but very much in the moment (yet no fear that it would disappear). I felt concern, care, total sensitivity from Him. He was not asserting Himself in any dominating way, yet I knew He was all there. Everything was part of or came from Him.

He was indescribably sweet, sincere, responsive to me, and there was even humor (like he was saying surprise surprise). He looked at me as if He was looking at something totally precious and dear to Him and I couldn't take my eyes away, I never felt love like that, complete love with no demands, just a total recognition I was wonderful and He knew it all along and wanted me to know it. Slowly it faded and I was back in the room, or rather the room returned to its normal state and I felt so, so grateful I had been given this gift, this knowledge.[6]

Whether by Jesus Christ, by Dead Saint Experience, or mystical revelation, God is where Love is, for God is Love. After love transforms our heart, then practicing kindness is our ongoing challenge. When I look for the *loving* memories of my life, I try to think about times when I was purposefully loving, when I did a kind act without thinking, or when I smiled at a stranger, politely held a door open, or said a kind word. I remember when I rescued a Japanese drunk woman from the street so she wouldn't be run over. I gave change to homeless people. I pray there are more good things I did than I can remember. I also remember all the times I didn't help people, became angry, and missed opportunities to help others when they were in need. When I built my company, I always tried to integrate a loving, kind approach to being a CEO. I didn't always succeed. It was difficult to always remember love and to run a business at the same time.

Love requires practice. According to Mary Jo's encounter with God, we can learn to unconditionally love the way God loves us:

> *I looked up and I saw this Light; it wasn't a normal light, it was different. It was luminescent. And it grew. I kept looking at it like, 'What is that?' Then it grew large and I went into it. 'I went into this tunnel, and I came into this room that was just beautiful. God held me. He called me by name and He told me, 'Mary Jo, you can't stay.' And I wanted to stay. I protested. I said, 'I can't stay? Why not?' And I started talking about all the reasons; I was a good wife, I was a good mother, I did 24-hour care with cancer patients.*
>
> *And He said, 'Let me ask you one thing. Have you ever loved another the way you've been loved here?'*
>
> *I said, 'No, it's impossible. I'm a human.'*
>
> *Then He just held me and said, 'You can do better.'* [7]

Teri's NDE: Even after Teri's transformational Dead Saint experience, he found his "buttons" were still pushed because people didn't believe him. It took him 30 years of practice to attain the unconditional love of God he found during his NDE:

> *What I found was no one believed my experience and that made me angry and hurt. None of that had changed. My "buttons" were still easily pushed which made me realize, just because I had understood what I needed to do, it didn't mean I had brought back anything that was going to make it happen automatically. I felt very alone, confused yet still very driven to find a way to change.*
>
> *...My experience was the catalyst that transformed me into a completely different person than what I was at the time of my NDE. It took about 30 years of trial and error and many scientific discoveries, but I have finally developed the ability to feel love for everyone, no matter what they do. That is a place of power I can now use to help others make positive changes in their lives and in the world. Instead of feeling anger over corruption and dishonesty I hear about in the news, I am able to create warm loving feelings and project that energy into the situation instead of fuming in anger. It's not always instantly, but I can get there 100% of the time.* [8]

Practice by Putting Smiles on Stranger's Faces

Bobby's NDE: *There comes a time in each person's life, when gold loses its luster and diamonds cease to sparkle; that special time, when we all start to search, and quest, and seek that hidden voice which speaks inside, yet no one hears; that special time when all the good we do means less than a simple smile put on a stranger's face by our own unselfish acts of kindness. You can take that to the bank, because money won't get you into Heaven.*[9]

The sage, Lao Tzu, gives advice about practicing kindness, "Kindness in words creates confidence. Kindness in thinking creates profoundness. Kindness in giving creates love."[10]

Love Is the Only Thing that Matters

The Apostle Paul speaks of the supremacy of love in I Corinthians:1-4 (ISV):

"If I speak in the languages of humans and angels but have no love, I have become a reverberating gong or a clashing cymbal. If I have the gift of prophecy and can understand all secrets and every form of knowledge, and if I have absolute faith so as to move mountains but have no love, I am nothing. Even if I give away everything I have and sacrifice myself, but have no love, I gain nothing."

Bobbie sums up unconditional love as the greatest testimony of the Dead Saints:

The greatest emphasis of this [NDE] experience is LOVE. You are so totally engulfed with a love that does not exist in our physical world. No matter how deep a love you feel for your children, it does not compare with this love. This love is the purest, truest, deepest, totally unconditional love you could EVER imagine your heart, as a feeling that you experience. It can bring your soul to its knees, in a sense, with a quick swoosh of sensation. Now, this is not overwhelming in a bad way. It is totally overwhelming in the best way imaginable. Once you have a taste of it, you will forever be changed. It is total bliss. What you've always wanted, and then so much more. I was awestruck that I was so loved. I still am, and I forever will be.[11]

Maria asked herself during her NDE what pure love is. She realized, *'Love is Light. I wanted it to never end.'* Then it occurred to her, *'Something so great could never end.'*[12]

Love is Living Water

Many times throughout the *Chronicles*, love has been described as living water. Earlier in the chapter, Robyn described pouring water over her attacker to forgive him. A year ago, I dreamed of Jeremiah's well of living water. A few months before publishing the *Chronicles*, I had a dream about unconditional love and living water:

Dream: *A camel that walked into my home and came over to me where I was sitting and lay its head on my lap. The camel exuded SO MUCH COMPASSION—Love without condition beyond any I have ever experienced. It was almost as if the beast was God Himself. I lovingly caressed its head and noticed an open wound mid-way down its neck. I began sobbing, sobbing, sobbing overwhelmed by the Camel's love for me, and the living water He carried in his hump. I knew the camel was Christ. Then I woke up.* **~Chronicle 847**.

One Dead Saint in prison experienced this same ocean of Love:

I was a withdrawing mess, suicidal, full of hate. Alone in the holding cell—or so I thought. Then it happened. In short, the cell took on a different light and color. There was a sound and intense feeling of rushing water, but it was not wet or physical, it was alive, moving and with voice, 'living water.' This gentle loving voice said it loved me and called me by name. By this time, I was pressed back on the bunk and could not move. Physical breathing became nil. These waters intensified, at a seemingly high vibrating rate penetrating every fiber of my being. I found myself basking in this ocean of Love, still held in total awe of what was happening to me.[13]

The Gospel of John describes Love as Living Water. John 7:38 says, "The one who believes in me, as the Scripture has said, will have rivers of living water flowing from his heart." And in John 4:10, "Jesus answered her, 'If you knew the gift of God, and who it is who is saying to you, 'Please give me a drink,' you would have been the one to ask Him, and he would have given you living water."

The unconditional Love described by the Dead Saint testimonials are these same living waters. They are sacred and their writings and experiences are as holy and as important as ancient near-death / born-again experiences of the Apostles. They add significantly to our understanding of Christianity and Scriptures of all Faiths.

Dead Saint face-to-face encounters with Light / Light Beings / God and Jesus Christ should give you comfort of the ONE TRUTH:

Our consciousness SURVIVES death. There is only the continuation of LIFE Everlasting IN HEAVEN FOR ALL WHO BELIEVE IN LOVE.

The testimonies of the Dead Saints are the crunching of the mountain gravel beneath our feet. Their stones speak out just as Christ declared in Luke 19:40, "And he answered and said unto them, I tell you that, if these should hold their peace, the stones would immediately cry out." Remember, not all follow the same granite path, but all granite paths have one destination—which is the Light.

So there you are. You have your walking stick. The gravel is crunching underfoot. In the quiet between footsteps, hear the miracles sparkling in the quartz hidden among the granite stones.

Walk in Faith. Call on Him when you are sick, weary, fighting, or fearful. Remember Matthew 11:28-30:

Come unto me, all ye that labor and are heavy laden, and I will give you rest. Take my yoke upon you, and learn of me; for I am meek and lowly in heart: and ye shall find rest unto your souls. For my yoke is easy, and my burden is light.

Ask for help. The Being of Light WILL respond. Christ proved it to my family and me in the final two weeks preparing a printing proof for our publisher. He added one last exclamation point to the last two pages of the book in a dramatic sequence of events occurring over a five-day period beginning January 23, 2016 and ending on January 28:

~Last night, January 23, 2016, as I was on my way to my 57th birthday party at Mom's around 4:30 pm, Delynn was driving her car to meet us, slid on the ice on a rural road during a snowstorm and plunged into several feet of ocean bay water. Because of the accident, she never arrived at the party. Her phone was lost under the freezing bay water and we never heard from her. Ben and I assumed, when Delynn didn't call, she would meet us at the birthday party. Two hours passed. No word. What happened to her? We called all the Hospitals and emergency room clinics. No one, not even her best friends had heard anything. No texts. By 7:00 pm, we thought the worst.

Was she dead?

From Delynn's memory of events, a passer-by helped her get home by 5:30 pm. Everything was a blur after that. Some things she remembered, other things she did not. Without going into personal details, Delynn, as caregiver and wife, had reached a mental breaking point that had been building for weeks.

My MRI was set for 4:00 pm Monday, January 26 at the Hampton, VA. After two-years of relative stability requiring no chemo, my brain tumor awoke from the dead and began growing explosively. MRI's over seven months revealed tumor growth from 3mm (pea sized) on May 26, 2015, to 1.5cm x 1.8 cm (15mm x 18mm) on December 1. At that time, our VA neuro-oncologist, Dr. Gupta, and Dr. Randazzo at Duke, sadly told us we had limited treatment options. I did not qualify for Avastin or any clinical trial. It was either heavy chemo or radiation. Both would sedate and depress my ability to think and talk clearly. I refused both.

Delynn was mentally drowning. Would the MRI Monday reveal further growth? Would it reveal the proverbial "handwriting on the wall?"

Now the accident.

Although Delynn was physically unhurt, her mind had reached its limit, and its ability to cope with anything. She literally "blacked out" and could only remember parts of her experience. Our family was in crisis and we desperately needed God's help. I prayed harder than I ever remember praying in my life. While Delynn was recovering from her accident, Mom took me to the Hampton VA medical center for my 4:00 pm MRI. Scan results showed the brain tumor had grown again to 2.2cm x 2.1cm, (22mm x 21mm) a 20% growth rate in seven weeks. T2 Flair, which is an indication the brain cancer was spreading, had increased dramatically.

It certainly did not look good.

Our brains can only take so much tumor growth before they begin to shut down. While the thinking part of my brain was very sharp, the brain tumor was putting pressure on the motor skill areas of my legs. I was beginning to have constant pressure headaches that felt like a vise-grip on the left side of my head. My right leg was becoming numb. I could still walk, but it felt twice as heavy as my left leg. I was losing more balance almost daily.

I felt like Dorothy from the Wizard of Oz with the sandglass of time running out. My fear was that I would not have time to finish the Chronicles. I had projected my fears onto Delynn. I didn't listen to Great Grampa's advice in June during his visit from Heaven that I should be like a Terrapin, a turtle – write slow and steady. I had become a hare, writing like a maniac, because I feared I would not have enough time to finish writing. I did not pay attention to my wife, my caregiver and her fears and feelings about losing the love of her life. Delynn wanted me to spend more quality family time with my kids and with her before I died.

It took a couple of days, but Delynn slowly recovered from her "breakdown." Mom was driving us around while we waited for a rental car replacement from our insurance company. On the evening of Monday, January 26, while out and about, we saw a black man shivering in the cold who seemed lost. He had just been released from the city jail and was holding only a plastic baggy containing his cell

phone. Without thought, Mom handed him a $50.00 bill she had tucked away in her purse for a rainy day.
   That's when our eyes met.
   I asked this gentle man with kind eyes, "What is your name?"
   He said, "Immanuel." God is with us. ~**Chronicle 955**

January 23, 2016

The tragic accident forced long held issues with my family to surface for Delynn and me. Dying is hard on everyone. Nobody talks about it. Resentments and misunderstandings build to a crescendo. Our family had reached that critical note. Then, God sent a message like thunder answering our prayers. *Immanuel is with you in this very moment.* These are the granite stones speaking! Hear them! See them! Dismiss them not! Healing will take time, but I am absolutely certain the process has begun.

However, God was not done with us yet. Another miraculous set of events transpired five days later on January 28, 2016:

12.01am. Text from Dannion Brinkley: David, [the Foreword] is on my computer in LA. I will try to get Kathryn to find the file and send it Sunday night (Jan 31)

12.06am. Five minutes later. *A text came in from my 17-year-old daughter Angela: I LOVE YOU DADDY. YOU'RE AMAZING AND I LOVE YOU. I 100% forgive you...*

She had had a hard time accepting the divorce between her mother and I. I had asked many times for Angela's forgiveness. This was a blessing to my heart and I know her's as well. I subsequently discovered Angela was awarded a life changing/life altering, first-of-a-kind, Internship from a national media company for her music and artistic video work. If she does well, it will most likely become her career...cementing University decisions here on the East Coast.

4:30pm: Final Editing. *Maggie and Steve Courter come over to work on the final editing before book layout of the Chronicles. I pulled out the book by* **Pin van Lommel M.D**, *Consciousness Beyond Life: The Science of the Near-Death Experience and showed it to Maggie, because I wanted to use it as an example for the Chronicles Bibliography.*

6:15pm: *Before leaving, Maggie told me a story about a miracle of kindness that happened to her the day before at grocery store.* **A total stranger walked up to her and gave her a dozen red roses!** *To Maggie, this "random act of kindness" was a sign from God. Their house* *in the Blue Ridge Mountains hadn't sold, straining their finances. The roses were a nod from God, 'I am aware of your burden. I am with you."*

6:30pm: When Maggie and Steve left, I did my daily check on the NDERF.org website for new NDE updates. The last NDERF posting was January 22, 2016. When I checked again, lo and behold, a new NDE blog dated January 28, 2016. #4087 posted by Anna NZ's had the mention of Pin van Lommel. As I glanced through her Dead Saint experience, tears ran down my face. I could hardly believe what I was reading. Anna, a physician, stopped breathing and died for 8 minutes during standard laparoscopic surgery. During her "death," she finds herself flying through a black tunnel before ending up in a brightly lit roofless hall made of glass that looked like the Greek Pantheon. She was sitting by a table with young people talking who looked 30-40 years old dressed in very bright colors of green, red, blue, and gold. Anna's NDE continues:

> *I sat at a wall and just looked around. I saw a dark passage with a table like in the Last Supper. The stools are placed like in a theatre... Sometime during this experience, my life was tested and I answered different questions [The Life Review and Judgment]. At the end of the table, I see my mother sitting, who died when she was 88 years old, except now she looks like she is 40 years old.* **She wears a dress that I know to be dark blue in reality, but this dress was white with red roses....** *From above, through the opening in the ceiling, I saw a great brightness like a beam of non-blinding, white Light.*
>
> *I kept saying repeatedly the whole time, 'My God, where am I?'*
>
> *Suddenly, I get it. I put two and two together; my mother, The Light, the table, and those people. I was dead. I said, 'No! No! I don't want to be here. I got here by mistake. What about my husband, my children and my grandchildren? And my patients?'*
>
> *My mother rose from the table, comes over to me and takes my hand. She leads me to the corridor and says, 'It's not your time yet. We must part. You must go back.'*
>
> *Then I remember I looked just like a ghost in a comic book, looking around the operating room and seeing my own heart defibrillation. I saw the way a woman was lying on the bed in the surgery room. I was wondering who it is lying there. The doctor said to the assisting staff, 'Now get away.' Then, he used the defibrillator on the woman.*
>
> *It was me.*

I also remember a priest giving me the last sacrament. The priest said, 'You'll go to Heaven.' [14]

It took 18 months for Anna to get back to normal from brain damage (neuroplasticity) caused by 8 minutes without breathing. During her recovery, she describes being "cared for by Heaven" and full of love, even to people to whom she shouldn't have any love. She read many books about love, but Anna was afraid of telling other people because she didn't want them to think she was crazy. She ends the January 28 blog by saying, "*In my opinion the most invaluable piece is* **'Consciousness Beyond Life' by Dr. Pim Van Lommel**. *I attended one of his conferences. The people I told about my experience, they say that I should not keep it to myself. I changed, and my life changed.*"[15] ~Chronicle 960.

Dr. Pin Von Lommel's name has NEVER been mentioned on the over 4000 NDERF postings since 1998 u*ntil this FIRST POSTING on January 28, 2016.*

I read about Anna's NDE two hours after discussing Dr. Lommel's book with Maggie. Then, there is Anna's mother's white dress with red roses and Maggie receiving Red Roses from a complete stranger the day before. I have never read of a dress of similar description posted on NDERF.

Two coincidences within two hours? God invoked the Law of 2's...showing His breadcrumbs again!

What did I think God was saying to Delynn and me?

I believe God was saying, "Be at peace. Everything is unfolding EXACTLY as planned."

Zen Closing to the Christian Afterlife

My wish for your journey remains; that beyond Faith, the *Chronicles* give you comfort that **death is not the end—a** realization that is the first step of a thousand miles. Take the walking stick and step forward. Hear the granite gravel crunch underfoot until you have a real EXPERIENCE of the BEING OF LIGHT, JESUS CHRIST, OR GOD. And whether the EXPERIENCE of the LIGHT is Born-Again Christian, Mystical-death, Holy Spirit, (non-religious or religious), Dead Saint, or Near-Death Lightning, the EXPERIENCE will forever transform your Heart.

From that moment on, it becomes a journey of following "the still small voice" that leads you like a child to the "living waters" of Life Everlasting. Cultivate these thoughts. Lessons you have struggled with your entire life will suddenly become easier to overcome, especially your ability to forgive. Then, as the Zen saying goes, you will begin to truly "see, hear, think, and speak" the TRUTH, the same freedom spoken of by Christ in John 8:32 (NIV): *And ye shall know the truth, and the truth shall set you free.*

Death is Graduation from Earth University

Death will be my graduation from Earth University... and what a fine Day it will be!

Remember when you graduated from High School, Military School, or University? I remember that day like yesterday, when all 683 seniors of the Princess Anne High Class of 77' graduated. It was awesome! After the last word was given, we threw our blue graduation caps high into the air. Classes were over! Thank God!

According to one Dead Saint, there are "announcement centers in Heaven and people are notified their loved ones are about to arrive."[16] It's a sad parting for friends and family. Goodbyes and farewells are difficult, BUT we will see each other again, sooner than we think. That's what I expect dying will feel like.

But not yet!

I certainly look forward to reuniting with long lost friends and the great cloud of witnesses[17] sitting in the bleachers welcoming me home at my appointed time. I suspect Great Grandpa Sarge has already alerted everyone to my upcoming arrival in the not-to-distant future. How long must they wait?

It is up to God and me. May the Lord Bless you all.

Maranatha.

---

1 Afshin Javid 2012. *You Tube Video interview of Afshin Javid.* Excerpted and transcribed. https://www.youtube.com/watch?v=Xe7fJOb9XGU
2 *Bridget F NDE*, #1654, 07.21.08, NDERF.org
3 *Robyn F NDE*, #3666, 05.03.14, NDERF.org
4 D.C. Lau 2001. *Tao Te Ching.* (New Bilingual Edition). Hong Kong: Chinese University Press.
5 *Barry C NDE*, #3236, 01.14.13, NDERF.org
6 *Stephanie L NDE*, #1005, 02.03.07, NDERF.org
7 Mary Jo Rapini, *describing her near-death experience,* http://ndestories.org/mary-jo-rapini/
8 *Teri R NDE*, #2301, 08.10.10, NDERF.org
9 *Bobby H's NDE*, #776, 02.19.06, NDERF.org
10 D.C. Lau 2001. *Tao Te Ching.* (New Bilingual Edition). Hong Kong: Chinese University Press.

11 *Bobbie D NDE*, #1936, 07.09.09, NDERF.org
12 *Maria R NDE*, #917, 07.29.06, NDERF.org
13 *My Story*, #92, aleroy.com/board92.htm
14 Anna NZ NDE, #4087, 01.28.16, NDERF.org
15 Anna NZ NDE, #4087, 01.28.16, NDERF.org
16 Richard Sigmund 2004 & 2010. *My Time in Heaven: A True Story of Dying…And Coming Back.* New Kensington, PA: Whitaker House. p. 20.
17 Hebrews 12:1-2, *Wherefore seeing we also are compassed about with so great a cloud of witnesses, let us lay aside every weight, and the sin which doth so easily beset us, and let us run with patience the race that is set before us, looking unto Jesus the author and finisher of our faith; who for the joy that was set before Him endured the cross, despising the shame, and is set down at the right hand of the throne of God.*

Foreword to the Afterword
By David Solomon

Cancer diagnosis June 13, 2013... Eleven days after a brain biopsy on July 1, 2013, we met with neuro-surgeon, Dr. Gwinn. He recommended surgery and we scheduled it for August 2 to remove the 20mm brain tumor. According to Gwinn, the resection of my tumor would likely leave my right leg, and possibly my right hand permanently nerve-damaged. Translation: following surgery there was a good chance I would be wheelchair bound.

If this turned out to be the reality, I wanted to get in as much physical activity as I could while I still could.

Walking! For instance...

In addition, as many of the other normal things I had always taken for granted. Sharing days camping, biking, hiking, skiing with my children. Caring for my gardens; or now, wrapping things up with my business partners; getting my affairs in order in case the worst went wrong with the surgery. Even if I survived, they said I might never be able to walk again. We wrote out a bucket list. I'd traveled the world the last twenty years, but had never been to Yellowstone Park or seen the Grand Tetons. So we plotted out an impromptu four-day trip there. Anna, my ex, loaned me her SUV. We stuffed all seven of us in, Patrick, Nathan, Angela, Matthew, Benjamin, Delynn and myself and off we went 12-hours to Yellowstone.

Departing for Yellowstone & Grand Tetons – Old Faithful & Prism Lake

The long drive sped by and we checked into our appropriately named Hotel Terra. Yellowstone geysers are scattered around a closed 75-mile-long loop. It's a full day of driving, "Old Faithful" of course, and a half-dozen other gorgeous, crystal clear boiling geysers. The most amazing was Prism Lake. A half-mile wide and 160 degrees, its intense deep blue was bordered by pumpkin orange, green and white sulfur crusts. A spooky mist wafted continuously over the lake. It looked like a scene out of a monster movie. *~Chronicle 37*

River Rapids

Last minute, we arranged a white water rafting trip. The rapids were low, level 2 or 3—nothing compared to the level 6 and 7 Grand Canyon rapids last year. But it was good for all of us to be together for this calm trip downstream. I remember the moment the huge yellow rubber raft came to rest at the end of the white water and I asked the tour leader if they ever allowed wheelchair-bound tourists aboard.

He said, "No."

Hearing that from the raft leader, Angela and I locked eyes for a moment. I could see her trying to accept what might be in store for me. It hit me in the gut. We both were in tears without a word being said.

Even so, it was a glorious trip. Now it was back home to Olympia.

Heading Home

Delynn and I woke up early and drove to Jenny Lake to watch the sun come up. I practiced my Tai Chi form on the banks of a nearby river as the sun brightened the cold morning. Purple and yellow wildflowers everywhere. A fitting finale to a glorious trip.

We drove back to the hotel to pick up the kids and their friends, repacked them back into the SUV, and headed west. A few hours into the drive, I was talking with Delynn about who might co-author, or ghost write or at least help edit the *Chronicles*.

I suddenly had a hunch to call my old friend, writer and much published rogue Egyptologist, John Anthony West. I'd enjoyed two tours to Egypt with him in 1992 and 2009, and funded his and geologist Robert M. Schoch's Goebekli-Tepi important research project in Turkey in 2011. Perhaps he'd be open to it? But would he have the time to commit to it? Could he take the risk? I might die in the middle of writing the book; in which case, no book.

So I called. He was not only enthusiastic about the idea, but had just terminated a long-term co-writing job. So he had the time. I hadn't written anything yet, not a word ...but I had a writing partner! That "still small voice" telling me to call John gave me hope. Who knows what might have happened if he didn't have the time, or had said no? It reassured me. The *Chronicles* would, indeed, be written. Talk about a "brainstorm?" ~**Chronicle 38**

David Solomon

AFTERWORD: *The Idea Whose Time Has Come?*

By John Anthony West

John Anthony West, rogue Egyptologist; guide; author of *Serpent in the Sky: The High Wisdom of Ancient Egypt* and *The Traveler's Key to Ancient Egypt: A Guide to the Sacred Places of Ancient Egypt;* and recipient of the 1993 News & Documentary Emmy Award for Best Research and a nomination for Best Documentary for the NBC Special *The Mystery of the Sphinx*, hosted by Charlton Heston.

"There is one thing stronger than all the armies in the world, and that is an idea whose time has come," said novelist, playwright and poet, Victor Hugo (France's most celebrated 19th Century literary figure.)

But good Victorian optimist that he was, Hugo failed to notice, "The second strongest thing in the world is the idea whose time has not yet gone."

And since, at any given time, all the armies in the world are formally or *de facto* in the service of the idea whose time has not yet gone, battle lines are drawn.

Scientific truth does not triumph by convincing its opponents and making them see the light, but rather because its opponents eventually die and a new generation grows up that is familiar with it.
~Max Planck, Nobel Prize winning physicist.

"All truth passes through four stages. First, they ignore you, then they laugh at you, then they oppose you, and then they say that everybody knew it all along. (Adapted from Arthur Schopenhauer, German Philosopher & Mahatma Gandhi, Indian Philosopher and Revolutionary)

These metaphorical armies are not military, of course, They do not look like "armies"; nor do they call themselves, or even regard themselves, as "armies". But they are armies nonetheless, and depending upon the nature of the challenging idea, these "armies" band together to protect their paradigm. While virtually every new idea is subject to the Schopenhauer/Gandhi "ignore/ridicule/oppose/accept" sequence, this is a strictly human phenomenon. It has no parallel in nature. Only human beings (as far as we know) dismiss, ridicule, oppose and (ultimately, if everything else is in place) accept.

To further complicate matters, that ignore-to-accept sequence operates within a grander cycle that is, in fact, cosmic.

As mathematician / philosopher / orientalist and practicing alchemist, R.A. Schwaller de Lubicz pointed out: everything in the universe is **organic**; the entire universe, in one way or another, is subject to the organic Laws of Manifestation; a cycle we all recognize as Fertilization / Gestation / Birth / Growth / Maturity / Senescence / Death / Renewal.

For the "idea whose time has come" to actually get there it must be guided through the painful psychological ignore-to-accept sequence while simultaneously developing through the necessary stages of the cosmic organic fertilization-to-rebirth cycle, a tricky process by no means either assured or predictable. Everything has to be in place at just the right time.

An Autobiographical Note

Back in 1992, when I first met David Solomon, he was already involved in serious research—research that had no connection at all to NDEs, but considerable connection to my own work on ancient Egypt and the Great Sphinx of Giza. I'd developed a revolutionary theory, inspired by an offhand remark of R.A. Schwaller de Lubicz—the genius Alsatian scholar who had reformulated the Sacred Science of the ancients— that the Sphinx had been weathered by water, not wind and sand. If proven correct via hard-nosed geology, this would push back the date the Sphinx was carved many thousands of years.

This would mean, in turn, that all of very ancient history had to be totally re-written from scratch, and with it, the accepted scholarly/scientific understanding of the origins of advanced civilization would have to be abandoned. Totally. In other words, a lot rested upon that single observation. David, at the time, was delving deep and systematically into ancient history, geology, archeology, anthropology and other disciplines dealing with the pre-historical past, looking for physical evidence that might directly or indirectly support references and prophecies in the Christian Bible, and in virtually all ancient religious traditions and innumerable myths and legends from peoples scattered all over the globe.

There were too many major themes, and often small and improbable details in common in this vast literature to attribute all of it to coincidence or to some sort of global romanticism where people with no known connections to each other were cooking up similar fanciful tales out of the blue all at the same time: Among these: A Deluge, vanished, high civilizations, sudden global catastrophes, complex but similar pantheons, mythologies and legends. This was a rich field for research. Much work had already been done (by Ignatius Donnelly, Carl Jung, Mircea Eliade, Joseph Campbell, Giorgio de Santillana/Herta von Dechend...and many others) igniting heated scholarly debates and irreconcilable competing theories in both the academic and religious worlds.

David was approaching it from a fresh and promising angle (to come to fruition more than twenty years later as *The Armageddon Stones*, Book III of this trilogy). But back in '92, with our Egypt trip over, we went our separate ways and lost touch, reconnecting only in 2009 for our second Egypt trip. Much had happened in the intervening years.

David's charismatic mentor (and adoptive father), Paul Solomon, had died and David had struck out on his own into the very alien world of business, swiftly finding out, to his surprise, that he had a real talent for it. Enough so that, on this second trip, he wanted to discuss financing us (myself and Dr. Robert Schoch) in our ongoing geological/Egyptological research.

That welcome news would lead to our week-long 2011 investigation at Goebekli-Tepe, the amazing, perfectly intact and highly sophisticated buried site in Turkey, (discovered 1994) and dated by the late Klaus Schmidt, the German archeologist in charge of the dig, at 10,000 BC or still earlier. For us, this was the "smoking gun." For never again could the Egyptological / Archeological establishment dismiss our Sphinx theory out of hand on the grounds that it was "impossible" — since there was no civilization capable of producing a Sphinx and its adjacent massive temples at that time. It was all hunter-gatherers back then. (Google up Goebekli-Tepe, if you don't yet know about it.)

Some hunter-gatherers!

As for our "idea" of pushing the age of the Sphinx thousands of years back into the past, even with Goebekli Tepe, perhaps its time had not yet quite come, *but we were getting close.*

Meanwhile, despite all his voluminous earlier research, David had abandoned, anyway indefinitely postponed, his plans for writing *The Armageddon Stones*. Instead, his indefatigable research fairy had been turned loose on the Near-Death Experience phenomenon, collecting, compiling, analyzing thousands of first hand testimonials, establishing thematic connections and weaving together innumerable disparate threads to produce in the end a coherent tapestry. As he described it, it sounded as though it might be a book of considerable value,

Except he had no serious intention of writing such a book, though he had toyed with the idea. Up to this point, it had been an all-absorbing "hobby." And then, with no warning signs apart from some persistent dizziness, came that thunderbolt glioma diagnosis that, barring a certifiable miracle, is a death sentence; its only variable the amount of time allotted to him. Overnight, his "hobby" was transformed into his "mission": ***The Dead Saints Chronicles***, with himself as author and also as his own ongoing scientific experiment as he wrote the book, I was drafted in as editor and literary consultant.

In this capacity, I appointed myself ombudsman to the Academic/Scientific Establishment, prepared to monitor and expose the predictable academic/scientific malpractices of its Paradigm Police, and, if possible, neutralize them. I'd been dealing with them in my own field for over forty years and liked to think I knew their ways and wiles as well as anyone.

A Very Brief Look at the Idea Whose Time Has Not Yet Gone

For roughly the last 150 years the Western world, and increasingly the Eastern world, has come under the sway of a set of ideas and principles brought together formally, since 1970 in *The Humanist Manifesto*, under the rubric—Secular Humanism.

Though presented as something new, Secular Humanism had its precursors in the Skeptics, Cynics and Stoics of ancient Greece and Rome. Essentially what it proposed then and what it proposes now—stripped of its deceptive academic dress is: "What you see, hear, smell, taste and feel is all there is, Buddy. Deal with it." While there is no formal Secular Humanist Non-Bible written for the unenlightened, if there were, its chapters might be headed:

The universe is an accident.

Matter precedes Mind.

Consciousness is a fortuitous spin-off of Matter.

Human life, indeed, all life, serves no higher purpose.

There is no consciousness higher than our own.

"Progress" ascends in a straight line from primitive hominids to ourselves.

Religion is delusion.

"Spiritual" and "sacred" are polite words for superstition.

Only modern science and the scientific method can reveal the objective Truth.

Contemporary man represents the most highly evolved level humanity has ever reached.

Unfortunately, for the Humanists, however, opposition to this dreary catechism is not restricted to the illiterate and the uncredentialed; the ignorant and the superstitious ...much as they would like to have the world believe.

> *The certainties of science are a delusion They are hedged round with unexplored limitations. Our handling of scientific doctrines is controlled by the diffused metaphysical concepts of our epoch. (italics mine – JAW) Even so, we are continually led into errors of expectation. Also, whenever some new mode of observational experience is obtained the doctrines crumble into a fog of inaccuracies.*
>
> ~Alfred North Whitehead, *Adventure in Ideas*, 1933, p.198

Mathematician and Philosopher, Whitehead was one of the most influential thinkers of his time. His severe doubts about relying overmuch upon science as a final arbiter of truth have been expressed and developed by innumerable eminent scientists since the above passage was penned. But this is a huge subject. (Readers who want to go deeper into this ongoing subject should google up renegade Biologist Rupert Sheldrake's website www.rupertsheldrake.org and surf thoroughly. Also google up Nobel Prize Winning Physicist Brian Josephson and follow his adventures countering the Paradigm Police as they witch hunted him for *daring* to support parapsychology. Also follow www.thedailygrail.com.

Not only has their Humanist's Manifesto been exposed irrevocably as scientifically fraudulent from within by a minority of their own scientific colleagues, its inescapable emotional / psychological / philosophical emptiness has also been noted by their own.

> **That man is** *the product of causes that had no prevision of the end they were achieving; that his origin, his growth, his hopes and fears, his loves and his beliefs, are but the outcome of accidental collocations of atoms; that no fire, no heroism, no intensity of thought and feeling, can preserve individual life beyond the grave; that all the labors of the ages, all the devotion, all the inspiration, all the noonday brightness of human genius, are destined to extinction in the vast death of the solar system, and that the whole temple of Man's achievement must inevitably*

be buried beneath the debris of a universe in ruins- all these things, if not quite beyond dispute, are yet so nearly certain that no philosophy which rejects them can hope to stand. "Only within the scaffolding of these truths, only on the firm foundation of unyielding despair, can the soul's habitation henceforth be safely built."

~Philosopher/mathematician *Bertrand Russell accepting the inevitability and consequences of the heat death of the Universe.*

While Russell's ecstatic embrace of nothingness verges on the orgasmic, it is unlikely to win converts for the cause. Some of Russell's less literary colleagues get right to the point in fewer words.

The more the universe seems comprehensible, the more it also seems pointless." ~Steven Weinberg, Nobel Prize Winning Physicist.

Interesting observation!

Presumably, Beethoven, when composing his Late Quartets, and Bach his B-Minor Mass, and Monteverdi his Vespers of 1610 did not feel the universe was pointless at all. But they, of course, were merely composers, not Nobel Prize winning physicists. And therefore, evidently, they must have known less about the Universe than Steven Weinberg.

The systematic denial of purpose is the cornerstone of the scientific method.
~Jacques Monod, Nobel Prize for Chemistry.

The above represent just a few insiders' quotes on the inherent and inescapable meaninglessness of our purportedly accidental and unconscious universe. Yet, it is a curious fact that these conclusions are never part of our standard Western education. We are never, ever taught that as we suffer our way through the obligatory tedium of Education.

Why not? Very simply, the Secular Humanist's *Paradigm Police* (comprised of Establishment Science, Government Mandated Education and the Corporate Owned Media) have hijacked and held hostage the curriculum.

Briefly, Science develops the doctrine. Education disseminates it. The Media makes it palatable, or at least tries. So if young people are to learn the bleak consequences of the Secular Humanist dogma (for dogma is what it is) getting stuffed down their throats, they are going to have to learn it for themselves.

And so they do. In droves—though it is true many still do not (google up Skeptics and follow the threads and comments). It is Education, strangely enough, that is the most resistant to change. Thus it is still generally *verboten* within a school setting to introduce students to anything and everything that in any way contradicts or even questions the Materialist Manifesto, in which only the Secular is sacred: : Astrology, Alternative medicine, Faith Healing, Zero Point Energy, telepathy, the paranormal or parapsychological, anything challenging Darwinian Evolution via Natural selection, UFO's, Crop Circles, "Nessie & Yeti", Ghosts, Life after Death, Reincarnation, Lost, advanced Civilizations, Spiritual Transformation through inner work, and the NDE, (To Secular Humanists, little or no distinction is made concerning the importance or potential importance of these subjects. All are derisively dismissed *en masse* and out-of-hand as "Woo.")

Even so, not all is in harmony within the ranks of the Paradigm Police themselves. Cutting edge science includes a handful of acknowledged mystics, and a larger number of closet mystics (if you read and listen carefully) though they do not get major press, professionally they have to be careful and their highly technical work tends to be comprehensible initially only to their own cutting edge peers.

The Media, however, much less concerned with Paradigm Correctness, is effectively impossible to control. Bluntly, if the media thinks it can make money out of any given subject, no matter how derided or reviled by the Paradigm Police, it will exploit it.

So it is that just about every one of the anathematized subjects listed above gets promoted (usually irresponsibly, this is true) in proportion to the amount of money it brings in. Since in virtually every instance there is at least suggestive; in some cases, absolutely compelling evidence that legitimizes the subject, there is no way in which this information can still be hidden from the electronically connected segment of the general public—which in effect means everyone...unless you happen to live in North Korea. The internet has changed the rules, and it is no longer possible to keep on moving the goalposts.

Secular Humanism, that Idea whose time has not yet gone, is rapidly losing ground to paradigm shifting books like *The Dead Saints Chronicles*. Increasingly buffeted by National Media coverage of NDEs and many other "woo" phenomena, Secular Humanism's day, if not done, is quickly dimming. All it takes is a metaphorical asteroid strike to "wipe out the dinosaurs." A new epoch, begins and new life forms arise out of the chaos. It might not be long now...

If humanity is going to extricate itself from the morass created (not so much by the "advance of learning" and "the development of modern science"—as the Paradigm Police imagine), but rather by the major traditional religious institutions degenerating to the point where they were unable to defend themselves from the shiny barbarism (they call it "Progress") of the Secular hordes, they will have to regain a sense of their original purpose—which in the words of Schwaller de Lubicz is "The return to the Source." (In Christianity: salvation).

As an essential first step, those who understand what is at stake must learn to distinguish between those "woo" subjects that matter and those that don't. No one is going to do that for us/them.

Some of this really shouldn't be that much of a problem. E.g., there is considerable support for many aspects of non-traditional medicine. Acknowledging that would not even oblige them to abandon their paralyzing paradigm. Other woo-isms, the Yeti and "Nessie" for instance, are minor issues; genuine curiosities, certainly, but hardly worth rousing celebration if found or derisive abuse if not. Rather like putting a robot appositely named "Curiosity" (the same that killed the cat) on Mars. Such things do not matter much in the grand scheme of things, and even secular science should be able to accommodate them if valid or dismiss them if not without (as the Brits say) "getting their knickers in a twist".

Other taboos, however, seem impossible to account for within the Materialist's paradigm. And they matter. Spiritual transformation matters; all that furthers our individual and collective inner work (all "woo" to the Humanists of course) has value. I believe the NDE phenomenon in particular has the potential to become that one rare paradigm-busting, game-changing "idea whose time has come." Though it does have a formidable, foreseeable hurdle to cross.

The Science department back at Secular A&M (Agricultural & Mechanical) has taken it upon itself to define what counts as evidence and what does not.

High on its what-does-not-count list is anecdotal evidence.

Just because someone claims to have witnessed/experienced something doesn't make it true, much less "Science." The same thinking (or lack of thinking as the case may be) applies to multiple people claiming to have witnessed the same thing.

Reincarnation, a favorite eternally popular cinema subject could be sneered away, (despite a lot of very serious and very careful work over the years) since there was no way to verify the many detailed and plausible accounts of reincarnation memories...until very recently when Jim Tucker was able to do just that; verify the detailed past life stories of a number of people alive now able to recall their past lives. Suddenly major media could no longer ignore the solid evidence. Cracks in the castle façade are becoming fissures. Unfortunately, this will refute that great and famous observation by one of America's most beloved philosophers, Yogi Berra.

It would appear that in this particular game we call life, "It ain't over till it's over," is true only up to a point. The evidence to the contrary is now commanding. "It ain't over then, either."

And the NDE may now become the *coup de grace* to the fraud that is Secular Humanism. At a certain point all those thousands of sifted and analyzed Dead Saint testimonials will have to count as real evidence— whether the Paradigm Police like it or not.

There is too much at stake. The Afterlife is real, and every one of us would do well to start preparing for it. (The Ancient Egyptians went to inordinate lengths to do just that.) The Humanist debunkers, huddled deep underground in their Debunker Bunkers won't, of course, but that's their dilemma.

David Solomon's unique treatment of the subject, his comprehensive familiarity with its many aspects, along with the emotionally charged circumstances surrounding the writing of *The Dead Saints Chronicles* put it in a position to make a difference—at a critical time in this epoch of otherwise seemingly irreversible chaos and conflict.

And there is something oddly satisfying in knowing that if this is, indeed an *"idea whose time has come"*, not only is it **not** a new idea, it is a much older idea than the upgraded, genetically-modified, scientifically-enriched cynicism / skepticism / stoicism of ancient Greece.

The Afterlife may be the very oldest human idea we have. As far as we know, burial practices go back to the earliest human times. In fact, any kind of burial practice or ritual by definition presupposes an Afterlife of some sort. Were that not the case, why would our distant ancestors go to the considerable trouble of digging a grave with primitive tools. The ancient practice of burying the dead in a fetal position strongly suggests our ancestors believed they would be born again—into the Afterlife.

The sheer volume of evidence for survival after death is so immense that to ignore it is like standing at the foot of Mount Everest and insisting you cannot see the mountain.

~Colin Wilson, author of *The Outsider and The Strange Life of P.D Ouspensky.*

To upset the conclusion that all crows are black, there is no need to seek demonstration that no crows are black; it is sufficient to produce one white crow; a single one is sufficient.
   ~Harvard Professor William James

David Solomon's *Dead Saints Chronicles* may have finally revealed the "white crow "we all have been looking for:

Conclusion: A surplus of white crows.

Acknowledgements

So many relatives, friends and even stranges have contributed encouragement and anecdote to the writing of this book that it is impossible to name them all.

First, however, to say how much I am indebted to Dr. Jeffrey Long is beyond words. His work to create the world's largest near-death website, NDERF.org, and its sister website, ADCRF.org, provided me the first inkling so many near-death blogs existed in 2011, where from among thousands of references, your easy to access databases helped me discover the hundreds of stunning Dead Saint stories that made the *Chronicles* possible. I am forever grateful for the research and support, you and your wife, Jodi, provided me during my race to write the book during my cancer struggle.

To the webmaster and "student of life" of aleroy.com. Your database of 300 NDE blogs offered several important Dead Saint anecdotes I quoted in the Chronicles. Thank you.

To Dannion Brinkley for an amazing and jaw dropping Foreword you completed while being so sick. Thank you for 'going the distance.' Even though we have never met, I feel we have become good friends after many hours of calls with Delynn and me, not just regarding the Foreword, but your sincere understanding of our struggles from 33 months of going through the "dying process" and its accumulative effects on the family. You practice what you preach. Blessings to the Veteran's "Twilight Brigade" established at VA Medical Centers throughout the US and the responsibility you take managing 5,500 Hospice volunteers.

We all need to remember your motto: "No one ever need to die alone." Blessings.

To John Anthony West, my chief editor and friend, who polished my average writing skills; who labored 18 months with me to have the Chronicles well-written. Thank you for your astounding Afterword. Thank you for believing in me and opening your mind and heart to the possibility of a real 'Jesus.'

To Dr. Wayne Wheeler for hundreds of editing corrections and several critical theological suggestions that came "just in time" on January 10, 2016. Your caring and attention made a monumental difference in the final published version of the *Chronicles*. Thank you.

To Maggie Courter for professional copyediting. You labored for weeks over the holidays and beyond to reach a final proof. You were an "extreme proofer" like the scriptoriums of old. Yet, you were much more than a proofer. Your Christian and spiritual background provided me with valuable observations to re-write crucial paragraphs to clearly elucidate this volumous work. You are an inspiration. God Bless you!

For editing assistance: Myles Tufts, the Writers Group of Key West, with special help from Robin Robinson. To Dawn, Marti Casey and Mary Ann, who spent the last days with us in Key West, as we raced towards final edit. Our evening spiritual conversations were awesome.

To Publicist, Dottie Dehart, Meghan Waters at Dehart and Company for your expert press, marketing and media assistance, and for one of the best book covers and website designs ever. You have angels on your staff who "got it." Thank you.

For the wonderful endorsements from Jeffrey Long M.D, Robert Pennington, Ph.D., Mary Elizabeth Marlow, Stephen Haslam, and many others yet to come. Thank you!

I owe a lifetime of gratitude to my spiritual father and teacher, Paul Solomon, who demonstrated in all sincerity and integrity, the love, wisdom, and intellect taught by our Lord and Savior, Jesus Christ. His eternal patience and knowledge empowered my journey to know the truth, without which this book could never have been written. To my Dad, who raised me the best he could, and instilled in me to always try to do things right. To my mother, who endlessly cared for me no matter what I did, or where I traveled, and who always told me to go after my dreams.

To my Japanese family; Emiko Takahashi, who translated and interpreted; Makoto Asano, who first invited Paul Solomon and me to Japan in 1987; Buddhist priest, Sugasawa san and priestess, Tamo san (Ryoju Kikuchi) who taught me the importance of being like a child; and Bonsai master, Takanohashi sensei, who took me under his wings and taught me everything he knew. To Akito Takahama san, who funded the *Chronicle's* initial research for *The Armageddon Stones* (third book of the *Dead Saints Chronicle* series), and to Anna Ebell, who helped, while I poured through books and spent endless hours rummaging in libraries around the country.

To Felton Jones who introduced the art of Bonsai to me. You gave me the walking stick and the wisdom that changed my life.

To Phil Hulbert, my good friend and teacher, whose Japanese garden and granite *Feng Shui* expertise made Akio Botanical one of the most beautiful gardens in Washington State, creating an enduring legacy for centuries to come. I cherish the friendship we made in the years we knew each other.

To Mike Zblewski, for your excavator work in lifting those ten-ton granite stones and imminently competent and insightful underground installation of all electrical, water, and irrigation systems that made everything above ground work.

To all my garden helpers, Ron, Pat, and Chris. I wish we could have kept our little "yeshiva" going. It was a Camelot for a time. And for the team who helped prepare the gardens before my treatments began. Pete, Achalla, Steve, Dyanne, Sarah, ,

To Saint Rick, a nickname I will always remember, and a friend at Akio I will never forget. You were "Boothby" to me.

To Grace de Rond and Sharon Solomon for digging up old files and photographs when I needed them.

To Dr. Angela Perry, who advised I get an MRI on the morning of June 13, 2013 to investigate my dizziness.

To Dr. Lee at the Virginia Beach, VA Medical Center, who always cared about my condition, responded immediately to requests for medication refills, and who listened to me when I talked about my book. He is a credit to the VA medical system. To Dr. Randazzo at Duke University—who tried everything she could to treat me. And to Dr. Gupta at the Hampton, VA Medical Center, who helped me choose the right therapeutic path. I will remember our last discussion on February 10, 2016 about dying *cancer patients and their families* recognizing their loved ones may have reached their "appointed time," and begin to accept their approaching death, and "let go." You just listened with tears in your eyes. You are one of the most caring doctors I have ever met.

To Christopher Russel, whose Dead Saint testimonial about Jesus, triggered my own Jesus encounter I would later call Near-Death Lightning. Without your near-death experience, this book may never have been written.

To Cheryl Broyles for your continuing fight, living 15 years with GBM, and your positive outlook on life despite the odds. I looked up to you more than you can know. Thank you for your support and encouragement.

To Dennis Raschka and his wife Nancy for your caring, prayers, and support when I was so sick. Our Christian banter about the Chronicles helped me write a better book. Thank you for writing every few months to ask how the book and me were coming along, and giving me the first thumbs up Christian conservative feedback.

To Colin Reed, a payment business colleague who was diagnosed with GBM a few months ago, and his wife Candice. We have become closer friend aside from business. Stay strong! To my many payment friends made over 15 years: Marty Wood, Jerry Lewis, Edward Slominski, Rick Taylor, Blake Martensen and all the staff at Meritcard. Thank you.

To James and Laurie Coffin, who purchased the first, early draft of the *Chronicles;* thank you for your support. And to Mikelynn for your beautiful spirit.

For loving support: Dawana and Shawn, John Forte and Paul Michels, Nancy and Joel, Jim and Laura Huayke, Rick and Lauri, Achala for her intense loving ways, Chrissi Sweet and Shelley at the 76 Station where I drove to get coffee, and who check on me almost every month even after I moved away. To Daniel Davis who cared enough to research and send me every health cure on the planet; to Howdy Kabrins who was a good friend, and who sadly lost his daughter a few months ago, hugs and sincere condolences. Thank you.

To Sharon and Emil in Florida. To David Bommerito who was a good friend. To Diane and Kurt. Thank you.

To Sarah Morris; take care of your Bonsai masterpiece!

To Iriana for her photographs used in the book, and for her ceiling painting of the Sistine Chapel at Akio and for your beautiful spirit. To Kerry Kodat who, after not hearing from him in nearly four years, called me on December 1, 2015, called unexpectedly to pray with me after a disappointing MRI news I received earlier in the day. Thank you.

Bruce and Martie Shelton, Robert Krajenke, Ruth Ann Pippenger and her daughter Lauri, Judith and Chris Van Cleave, James Yax, Jerry Teplitz, Sam and Dax, Myrrh Haslam, Niti Zudsiri, Susan Thomas, Sarah and Jacob Anderson, Annaleah and Joshua Atkinson, Dick Dingus, John Krysco, Joy Talley, Francis Sporer, Jill Albrandt, Cynthia Funk, Larry Jennings, George Michelow for his jovial countenance, Heidi Gibson who was our champion to raise funds for the needy, local and worldwide, to David Brian Berry for your spiritual support and wisdom, and Sheila Killmon for helping Delynn when she most needed it. To Marsha whose drawings I so admired.

To Steve Courter who has the patience and quietness of a Saint.

To Terrance Melchar for the 35 million year-old fossils from the Chesapeake Bay, the Japanese Maples, and our theological discussions. And to Rev. Jeanette Vivier, who died suddenly on December 12, 2015, before I could say goodbye. You will be missed.

And all those at the Fellowship I have not named, thank you.

To all those at Nick's Restaurant where I spent hundreds of hours writing during breakfast: Pooch, Valerie, Cheryle, Chookie, breakfast cooks Tim and Trish, and to Francisco who cared enough to check on how I was doing every day. Special thanks to the proprietors "Pooch" and Frank for your $3.50 Pooch Eggs, bacon, potatoes and toast, plus the waffles and hot syrup, and the ceiling tile with the *Chronicles* book cover that looks down on my favorite breakfast booth sitting under the picture of the 18th hole of St. Andrews in Edinburgh, Scotland.

To my payment industry friends; Blake Martensen, Gabe Nickens, Chris Thill, Joe Cloud, Frederick Wilgram, and all the employees of Meritcard, thank you. To Richard Davis, Rick Taylor, CEO of Bridgepay, Marty Wood, and Edward Slominski.

To Lisa Rivera, Mandy Winegarner, Ginger, Kathy Charlee, and all my former friends and employees of Fast Transact, thank you. To Locke Walsh and Frederick at Ezic; without you, Fast Transact would never have existed and Akio Botanical G1ardens would never have been built. Thank you.

Special hugs, appreciation and thanks, to my family; my Dad and his wife Lou, Michelle and her husband David, Alex, Josh and his wife Melissa, Terri and her husband John, Isabella, Zach, Leah, James, Jason, grandchildren, Liam, Aiden, and new born granddaughter, Mila; my nephew, Scott and his wife, Doreen, Ralph and Sue Petty, Linda and Steve Woodruff, Paul and Sonia Ferris, Stephanie Jekel, and my spiritually adopted sons, Patrick Jekel and Nathan Blood.

To Delynn's huge family —too many to say thank you by name; but especially to brother Kevin, sister Loretta and Doug, brother Jay and loving wife Sue. Jay thank you for the 15 games of cribbage in February. I won fair and square! I hope you enjoy the near-death books from my library. Bring them back in late March and we'll play another set of cribbage matches!

To Ann Marie and Ranny, who rented their beautiful Bay Colony home to us; the gardens, screened porch, wood fireplace, brought peace to our family. Thank you.

To Jimmy Stratton (Zenbilly) who took my last headshots for Facebook and the Chronicles. Thank you for the "heart agate" stone. It is special to me. Thank you brother.

To Benjamin and Angela, my beloved children, who eagerly awaited these long years to see the fruits of my thoughts actually make it to print; this book is dedicated to you. Always know how much I love you and will be sitting on Heaven's balcony looking down on you, helping when I can. I hope Heaven has Earth TV, so I can watch football and Stargate with you in spirit!

To Delynn, my lovely wife with a commanding heart, who patiently saw my attention ever diverted to this book; whose contribution in both writing and editing helped me when I was unclear; who gently and firmly pushed me when I felt ill: who gave up her dreams to help me fulfill mine; who suffered through doctors, hospitals, fearful decisions and financial collapse; who persisted through my family strife and my suffering; who relived your mother's death from GBM; and watched me slowly die from the same disease; who took upon your shoulders the great responsibility for my care and the stress of publishing of the *Chronicles* and its sequels. You never gave up. You are a hero to me. I love you much and will so miss you when I am gone.

To all my friends and family on the "other side" whose visitation in my dreams gave me hope and the knowledge all was on track. You were there when I needed you. And finally, to Jesus Christ, who gave me the shmeda to make Holy and a camel to traverse the desert of the impossible in just enough time, who trusted me to deliver this message before it was too late.

Bibliography

Literature

Alexander, Eben 2012. *Proof of Heaven, A Neurosurgeon's Journey into the Afterlife.* New York: Simon and Schuster Paperbacks.

Anathemas against Origen 545 A.D. Attached to the decrees of the Fifth Ecumenical Council, in Nicene and Post-Nicene Fathers, 2d ser., 14: 318.

Atwater, P.M.H. 2007.*The Big Book of Near-Death Experiences.* Charlottesville, VA: Hampton Roads Publishing Co.

Atwater, P.M.H., LH.D. 1999 & 2003. *The New Children and Near-Death Experiences. Rochester, VT: Bear & Co.* Originally published in 1999 by Three Rivers Press under the title: *Children of the New Millennium: Children's Near-Death Experiences and the Evolution of Humankind.*

Beauregard, Mario 2012. *Near death, Explained.* http://www.salon.com/2012/04/21/near_death_explained/Mario Beauregard/

Bible in the Church, the Encyclopedia of Religion and Ethics.

Brinkley, Dannion and Paul Perry 1994. *Saved by the Light: The true story of a man who died twice and the profound revelations he received.* New York: Villard Books.

Brinkley, Dannion. *The Twilight Brigade*, PO Box 84013, Los Angeles, CA 90073; (310) 473-1941; fax (310) 473-8249. Website www.thetwilightbrigade.com/dannion-info.htm. Further contact: West Los Angeles VA Medical Center, 11301 Wilshire Blvd, Bldg. 258, Room 113, Los Angeles, CA 90073.

Broyles, Cheryl L. 2012. *Life's Mountains. Published with Create Space. Originally published with Xlibris in 2008.*

Callanan, Maggie and Patricia Kelly 1992. *Final Gifts.* New York: Bantam Dell.

Catherine Hezser 2001. *Jewish Literacy in Roman Palestine.* Turbingen: Mohr/Siebeck.

Catholic Encyclopedia, vol. VI., 655-656; 132, Gnostic Gospels.

Catholic Encyclopedia, vol. VI, 543; the Dogma of the Infallible Church was reaffirmed by the Sacred Vatican Council in 1870 C.E., and again by Pope Leo XIII, in his Encyclical Prov. Deus in 1893.

Clement, Stromata, 7.1. *The Gnostic alone is truly pious...the true Christian is the Gnostic.*

Cott, Jonathan 1987. *The Search for Omm Sety.* Parktown, South Africa: Studio 33 Books, Random House Group, Ltd., UK.

De Rond, Grace 2000. *The Fellowship Primer,* Paul Solomon. Ireland, UK. The Paul Solomon Foundation.

Eadie, Betty J. 1992. *Embraced By The Light.* Placerville, CA: Gold Leaf Press.

Ecology.com. Birth and Death Rates. http://www.ecology.com/birth-death-rates/

Ehrman, Bart D. 2005. *Misquoting Jesus: The Story Behind Who Changed the Bible and Why.* San Francisco: Harper Collins/HarperOne.

Eliade, Mircea 1964. *Shamanism: Archaic Techniques of Ecstasy,* tr. Willard Trask. Princeton, NJ: Princeton University Press.

Examiner.com. http://www.examiner.com/article/do-gnostics-believe-reincarnation

Fanti, Guilio and Malfi, Pierandrea 2015. *The Shroud of Turin: First Century after Christ!* Singapore: Pan Stanford.

Faulkner, R.O. 1985. *The Ancient Egyptian Book of the Dead,* (revised ed. C. A. R. Andrews). London: The British Museum Press.

Fischer, Michael J. 2016. *The Shroud of Turin, Evidence it is authentic?* Adapted from the original article by John C. Iannone.

Flipp, Michael 2012. *!2 Signs and Coincidences from God.* Amazon Digital Services, LLC.

Fortune, Dion 1968. *Through the Gates of Death.* Great Britain: Society of Inner Light.

Frale, Barbara April 2004. Abstract. *The Chinon chart*: *Papal absolution to the last Templar, Master Jacques de Molay.* Journal of Medieval History, 30,.2, pp. 109–134., 30,.2.

Frale, Barbara 2012. *The Templars and the Shroud of Christ.* Skyhorse Publishing.

Freke, Timothy and Peter Gandy 1999. *The Jesus Mysteries.* Three Rivers Press, Crown Publishing Group.

Fulke, William D.D. 1843. *Master of Pembroke Hall, Cambridge. A Defence of the Sincere and*
True Translations of the Holy Scriptures into the English Tongue, Against the cavils of George Martin. Printed at University Press.

Gallup, G. and Proctor, W. 1982. *Adventures in Immortality: A Look Beyond the Threshold of Death.* New York: McGraw-Hill.

Garlow, James L and Keith Wall 2010. *Encountering Heaven and the Afterlife.* Bloomington, Minnesota: Bethany House Publishers.

Helm, Neil, M.A. 1989. Scholar in Residence, Atlantic University. *Did Edgar Cayce Have a Near-Death Experience?*

Hensley, Mary Dr., August 10, 2014. Sermon at the *Fellowship of the Inner Light*. Excerpts taken from You Tube. https://www.youtube.com/watch?v=nbVIp2qq2QQ

Hezser, Catherine 2001. *Jewish Literacy in Roman Palestine*. Turbingen: Mohr/Siebeck.

Hoffman, R.F. 1995. Disclosure Habits After Near-Death Experience: Influences, Obstacles, and Listener Selection. *Journal of Near-Death Studies* 14: 29-48.

Holden, Janice Minor, Ed.D. Greyson, Bruce M.D., and James, Debbie. RN/MSN, 2009. *The Handbook of Near-Death Experiences, Thirty Years of Investigation*. Santa Barbara, CA: Denver, CO. Oxford, England: Praeger Publishers, an imprint of ABC-CLIO, LLC.

Hughes, H.G. 2015. *Saint Francis of Assisi in a New Light*. See https://www.catholicculture.org/culture/library/view.cfm?recnum=8119

Inge, W.R. 1899. *Christian Mysticism*. London: Methuen.

Javid, Afshin Aug 23, 2011. *You Tube Video interview, Afshin Javid*. Public Domain. Excerpted and transcribed. https://www.youtube.com/watch?v=Xe7fJOb9XGU

Jewish Quarterly Review vi., p. 327.

Jobs, Steve Monday, October 30, 2011. *The Memorial service for Steve Jobs*, New York Times Online.

Jones, Stephen E. July 9, 2009. *The Shroud of Turin. My commentary on Shroud of Turin related matters*. http://theshroudofturin.blogspot.com/2009/07/re-there-is-compelling-evidence-it-is.html

King, Martin Luther, Jr. April 3, 1968. Edited from *I've Been to the Mountaintop* speech at the World Headquarters for the Church of God in Christ. Wikipedia.

Lambdin, Thomas O. Translation 2014. *The Gospel of Thomas*. The Gnostic Society Library, The Nag Hammadi Library, http://gnosis.org/naghamm/nhl_thomas.htm.

Lau, D.C. 2001. *Tao Te Ching. (New Bilingual Edition)*. Hong Kong: Chinese University Press.

Lewis, C.S. 1942, 1961, 1996. *The Screwtape Letters (New York: Touchstone)*, 61, Lewis, ix.

Liichow S., Rev. Robert October 2007. *THE SUFFICIENCY OF SCRIPTURE*. Truth Matter Newsletters. Vol 12, Issue 10.

Lommel, Van Pim M.D. 2007. *Consciousness Beyond Life, The Science of the Near-Death Experience*. New York: HarperCollins.

Long, Jeffrey M.D. with Paul Perry 2010. *Evidence of the Afterlife: The Science of the Near-Death Experience*. New York: HarperCollins.

Maclaine, Shirley 1983. *Out on a Limb*. New York: Bantam Books.

Marion, Andre and Courage, Anne-Laurie, *Nouvelles dècouvertes*, forward by Christian Imbert (director in chief, Institute d'Optique and of l'Ecole Superieure d'Optique d'Orsay).

Metzgre, Bruce M. 1968. *"Explicit References in the Works of Origin to Variant Readings in New Testament Manuscripts,"* in Biblical and Patristic Studies in Memory of Robert Pierce Casey, ed.

Migliore, Vince 2009. *A Measure of Heaven.* Folsom, CA: Blossom Hill Books.

Moody, R.A. Jr., M.D., and P. Perry 1988. *The Light Beyond.* New York: Bantam Books.

Moody, R.A. Jr., M.D., and P. Perry 1991. *Coming Back: A Psychiatrist Explores Past-Life Journeys.* New York: Bantam.

Moody, R.A. Jr., M.D. 1977. *Life after Life,* Covington GA: Mockingbird Books.

Moroni, M., 1991, "Pontius Pilate's Coin on the Right Eye of the Man in the Holy Shroud, in the Light of the New Archaeological Findings," in Berard, A., ed., 1991, "History, Science, Theology and the Shroud," Symposium Proceedings, St. Louis Missouri, June 22-23, 1991, The Man in the Shroud Committee of Amarillo, Texas: Amarillo TX, p.286.

Oswald, Bayer 2007. *Theology the Lutheran Way.* Grand Rapids, MI: Eerdmonds.

Owen, Richard November, 21, 2009. "Death certificate is imprinted on the Shroud of Turin," says Vatican scholar." Times of London.

Pew Forum on Religion and Public Life, U.S. *Religious Landscape Survey, Summary of Key Findings*, http://www.pewforum.org/2009/12/09/many-americans-mix-multiple-faiths/

Price, John W. 2013. *Revealing Heaven, The Christian Case for Near-Death Experiences.* New York: HarperCollins.

Rogers, Raymond N. September 2004. Abstract. *Thermochimica Acta* 425 (2005) 189–194.

Reyes, Christopher E. 2014. *In His Name, Vol. IVC, Who wrote the Gospels?* North America and International: Trafford Publishing.

Ritchie, George G Jr., M.D. 1991. *My Life After Dying, Becoming Alive to Universal Love.* Norfolk, Virginia: Hampton Roads Publishing.

Saint Francis of Assisi, Spring 1225 A.D. *The Canticle of the Creatures,* (FAED I, 113-114).

Shroud of Turin Blogspot. http://theshroudofturin.blogspot.com/2009/07/re-there-is-compelling-evidence-it-is.html

Simon, Richard 1689. *A Critical History of the Text of the New Testament. London: R. Taylor, pt. I.*

Sabom, Michael M.D. 1998. *Light and Death, One Doctor's Fascinating Account of Near-Death Experiences.* Grand Rapids Michigan: Zondervan Publishing House.

Semkiw, Walter M.D. 2003. *Born Again and the Revolutionaries. Pluto Project; Exp Int edition.* Charlottesville, VA.: Hampton Roads Publishing.

Solomon, Paul 2003. *The Meta-Human, Twice-Born.* Ireland, UK. Paul Solomon Foundation. Originally published by the Master's Press, 1985.

Solomon, Paul and Keller, Gary and Mary Anna 1985. *Love and Fear, Only Two Powers Exist.* Timberville, VA: The Master's Press.

Solomon, Paul Source Reading Excerpt, February 15, 1972. Transcribed Excerpt. Ireland, UK. Paul Solomon Foundation.

Solomon, Paul 1984. Lecture, *The Physics of Light and Darkness.* Excerpted from David Solomon's Journal notes.

Solomon, Paul 1982. *A Closer Walk with Jesus.* 8 CD set. Quoted from Excerpts. Ireland, UK: Paul Solomon Foundation. www.paulsolomon.com.

Sparrow, G. Scott 1996. *I Am With You Always. True Stories of Encounters with Jesus.* Bantam Books.

St. Irenaeus 170 A.D. *Against Heresies.*

Stevenson J. and Frend, W.H.C. 1957. *A New Euesbius, SPCK Church History. Documents illustrating the History of the Church to AD 337.* First Edition published 1957. Revised Second Edition published 1987. See J. Stevenson and W.H.C Frend 1957. A New Euesbius, SPCK Church History. Documents illustrating the History of the Church to AD 337. First Edition published 1957. Revised Second Edition published 1987. 814ff.

Sigmund, Richard 2004 & 2010. *My Time in Heaven: A True Story of Dying...And Coming Back.* New Kensington, PA: Whitaker House.

Sullivan, Lawrence E. 1988. *Icanthus Drum: An orientation to the Meaning of the South American Religions.* New York: Macmillan.

Swedenborg, Emanuel 2012. *Heaven & Hell,* Swedenborg Foundation Press, USA.

Telpner, Heidi R.N. 2007. *One Foot in Heaven, Journey of a Hospice Nurse.* Author.

Tenen, Stan 2011. The Alphabet That Changed the World: How Genesis Preserves a Science of Consciousness in Geometry and Gesture. Berkley, California: North Atlantic Books: Penguin Random House.

Tucker, Jim B. M.D., 2008. *Life before Life.* New York: St Martin's Press.

Van Laeys, Emily L. 1994. *Life Review revealed in near-death experience.* Venture Inward (July/August).

Vaughan, Henry (1621-1695). Poem, *The Night.* John 2.3.

Vincent, Kenneth R., Ed.D. 2005. Journal of Near-Death Studies. Abstract, *Resurrection Appearances of Jesus as After-Death Communication*. Houston, TX. Excerpts taken from (Maxwell & Tschudin. pp. 77–78).

Weiss, Joseph A. 1972.The *Gospel in the Stars*. Originally published in 1882, *The Gospel in the Stars: or, Primeval Astronomy*. Grand Rapids, MI: Kriegal Publications.

Wisenberg, Wesley W. 2016. Translation of The Gospel of Philip. The Gnostic Society Library, The Gnostic Society Nag Hammadi Library. http://gnosis.org/naghamm/gop.html.

Yogananda, Paramahansa 1981, 1987, 2007. *Autobiography of a Yogi*. Authorized by the International Publications Council of Self-Realization Fellowship.

Zanger, Walter August 24, 2014. *Jewish Worship, Pagan Symbols*. Bible History Daily.

Tables
Table 1

Seven Near-Death Triggers	Description
#1: Physical-Death	Clinical Death of the physical body
#2: Near-Death	Severe/moderate injury to the physical body, including coma
#3: Multiple-Death	Severe/moderate injury to the physical body during a multiple casualty event. NDE survivor witnesses and communicates with non-survivors as they die.
#4: Fear-Death	Non-injury, core-dying event caused by belief death is imminent. *(Term coined by Dr. Jeffery Long, M.D.)*
#5: Shared-Death	Non-injury core dying event experienced by the Living in the presence of a dying person. Living are acutely conscious and awake during the experience. (Term used by Dr. Jeffery Long, M.D., and Dr. Moody, M.D., Ph.D.)
#6: Mystical-Death	Non-injury core dying event triggered by deep meditation, prayer, hypnosis, astral travel, Near-Death Lightning, Holy Spirit, (i.e., Christian born-again), or appear spontaneously without cause. Sometimes referred to as an STE. (Spiritual Transformative Experience) or SOBE (Spiritual Out-of-Body Experience)
#7: ADC (after-death communication) / NELE (near-end of life event)	Non-injury core dying event experienced through a dream involving an after-death communication (ADC) from deceased loved ones, (which may occur years, months or days before death) or a near-end of life event (NELE) (seeing and talking while conscious or semi-conscious to deceased friends and family, weeks, days or hours before death.

Table 2

Death Element	Moody, M.D., Ph.D.	Solomon
#1		Sense of Impending Death or Doom
#2	Hearing Yourself Pronounced Dead	Realization Physical Body is Dead
#3	Hearing Unusual Noises	Hearing Unusual Noises (Pop, or loud buzzing, or humming sound)
#4	Finding Self outside the Physical Body Feelings of Peace and Quiet A Sense of Alteration of Time and Space	Finding Self outside the Physical Body: (includes 12 common phenomena associated with an OOBE. Divided into two categories, "Effects" and "Abilities") **Effects:** 1. No Pain 2. Profound Feelings of Peace, Quiet, and Incredible Joy 3. Perceived Alteration of Time and Space 4. Realization Spiritual-Self Separate from the Physical Body 5. A Remarkable Detached Point of View **Abilities:** 6. External Observation of Events 7. Heightened Awareness / Hyper-alertness 8. 360 Degree Vision 9. Acute Vision 10. Movement of Spiritual-Self Caused by Thought 11. Increased Intelligence 12. Telepathic Ability
#5	A Black Void or Dark Space	A Black Void or Dark Space
#6		Perception of a Veil
#7	Traveling through a Tunnel	Traveling through a Tunnel
#8		The Grand Central Station of Death
#9	Perception of an Unearthly	Perception of an Unearthly

	Environment and Heavenly Gardens	Environment and heavenly Gardens
#10	Experiencing a Bright Light / Being of Light	Experiencing a Bright Light / Being of Light (God, Jesus, or Bright Being).
#11	Meeting Spiritual Beings (Dead Friends, Relatives, or Angels)	Meeting Spiritual Beings (Dead Friends, Relatives, or Angels)
#12	Panoramic Life Review (includes the Judgment)	Panoramic Life Review
#13		The Judgment
#14	Access to All Knowledge	Access to Special Knowledge
#15	Shown Cities of Light	Cities of Light / City of God
#16	Realm of Bewildered Spirits	Realm of Bewildered Spirits / Realm darkness (Hell)
#17	Sensing a Border where you cannot go	Sensing a Border where you cannot go
#18	Coming Back to your Physical Body	Coming Back to your physical Body: (2 options) Mission unfulfilled: You must go back because you are not finished. (It's not your time.) Life Extension: You have a choice to return
#19	Ineffability—Inability to put into words	Ineffability – Inability to put into words
#20	Change of Life—Subtle "Broadening and Deepening" of the life afterward	Change of Life: 85% positive/ 15% negative (alcoholism, suicidal thoughts, inability to cope)
#21	Elimination of the Fear of Death	Elimination of the Fear of Death
#22	Corroboration of Events while Outside of your Body	Corroboration of Events while outside of your Body
#23	Supernatural Rescues	Supernatural Rescues & Events

~Chronicle Index – Table 3

Chapter	~Chronicle #	Date
Ch.5	174	04-Dec-13
Ch.23	193	23-Dec-13
Ch.14	197	27-Dec-13
Ch.22	199	29-Dec-13
Ch.20	201	31-Dec-13
Ch.22	231	30-Jan-14
Ch.14	332	11-May-14

Ch.15	333	12-May-14
Ch.6	358	06-Jun-14
Ch.23	424	11-Aug-14
Ch.12	428	15-Aug-14
Ch.6	481	07-Oct-14
Ch.6	504	30-Oct-14
Ch.6	505	31-Oct-14
Ch.23	518	13-Nov-14
Ch.6	524	19-Nov-14
Ch.23	558	23-Dec-14
Ch.23	568	01-Jan-15
Ch.16	586	20-Jan-15
Ch.4	589	23-Jan-15
Ch.6	593	27-Jan-15
Ch.6	596	30-Jan-15
Ch.8	596	30-Jan-15
Ch.17	604	07-Feb-15
Ch.15	311	20-Apr-15
Ch.19	730	12-Jun-15
Ch.12	775	27-Jul-15
Ch.13	780	01-Aug-15
Ch.6	782	03-Aug-15
Ch.3	794	15-Aug-15
Ch.6	815	05-Sep-15
Ch.3	819	09-Sep-15
Ch.8	821	11-Sep-15
Ch.12	826	16-Sep-15
Ch.24	847	07-Oct-15
Ch.11	858	18-Oct-15
Ch.24	865	25-Oct-15
Ch.10	889	17-Nov-15
Ch.16	890	18-Nov-15
Ch.15	905	04-Dec-15
Ch.9	908	07-Dec-15
Ch.14	911	10-Dec-15
Ch.18	927	27-Dec-15
Ch.14	937	05-Jan-16
Ch.24	955	23-Jan-16
Ch.24	960	28-Jan-16
Ch.23	965	02-Feb-16
Ch.12	976	13-Feb-16

Appendix A

NDERF.org
About NDERF

Founded by Jeffrey Long, M.D. and Jody Long, the Near Death Research Experience Foundation is the largest NDE website in the world with over 4000 Experiences in over 23 Languages collected since 1998. They provide Main pages in desktop, tablet, and smart phone formats.

NDERF PHILOSOPHY/MISSION STATEMENT

If enough people read about love, peace and hope; maybe they can change to become more loving, compassionate people who truly live their lives without fear. We can then change the world to become a better place like Heaven on Earth - as above, so below.

Jeffrey Long, M.D.

Jeffrey Long is a medical doctor specializing in the practice of radiation oncology, using radiation to treat cancer in Houma, Louisiana.

As a scientist, Jeff founded NDERF in 1998. He wanted to know if NDEs were real by directly asking the NDErs themselves. The answer is a resounding YES! As a result of his research, he is the author of the New York Times Best Seller, "Evidence of the Afterlife: The Science of Near-Death Experiences."

As a leading NDE researcher and a medical doctor, Jeff has appeared on national media including O'Reilly Factor, NBC today, ABC with Peter Jennings, the Dr. Oz Show, the History Channel, the Learning Channel, and National Geographic. He has also appeared on Fox News Houston and at the New York Academy of Sciences.

Jody Long

Jody Long is an attorney, and has been licensed in Washington, New Mexico, Louisiana, and the Navajo Nation. She is webmaster for the Near Death Experience Research Foundation (NDERF) www.NDERF.com for the past 15 years and provides support and a forum for NDErs and those who want to know about the Afterlife. She has several decades of experience researching paranormal and related phenomena. She is also webmaster for After Death Communication Research Foundation (ADCRF) www.adcrf.org and the other consciousness experience website which is everything that is not an NDE or ADC (OBERF) www.oberf.org.

Jody helped with *Evidence of the Afterlife*, the New York Times best-selling NDE book. She has written *God's Fingerprints: Impressions of*

Near Death Experiences, From Soul to Soulmate: Bridges from Near Death Experience Wisdom, and *Repeal Obamacare: A Critical Look at Why it isn't Fixable.*

Instruction: Understanding NDERF Quote Edits

Due to space limitation or length, some NDERF testimonials are abbreviated to highlight the kernel of their experience.

Example:
"I died and saw a Being of Light..." If the NDERF testimonial is abbreviated (sometimes in several places) then the next paragraph will start:
"...I came back to life because God told me I had a Mission to fulfill." (NDERF reference # at end of quotes.

How to Find NDERF References:

Example: NDERF.org reference: Teri R NDE, #2301, 08.10.10, NDERF.org.

We decided rather than include a lengthy web address of 210 NDERF testimonials in the reference notes, it would work to simply go to: www.nderf.org. Move your mouse over *NDE Stories* tab at the top right of the web page. The drop down box offers 4 archives that are dated. Look for the date range from the 4 archives for the example above: 08.10.10.

You will see the date of Teri's NDE listed in archive 2: (07.01.10 – 09.30.10)

Click here for More Archived NDEs (7/1/10-12/31/10) part I

This opens a webpage showing NDEs 2260 through 2284. Look for 2301. Teri R NDE. English expanded version. 8/10/10. Click on the link to see his entire experience. Alternately, you can go directly to the archives page at this link:

http://www.nderf.org/NDERF/NDE_Archives/archives_main.htm.

Appendix B

Websites

www.nderf.org
www.adcrf.org
www.oberf.org
www.near-death.com
www.aleroy.com
www.deadsaints.org
www.deadsaintschronicles.com
www.paulsolomon.com
www.FellowshipoftheInnerLight.com
www.maryelizabethmarlow.com

About The Author

David Solomon is a Christian minister. He is regarded as a leading philosopher and exponent of cosmological mythology, Bible interpretation, and prophecy. David brings to the table decades of personal experience with world religion. A full-time apprentice to Paul Solomon for 15 years (1979-1994), David documented Paul's life during world tours to Egypt, Israel, Europe, Australia, and Japan. During this period of teaching and apprenticeship, Paul Solomon directed David to study under many teachers, including: in the U.S., T'ai Chi master Da Liu; in Japan, renowned bonsai master Takanohashi Sensei, and Tamo San (born Ryoju Kikuchi), the first recognized enlightened Buddhist priestess in 500 years. In 1992 and 2010 Mr. Solomon assisted Egyptologist John Anthony West and geologist Dr. Robert M. Schoch in re-dating the Sphinx, as well as other Egyptian and Turkish monuments (proving them many thousands of years older than previously thought). Mr. Solomon's earlier extensive comet impact research supported the re-dating of these ancient sites. In 1994, he appeared in a supportive role on the national telecast NBC special Ancient Prophecies II, where he discussed the life and prophecies of Paul Solomon.

After Paul Solomon's death in March 1994, David moved to Washington State and "retired" from spiritual studies to build a family and business. Though lacking a college degree and with no business experience, he founded Fast Transact, Inc. Over the next 15 years it became one of the largest online payment processing companies in the Pacific Northwest, handling nearly $1 billion in annual payments for clients including GoDaddy.com, Dr. Phil, and 5,000 online and retail merchants. Mr. Solomon sold his company in a multi-million-dollar deal in January 2010. With the proceeds of the sale, he returned to his spiritual roots, beginning a seven-year project to build Akio Botanical Japanese Gardens around his five-acre home.

In July 2011, as the Japanese gardens transformed his property, Mr. Solomon began intensive research into the near-death experience, a project he would subsequently call The Dead Saints Chronicles. His research was 95 percent complete when severe equilibrium problems drove him to a hospital ER, where a CT scan found a one inch (20mm) brain tumor. A subsequent brain biopsy confirmed that the tumor was Glioblastoma Multiforme IV (GBM), a rare, aggressive brain cancer that kills 50 percent of its victims within 15 to 18 months. Despite months of debilitating radiation and chemotherapy, and faced with his own death, Mr. Solomon began writing The Dead Saints Chronicles with a Blues-Brothers-Mission-from-God vigor. During this difficult situation, an unresolvable financial crisis exhausted his project funds. He was forced to sell Akio Botanical Japanese Gardens and most of his assets, and relocated his family to Virginia Beach in late November 2013 so that he could receive ongoing cancer therapy at Duke University.

Mr. Solomon commissioned John Anthony West to edit the Chronicles from April 2014 to its exciting completion in late November 2015. Mr. Solomon continues to live in Virginia Beach with his family, enjoying the ocean and his small bonsai garden. With the help of his wife, Delynn, he is in the process of completing the second book in *The Dead Saints Chronicles* series, Training Wires of the Soul.

About John Anthony West

Author, lecturer, and guide, John Anthony West delivered a seismic shock to archaeology in the early 1990s when he and Boston University geologist Dr. Robert Schoch revealed that the Great Sphinx of Giza, Egypt, showed evidence of rainfall erosion. Such erosion could only mean that the Sphinx was carved during or before the rains that marked the transition of northern Africa from the last Ice Age to the present interglacial epoch, a transition that occurred in the millennia from 10,000 to 5,000 BC. To learn more, please visit www.jawest.com.

"Egyptian civilization was not a development, it was a legacy."
— John Anthony West

www.ingramcontent.com/pod-product-compliance
Lightning Source LLC
Chambersburg PA
CBHW060028180426
43195CB00051B/2209